Pensions on Divorce
A Practitioner's Handbook

Pensions on Divorce
A Practitioner's Handbook

Fiona Hay BSc BA (Hons) (Exon)
Barrister, Inner Temple

Edward Hess MA (Cantab)
Barrister, Middle Temple
District Judge, Principal Registry of the Family Division

David Lockett MA (Oxon), FIA
Actuary, Actuaries for Lawyers Limited

SWEET & MAXWELL

Second Edition   2013   by Hay, Hess & Lockett

Published in 2013 by Sweet & Maxwell, 100 Avenue Road, London NW3 3PF part of Thomson Reuters (Professional) UK Limited (Registered in England & Wales, Company No 1679046.
Registered Office and address for service: Aldgate House, 33 Aldgate High Street, London EC3N 1DL)

For further information on our products and services, visit *www.sweetandmaxwell.co.uk*

Typeset by Letterpart Limited, Caterham on the Hill, Surrey CR3 5XL

Forms typeset by Interactive Sciences Ltd, Gloucester

Printed and bound in Great Britain by CPI Group (UK) Ltd, Croydon, CR0 4YY.

No natural forests were destroyed to make this product; only farmed timber was used and re-planted.

A CIP catalogue record of this book is available for the British Library.

ISBN: 978-1-908-01319-4

Thomson Reuters and the Thomson Reuters logo are trademarks of Thomson Reuters.

Sweet & Maxwell ® is a registered trademark of Thomson Reuters (Professional) UK Limited.

Crown copyright material is reproduced with the permission of the Controller of HMSO and the Queen's Printer for Scotland.

All rights reserved. No part of this publication may be reproduced or transmitted in any form or by any means, or stored in any retrieval system of any nature without prior written permission, except for permitted fair dealing under the Copyright, Designs and Patents Act 1988, or in accordance with the terms of a licence issued by the Copyright Licensing Agency in respect of photocopying and/or reprographic reproduction. Application for permission for other use of copyright material including permission to reproduce extracts in other published works shall be made to the publishers. Full acknowledgement of author, publisher and source must be given.

Disclaimer: This work is not a substitute for legal advice in relation to any particular case. Although the authors have attempted to produce a work which is designed to assist the practitioner, neither they or the publishers undertake any duty of care to any person or entity whatsoever, without limitation, in relation to statements in, or omissions from this work, and accepts no legal liability or responsibility in respect of any statements in or omissions from this work.

© 2013 Fiona Hay, Edward Hess and David Lockett

Foreword to Second Edition

The Hon. Mr Justice Mostyn

In his foreword to the first edition of this masterly work Lord Justice Thorpe, writing in April 2008, anticipated that the Court of Appeal would soon be offering clear guidance on the new law of pension sharing following divorce. Surprisingly, there has been an almost complete dearth of authority ever since. Perhaps that is a tribute to the simplicity of the new law and its exposition in this book. If a law is simply expressed by the legislature and clearly explained by commentators then legal controversy ought not to require resolution exposition and clarification by the higher courts. Indeed the only appellate authority devoted to this subject is *Martin-Dye v Martin-Dye*, and in truth nothing of any great moment was decided there.

The particular merit of this work is its exceptional clarity of expression. In the field of what was known as ancillary relief clarity is an often absent commodity. Instead controversy tends to rage over the most subtle nuances found in legion and often conflicting judgments, some of which have an almost metaphysical quality. Happily there is little scope for the legal profession to mine equivalently that part of the field designated pensions given the almost encyclopaedic content of the second edition of this work.

There is however one area of controversy. I have read with great interest the discussion at 12–007 et seq. about the tension between equality of division and equality of outcome when making a sharing order. For my part I am firmly in the former camp as the latter exercise must surely bring into account the inestimable benefit of being actually alive when the other party is dead! In my book it is an equal outcome for the husband to receive £20,000 annually for 10 years and for his younger wife to receive £10,000 for 20 years. But I acknowledge that my view is not shared by all and we may have to await a decision from a higher court to resolve the issue. Both sides of the divide are very fairly put by the authors in this edition.

Chapters 15–17 examine certain public and private sector pension schemes. The analysis is extremely detailed and very useful. I would hope that in the next edition, for reasons on which I perhaps do not need to expand, that these chapters will be enlarged to include the judicial pension scheme.

In my opinion this work has rightly assumed the role of the leading commentary in this specialist field. The second edition takes the quality of the

FOREWORD TO SECOND EDITION

first to a new plane. It is an indispensable text for anyone practising in the field of matrimonial finance, where the treatment of pensions will likely loom large. I recommend it enthusiastically.

Nicholas Mostyn
July 12, 2013

Foreword to First Edition

The Rt Hon. Lord Justice Thorpe

Fiscal and economic factors have driven pension rights from the wings to centre stage in many marriages that end in divorce and contested ancillary relief proceedings. The enlargement of the court's statutory powers did not lag so far behind the changing times. The call for legislation by Lord Nicholls in *Brooks v Brooks* [1996] A.C. 375 was answered surprisingly swiftly in the shape of Pensions Act 1995. However the enlargement was cautious and can be seen as no more than a first step on the road to the realistic powers that the judge now exercises. The legislative progress can be ascribed to the facts that the issues were hardly contentious and the enlargements could be achieved by simple additions to pre-existing sections.

The law relating to pensions on divorce is necessarily complex. The statutory extensions and their subsequent exercise are nor even primarily the territory of family lawyers. The various changes engage the interface between family and pension law. Pension lawyers, responsible for designing and managing vast and complex schemes, government lawyers, responsible for state schemes, actuaries and financial advisers all raised issues and set bounds on policy debates preceding reform.

Thus there is no other area of ancillary relief practice more technical and pitfall-strewn than this. It justifies, probably demands, its own text book. Our two authors are eminently equipped to guide us, each having years of experience at the specialist bar. I particularly commend the layout and clarity of chapters 1 to 10 which lead us through the decade of reform that commenced in 1996. With tactful delicacy they observe that the Court of Appeal has yet to offer guidance of comparable clarity. The next time opportunity arises we can expect Hess and Hay to be on our list of authorities.

Some eminent lawyers fail as authors as they strive to share all their knowledge of some specialist field. The result for the comparatively ignorant readers is obscurity. The greatest virtue that I found in these chapters was the simplicity of language. The authors have made an easy read of what might have been arduous.

I hope this venture receives the enthusiastic response it deserves.
Royal Courts of Justice
April 1, 2008

Preface

Scheme of this book When a husband and wife decide to divorce it is frequently the case that one of them will own valuable pension rights and the other will not, or will own such rights of a smaller value.

The interests of fairness may justify court intervention to redistribute these rights or make some other provision as compensation. This book is targeted at legal practitioners or other individuals involved in this process and attempts to explain and explore in an accessible fashion:

(i) what powers the court has to intervene and redistribute these rights;
(ii) the procedural mechanisms which the court will follow in carrying out this intervention and redistribution;
(iii) the circumstances in which the court will consider it necessary or appropriate to intervene and redistribute these rights or make some other provision as compensation;
(iv) the actuarial issues which may arise from such considerations; and
(v) the particular features of a selection of some of the larger pension schemes.

Nomenclature The nomenclature used in the relevant statutes and statutory instruments can be wordy and is neither uniform nor simple and the use of different terms can make issues appear more complicated than they really are. Accordingly, for the sake of simplicity, accessibility and gender neutrality, this book will, wherever possible and appropriate, use the following nomenclature.

The spouse who has the rights in a pension which may be the subject of a Pension Sharing Order or a Pension Attachment Order, whatever the nature of the pension rights involved, including shareable state scheme rights, will be referred to as **"the member spouse"**. This is intended to cover (and be of wider application and/or more accessible than) a range of terms used in the various statutes and statutory instruments, including "the party to the marriage who is or is likely to have benefits under a pension arrangement", "the party with pension rights" or "transferor".

The other spouse will be referred to as **"the non-member spouse"**. In so doing it is recognised that this term may be confusing, for example, where both parties are members of the same pension scheme. Use of the expression "the other party", however, can be even more confusing in certain circumstances and is only helpful when linked to the original reference which can be a cause of unnecessarily complicated sentences. Likewise, the word "transferee" is appropriate only in some places.

PREFACE

In referring to a "**pension scheme**", this book intends to include, unless expressly stated otherwise, pension schemes, policies, contracts, funds, entitlements or shareable state scheme rights. A detailed description of the distinguishing features of various different types of pension likely to be encountered by the practitioner is set out in Chapter 1 below.

On the same basis this book will refer to "**the pension provider**" whether this is intended to cover the Government in relation to "shareable state scheme rights", or any other "person responsible for a pension arrangement" in relation to other pension schemes. The pension provider may perform its functions through trustees, managers or some other management vehicle and the use of the expression "pension provider" is intended to cover whatever management vehicle applies to a particular pension scheme.

The law relating to **Pension Sharing Orders** and **Pension Attachment Orders** applies only to what one might describe as genuine pension rights. Individuals, of course, provide for their retirement in many other ways through property portfolios or other investments, but these are outside the scope of this book, save in so far as they provide grounds for a court in financial order proceedings to offset such investments against genuine pension rights.

The coming into force of the **Family Procedure Rules 2010** has led to an updating of some of the general nomenclature in this area and this book generally adopts the new terms. For example, "ancillary relief proceedings" now become "**financial order proceedings**" and CETVs and CEBs now become **CE**s. We shall, however, continue to refer to "divorce petitions" and "divorce proceedings" rather than "applications for matrimonial orders" because the authorised forms still use this nomenclature, notwithstanding the wording in the body of Family Procedure Rules 2010.

Date of law in this book The law dealt with is the law of England and Wales as at April 1, 2013.

About the authors

Fiona Hay, BSc BA (Hons)(Exon), Barrister of the Inner Temple, read Law and Chemistry at Exeter. She is a Barrister practising from Harcourt Chambers, London and Oxford.

Edward Hess, MA (Cantab), District Judge of the Principal Registry of the Family Division of the High Court of Justice, Barrister of the Middle Temple, read Mathematics and then Law at Peterhouse, Cambridge.

David Lockett, MA (Oxon), FIA, Senior Actuary, read Mathematics with Philosophy at Jesus College, Oxford. He practises as a Pensions Actuary through his company, Actuaries for Lawyers Limited.

TABLE OF CONTENTS

	PAGE
Foreword to Second Edition	v
Foreword to First Edition	vii
Preface	ix
About the authors	xi
Table of Cases	xxv
Table of Statutes	xxix

PARA

Part A
LAW AND PROCEDURE

1. Different Types of Pension 1–001
    Defined Contribution Schemes 1–002
    Defined Benefit Schemes 1–003
    State Pension Provision 1–006
        State Pension Age 1–007
        Basic State Pension (for those retiring before April 2016) 1–008
        Additional State Pensions 1–009
        Graduated Retirement Benefit 1–010
        Contracting out 1–011
        Valuation of State Pensions 1–012
        Sharing State Pensions 1–013
    White Paper Proposals to change the State Pension 1–014
    Occupational unfunded pensions from public service
        employers 1–016
    Occupational funded pensions 1–017
        Small Self Administered Pension Schemes (SSASs) 1–019
        Unapproved retirement benefits schemes, funded and unfunded
            (FURBS and UURBS) 1–020
    Personal Pension Arrangements 1–021
        Stakeholder Pensions 1–023
        Guaranteed Annuity Options 1–024
        Retirement Annuity Contracts 1–025
        Self Invested Pension Plans (SIPPs) 1–026
    Pensions in payment
        Annuities 1–027

CONTENTS

   Drawdown, Unsecured and Alternatively Secured
      Annuities 1–028
      Flexible Drawdown 1–030
      The Hutton Report 1–031

2. Cash Equivalents
   Definition of Cash Equivalent (CE) 2–001
   Issues affecting calculation of CE 2–002

3. Historical Overview of Pension Redistribution by the Courts on Divorce
   Prior to 1996
      Traditional remedies 3–001
      Winds of change 3–004
   1996 to date
      The arrival of earmarking..3–005
      The arrival of pension sharing 3–006
      The present 3–007
      The future 3–009

4. Law and Procedure in Relation to Pension Sharing Orders
   Law
      Statutory framework 4–001
      Definition of a Pension Sharing Order 4–002
      Availability of Pension Sharing Orders 4–003
      Implementation of Pension Sharing Orders..........................4–004
   Procedure
      Statutory Framework 4–005
      Commencing an application..4–006
      Gathering valuations..4–007
      Further information: Pension Inquiry Forms (Form P) or
         Actuary's Report?...4–008
      Making an order 4–009
      Implementing the order 4–011
      Pension credits...4–012
      Completing the process 4–013
   Appeals and applications to set aside or vary an order
      Appeals 4–014
      Applications to vary 4–015
   Double orders
      Earlier Pension Attachment Order 4–016
      Earlier Pension Sharing Order 4–017
      More than one Pension Sharing Order in one divorce 4–018
   Pre-legislation divorces..4–019
   Pensions and the statutory charge...4–020
   Orders under the Matrimonial Causes Act 1973 s.37 4–021

CONTENTS

5. Law and Procedure in Relation to Pension Attachment Orders
Law
- Statutory framework 5–001
- Definition of a Pension Attachment Order 5–002
- Nature of a Pension Attachment Order 5–003
- Subsidiary powers 5–004

Procedure
- Statutory Framework 5–005
- Commencing an application 5–006
- Gathering valuation information 5–008
- Making an order 5–009
- Implementing an order 5–010

Appeals and applications to set aside or vary an order
- Appeals and applications to set aside 5–011
- Applications to vary 5–012

Double orders
- Earlier Pension Sharing Order 5–013
- Pre-legislation divorces 5–014
- Pensions and the statutory charge 5–015
- Orders under Matrimonial Causes Act 1973 s.37 5–016
- Summary of pension attachment order procedure

6. International Issues
- Pension sharing and attachment across borders within the United Kingdom 6–001
- Pension sharing and attachment across borders between the United Kingdom and other countries
  - The problem 6–002

Possible solutions
- Exporting or importing the pension rights 6–004
- Securing a commitment by way of undertaking in a United Kingdom court order to the obtaining of an equivalent pension order in an overseas country 6–005
- Applications under Matrimonial and Family Proceedings Act 1984 6–006

7. Pensions on Divorce and Insolvency 7–001
Individual insolvency
- Property Adjustment or lump sum orders 7–002
- Income Payment Orders 7–004
- Pensions 7–005
- Excessive contributions—recovery by trustee 7–006
- Excessive contributions—setting aside of Pension Sharing Order 7–007
- Underfunded Occupational Pension Schemes 7–008
- Market Value Reductions 7–011
- The Pension Protection Fund
  - Notification of an Insolvency Event 7–012

CONTENTS

    Introduction of the Pension Protection Fund 7–013
    Funding 7–014
    Eligibility and assessment period 7–015
    Transfer Notice, Compensation 7–016
    Matrimonial Causes Act 1973 s.25E and Family Procedure Rules
        2010 rr.9.37–9.45 7–017
    Pre-existing Pension Sharing Orders 7–018
    Pension sharing in the assessment period 7–019
    Pension Compensation Sharing Orders 7–020
    Pre-existing Pension Attachment Orders 7–021
    Pension Attachment Orders against PPF compensation
        rights 7–022
    Pension Protection Fund Charges 7–023
  Civil Partnership 7–024
  Pension schemes being wound up 7–025
  Fraud Compensation 7–026

8. Solutions for Cases in which Pension Sharing Orders are Not Appropriate 8–001
  Small Self-Administered Pension Schemes ("SSASs") 8–002
  Self-Invested Personal Pension Schemes 8–003
  Unapproved Retirement Benefit Schemes (Funded and
    Unfunded) 8–004
  Pension Sharing resulting in diminution of assets
    Transfer out of defined benefit schemes with disadvantageous
        CEs 8–005
    Guaranteed Annuities 8–006
  Income Gap 8–007
  Pension Protection Fund 8–008
  Other cases 8–009
  Solutions in cases where pension sharing is not appropriate
    Deferring pension sharing 8–010
    Offsetting 8–011
    Lump sums in instalments/series of lump sums 8–012
    Pension attachment 8–013
    Joint lives maintenance orders 8–014
    Imaginative Actuarial Solution 8–015

9. The Work of the Pensions Ombudsman
  Status of the Pensions Ombudsman 9–001
  Relevance to a divorce practitioner 9–002

10. Implementation Issues
  Unexpected death
    Basis of Pension Sharing Orders 10–001
    Death by either party before Decree Absolute 10–002
    Barder appeals 10–003

CONTENTS

Death of either party after Decree Absolute but before order has taken effect 10–004
Death of non-member spouse after order has taken effect, but before implementation 10–005
Death of member spouse after order has taken effect, but before implementation 10–006
Death of either party after implementation of Pension Sharing Order 10–007
Effect of death on a Pension Attachment Order 10–008
Moving Target Syndrome and Clawback
    CE valuation changes between the Pension Sharing Order and Valuation Day—Moving Target Syndrome 10–009
    Clawback 10–011
    Income Gap 10–012

11. Pension Sharing and Attachment on Dissolution of Civil Partnership

Civil partnerships
    The Statutory provisions 11–001
Entitlement to pension provision on death of the other civil partner 11–002
Pension sharing and attachment in civil partnership dissolution—provisions and regulations 11–003
Pension Sharing Orders after remarriage/new civil partnership 11–004
The PPF and pension sharing in civil partnership proceedings 11–005
Pre-existing orders 11–006
The PPF and Pension Compensation Attachment Orders in civil partnership proceedings 11–007
The PPF and pre-existing Pension Attachment Orders 11–008

12. The Section 25 Factors, Fairness and Equality in Relation to Pensions 12–001

Foreseeable future 12–002
The relevant s.25 factors 12–003
Quantification of the asset 12–004
    Widow's/Widower's pensions 12–006
Financial Needs and Obligations
    Equalisation of CE or of income? 12–007
    Maintaining the value of the pension 12–009
Health 12–010
Matrimonial acquest/Contributions 12–011
Pre-marital contributions
    H v H 12–012
    Harris v Harris 12–013
    The straight-line discount 12–014

CONTENTS

White v White, Miller, McFarlane, Charman and *N v F*—cases involving pre-marital contributions 12–015
Pre-marital contributions—cases involving pensions 12–016
Summary of the position where pension assets are "pre-marital property" 12–017
Contributions between separation and final hearing 12–018
    N v N, Cowan v Cowan 12–019
    Miller, McFarlane 12–020
    Rossi v Rossi 12–021
    Summary of the position in relation to post separation accrual 12–024
    Delay 12–025
Future Accrual 12–026
Age and duration of the marriage 12–027
    Pension Sharing Orders and continuing periodical payments 12–028
    Re-building 12–029

13. OFF-SETTING

Circumstances in which off-setting may be appropriate 13–001
The Courts' approach to offsetting
    Maskell v Maskell: pension CE cannot be treated as equivalent to a realisable asset 13–002
    Norris v Norris, GW v GW and *S v S* 13–003
    Martin-Dye 13–004
    Vaughan v Vaughan 13–006
    Summary of position in relation to Courts' approach to offsetting 13–007
Valuation of the set off
    Utilising CE and cases in which that may be appropriate 13–008
Offset without expert evidence
    Offset based on the Cash Equivalent 13–009
    Simple cases 13–010
Actuarially calculated offset 13–011
    Full Replacement Value 13–012
    Net Full Replacement Value 13–013
    Fund Account Value 13–014
    The Net Actuarial Value 13–015
    Replacement of pension sharing value 13–016
    Duxbury value 13–017
    Comparison of the approaches 13–018
    Conclusion 13–019
Capitalisation of periodical payments after offset 13–020

CONTENTS

Part B
ACTUARIAL SECTION

14. Actuarial Issues Arising from the use of CEs 14–001
    The nature of the CE as a method of valuation 14–002
    Security of benefits in a final salary scheme 14–005
    The CE and the external option.. 14–009
        Example 1 14–011
        Example 2 14–012
        Example 3 14–013
        Example 4 14–014
    Guaranteed Annuity Rates 14–015
    Market Value Adjustment Factors 14–018
    The Income Gap and Adjournment 14–020
        Pitfall A... 14–022
        Pitfall B 14–023
        Pitfall C 14–024
        Pitfall D... 14–025
        Pitfall E 14–026
        Pitfall F 14–027
        Pitfall G... 14–028
        Pitfall H... 14–029
        Pitfall I 14–030
        Pitfall J 14–031
    Apportioning Pension Rights.. 14–033
    Pension Rights at Different Dates 14–036
        Method I 14–037
        Method II 14–038
        Method III 14–039
    Health Issues 14–040

15. The Shorter Career Public Sector Pension Schemes
    Armed Forces Pension Scheme 1975 (AFPS 1975)—Non-Officers
        Section
        Contact details
        Eligibility 15–002
        Main features of the scheme 15–003
        Cash Equivalents 15–005
        Pension sharing.. 15–006
        Equal income calculations for pension sharing within the AFPS
            1975 15–007
        Case study one
        Case study two
        Case study three... 15–011
        Miscellaneous other matters.. 15–012
    Armed Forces Pension Scheme 1975 (AFPS 1975)—Officers
        Section
        Contact details

CONTENTS

Eligibility 15–014
Main features of the scheme 15–015
Cash Equivalents 15–017
Pension sharing 15–018
Equal income calculations for pension sharing within the AFPS
    1975 15–019
Case study one
Case study two
Case study three 15–023
Miscellaneous other matters 15–024
Armed Forces Pension Scheme 2005 (AFPS 2005)
    Contact details
    Eligibility 15–026
    Main features of the scheme 15–027
    Cash Equivalents 15–029
    Pension sharing 15–030
    Equal income calculations for pension sharing within the AFPS
        2005 15–031
    Case study one
    Case study two 15–034
    Miscellaneous other matters 15–35
Police Pension Scheme 1987
    Contact details
    Eligibility 15–037
    Main features of the scheme 15–038
    Cash Equivalents 15–040
    Pension sharing 15–41
    Equal income calculations for pension sharing within the Police
        Pension Scheme 1987 15–042
    Case study one
    Case study two 15–045
    Miscellaneous other matters 15–046
Police Pension Scheme 2008
    Contact details
    Eligibility 15–048
    Main features of the scheme 15–049
    Cash Equivalents 15–051
    Pension sharing 15–052
    Equal income calculations for pension sharing within the Police
        Pension Scheme 2008 15–053
    Case study one 15–055
    Miscellaneous other matters 15–056
Firefighters' Pension Scheme
    Contact details
    Eligibility 15–058
    Main features of the scheme 15–059
    Cash Equivalents 15–062
    Pension sharing 15–063

CONTENTS

Equal income calculations for pension sharing within the
    Firefighters' pension Scheme 15–064
Case study one
Case study two 15–067
Miscellaneous other matters 15–068
Firefighters' Pension Scheme 2006
  Contact details
  Eligibility 15–070
  Main features of the scheme 15–071
  Cash Equivalents 15–073
  Pension sharing 15–074
  Equal income calculations for pension sharing within the
    Firefighters' Pension Scheme 2006 15–075
  Case study one 15–077
  Miscellaneous other matters 15–078

16. Some "Longer Career" Public Sector Schemes
Local Government Pension Scheme
  Contact Details
  Eligibility 16–002
  Main Features of the scheme 16–003
  Cash Equivalents 16–005
  Pension sharing 16–006
  Miscellaneous other matters 16–007
Teachers' Pension Scheme (Section for members in service before
  January 1, 2007)
  Contact Details
  Eligibility 16–009
  Main Features of the scheme 16–010
  Cash Equivalents 16–012
  Pension sharing 16–013
  Miscellaneous other matters 16–014
National Health Service Pension Scheme (1995 Section)
  Contact Details
  Eligibility 16–016
  Main Features of the scheme 16–017
  Cash Equivalents 16–019
  Pension sharing 16–020
  Equal income calculations for pension sharing within the NHS
    Pension Scheme 16–021
  Case Study One
  Case Study Two
  Miscellaneous other matters 16–024
National Health Service Pension Scheme (2008 Section)
  Contact Details
  Eligibility 16–026
  Main Features of the scheme 16–027
  Cash Equivalents 16–029

CONTENTS

    Pension sharing..16–030
    Miscellaneous other matters..16–031
  Principal Civil Service Pension Scheme (Classic Plus Section)
    Contact Details
    Eligibility...16–033
    Main Features of the scheme..16–034
    Cash Equivalents...16–036
    Pension sharing..16–037
    Miscellaneous other matters..16–038
  Principal Civil Service Pension Scheme (Classic Section)
    Contact Details
    Eligibility...16–040
    Main Features of the scheme..16–041
    Cash Equivalents...16–043
    Pension sharing..16–044
    Equal income calculations for pension sharing within the
        Principal Civil Service Pension Scheme...16–045
    Case Study One
    Miscellaneous other matters..16–047
  Principal Civil Service Pension Scheme (Nuvos Section)
    Contact Details
    Eligibility...16–049
    Main Features of the scheme..16–050
    Cash Equivalents...16–052
    Pension sharing..16–053
  Principal Civil Service Pension Scheme (Premium Section)
    Contact Details
    Eligibility...16–055
    Main Features of the scheme..16–056
    Cash Equivalents...16–058
    Pension sharing..16–059
    Miscellaneous other matters..16–060

17. Some Private Sector Schemes
  British Airways Pension Schemes—Airways Pension Scheme
    Contact Details
    Eligibility...17–002
    Main features of the scheme...17–003
    Cash Equivalents...17–006
    Pension sharing..17–007
    Miscellaneous..17–008
  British Airways Pension Schemes—New Airways Pension Scheme
    Contact Details
    Eligibility...17–010
    Main features of the scheme...17–011
    Plan 65—increasing the build up rate...17–012
    Option 55...17–018
    Cash Equivalents...17–019

CONTENTS

Pension sharing 17–020
Miscellaneous 17–021
BP Pension Scheme—Final Salary section
   Contact Details
   Eligibility 17–023
   Main features of the scheme 17–024
   Cash Equivalents 17–028
   Pension sharing 17–029
   Miscellaneous 17–030
British Telecom Pension Schemes—Defined Benefit Sections
   Contact Details
   Eligibility 17–032
   Main features of the scheme 17–033
   Contributions 17–035
   Cash Equivalents 17–040
   Pension sharing 17–041
   Miscellaneous 17–042
Shell Contributory Pension Scheme
   Contact Details
   Eligibility 17–044
   Main features of the scheme 17–045
   Cash Equivalents 17–047
   Pension sharing 17–048
   Miscellaneous 17–049
Shell Overseas Contributory Pension Scheme
   Contact Details
   Eligibility 17–051
   Main features of the scheme 17–052
   Cash Equivalents 17–054
   Pension sharing 17–055
Universities Superannuation Scheme—Final Salary Section
   Contact Details
   Eligibility 17–057
   Main features of the scheme 17–058
   Cash Equivalents 17–060
   Pension sharing 17–061

Part C
RELEVANT LEGISLATION
                                                                                                                             PAGE

Statutes and Statutory Instruments 201

CONTENTS

Part D
MISCELLANEOUS MATERIALS

PAGE

Forms 299

Sample Letters of Instruction to a Pensions Actuary for an Expert's Report 339

Income Equality and Pension Age Tables...349

Index 363

TABLE OF CASES

Agbaje v Agbaje [2010] UKSC 13; [2010] 1 A.C. 628; [2010] 2 W.L.R. 709; [2010] 2 All E.R. 877; [2010] 1 F.L.R. 1813; [2010] 2 F.C.R. 1; [2010] Fam. Law 573; (2010) 107(12) L.S.G. 20; (2010) 154(11) S.J.L.B. 29 .... 6–006, 6–007
AR v AR (Treatment of Inherited Wealth) [2011] EWHC 2717 (Fam); [2012] 2 F.L.R. 1; [2012] W.T.L.R. 373; [2012] Fam. Law 15; (2011) 109(44) L.S.G. 19 12–011
B v B (Assessment of Assets: Pre-Marital Property) [2012] EWHC 314 (Fam); [2012] 2 F.L.R. 22; [2012] Fam. Law 516 .... 12–005, 12–007, 12–016
B v B [2010] EWHC 193 (Fam); [2010] 2 F.L.R. 1214; [2010] Fam. Law 905 .... 12–023, 12–024, 12–026
Ball v Jones [2008] B.P.I.R. 1051 ..... 7–003, 7–007
Barder v Barder (Caluori intervening). See Barder v Caluori
Barder v Caluori; sub nom Barder v Barder (Caluori intervening) [1988] A.C. 20; [1987] 2 W.L.R. 1350; [1987] 2 All E.R. 440; [1987] 2 F.L.R. 480; [1988] Fam. Law 18; (1987) 84 L.S.G. 2046; (1987) 137 N.L.J. 497; (1987) 131 S.J. 776 HL 10–003, 10–005
Boughton v Punter Southall and Trs of the Bell Clements Group Pension (2009) ref 74851/1 Pensions Ombudsman 4–004, 4–011, 9–002
Brooks v Brooks [1996] A.C. 375; [1995] 3 W.L.R. 141; [1995] 3 All E.R. 257; [1995] 2 F.L.R. 13; [1995] 3 F.C.R. 214; [1995] Pens. L.R. 173; [1995] Fam. Law 545; (1995) 145 N.L.J. 995; (1995) 139 S.J.L.B. 165 .... 3–001, 3–002, 3–004, 3–005
Burrow v Burrow [1999] 1 F.L.R. 508; [1999] 2 F.C.R. 549; [1999] Fam. Law 83 3–005
Charman v Charman [2006] EWHC 1879 (Fam); [2007] 1 F.L.R. 593; [2007] 1 F.C.R. 33; [2006] W.T.L.R. 1349; (2006-07) 9 I.T.E.L.R. 173; [2006] Fam. Law 1018; (2006) 103(35) L.S.G. 33; (2006) 150 S.J.L.B. 1111 ... 12–015, 12–017, 12–020, 12–021, 12–022
Cleworth v Teachers' Pension Scheme (2012) 21 December 2012, ref 87725/2 Pensions Ombudsman 9–002, 10–011
Coleman v Coleman [1973] Fam. 10; [1972] 3 W.L.R. 681; [1972] 3 All E.R. 886; (1972) 116 S.J. 746 Fam Div 8–012

Cowan v Cowan [2001] EWCA Civ 679; [2002] Fam. 97; [2001] 3 W.L.R. 684; [2001] 2 F.L.R. 192; [2001] 2 F.C.R. 331; [2001] Fam. Law 498 .... 3–001, 12–019, 12–020, 12–024, 12–025
Crabtree v BAE Systems Executive Pension Scheme (2008) 19 May, ref S00522 Pensions Ombudsman 9–002, 10–010
Culverwell v Teachers' Pension Scheme (2012) 13 November, ref 82981/3 Pensions Ombudsman 9–002, 10–010
D v D (Financial Provision: Periodical Payments) [2004] EWHC 445 (Fam); [2004] 1 F.L.R. 988; [2004] Fam. Law 407 12–028
Davis v Windsor Life Assurance Company (2012) 6 March, ref 80998/1 Pensions Ombudsman 9–002, 10–011
Duxbury v Duxbury [1987] 1 F.L.R. 7; [1987] Fam. Law 13 CA (Civ Div) 8–014, 13–003, 13–014, 13–017
Edgar v Edgar [1980] 1 W.L.R. 1410; [1980] 3 All E.R. 887; (1981) 2 F.L.R. 19; (1980) 11 Fam. Law 20; (1980) 124 S.J. 809 CA (Civ Div) 8–010
G (Children Act 1989 Sch.1), Re [1996] 2 F.L.R. 171; [1997] 1 F.C.R. 261; [1996] Fam. Law 534; (1997) 161 J.P.N. 138 Fam Div 7–002
GS v L (Financial Remedies: Pre-acquired Assets: Needs) [2011] EWHC 1759 (Fam); [2013] 1 F.L.R. 300; [2012] Fam. Law 800 12–016
GW v RW (Financial Provision: Departure from Equality) [2003] EWHC 611 (Fam); [2003] 2 F.L.R. 108; [2003] 2 F.C.R. 289; [2003] Fam. Law 386 13–003
H v H (Financial Provision: Capital Allowance) [1993] 2 F.L.R. 335; [1993] 2 F.C.R. 308; [1993] Fam. Law 520 .... 12–012, 12–014
H v H (Financial Relief: Pensions) [2009] EWHC 3739 (Fam); [2010] 2 F.L.R. 173; [2010] Fam. Law 575 ..... 4–002, 8–002, 10–009
H v H (Pension Sharing: Rescission of Decree Nisi) [2002] EWHC 767 (Fam); [2002] 2 F.L.R. 116; [2002] Fam. Law 591 4–019
H v H [2007] EWHC 459 (Fam); [2007] 2 F.L.R. 548; [2008] 2 F.C.R. 714; [2007] Fam. Law 578; (2007) 151 S.J.L.B. 503 .... 12–008, 12–022, 12–024, 12–026

TABLE OF CASES

Haines v Hill. *See* Hill v Haines
Hamilton v Hamilton [2013] EWCA Civ 13; [2013] Fam. Law 539; (2013) 157(4) S.J.L.B. 43 8–012
Hamlin v Hamlin [1986] Fam. 11; [1985] 3 W.L.R. 629; [1985] 2 All E.R. 1037; [1986] 1 F.L.R. 61; [1985] Fam. Law 321; (1985) 82 L.S.G. 3173; (1985) 135 N.L.J. 582; (1985) 129 S.J. 700 6–003
Harris v Harris Unreported November 23, 2000 CA 12–013
Hellyer v Hellyer (Lump sum payments) [1996] 2 F.L.R. 579; [1997] 1 F.C.R. 340; [1997] B.P.I.R. 85; [1997] Fam. Law 14 CA (Civ Div) 7–002
Hendry v Tarmac UK Pension Scheme (2012) 6 March, ref 85218/1 Pensions Ombudsman 9–002, 10–002
Hill v Haines; sub nom Haines v Hill [2007] EWCA Civ 1284; [2008] Ch. 412; [2008] 2 W.L.R. 1250; [2008] 2 All E.R. 901; [2008] 1 F.L.R. 1192; [2007] 3 F.C.R. 785; [2007] B.P.I.R. 1280; [2008] W.T.L.R. 447; [2008] Fam. Law 199; [2007] 50 E.G. 109 (C.S.); (2007) 151 S.J.L.B. 1597; [2007] N.P.C. 1 .... 7–003, 7–007
J v J (Financial Orders: Wife's Long-term Needs) [2011] EWHC 1010 (Fam); [2011] 2 F.L.R. 1280; [2011] Fam. Law 684 13–006
Jones v Jones [2011] EWCA Civ 41; [2012] Fam. 1; [2011] 3 W.L.R. 582; [2011] 1 F.L.R. 1723; [2011] 1 F.C.R. 242; [2011] Fam. Law 455; (2011) 161 N.L.J. 210 .... 12–011, 12–015
K v K (Financial Relief: Widow's Pension) [1997] 1 F.L.R. 35; [1996] 3 F.C.R. 158; [1997] Fam. Law 162 Fam Div 3–002
K v L (Ancillary Relief: Inherited Wealth) [2011] EWCA Civ 550; [2012] 1 W.L.R. 306; [2011] 3 All E.R. 733; [2011] 2 F.L.R. 980; [2011] 2 F.C.R. 597; [2012] W.T.L.R. 153; [2011] Fam. Law 799; (2011) 108(21) L.S.G. 18; (2011) 161 N.L.J. 742 12–011
Kemp v Axle Group Holdings Ltd Directors and Executives Pension Scheme (2010) 1 September, ref 76194/1 Pensions Ombudsman. 5–016, 9–002
Kerbel v Southwark Council (2009) 26 January, ref 72577/1 Pensions Ombudsman 9–002
Kilvert v Flackett (A Bankrupt) [1998] 2 F.L.R. 806; [1998] B.P.I.R. 721; [1998] O.P.L.R. 237; [1998] Pens. L.R. 289; [1998] Fam. Law 582 Ch D 7–004
Lambert v Lambert [2002] EWCA Civ 1685; [2003] Fam. 103; [2003] 2 W.L.R. 631; [2003] 4 All E.R. 342; [2003] 1 F.L.R. 139; [2002] 3 F.C.R. 673; [2003] Fam. Law 16 12–024

Lauder v Lauder [2007] EWHC 1227 (Fam); [2007] 2 F.L.R. 802; [2008] 3 F.C.R. 4 Fam Div 8–014
Le Marchant v Le Marchant [1977] 1 W.L.R. 559; [1977] 3 All E.R. 610; (1977) 7 Fam. Law 241; (1977) 121 S.J. 334 CA (Civ Div) 3–002
M v M (Financial Relief: Substantial Earning Capacity) [2004] EWHC 688 (Fam); [2004] 2 F.L.R. 236; [2004] Fam. Law 496 12–022
Martin-Dye v Martin-Dye [2006] EWCA Civ 681; [2006] 1 W.L.R. 3448; [2006] 4 All E.R. 779; [2006] 2 F.L.R. 901; [2006] 2 F.C.R. 325; [2006] Fam. Law 731; (2006) 156 N.L.J. 917 ... 4–008, 12–004, 12–008, 13–004, 13–005, 13–007
Maskell v Maskell [2001] EWCA Civ 858; [2003] 1 F.L.R. 1138; [2001] 3 F.C.R. 296; [2003] Fam. Law 391 13–002
McFarlane v McFarlane. *See* Miller v Miller
Miller v Miller; McFarlane v McFarlane [2006] UKHL 24; [2006] 2 A.C. 618; [2006] 2 W.L.R. 1283; [2006] 3 All E.R. 1; [2006] 1 F.L.R. 1186; [2006] 2 F.C.R. 213; [2006] Fam. Law 629; (2006) 103(23) L.S.G. 28; (2006) 156 N.L.J. 916; (2006) 150 S.J.L.B. 704 .... 12–011, 12–015, 12–016, 12–017, 12–020, 12–021, 12–024, 12–026, 12–027, 13–003
Milne v Milne [1981] 2 F.L.R. 286 3–002
Minton v Minton [1979] A.C. 593; [1979] 2 W.L.R. 31; [1979] 1 All E.R. 79; (1978) 122 S.J. 843 HL 4–018
Morton v MJF Associates Private Pension Scheme (2010) 4 July, ref 77828/2, Pensions Ombudsman 5–004, 9–002
Mountney v Treharne [2002] EWCA Civ 1174; [2003] Ch. 135; [2002] 3 W.L.R. 1760; [2002] 2 F.L.R. 930; [2002] 3 F.C.R. 97; [2002] B.P.I.R. 1126; [2002] Fam. Law 809; (2002) 99(39) L.S.G. 38 7–002
N v F (Financial Orders: Pre-Acquired Wealth) [2011] EWHC 586 (Fam); [2011] 2 F.L.R. 533; [2012] 1 F.C.R. 139; [2011] Fam. Law 686 .... 12–011, 12–015
N v N (Financial Provision: Sale of Company) [2001] 2 F.L.R. 69 Fam Div 12–019, 12–020
Norris v Norris [2003] 1 F.L.R. 1142, [2002] EWHC 2996 (Fam). 13–003
P v P (Post-Separation Accruals and Earning Capacity) [2007] EWHC 2877 (Fam); [2008] 2 F.L.R. 1135; [2008] Fam. Law 614 .... 12–023, 12–024, 12–026
Parker v Parker [1972] Fam. 116; [1972] 2 W.L.R. 21; [1972] 1 All E.R. 410; (1971) 115 S.J. 949 Fam Div 3–002

TABLE OF CASES

Pearce v Pearce [2003] EWCA Civ 1054; [2004] 1 W.L.R. 68; [2003] 2 F.L.R. 1144; [2003] 3 F.C.R. 178; [2003] Fam. Law 723; (2003) 100(36) L.S.G. 39 8–014

Pike v Teachers' Pension Scheme (2008) 26 March, ref 26355 Pensions Ombudsman 9–002, 10–011

R. (on the application of Smith) v Secretary of State for Defence [2004] EWHC 1797 (Admin); [2005] 1 F.L.R. 97; [2004] Pens. L.R. 323; [2005] A.C.D. 15; [2004] Fam. Law 868; (2004) 101(34) L.S.G. 30 . . . . . 10–012, 15–006, 15–018, 15–030

R. (on the application of Thomas) v Ministry of Defence [2008] EWHC 1119 (Admin); [2008] 2 F.L.R. 1385; [2008] Fam. Law 731 . . . . 10–012, 15–006, 15–018, 15–030

Raithatha v Williamson [2012] EWHC 909 (Ch); [2012] 1 W.L.R. 3559; [2012] 3 All E.R. 1028; [2012] B.P.I.R. 621 7–004

Robson v Robson [2010] EWCA Civ 1171; [2011] 1 F.L.R. 751; [2011] 3 F.C.R. 625; [2011] Fam. Law 224; (2010) 107(43) L.S.G. 20; (2010) 160 N.L.J. 1530 . . . . 12–011, 12–015

Rossi v Rossi [2006] EWHC 1482 (Fam); [2007] 1 F.L.R. 790; [2006] 3 F.C.R. 271; [2007] Fam. Law 104 . . . 12–021, 12–022, 12–024, 12–025

RP v RP [2006] EWHC 3409 (Fam); [2007] 1 F.L.R. 2105; [2008] 2 F.C.R. 613; [2007] Fam. Law 581 . . . . 12–007, 12–026

S v S (Ancillary Relief after Lengthy Separation) [2006] EWHC 2339 (Fam); [2007] 1 F.L.R. 2120; [2007] 2 F.C.R. 762; [2007] Fam. Law 482 . . . . 12–008, 12–022

S v S (Financial Provision: Delay) [1990] 2 F.L.R. 252; [1989] F.C.R. 582 CA (Civ Div) 12–025

S v S (Non-Matrimonial Property: Conduct) [2006] EWHC 2793 (Fam); [2007] 1 F.L.R. 1496; [2007] Fam. Law 106 . . . . . 12–016, 12–017, 12–024, 13–003

S v S (Rescission of Decree Nisi: Pension Sharing Provision) [2002] 1 F.L.R. 457; [2002] 1 F.C.R. 193; [2002] Pens. L.R. 219; [2002] Fam. Law 171 Fam Div 4–019

S v S [2011] EWCA Civ 174; [2011] 1 F.L.R. 2129; [2011] Fam. Law 570 6–007

Sandford v Sandford [1986] 1 F.L.R. 412; [1986] Fam. Law 104 CA (Civ Div) 4–018

Shagroon v Sharbatly; sub nom Sharbatly v Shagroon [2012] EWCA Civ 1507; [2013] 2 W.L.R. 1255; [2013] 1 F.C.R. 467; [2013] Fam. Law 394 6–006

Sharbatly v Shagroon. *See* Shagroon v Sharbatly

Shepherd v Trs of the Air Products Pension Plan (2006) 21 September, ref Q00278 Pensions Ombudsman 9–002, 10–011

Slattery v Cabinet Office (Civil Service Pensions) [2009] EWHC 226 (Ch); [2009] I.C.R. 806; [2009] 1 F.L.R. 1365; [2009] 3 F.C.R. 558; [2009] Pens. L.R. 129; [2009] Fam. Law 398 . . . . 4–004, 10–010

Staley v Marlborough Investment Management Ltd Retirement Scheme (2012) 31 July, ref 81482/2 Pensions Ombudsman 9–002, 10–010

Symons v Astra Zeneca Pension Trustees Ltd (2011) 15 July, ref 83880/2 Pensions Ombudsman 9–002

T v T (Financial Relief: Pensions) [1998] 1 F.L.R. 1072; [1998] 2 F.C.R. 364; [1998] O.P.L.R. 1; [1998] Pens. L.R. 221; [1998] Fam. Law 398 Fam Div 3–005

Traversa v Freddi [2011] EWCA Civ 81; [2011] Fam. Law 464 . . . . 6–006, 6–007

Twiname v Twiname [1992] 1 F.L.R. 29; [1992] F.C.R. 185; [1991] Fam. Law 520 CA (Civ Div) 12–025

Vaughan v Vaughan [2007] EWCA Civ 1085; [2008] 1 F.L.R. 1108; [2007] 3 F.C.R. 533; [2008] Fam. Law 14; (2007) 151 S.J.L.B. 1435; (2007) 151 S.J.L.B. 1499 . . . . 12–008, 12–016, 13–006

Warwick (formerly Yarwood) v Yarwood's Trustee in Bankruptcy [2010] EWHC 2272 (Ch); [2010] 3 F.C.R. 311; [2010] B.P.I.R. 1443; (2010) 154(36) S.J.L.B. 33; [2010] N.P.C. 93 7–002

Westbury v Sampson [2001] EWCA Civ 407; [2002] 1 F.L.R. 166; [2001] 2 F.C.R. 210; [2002] Fam. Law 15; (2001) 98(20) L.S.G. 44 . . . . 5–003, 5–012

Whaley v Whaley [2011] EWCA Civ 617; [2012] 1 F.L.R. 735; [2011] 2 F.C.R. 323; [2011] W.T.L.R. 1267; 14 I.T.E.L.R. 1; [2011] Fam. Law 804; [2011] N.P.C. 53 12–011

White v White [2001] 1 A.C. 596; [2000] 3 W.L.R. 1571; [2001] 1 All E.R. 1; [2000] 2 F.L.R. 981; [2000] 3 F.C.R. 555; [2001] Fam. Law 12; (2000) 97(43) L.S.G. 38; (2000) 150 N.L.J. 1716; (2000) 144 S.J.L.B. 266; [2000] N.P.C. 11 HL . . 3–006, 12–007, 12–012, 12–015

TABLE OF STATUTES

1973	Matrimonial Causes Act (c.18) . . 3–004, 4–001, 4–021, 5–001, 11–003, 11–004, 11–005
	s.5 3–002
	s.10(2) 3–002
	Pt II 4–001, 5–001
	s.21A 4–002
	s.21B 7–020, 8–008, 11–005
	s.23 5–003
	(5) 10–002, 10–008
	s.24 3–006
	(1)(c) 3–004
	(3) 10–002
	s.24A(3) 10–002
	s.24B . . 4–003, 4–009, 4–017, 4–018
	(3) 4–017
	(5) 4–016, 8–014
	s.24C(1) 4–010
	s.24E 7–020
	(3) 7–020
	s.25 . 4–003, 7–003, 12–001, 12–003, 13–008, 13–010
	(2)(a) 12–002, 12–003
	(f) 12–011
	s.25A 3–001, 3–003, 4–003
	s.25B 4–003
	(1) 12–002, 12–004
	(a) 12–003
	(b) 12–003
	(2)(b) 12–003
	(d) 12–003
	(e) 12–003
	(f) 12–003
	(h) 12–003
	(3) 5–002, 5–003
	(4) 5–002, 8–013
	(5) 5–002
	(7) 5–002, 5–004
	(7B) 4–017, 5–013
	s.25C 5–002, 8–013, 10–008
	(2) 5–004
	(4) 4–017, 5–013
	s.25D(1) 5–016
	(3) 5–002
	s.25E 7–017, 7–019, 7–021
	s.25F 7–022
	s.28(1)(a) 10–008, 12–028
	(3) . . 4–006, 5–006, 6–006, 8–010, 11–004
	s.31 . . . 4–015, 4–018, 5–012, 8–010, 8–014
	(2)(b) 5–003
	(d) 8–012
	(dd) 5–003, 5–012, 8–013
	(g) 4–015
	(2B) 5–003, 8–013
	(4A)(a) 4–015
	(7A) 12–013
	(7B)(a) 5–012
	(ba) 4–015, 4–017, 13–020
	s.37 . . . . 4–021, 5–016, 9–002
	(1) 4–021
	s.40A(2)–(4) 4–014
	(5) 4–014
1975	Social Security Pensions Act (c.60) 2–001
	Inheritance (Provision for Family and Dependants) Act (c.63) 3–003, 10–002, 10–004
1984	Matrimonial and Family Proceedings Act (c.42) 6–006, 6–007
	s.3 . . . . 3–001, 3–003
	s.12(2) 6–006
	s.13 6–006
	s.15 6–006
	s.16 6–007
	s.17(1)(b) 6–006
	(c) 6–006
	s.20 6–006
	s.21(1)(bd) 6–006
	(bg) 6–006
1985	Social Security Act (c.53) 2–001
1986	Insolvency Act (c.45)
	s.281(5) 7–003
	s.283 7–005
	s.284 7–002
	s.310 7–004
	(6) 7–004
	(7) 7–004
	s.310A 7–004
	s.339 . . . . 7–003, 7–007
	s.340 7–007
	s.342A–C 7–006
	s.385 7–004
1988	Income and Corporation Taxes Act (c.1)
	s.612 4–002
1992	Social Security Contributions and Benefits Act (c.4)
	s.44(3)(a) 4–002
	(b) 4–002
	s.48(1) 1–008
	(3) 1–008
1993	Pension Schemes Act (c.48)
	Pt IV 14–034
	Ch.IV 2–001
	s.93 2–001
	Pt X 9–001
1995	Pensions Act (c.26) 2–001, 3–006, 3–007
	ss.73–77 7–001
	s.74 7–025
	(6) 14–034
	s.152 2–001

TABLE OF STATUTES

s.166 . . . . . . 3–005, 5–001, 12–002	
Sch.4 1–007	
1996 Family Law Act (c.27)	
Pt II 4–001	
1999 Welfare Reform and Pensions Act	
(c.30) . . 1–023, 3–006, 3–007, 4–001, 8–014	
s.2 1–023	
s.11 7–005	
(2) 7–005	
s.12 7–005	
s.15 7–006	
(6) 7–006	
s.28 6–001	
(1)(a) 10–004	
s.29 10–006	
(1) 10–004	
(2) 4–004, 10–009	
(4) 4–004, 10–010	
(5) 4–004, 10–010	
(7) 4–004, 4–011, 10–009	
(8) 4–004, 10–010	
s.31 . . . . 4–002, 4–004	
s.34 . . . . 4–004, 10–009	
(1) 4–011	
s.35(1) 4–012	
(2)(b) 10–005	
s.41(3)(b) 4–009	
s.46 4–002	
s.47 4–002	
s.49 4–011	
s.85(3) 3–006, 4–019	
(b) 4–015	
Sch.3 4–001	
para.3 3–006	
para.9 4–021	
Sch.5 . . . . 4–004, 4–012	
para.8 . . . . 7–008, 7–010	
para.10 4–012	
Sch.12 4–001	
2004 Finance Act (c.12) 1–002, 1–026, 1–028, 9–001	
Civil Partnership Act (c.33) 3–007, 4–003, 11–001, 11–002, 11–003	
Pt 2 11–001	
s.3 11–002	
ss.16–19 11–003	
ss.19A–19F 11–003	
ss.24–29 11–003	
Pt 4 11–003	
Pt 4A 11–003	
Pt 6 11–003	
Sch.5 . . . . 11–001, 11–003	
para.4A 11–005	
para.7 11–007	
Pensions Act (c.35) 7–013, 7–019, 7–026	
Pt 2 7–013	

ss.107–120 7–013	
s.121 . . . . . . 7–001, 7–012, 7–015	
s.122(2) 7–015	
(6) 7–015	
s.126 7–015	
s.127 7–001	
s.132 7–015	
(2)(b) 7–015	
s.133 7–019	
(8) 7–018	
s.138 7–019	
(2) 7–018, 11–006	
s.149 7–015	
s.154 7–015	
s.160(a) 7–015	
s.175 7–014	
s.187 7–026	
s.189 7–014	
s.319(1) 7–017	
Sch.5 para.31 11–008	
Schs 5–9 7–013	
Sch.7 7–016	
para.3 7–016	
para.4 7–016	
para.5 7–016	
para.6 7–016	
para.8 7–016	
para.9 7–016	
para.11 7–016	
para.13 7–016	
para.15 7–016	
para.18 7–016	
para.21 . . . . 7–018, 11–006	
para.24 7–016	
para.26 7–016	
Sch.12 7–017	
2007 Pensions Act (c.22) 1–007, 1–008	
Pt 2 1–011	
2008 Pensions Act (c.30) 4–021, 10–012, 11–005	
Pt 3 3–008	
ss.107–123 . . . . 7–020, 11–005	
Sch.5 . . . . 7–020, 11–005	
Sch.6 . . . . 7–020, 11–005	
2010 Equality Act (c.15)	
s.18(1) 11–002	
Sch.9 11–002	
2011 Pensions Act (c.19) 1–007, 8–008	
ss.107–123 8–008	
Sch.5 8–008	
Sch.6 8–008	
2013 Public Services Pensions Act (c.25) 4–002	
Children and Families Act (draft)	
s.18 4–001	

PART A

LAW AND PROCEDURE

PART A

LAW AND PROCEDURE

CHAPTER 1

Different Types of Pension

The pension provision which an individual may accrue in the United Kingdom can come from any of three generic sources. First, the state provides some pension rights. Secondly, there is provision made by employers for their employees. Thirdly, there is provision made by individuals themselves outside the first two sources.

There are two basic types of pension; the first can be termed "Defined Contribution" and the second "Defined Benefit". There are some schemes that include both types of benefit on a "Best of Both Worlds" promise and many that offer both styles within the same scheme.

1–001

DEFINED CONTRIBUTION SCHEMES

Defined Contribution Schemes are often called money purchase schemes and are becoming increasingly popular with employers. They are so named because the terms are such that a defined amount is paid into the policy or Scheme. In the simplest form of this type of pension, money is paid regularly (often monthly) into a policy and the contributions purchase units in a pooled investment fund. The value of the units accumulated will then be available at retirement to purchase pension benefits.

The amount of pension that is then provided depends on the contributions made, the investment return on those contributions and on the terms available at the date of retirement. The member does not know until retirement how much will be received as retirement income.

Traditionally, Defined Contribution Schemes offer scheme members the option of taking a proportion of the fund as tax-free cash (currently most policies allow 25 per cent of the fund to be taken as cash). The remainder of the fund traditionally was used to purchase an annuity from a pension provider. Where an annuity is purchased, the fund is passed to the annuity provider who will then contract to pay a series of payments in future. If the annuity selected is a pension annuity, then the payments will be paid for life. The member will usually (unless the contract states otherwise) have a choice about the type of annuity and can opt for a series of payments that do not increase or one that increases in line with inflation each year or at a fixed rate each year. The member can also opt for a pension to be payable to a spouse or dependant on their death.

1–002

DIFFERENT TYPES OF PENSION

Changes in legislation[1] have meant that there are now other options available to the member with the funds (unless the original contract prohibits this). One option is to place the funds in drawdown where the funds remain invested and the member has the option to take an income (up to a defined limit) each year. However, there is a risk in this option and unless the invested funds perform well, the income in the later years of retirement can be lower using this method.[2]

DEFINED BENEFIT SCHEMES

1–003 A Defined Benefit Scheme is one where the benefit payable is defined as an amount or according to a formula at retirement. Typically the benefit is an income payable in retirement although there are some schemes in the UK (and many more in Europe) that simply pay a defined sum at retirement and no income.

Such schemes are provided by the state and by employers. Schemes provided by employers include funded and unfunded schemes. If it is an employer offering a scheme and that employer is not a public sector employer, then in order for the scheme to qualify for tax benefits, it has to be funded. Thus, it has to have funds invested separately (outside the employing or sponsoring company) that are used to pay the benefits that it has promised to its employees as a result of their service in the scheme.

The public sector schemes (including the NHS Pension Scheme, the Teachers' Pension Scheme, the Firefighters' Pension Scheme, the Police Pension Scheme, the Armed Forces Pension Scheme and the Principal Civil Service Pension Scheme) and state benefits are not funded and are the responsibility of the Treasury.

1–004 The typical Defined Benefit Scheme from an employer pays a proportion of the final pensionable salary at retirement (most commonly one-sixtieth) for every year of service. Therefore, a member having done, say, 30 years' service and having a pensionable salary of £50,000 per annum at retirement would have accrued a pension of £25,000 per annum (1/60 x 30 x £50,000 = £25,000).

Some of the older format public sector pension schemes (for example the Teachers' Pension Scheme) accrue benefits in a slightly different way in that they will accrue a pension at a lower rate (one-eightieth) but will accrue an additional tax-free cash lump sum at retirement. Therefore under the same circumstances as above, the member would have accrued a pension of £18,750 per annum (1/80 x 30 x £50,000 = £18,750) plus an automatic lump sum of £56,250.

In the first example, the member will usually be able to receive a tax-free cash lump sum at retirement by reducing the pension and therefore the two types of pension rights are similar in the benefits provided.

Another type of Defined Benefit pension that is becoming increasingly popular with employers is the "career average revalued earnings scheme" (often termed CARE schemes, based on "Career Average Revalued Earnings"). This operates in a different way whereby each year's earnings are revalued in line with

---

[1] Finance Act 2004.
[2] See paras 1–022—1–026 below.

an index, which historically has usually been the Retail Prices Index ("RPI")[3] until retirement and the final pension is then a proportion of the aggregate earnings throughout a working life.

The attraction of a CARE scheme to employers can be demonstrated by an example. Take two hypothetical employees: both are employed by the same company for 30 years. Employee A is employed initially in a modest position but has worked his way steadily up the ladder to Chief Executive at retirement. Employee B is employed as Chief Executive and remains in that position until retirement. If the company had a final salary scheme both employees would receive the same pension. If the scheme is a career average revalued earnings scheme Employee A will receive a significantly smaller pension than Employee B.

Career average revalued earnings schemes are less expensive for the employer as they would usually pay lower benefits as most members' pensionable salaries are highest in real terms at or close to the time of leaving.

1–005

STATE PENSION PROVISION

State pension provision for those retiring before April 2016 comes from three different sources: the Basic State Pension, the Additional State Pensions and the Graduated Retirement Benefit. There is at the time of writing, a White Paper and draft Pensions Bill in circulation which proposes a major overhaul of the State Pension provision for those reaching State Pension Age after April 2016, meaning that the majority of people reaching State Pension Age after April 2016 will have their State pension based on the new flat rate State Pension.

1–006

State Pension Age

State Pension Age was for many years 65 for men and 60 for women. This situation has been changed by the Pensions Act 2007 and the Pensions Act 2011. Women born on or after April 6, 1950 have a higher State Pension Age than 60 and, for those born on or after December 6, 1953, there is no difference between the genders.

1–007

For those born on or after December 6, 1953 the State Pension Age will gradually increase, depending upon their date of birth, so that those born on or after April 6, 1978 will have a state pension age of 68.[4] The changes already implemented by the Pensions Act 2007 and the Pensions Act 2011 are unlikely to be the last in this area and the Chancellor's Autumn statement (November 29, 2011) announced specific plans to legislate to accelerate the move to a State Pension Age of 67 and to give further thought to accelerating the move to a State Pension Age of 68. These changes form part of the draft Pensions Bill.

---

[3] Some schemes have in recent times moved to using Consumer Price Index ("CPI") rather than RPI and some others are currently considering this change. See "Pension Related Actuarial Reports in Financial Order Cases: Recent Developments" [2011] Fam Law 1138.

[4] Pensions Act 1995 Sch.4 as amended by the later legislation.

DIFFERENT TYPES OF PENSION

In Section D of this book, a table has been produced from which State Pension Ages can be calculated for any given individual according to their age. A similar exercise can be carried out on The Pension Service website's State Pension Age Calculator.[5]

Basic State Pension (for those retiring before April 2016)

1–008 The Basic State Pension is dependent on National Insurance contributions.[6] Formerly, those receiving the Basic State Pension would only be entitled to receive the full Basic State Pension if they were men having 44 years qualifying years or women with 39 qualifying years. (This is equivalent to approximately 90 per cent of an individual's working life between the age of 16 and State Pension Age.)

By virtue of the Pensions Act 2007, those reaching State Pension Age from April 5, 2010 will receive the full Basic State Pension as long as they have 30 qualifying years. For the tax year 2013/14 the full Basic State Pension is £5,727.80. This increases in line with a triple guarantee where it is the best of (i) the increase in earnings, (ii) increase in prices and (iii) 2.5 per cent per annum.

On divorce a spouse reaching State Pension Age before April 2016 can claim credits towards their Basic State Pension for their former spouse's National Insurance contributions for years up to the year of divorce when they do not have a full contribution history using a procedure known as substitution. Note, however, that this will not apply if the claiming spouse re-marries before State Pension Age. The member does not lose any benefits as a result of this.[7]

Additional State Pensions

1–009 The Additional State Pension comprises two different pensions: the State Earnings Related Pension Scheme ("SERPS") and the State Second Pension ("S2P"). SERPS rights were accrued between 1978 and 2002. SERPS was a revalued average earnings scheme which applied to earnings between a Lower Earnings Limit (£5,668 per annum for 2013/14 and historically similar to the amount of the Basic State Pension) and an Upper Earnings Limit (currently £42,475 per annum for 2013/14 and historically similar to the National Average Earnings amount). Employees earned a pension which was then revalued each year until and during retirement. The initial target was a pension of 25 per cent of Middle Band Earnings; the amount between the Lower Earnings Limit and the employee's earnings (up to a maximum of the Upper Earnings Limit). This target reduced to 20 per cent of Middle Band Earnings in 1988.

In 2002 the SERPS system was effectively replaced by the S2P. The S2P is similar except that those earning between the Lower Earnings Limit and £13,000 per annum are treated as if they earn £13,000 per annum. The accrual rate for these individuals was doubled and the accrual above £13,000 per annum reduced

---

[5] Visit www.thepensionservice.gov.uk/resourcecentre/statepensioncalc.asp.
[6] If an individual wants to obtain their full NI history, they can request a statement of account from H M Revenue & Customs who can be telephoned on 0845 604 2931.
[7] Social Security Contributions and Benefits Act 1992 s.48(1), (3).

to provide improved benefits for all those whose earnings are below the Upper Earnings Limit and the same benefit for those above the Upper Earnings Limit.

It has previously been possible to contract out of the S2P into private schemes and stakeholder pensions. It is possible to contract out of the S2P into occupational schemes until April 2016.

The Government proposes to reform State Pensions and this will serve to remove the Additional State Pensions.

Graduated Retirement Benefit

The Graduated Retirement Benefit was effective from April 6, 1961 until April 5, 1975. It is calculated by reference to a number of units purchased; that number being converted to a pension benefit which is revised annually. 1–010

Even those who earned the maximum number of units receive less than £13 per week and therefore this is not a significant benefit.

Contracting out

Occupational schemes could contract out of the Graduated Retirement Benefit by agreeing to pay an "Equivalent Pensions Benefit". From 1978 to 1997, schemes could contract out of SERPS by guaranteeing to pay at least a Guaranteed Minimum Pension ("GMP") which would be roughly the same as the employee member would have received under SERPS. Since 1997 schemes have still been able to contract out, although since then it has either been by having a separate fund to cover the benefits (Protected Rights Fund Method) or by confirming the Scheme offers benefits at least as good as a prescribed scheme (the "Reference Scheme Test"). As referred to above it is still (at present) possible to contract out of S2P, although this is likely to cease to be a possibility if provisions in Part 2 of the Pensions Act 2007 are implemented. 1–011

Valuation of State Pensions

The amount of weekly State Pension accrued to date and the expected pension at State Pension Age can be obtained by completing Form BR19[8] and sending it to the Pension Service. 1–012

The State Pension schemes do not involve the payment of lump sums, although if an individual delays retirement, the missed payments can be received as a cash lump sum when the individual finally retires (although this is subject to income tax at the marginal rate of income).

Sharing State Pensions

The Basic State Pension and the Graduated Retirement Benefit are not shareable and although the Additional State Pension is shareable (and the value can be obtained from the Pension Service by completing Form BR20[9] and sending it to The Pension Service) the proposal is to remove this option in April 2017. 1–013

---

[8] For information on how to do so see Section D below.
[9] For information on how to do so see Section D below.

WHITE PAPER PROPOSALS TO CHANGE THE STATE PENSION

1–014   In January 2013, a White Paper and draft Bill were published which proposed a radical overhaul of the State Pension and that a flat rate State Pension would be introduced of the equivalent of £144 per week for anyone reaching State Pension Age after 2016. This would be payable to anybody with 35 years' worth of National Insurance contributions. At the same time, the State Second Pension would cease to accrue.

At April 2016, all those below State Pension Age will have their accrued State Pension set as a "Protected Amount" and will receive at least this amount at State Pension Age. Thus someone who had accrued the full Basic State Pension of £107.45 per week plus an Additional State Pension of £70.00 per week would have a protected amount of £177.45 per week and would receive at least that (which would be better than the £144 per week accrued under the new regime). These figures are in today's terms as an example.

However, a 55 year old with 20 years of contributions and an Additional State Pension of £60 per week would only have accrued £131.63 per week. Their forecast under the old system would be £167.45 per week (full Basic State Pension with another 10 years' contributions plus £60 per week) but their Protected Amount would only be that accrued to April 2016 of £131.63. This is significantly less than they might be expecting based on the pre-2016 accrual of benefits. Their pension under the new system if they worked to 67 would be 32 years' worth (32/35 x £144) which is £131.66 per week and therefore they would receive this. This is significantly less than they might be expecting now and they might even be expecting further Additional State Pension accrual to say £180 per week.

1–015   Conversely, the self-employed will see an overnight enhancement to their prospective State Pension.

Under the proposal, April 2016 will see an end to sharing the Additional State Pension even where the Protected Amount still bites and the member is going to receive an Additional State Pension.

It is also proposed to end State Pension substitution for spouses so they will no longer be able to claim against the former spouse's record to get a State Pension. There will be an introduction of more ways to have credits applied to an individual's record for family responsibilities but the automatic right is removed.

Practitioners should take great care when dealing with State Pensions. Sharing an Additional State Pension before April 2016 could provide the recipient with a benefit that will then be absorbed into a State Pension they would have received anyway if they reach State Pension Age after April 2016. Likewise, for those reaching State Pension Age after April 2016, taking into account current State Pensions may be detrimental to one party and the proposals would need careful consideration on a case by case basis.

OCCUPATIONAL UNFUNDED PENSIONS FROM PUBLIC SERVICE EMPLOYERS

The public sector historically offered all of its employees a very good defined benefit scheme. The main public sector schemes are the:

- NHS Pension Scheme;
- Teachers' Pension Scheme;
- Firefighters' Pension Scheme;
- Police Pension Scheme;
- Principal Civil Service Pension Scheme;
- Armed Forces Pension Scheme.

1–016

The Judicial Pension Scheme and the MPs' Pension Scheme are also unfunded public schemes which are similar but not the same as the schemes above. In a category of its own is the Local Government Pension Scheme which is funded but otherwise has many similar features to the above schemes.

The main feature of these schemes is that they are unfunded in that there is no fund anywhere to meet future payments. The benefits will be paid out of future taxation and future members' contributions. For this reason, on the making of a Pension Sharing Order, all of the schemes listed above only offer the non-member spouse a pension within the scheme (the internal option); they do not allow the non-member spouse to transfer out of the scheme (external option). One consequence of this is that the non-member spouse sometimes has to wait until Scheme Retirement Age to receive benefits.[10]

OCCUPATIONAL FUNDED PENSIONS

Traditionally the majority of these schemes are Defined Benefit Schemes offering a pension as a proportion of final salary with the option to take a tax-free cash lump sum at retirement. One of the features of these schemes is that they offer any member who is not yet in receipt of benefits but who has accrued benefits under the scheme, a transfer value and the right to transfer out of the scheme into a personal pension.

1–017

The limits on how much an employee can accrue in these schemes have changed recently. It is now the case that a member can accrue up to the Lifetime Allowance (£1.25 million from April 2014) in all schemes. In order to calculate the Lifetime Allowance any promised pension is multiplied by a factor of 20. Any accrual over and above that is subject to a penal tax charge.

There are also limits on the amounts that can be contributed each year (£40,000 from April 2014) and the rules regarding this mean that the deemed

---

[10] At the time of writing, the Police Pension Scheme and the Firefighters' Pension Scheme insist on this whilst pension credit members of other public sector schemes such as the Armed Forces Pension Scheme can take benefits from age 55 although this is still a higher age than the member can often take benefits. See paras 10–012 and 14–020 below.

accrual is based on the increase in benefits so long serving members can find that an above inflation increase in salary in a final salary scheme could trigger a tax charge.

The right to transfer out of any occupational pension scheme became available to all scheme members not in receipt of a pension on April 29, 1988. This led to many millions of employees being persuaded to leave their company pension schemes in favour of personal arrangements. Many of these transfers were procured by misrepresentations (in what became known as "the Pensions Mis-selling Scandal") and led to an industry review of all of the sales. The overall cost of compensation and expenses involved with calculating and administering the review has been estimated at a figure in the region of £10 billion.

1–018   It is now unusual for employees to consider leaving a Defined Benefit Scheme.

These schemes, however, have become much less popular with the employers. A variety of factors including poor stock market returns, improvements in mortality rates (increases in longevity), the requirement to contribute to the Pension Protection Fund and increased regulatory requirements have meant that the schemes are becoming increasingly more expensive both to fund and to administer. A considerable number of schemes have been closed to new employees joining the company and some have even closed the scheme to future accrual so that existing members retain their rights earned to date but are prevented from earning any further rights in the scheme.

A number of employers now offer Defined Contribution Schemes where employees can purchase an investment in a fund or choice of funds to provide pension benefits at retirement. These will usually receive both the employees' contributions and the employers' contributions although there is no legislation that provides that employees have to contribute.

In a small number of cases, an employer's money purchase scheme for a key employee may be a targeted benefit scheme. In this type of scheme, although it is a money purchase fund with benefits dependent on the funds at retirement and rates available at that time, the employer's contribution is variable in order to target a level of benefit (or proportion of salary) at retirement. Thus the employer's contribution will be refined over the period of the policy to try to ensure that the funds at retirement achieve a set level of benefits.

Small Self Administered Pension Schemes (SSASs)

1–019   These schemes, typically, were for one or more senior employees of a company. Until "A-Day" (April 6, 2006) they offered more investment freedom than a personal pension policy. Many were used by smaller companies to purchase the business premises and lease it back to the company. In circumstances where there is only one member, the intention would be to sell the premises when the member retired and thus help provide a retirement fund.

These schemes can present difficulties for pension sharing. Frequently the scheme assets consist of a commercial property, perhaps with a mortgage on that property and a limited amount of cash or other liquid investments. If the court were to make a significant Pension Sharing Order in relation to this type of scheme it is possible that there would be insufficient liquid funds to pay a transfer value to the spouse equal in value to her entitlement. In order to provide the funds, it may be possible to arrange a loan or further loan on the property but there are limits on the amount of borrowing that such a scheme can make and any lender would need to be convinced that mortgage repayments could be met.

In the above circumstances, an option would be for the non-member spouse to have an internal option and become a scheme member. However, legislation implemented on March 9, 2002[11] required all members to be trustees (or alternatively directors of a company that is a sole trustee) and all decisions unanimous except where an independent trustee is appointed. For this reason, making the non-member spouse a trustee of the pension scheme that invests in the company premises of the member spouse's company is unlikely to be a practicable solution.

Further complications arise where the scheme already has more than one member. The most likely scenario is that the partners in the business are all members of the scheme. In this case, even if there is liquidity in the scheme to be able to provide the non-member spouse with a transfer value, it is quite likely that the other members will refuse (as trustees) to allow a transfer out, as this will reduce the liquidity of the scheme. This is an example of a situation in which the parties may prefer a solution other than pension sharing. A summary of situations in which such solutions may be preferable is contained in Chapter 8.

Unapproved retirement benefits schemes, funded and unfunded (FURBS and UURBS)

Historically the unapproved schemes were largely set up for senior employees who had remuneration packages which exceeded the "cap" placed on benefits in approved schemes. Employers would therefore set up unapproved schemes as top ups but these schemes would have fewer tax advantages.

1–020

Unapproved schemes can be the subject of pension sharing, although the Scheme does not have to offer this option, and considerable care needs to be taken as the rules of the scheme may provide that the pension credit has to remain in the scheme or be paid in a specified form. Benefits may also have conditions attached to them. One such scheme of which the authors are aware had the condition that the member (an ex-partner) lost all of his rights if he were to work for a competitor or provide any information to a competitor about the company. Thus the benefits may be contingent on the conduct of the member.

PERSONAL PENSION ARRANGEMENTS

In their simplest form, the individual pays contributions to a pension provider who purchases units in a managed fund or similar product. The funds then grow with investment growth and additional contributions until retirement. The policyholder can choose, within limits, when to retire. The benefits available

1–021

---

[11] The Occupational Pension Schemes (Investment of Schemes Resources) Regulations 1992 (SI 1991/246) now revoked and replaced by The Occupational Pension Schemes (Investment) Regulations 2005 (SI 2005/3378).

depend on the amount of contributions, investment growth and the terms for purchasing benefits at retirement, which in turn are age dependent.

Such policies typically offer up to 25 per cent of the fund to be taken as tax-free cash at retirement and can be converted to an annuity at retirement or used to provide incomes in retirement from an Unsecured Pension Fund or an Alternatively Secured Pension Fund or used for Flexible Drawdown.

Furthermore, there are rules whereby if an individual has secured an income of £20,000 gross per annum (any income has to be guaranteed at that level and not able to reduce in future) can then take the whole of a fund as a cash sum, although only 25 per cent is tax-free and the remainder subject to income tax.

1–022 There is a limit to the amount that an individual can contribute to such pension schemes in any one year. The Annual Limit is the amount of the individual's annual salary or £40,000 (in the tax year 2014/15) if lower.

Prior to Stakeholder Pensions many of the personal pension policies that were sold in the late 1980s and 1990s were unit-linked policies invested in a "Managed" fund. Each contribution bought a number of units in the fund and the value of the units would fluctuate with the value of the investments in the fund. These have largely been superseded by Stakeholder Pensions because many had charging structures which were expensive, complex and often felt to be misleading.

As well as investing in Managed funds some providers offered the option to invest in a "With Profits" fund, which participated in the profits of the company. This was good news when the company was performing well and the principle of a smoothed investment return (those encashing when the value of the fund was high getting less than their true value and those when the value of the fund was low receiving more) appealed to more cautious investors.

Stakeholder Pensions

1–023 Introduced by Welfare Reform and Pensions Act 1999, these schemes are a type of personal pension arrangement. The schemes must be registered under Welfare Reform and Pensions Act 1999 s.2 and must satisfy certain conditions to achieve that registration. The annual charges that may be imposed by providers are limited to 1.5 per cent of the value of the fund. Members of Stakeholder Pension Schemes need not be employed and an individual can invest in the scheme for the benefit of a partner or children. The vast majority of personal pensions now sold in the UK are Stakeholder Pensions.

Guaranteed Annuity Options

1–024 Guaranteed Annuity Options became very well known in the late 1990s following a House of Lords ruling against Equitable Life which led to its near collapse. Policies with Guaranteed Annuity Options work in a very similar way to the more standard money purchase policies except that at the specified retirement age (or at a selection of ages), the funds can be converted to an annuity at the rates specified in the contract. The rates were specified at the start of the contract and due to the fact that annuity rates have worsened steadily over the past 20 years or more, the benefit available from utilising these rates can be substantially more than the amount that could be bought on the open market. Guaranteed Annuity Option policies are no longer sold but there are many that are still in force and most pension providers offered the contracts in the 1980s and 1990s.[12]

Retirement Annuity Contracts

A predecessor of the Stakeholder Pension was "the Retirement Annuity Contract". Some Retirement Annuity Contracts offer a fixed pension at retirement (as long as all premiums are paid) rather than building up a fund to buy pension benefits at retirement. These offer Guaranteed Benefits but should not be confused with Guaranteed Annuity Rates as these policies will usually have CEs that represent the true value of the policy.

1–025

Self Invested Pension Plans (SIPPs)

Self Invested Pension Plans are a form of a personal pension plan which allows the member more freedom of investment. The Pensions Act 2004 originally proposed that any assets could be held in a SIPP but, prior to implementation, this proposal was modified so that members could not invest in their own property or second homes or "Pride in Possession" assets such as works of art, vintage cars or yachts.

1–026

SIPPs are still popular and members can use them to invest in assets of their choice subject to the above restrictions. Members are able to invest in property and the scheme can take a loan up to 50 per cent of the value of the assets in the scheme. The loan interest is tax deductible against rental income.

SIPPs can be used to receive "pension credits" where a Pension Sharing Order is implemented and discharged by means of the external option.

SIPPs can, however, present particular difficulties for pension sharing. A SIPP fund will have to be valued carefully and may contain assets that are integral to the member's business (and therefore future income).[13]

PENSIONS IN PAYMENT

Annuities

Where the pension has been invested in a personal pension plan of one type or another, then one option at retirement is to purchase an annuity from an annuity provider. This provides a level of benefits in retirement according to payments as defined at the time that the annuity is purchased. The authors have known annuity providers to re-draw annuities once purchased but only in exceptional circumstances and high value cases. The standard annuity that is purchased is unlikely to be able to be changed once it is in payment. It is possible to use pension sharing on an annuity in payment and the pension income will be

1–027

---

[12] See para.14–015 below.
[13] See Ch.8 below.

Drawdown, Unsecured and Alternatively Secured Annuities

1-028   Drawdown has become increasingly popular and the regulations were revised in Finance Act 2004[14] which introduced the rules regarding Unsecured Pensions and Alternatively Secured Pensions. There are different views on this method of providing retirement income and the financial regulator, the Financial Services Authority (FSA), regards income drawdown as a complex product and strongly recommends that pension investors seek professional advice and understand the risks before choosing this option.

The biggest risk of income drawdown is that the fund could be significantly (if not completely) eroded in adverse market conditions, or if the member makes poor investment decisions. This will in turn lead to a lower (or perhaps no) income in retirement.

As well as the risk of the drawdown fund being significantly reduced, the investment return will have to be very good to keep up with maximum income withdrawals, charges and inflation. This means that anyone considering income drawdown needs a more adventurous attitude to investment risk than someone buying a lifetime annuity.

1-029   Lower-risk investments will struggle to keep pace with the income withdrawn, while higher risk investments could mean the capital will be subject to large fluctuations. Where a pension fund is used to draw an income before the age of 75, the funds are placed in an "Unsecured Pension Fund". The scheme administrator of an Unsecured Pension Fund has to determine the maximum level of Unsecured Pension that can be paid from the fund. The amount is defined in the regulations and is approximately equal to the amount of non-increasing annuity the member could purchase with the full fund. Thus it provides the option of a high initial income but if the maximum income is drawn the fund is likely to be depleted.

The maximum level of pension has to be re-calculated every five years and therefore if the fund has not maintained its value the maximum possible withdrawal will reduce. If the fund investments have increased enough to cover the income withdrawals and more, then the maximum income will increase.

The income is uncertain in future using this method. The other main feature of the benefits is that the fund is returned on death (subject to tax in some cases) so in the event of death in the early years of retirement, the death benefit may be greater than if an annuity is purchased even if the annuity has a guarantee for the first ten years in payment.

Pension funds placed in a drawdown fund can be subjected to a Pension Sharing Order both before and after they are placed in an Alternatively Secured Pension Fund.

---

[14] Finance Act 2004 and the Registered Pension Schemes (Relevant Annuities) Regulations 2006 (SI 2006/129).

Flexible Drawdown

Flexible drawdown is a facility that has been available since April 6, 2011. It allows some individuals the opportunity to withdraw as little or as much income from their pension fund as they choose and can do so as and when they need it. This income is subject to Income Tax. In order to qualify the individual has to declare that they are already receiving a secure pension income[15] of at least £20,000 per annum[16] and the present understanding is that secured income is taken as the gross annual amount of pension. In addition flexible drawdown can only be taken once the member has finished saving into pensions. If pension contributions have been made to any pension in the same tax year or if the member is still an active member of a defined benefit scheme, it is not possible to start flexible drawdown.[17] Once in flexible drawdown, it is not possible to make further pension contributions.

1–030

THE HUTTON REPORT

On March 10, 2011 the Independent Public Service Pensions Commission, a group chaired by Lord Hutton, produced its final report, commonly known as "The Hutton Report". This report produced a number of recommendations, including:-

1–031

(i) that a new career average re-valued earnings scheme should generally be utilised in public sector pension schemes in place of final salary schemes (the effect of which would be to reduce the benefits of many public sector pension schemes);
(ii) that personal contributions should be substantially increased; and
(iii) that the normal pension age in public sector pensions should coincide with the State Pension Age (which it very often does not at present).

The Coalition Government has indicated an intention to implement the recommendations of this report by 2015; but the proposals have engendered hostility from many of those adversely affected. At the time of writing this book negotiations were very much ongoing between interested parties; but it seems likely that public sector schemes will be changed in accordance with the thrust of the recommendations of the Hutton Report. This is contained in the Public Sector Pension Schemes Bill 2013.

---

[15] Secured pension income includes a Company Pension being paid either from an UK or Overseas Company, an annuity being paid from a Personnel pension or a company pension again either from the UK or Overseas, or Estate Pension being paid either from the UK or Overseas. It does not include drawdown pension income, a dependent drawdown pension income, payments from a relevant non UK scheme which are classified as drawdown pension, a purchase life annuity or a scheme pension from an SSAS.

[16] The requirement for the income to be £20,000 per annum may change in future and the level of income required might increase. As well as securing the pension, it is a rule that the payment must have started from the pension so you cannot claim to have secured the pension if it is even a state pension that is not payable immediately but only payable in the future.

[17] In order to effect flexible drawdown as well as the conditions being met, the member needs to make a declaration and the scheme administrator accepts a declaration to that effect.

DIFFERENT TYPES OF PENSION

It is still not certain what the precise details will be although changes will only affect accrual after April 2015 and any rights built up to that time will be unaffected. In addition, anyone within 10 years of retirement age (under scheme rules not State Retirement Age) will be unaffected. Therefore although this will not affect the value of accrued rights for some time, for those who are not protected by the rule regarding being within 10 years of retirement at April 2012 may have a different decision to make about when they retire than those currently retiring or protected by this rules.

CHAPTER 2

Cash Equivalents

DEFINITION OF CASH EQUIVALENT (CE)

The Cash Equivalent[1] ("the CE"), which was formerly called the Cash Equivalent Transfer Value or "CETV", is, essentially, the amount of money which a pension provider will transfer to an alternative pension arrangement to extinguish their liability to a member of a scheme. The CE was defined for this purpose. It was originally designed for occupational pension schemes where an individual moved from one employer to another and could, if the former employer's scheme agreed, transfer the benefits to the new employer's scheme.

2–001

The provisions of Social Security Act 1985[2] allowed all employees leaving an occupational pension scheme on or after January 1, 1986 to have an enforceable right to transfer their pension to a new employer's occupational pension scheme or a "buy-out bond" or other pension arrangement. The provisions of the Pensions Act 1995[3] extended that right to all pre-1986 leavers except that it is not available within one year of Normal Retirement Date. Such a transfer discharges the trustees of the ceding scheme of all liability.[4]

The right to transfer the pension and therefore to a transfer value does not extend to pensions already in payment.

As it is not possible to transfer out a pension that is already in payment, there can be no transfer value. The Pensions on Divorce etc (Provision of Information) Regulations 2000[5] provide that where a pension is already in payment the cash equivalent of the benefits (formerly called "the CEB") shall be calculated. Once again, this is now just called the "Cash Equivalent". The CE of the pension in

---

[1] The expression CETV (originally devised, long before pension sharing was invented, to assist individuals to transfer between competing pension providers) had been widely adopted by family lawyers in the context of pension sharing. The expression owed its use not to its inclusion in any of the myriad of pension sharing related statutes or statutory instruments, but to its inclusion in the standard form of Form E in use between 2000 and 2011. Accordingly the expression could be, and was, abolished simply by the drafting of the new standard form of Form E with the term CETV replaced by the term CE. Curiously, the Form P1 uses the expression CEV, but the expression CE has the wider currency.

[2] By means of an amendment to the Social Security Pensions Act 1975. These provisions are now consolidated in the Pension Schemes Act 1993Ch.IV and The Occupational Pension Schemes (Transfer Values) Regulations 1996.

[3] Pensions Act 1995 s.152 amending the Pension Schemes Act 1993 s.93.

[4] The Occupational Pension Schemes (Miscellaneous Amendments) Regulations 1986 (SI 1986/2171).

[5] SI 2000/1048.

payment can be considered as equivalent to that of the CE not in payment, although some schemes use different valuation methodology as between the two categories.

ISSUES AFFECTING CALCULATION OF CE

2–002   For a Stakeholder Pension, the CE will simply be the value of the funds attributable to the member at the time of the request. Many other personal pensions will have CEs that are simply the value of the funds. Occasionally, however, there will be surrender penalties or market value adjustments which distort the value.

Prior to October 2008 valuations of occupational schemes were calculated by reference to Guidance Note 11 ("GN11") published by the Institute of Actuaries and the Faculty of Actuaries. Calculations under GN11 very often undervalued occupational schemes. Since October 1, 2008 these figures will have been calculated under The Occupational Pension Schemes (Transfer Values)(Amendment) Regulations 2008 (SI 2008/1050). These regulations have generally had the effect of rendering CEs more representative of their true value, but this is not always the case and practitioners should always be wary of its reliability, as the use of different mathematical assumptions can produce very different end valuations. It is now the Trustees' responsibility to state what the expected return on assets should be and set the basis for the calculations.

There are a number of factors that will influence the actuarial value:

- the amount of annual pension promised to the member;
- any additional benefits promised, such as tax-free cash at retirement, spouse's and children's pensions and the guarantee period on the pension;
- the rate of increase of the pensions benefits when in payment[6];
- the length of time until the pension rights become payable;
- the increases to the pension benefits until the pension becomes payable;
- benefits that would be payable on the death of the member before the pension becomes payable;
- the length of time that the pension is expected to be payable (taking into account mortality rates); and
- the rate at which future payments are discounted.[7]

The top six above factors will usually be defined in the scheme rules. Transfer value legislation states that a CE for an active member must assume that the member leaves service on the date of the CE calculation.[8] Therefore the increases to the benefits will usually be in line with legislation that prescribes increases in deferment to match an inflation index at least up to a maximum that depends on when the benefit accrued.

---

[6] For example, the decision as to whether to use RPI or CPI can make a great deal of difference to the calculation of CE.

[7] The more optimistic the trustees are about the investment returns they expect to achieve the lower will be the CE.

[8] Pensions on Divorce etc. (Provision of Information) Regulations 2000 (SI 2000/1048) reg.3(4).

ISSUES AFFECTING CALCULATION OF CE

The key factors which can be different between one calculation and another and which are subject to the discretion of the actuary are the rate of discount and the mortality rates that are used. If a payment is to be made some years in the future then the higher the rate of discount that is used the lower the current value will be. This can have a very significant impact on the overall value. Similarly the more optimistic the assumption is about future life expectancies, the longer the pension will be paid for and the higher the value will be.

2–003

These factors can lead to a range of values being provided for the same benefit and as the scheme has to consider the discount rate in the light of the investments, one scheme may take a more optimistic view regarding the performance of its investments than another.

This issue is discussed further when considering the use of the CE later in this book.[9]

In summary the practitioner has to be aware that CEs are inconsistent between schemes and can be a poor or misleading representation of the true value of the benefits.

---

[9] See Ch.14.

CHAPTER 3

Historical Overview of Pension Redistribution by the Courts on Divorce

PRIOR TO 1996

Traditional remedies

It is remarkable today to recall that prior to 1996 the courts had no powers on a divorce to interfere with the rights held by an individual in a pension scheme. The existence of such rights could be taken into account in apportioning other assets and income between the spouses but the pension rights were themselves, for most purposes, unimpeachable.

3–001

In practice the courts were obliged to use such powers as they then had to compensate the non-member spouse, whilst leaving the actual pension rights of the member spouse unaffected. The remedies at the court's disposal were in practice much less satisfactory than those now available. Broadly, they were remedies such as divorce avoidance, lump sum orders, joint lives periodical payments orders, off-setting and, latterly, Brooks[1] orders. With the exception of Brooks orders, all of these remedies remain available. Indeed there are still circumstances in which one or more of these remedies may still be more appropriate than a Pension Sharing Order or a Pension Attachment Order (see Chapter 8 below).

Although these remedies were available and were utilised from time to time it was quite often the case (even in the relatively recent past) that pensions were not identified as a substantial matrimonial asset to which the court should direct its mind. Prior to 1996 there was no evidential requirement for the disclosure of a pension CE in financial order proceedings. The lack of attention paid to pensions was no doubt partly due to a lack of awareness of the true value of the asset but it was also attributable to the common application of the doctrine of reasonable requirements[2] and the hitherto more frequent use of the joint lives periodical payments order.[3]

Divorce avoidance, or the use of financial grounds by the court to refuse to dissolve a marriage where the basis of the divorce was a period of separation,

3–002

---

[1] See *Brooks v Brooks* [1996] A.C. 375 HL; [1995] 2 F.L.R. 13.
[2] An analysis of the doctrine can be found in Thorpe L.J.'s speech in *Cowan v Cowan* [2001] 2 F.L.R. 192; (2001) EWCA Civ 679 at para.24.
[3] The "clean break provisions" were introduced by Matrimonial and Family Proceedings Act 1984 s.3, which introduced Matrimonial Causes Act 1973 s.25A.

used not to be uncommon. The statutory powers to do this remain in force.[4] In *Le Marchant v Le Marchant*,[5] a case in which the wife sought to resist the grant of decree nisi on the grounds that she would lose her rights under her husband's generous Post Office pension scheme, Ormrod L.J. observed that:

> "There are many cases, and this is one, in which the powers of the court, extensive as they are under sections 23 and 24 as well as section 10, are not wide enough to enable the court to carry out by order various things which a petitioner husband can do voluntarily".

The Court of Appeal adopted the approach of Cumming-Bruce J. in *Parker v Parker*,[6] made a prima facie finding as to grave hardship and expressed a willingness to dismiss the petition unless the husband was able to satisfy the court that he had made provision for the wife to alleviate that hardship.[7] In theory this remains an available remedy for the court, but it is most unlikely that the facts of any case would justify such an approach today.

A more common approach was to recognise the capital which a member spouse would receive from the pension scheme and structure a lump sum order around it. For example, in *Milne v Milne*,[8] the Court of Appeal, overturning an order that the husband should set up and maintain an insurance policy on his life for the benefit of the wife, instead directed that:

> "... providing the wife is surviving at the material time, the husband shall pay a sum equal to one half of the sum that he or his estate would be entitled to under the pension scheme if the appropriate option were exercised. That should be payable at the husband's death or on his retirement, as I have said, providing the wife is still living at the time".[9]

Ewbank J., giving judgment in the first appeal (of three) in *Brooks v Brooks*,[10] observed that the payment to the wife of a proportion of the husband's commuted lump sum was "the usual and conventional route by which a wife who is divorced can obtain part of the husband's pension".[11]

3–003 In very many cases a joint lives periodical payments order was the means by which the court secured the non-member spouse's income in retirement. The use of such orders was, of course, affected by the development of the "clean break" principle.[12] This had its own difficulties. The non-member spouse was not protected in the event of the member spouse's death, re-marriage by the non-member spouse brought about a termination and the non-member spouse had little if any control over the pension scheme itself or over levels of commutation or dates of retirement. To provide a level of security, joint lives periodical

---

[4] Matrimonial Causes Act 1973 ss.5 and 10(2).
[5] [1977] 1 W.L.R. 559.
[6] [1972] 1 All E.R. 410.
[7] See also *K v K* [1997] 1 F.L.R. 35. In *Parker, Le Marchant* and *K v K* arrangements satisfactory to both parties were made eventually and decrees were granted.
[8] [1981] 2 F.L.R. 286 CA.
[9] Above p.289 D.
[10] [1993] 2 F.L.R. 491.
[11] Above p.494 F.
[12] Matrimonial Causes Act 1973 s.25A, as inserted by Matrimonial and Family Proceedings Act 1984 s.3.

payments orders were generally combined with undertakings in relation to insurance provision and/or nominations of death benefits but these were voluntary and involved problems of enforcement. As a safety net the surviving dependant non-member former spouse could make an application under the Inheritance (Provision for Family and Dependants) Act 1975. There may, however, still be (fairly rare) situations, even where the member spouse has a significant pension scheme, in which a joint lives periodical payments order is appropriate to provide income in retirement after divorce for the non-member spouse.[13]

It was also common practice, in order to circumvent the absence of powers to intervene in the pension schemes themselves, to off-set the existence of pension schemes against other assets so that the non-member spouse would receive more of the non-pension assets and the member spouse receive commensurately less. There remain many cases today where this is the appropriate way of dealing with pension issues and the principle of off-setting remains very much alive. The valuation and actuarial issues arising from such an exercise continue to trouble the courts and are discussed in detail below.[14]

Winds of change

As the law relating to financial order proceedings gradually developed through the divorce reforms of the 1960s into the Matrimonial Causes Act 1973 and then towards an increasingly interventionist judicial construction of this Act, the absence of powers to interfere with pension rights increasingly became an anomaly.

3–004

The absence of such powers was analysed and criticised in 1995 by Lord Nicholls in the House of Lords in *Brooks v Brooks*.[15] He referred to attempts over many years by the Law Commission and others[16] to address the problem and suggested that "for many married people their two single assets of greatest value are the house in which they live and, as time passes, the accumulating pension provision of the money-earner"[17] and that there was "general dissatisfaction with the state of the law".

The particular innovative solution found to the problem in *Brooks v Brooks*, i.e. treating a pension fund as a post-nuptial settlement within the meaning of Matrimonial Causes Act 1973 s.24(1)(c), could not be used where there were third party scheme members and was therefore of limited application and did not provide a general solution to the problem. The far more common instance of an individual having rights in a multi-member pension scheme could not be addressed by such a solution and Lord Nicholls commented, "legislation will still be needed". Lord Nicholls probably had in mind the introduction of powers to enable the courts to engage in what was then known as pension "splitting".

---

[13] See the discussion in Ch.8 below.
[14] See Ch.13 below.
[15] [1996] A.C. 375 HL at p.388.
[16] For example, a paper commissioned by the Pensions and Management Institute in 1993 concluded that legislation should be introduced to facilitate pension "splitting" on divorce.
[17] Indeed, as Rae and Ellison observed in 2001 in *Family Breakdown and Pensions* (2nd edn), there will be very many marriages in which the pension is by far the most valuable matrimonial asset.

1996 TO DATE

The arrival of earmarking

3–005　The call by Lord Nicholls for legislation was heeded and the case of *Brooks v Brooks* will remain an important footnote in the history of divorce law reform. Reformers seeking the full powers of pension splitting had to be patient, however, for a few more years. The Government of the time was not prepared to extend powers this far at this stage, citing the availability of the remedy in *Brooks v Brooks*, together with the estimated cost to the taxpayer of pension "splitting" (£200 million by 2037)[18] as reasons for not introducing pension "splitting".

The Government was convinced, however, of the need for some legislation. A first attempt at such legislation followed in the form of the Pensions Act 1995 s.166. In relation to divorce proceedings from July 1996 onwards[19] the courts could direct the pension providers, at the time they were due to make payments to the member spouse (or to others on the death of the member spouse), to divert a portion of these payments to the non-member spouse. This was generally known as "pension earmarking", although this term was not actually used in the legislation.

Experience in the succeeding years established that earmarking was a less than wholly satisfactory remedy from a number of points of view. Earmarking orders, particularly of income,[20] were capable of variation and thus had limited finality. Early termination by court order or as a result of the member spouse's death created uncertainty. Non-member spouses had no control over when the member spouse retired and thus when the benefits were to be received. Furthermore, a number of the early reported cases on earmarking tended to discourage the use of the powers, certainly in relation to long-term provision.[21]

The arrival of pension sharing

3–006　Inevitably, the pressure for the courts to have fuller powers grew and in due course gained wide support. There followed the Welfare Reform and Pensions Act 1999. In relation to divorce proceedings from December 2000 onwards[22] the court in financial order proceedings acquired additional powers to make Pension Sharing Orders (these had previously been known informally as pension splitting orders, but this term disappeared on the passing of the new Act). These orders allowed the court to take the existing pension scheme and direct the pension provider to divide the rights under the scheme between the spouses so that each would have their own independent rights under that scheme or under two separate schemes.

---

[18] House of Commons Hansard debates, July 4, 1995.

[19] i.e. in any divorce proceedings commenced on or after July 1,1996: see Pensions Act 1995 (Commencement)(No. 5) Order 1996 (SI 1996/1675) para.4.

[20] As well as, although more rarely, of capital.

[21] See, for example, Singer J. in *T v T* (Financial Relief: Pensions) [1998] 1 F.L.R. 1072 and Cazalet J. in *Burrow v Burrow* [1999] 1 F.L.R. 508.

[22] i.e. in divorce proceedings commenced on or after December 1, 2000: see Welfare Reform and Pensions Act 1999 (Commencement No.5) Order 2000 (SI 2000/1116) para.2 and Welfare Reform and Pensions Act 1999 s.85(3).

Earmarking orders were retained in substantially the same form as had been introduced by the Pensions Act 1995, but now became known as "Pension Attachment Orders". Brooks orders under Matrimonial Causes Act 1973 s.24 were abolished.[23]

At almost exactly the same time as Pension Sharing Orders became available the House of Lords, on October 26, 2000, made a decision which radically changed the courts' approach to the overall division of assets in financial order cases.[24] The "yardstick of equality" moved to centre stage. These two developments have radically changed the way in which the courts intervene and redistribute rights in pension schemes on divorce.

The present

The regimes implemented by the Pensions Act 1995 and the Welfare Reform and Pensions Act 1999 for divorcing couples are substantially the ones in force today and will be considered in detail in the succeeding chapters.

3–007

The principle of pension sharing is now well established and Pension Sharing Orders are usually the first port of call for those cases in which pensions come to be considered. Pension Attachment Orders have become quite rare in practice, although they do arise from time to time.

Once the principle of pension sharing became well established, the attention of legislators was drawn to ways in which such remedies could be extended beyond divorcing couples. Following the Civil Partnership Act 2004 same sex couples who have entered into a civil partnership which has later been dissolved became subject to a statutory structure for pension sharing and pension attachment which is very similar to that operating for divorcing couples.[25] Most of the substantive law and procedure and the use of forms are identical, subject to some changes in terminology.

A closer look at the statistics reveals, however, that there are perhaps fewer orders interfering with pension rights than might be expected. The following table[26] illustrates the use of Pension Sharing Orders and Pension Attachment Orders in the years since 2004. It can be seen that the statistics appear to have settled down with (for whatever reason) fewer than 10 per cent of divorces/nullities/dissolutions leading to financial resolution involving a Pension Sharing Order or a Pension Attachment Order.

Year	Decree Absolutes of Divorce or Nullity and Civil Partnership Dissolutions in England and Wales	Court orders made which include either a Pension Sharing Order or a Pension Attachment Order (or both)	Percent-age (%)
2004	154,031	3,714	2.41
2005	142,770	2,943	2.06

---

[23] Welfare Reform and Pensions Act 1999 Sch.3 para.3.
[24] See *White v White* [2000] 2 F.L.R. 981.
[25] See Ch.11 below for a full analysis.
[26] All the data in this table is taken from the "Judicial and Court Statistics" reports produced annually by the Ministry of Justice.

HISTORICAL OVERVIEW

2006	133,026	13,630	10.25
2007	129,146	11,564	8.95
2008	122,861	10,417	8.48
2009	115,372	9,218	7.99
2010	121,421	10,205	8.40
2011	119,610	9,973	8.34

3–008 Another recent development (with effect from April 6, 2011) has been the introduction of two new species of order, the Pension Compensation Sharing Order and the Pension Compensation Attachment Order. Introduced by means of the Pensions Act 2008 Pt 3, and enjoying their own procedural chapter,[27] these species of order enable a court to redistribute between spouses the benefits arising from pensions for which the Pensions Protection Fund has assumed responsibility. These orders are considered in detail in Chapter 7 below.

The future

3–009 For the time being, cohabiting couples who never marry (or enter into a civil partnership) cannot invite the court, even if they both agree, to intervene in their pension arrangements by way of Pension Sharing Orders. The Law Commission has recommended that in certain circumstances pension sharing remedies be extended to cohabiting couples who have never married.[28] Whilst this possibility remains on the agenda, supporters of such a reform have seen little evidence of activity to encourage them that such a change is likely to be implemented in the foreseeable future, certainly not in the 2010–2015 parliamentary term.[29]

---

[27] Family Procedure Rules 2010 Pt 9 Ch.9.
[28] See The Financial Consequences of Relationship Breakdown, published July 31, 2007.
[29] See Written Ministerial Statement dated September 6, 2011 (*Hansard*, HC Deb 6 September 2011 cc15-16WS).

CHAPTER 4

Law and Procedure in Relation to Pension Sharing Orders

LAW

Statutory framework

A practitioner dealing with a financial order case involving the possibility of a Pension Sharing Order needs to have some familiarity with a core number of provisions to be found in various statutes and statutory instruments, some of which are necessarily highly technical. The appendices to be found at the end of this book provide full extracts of most relevant materials likely to be encountered by the practitioner in this area. This chapter attempts to summarise the significance of the more important of these provisions to assist the digestibility of a more detailed reading of the extracts.

4–001

The main statutory provisions in relation to Pension Sharing Orders were introduced by the Welfare Reform and Pensions Act 1999. Most importantly, Sch.3 of that Act had the effect of amending important parts of the Matrimonial Causes Act 1973[1] Pt II and it is appropriate in this context to refer to the amended sections of the Matrimonial Causes Act 1973.

Definition of a Pension Sharing Order

A Pension Sharing Order is defined in the Matrimonial Causes Act 1973 s.21A as an order which specifies that a particular percentage[2] of the value of the member spouse's shareable pension rights will be transferred to the non-member spouse. If there is a main scheme and an accompanying Additional Voluntary Contribution (AVC) scheme then some pension providers insist that the same percentage must apply to both.[3] It must be a simple percentage figure between 0

4–002

---

[1] By virtue of the Welfare Reform and Pensions Act 1999 Sch.12 many of these provisions were also inserted into the Family Law Act 1996 Pt II in anticipation that the relevant part of this Act might in due course be implemented. It never was implemented and was finally repealed by the Children and Families Act 2013 s.18.

[2] Some pension providers are relaxed about the number of decimal points to which the percentage may descend. Others will (curiously) not allow more than one decimal place. If this is a matter of importance it may be sensible to check with the pension provider before inviting a court to make an order with more than one decimal place in the percentage.

[3] If they do insist on this then they normally rely upon the Welfare Reform and Pensions Act 1999 s.31. The authors' experience is that some pension providers insist on this (for example the British Airways Pension Scheme and the IBM Pension Scheme) whereas others do not (for example the

and 100, not a fixed sum of money or a percentage calculable by reference to a formula. For example, formulas such as "that percentage which will produce £10,000 pa income" or "that percentage which will produce a transfer of £100,000" are not permitted. In so far as there was previously any debate about this,[4] the judgment of Baron J. in *H v H* (Financial Relief: Pensions) [2010] 2 F.L.R. 173 laid this to rest. In her words at p.176: *"I am clear that the court must make a percentage order"*.

These "shareable rights" can be "shareable rights under a specified pension arrangement" or "shareable state scheme rights". The reference to "specified" in this context means that the particular scheme must be identified in the order. A "pension arrangement" is widely defined in the Welfare Reform and Pensions Act 1999 s.46, and almost any kind of pension scheme held by an individual which is not a state scheme, whether or not it is in payment, falls within this category. This includes rights in schemes held by public employees. There are only very limited exceptions to this general rule and very few United Kingdom pension arrangements are not susceptible to Pension Sharing Orders.[5] Even where a pension arrangement can be subjected to a Pension Sharing Order, not all of the rights under it are considered "shareable". The exceptions are, however, limited.[6]

A "shareable state scheme right" is defined in the Welfare Reform and Pensions Act 1999 s.47, and for all practical purposes means all entitlements of an individual under SERPS or S2P.[7] Entitlements to the basic state retirement pension do not fall within this category and cannot be subjected to a Pension Sharing Order.[8]

Universities Superannuation Scheme). If this is likely to be an issue in a particular case a prudent practitioner should ask the pension providers for their view before any Pension Sharing Order is made.

[4] See the article by David Salter: "The Hallam Pensions Formula: RIP?" [2010] Fam Law 722.

[5] Curiously, the pension schemes of the Prime Minister, Lord Chancellor and the Speaker of the House of Commons have been exempt under The Pension Sharing (Excepted Schemes) Order 2001 (SI 2001/358), but the separate pension arrangements for holders of these offices will be abolished by the Public Services Pensions Act 2013 and such justification as ever existed for this anomaly removed.

[6] Most significantly, rights which a person has by virtue of being a widow/widower of a deceased person and rights resulting from disablement or death by accident of a person during his service do not count as shareable rights: The Pension Sharing (Valuation) Regulations 2000 (SI 2000/1052) regs 1 and 2 and Income and Corporation Taxes Act 1988 s.612.

[7] In January 2013 the Coalition Government announced (see "The single-tier pension: a simple foundation for saving") an intention to cut off fresh accruals to rights under the S2P and implement a single-tier state pension with effect from 2016, and published a draft Pensions Bill 2013 to bring this about. If this is implemented then rights accrued up to that date will continue to be potentially subject to pension sharing for divorces up to 2016, but thereafter there will be no pension sharing of state pensions.

[8] This is because it is paid pursuant to Social Security Contribution and Benefits Act 1992 s.44(3)(a) and not s.44(3)(b).

Availability of Pension Sharing Orders

By virtue of the Matrimonial Causes Act 1973 s.24B, a Pension Sharing Order can be made against one spouse in favour of the other only on the granting of a decree of divorce or nullity of marriage or at any time thereafter. It cannot be made between two parties who were never married[9] nor on a decree of judicial separation nor without a court order. 4–003

The court is not obliged to make a Pension Sharing Order in all circumstances. Even where a Pension Sharing Order is technically available the court has a discretion not to make such an order, having considered all the relevant factors in the case under the Matrimonial Causes Act 1973 s.25, 25A and 25B, including of course the pension benefits which each spouse has and the consequences for the other of losing a possible entitlement to such benefits as a result of the divorce.

In deciding whether or not to make a Pension Sharing Order the court will need to have, at least, a "relevant valuation", that is a fairly up to date[10] basic statement of the value of the rights or benefits accrued under any relevant pension scheme.[11]

This "value" figure was formerly known as the "cash equivalent transfer value" (CETV) or the "cash equivalent of benefits" (CEB) (where the pension was already in payment). These terms should have fallen into disuse as a result of the amended version of Form E[12] appearing in Practice Direction 5A made under Family Procedure Rules 2010. The approved term now is Cash Equivalent (CE).[13] The CE will appear in paragraph 2.13 of the Form E of the spouse with the pension rights. This figure will have been supplied by the pension provider and should have been properly calculated in accordance with detailed technical guidance and regulations.[14]

---

[9] Save in relation to dissolving civil partnerships under Civil Partnership 2004, where almost identical provisions of law and procedure exist, for a detailed analysis of which see Ch.11 below.

[10] Family Procedure Rules 2010 r.9.3(1) defines "relevant valuation" as being a valuation at a date not more than twelve months before the date fixed for the First Appointment date. The Divorce etc. (Pensions) Regulations (SI 2000/1123) reg.3 suggests a valuation no earlier than one year before the divorce petition. Ideally the valuation should be as recent as possible.

[11] Family Procedure Rules 2010 r.9.30(1) and The Pensions on Divorce (Provision of Information) Regulations 2000 (SI 2000/1048) reg.2(2).

[12] The expression CETV (originally devised, long before pension sharing was invented, to assist individuals to transfer between competing pension providers) had been widely adopted by family lawyers in the context of pension sharing. The expression owed its use not to its inclusion in any of the myriad of pension sharing related statutes or statutory instruments, but to its inclusion in the standard form of Form E in use between 2000 and 2011. Accordingly the expression could be, and was, abolished simply by the drafting of the new standard form of Form E with the term CETV replaced by the term CE. Curiously, the Form P1 uses the expression CEV, but the expression CE has the wider currency.

[13] In relation to the Additional State Pension and PPF compensation entitlement this will be a "valuation" rather than a CE.

[14] Prior to October 2008 valuations of occupational schemes were calculated by reference to Guidance Note 11 published by the Institute of Actuaries and the Faculty of Actuaries. Calculations under GN11 very often undervalued occupational schemes. Since October 1, 2008 these figures will have been calculated under The Occupational Pension Schemes (Transfer Values)(Amendment) Regulations 2008 (SI 2008/1050). These regulations have generally had the effect of rendering CEs more representative of their true value, but this is not always the case and practitioner should always be wary of its reliability, as the use of different mathematical assumptions can produce very different end valuations: see the discussion in Ch.2 above.

LAW AND PROCEDURE IN RELATION TO PENSION SHARING ORDERS

Implementation of Pension Sharing Orders

4–004   Once a Pension Sharing Order is made, its implementation will in due course take place by reference to the percentage identified in the Pension Sharing Order, but not of the CE figure which the court will have had before it on the day the order was made, but instead a fresh valuation figure of the CE. This fresh valuation will be made as at "the valuation day".[15] The valuation day will ordinarily be some months after the court hearing and will be a date selected by the pension provider within a four month implementation period.[16] The rights which are valued, however, will be those which the member spouse has at the date the order "takes effect",[17] also known as "transfer day".[18] These distinctions are unlikely to make much difference in most cases, but might do so, for example, in the event of a significant change in market conditions or valuation methodology in the course of the process of making and implementing a Pension Sharing Order.[19]

The non-member spouse is not entitled to receive the benefits of the order in cash, but will receive an appropriately calculated[20] pension credit which will be used to create fresh pension rights for the non-member spouse.[21] The fresh pension rights will sometimes be within the same scheme (an internal transfer) and will sometimes be within a different scheme (an external transfer).[22] The member spouse will commensurately be subjected to a pension debit, reducing the value of the rights under the original pension scheme.[23]

PROCEDURE

Statutory Framework

4–005   Since April 6, 2011 the framework for pension sharing procedures has been largely governed by Family Procedure Rules 2010 Pt 9 Ch.8.[24] These rules, via Practice Direction 5A, provide guidance on the pension parts of Form E (Statement of Means) and also Forms P (Pension Inquiry Form), P1 (Pension

---

[15] Welfare Reform and Pensions Act 1999 s.29(2).
[16] Welfare Reform and Pensions Act 1999 ss.29(7) and 34. If, however, the pension provider unnecessarily delays the implementation within the four month period and losses arise as a result then the victim of the losses may have a remedy for maladministration on application to the Pensions Ombudsman: see *Boughton v Punter Southall & the Trustees of the Bell Clements Group Pension* (2009) ref 74851/1.
[17] See para.4–010 below and see *Slattery v Cabinet Office (Civil Service Pensions) and Another* [2009] 1 F.L.R. 1365.
[18] Welfare Reform and Pensions Act 1999 ss.29(4), 29(5) and 29(8).
[19] See Ch.10 in which various "implementation issues" are discussed in detail.
[20] i.e. the percentage identified in the order multiplied by the value of the shareable rights on valuation day.
[21] For Pension Sharing Orders taking effect after "A-Day" (April 6, 2006) the amount of the pension credit will count towards the non-member spouse's lifetime pension allowance for the purposes of the Finance Act 2004. Commensurately the fact of the pension debit will be taken into account in calculating the member spouse's lifetime allowance.
[22] Welfare Reform and Pensions Act 1999 Sch.5.
[23] Welfare Reform and Pensions Act 1999 s.31.
[24] SI 2010/2955. The procedural framework in fact largely follows the rules introduced by The Family Proceedings (Amendment) (No.5) Rules 2005 (SI 2005/2922).

Sharing Annex), P2 (Pension Attachment Annex), PPF (Pension Protection Fund Inquiry Form), PPF1 (Pension Protection Fund Sharing Annex) and PPF2 (Pension Protection Fund Attachment Annex). Form P1 was amended with effect from April 6, 2012[25] to delete the (largely ignored) requirement for the obtaining of Form P and its attachment to the order. Form PPF1 was not simultaneously amended and continues to include the requirement discarded from Form P1.

Commencing an application

The divorce petition (in Form D8) can contain an application for a Pension Sharing Order if it is to be sought.[26] Alternatively, either party can make a later free-standing application for a financial order, including a Pension Sharing Order (in Form A),[27] in the same court as the one in which the divorce is proceeding.[28] 4–006

Curiously, unlike other financial orders, a non-member spouse can apply for a Pension Sharing Order even when re-married.[29]

If Form A contains an application for a Pension Sharing Order (or if it is added later) then a copy of the Form A must be sent by the applicant to the pension provider for the pension scheme concerned.[30] This rule, on its face, requires this step to be taken at the time that Form A is issued (or amended). In practice, the non-member spouse may not, at that time, know the details necessary to comply with this rule and may not even know in which pension scheme the member spouse has interests. It will probably suffice to carry out the service as soon as these details are known and as far as possible in advance of any court date where the making of a Pension Sharing Order might occur. A sensible hedge against the possible costs consequences of not complying with this rule would be to put the other side on specific written notice that more details are required to permit compliance with this rule. In practice pension providers rarely do anything other than acknowledge receipt of the Form A so complying with this requirement later rather than earlier usually causes no great problem; but the step is a necessary pre-requisite for obtaining a Pension Sharing Order and a practitioner who fails to execute a timely service of the Form A might regret the omission in the event that there is a particular previously undiscovered problem with the pension scheme involved.

Gathering valuations

Once Form A is issued, even where pension sharing is not specifically requested, any member spouse should, within 7 days of receiving notification of the date of the First Appointment, unless already in possession of an up to date valuation (i.e. one taken less than one year prior to the First Appointment[31]), request from the pension provider of each pension scheme in which rights exist, including any 4–007

---

[25] Family Procedure (Amendment) Rules 2012 (SI 2012/679).
[26] Family Procedure Rules 2010 r.9.4(a).
[27] Family Procedure Rules 2010 r.9.4(b).
[28] Family Procedure Rules 2010 r.9.5.
[29] Matrimonial Causes Act 1973 s.28(3). See also Ch.6 in relation to the position following an overseas divorce.
[30] Family Procedure Rules 2010 r.9.31.
[31] Family Procedure Rules 2010 rr.9.3 and 9.30(4).

LAW AND PROCEDURE IN RELATION TO PENSION SHARING ORDERS

SERPS or S2P rights or PPF compensation entitlements, a basic valuation of such rights.[32] This will be the "cash equivalent" (CE) or, in relation to SERPS, S2P or PPF compensation entitlements, simply a "valuation".[33]

The pension provider, if informed that divorce proceedings have been commenced, should furnish the above information within six weeks of receiving this request,[34] although this doesn't always happen in practice. Within 7 days of receiving the information the member spouse should provide it to the non-member spouse, together with the name and address of the pension provider.[35] In practice this information is usually supplied within Form E and the requirement to supply it separately might be thought to be an unnecessary duplication of effort. In any event, even if already supplied, this information, together with some other information, needs to be within the completed Form E within paragraph 2.13 in the form provided by Practice Direction 5A. The information required includes the following:

1) the name and address of pension provider or PPF Board;
2) the member spouse's National Insurance Number;
3) the reference number of the pension scheme or the PPF compensation entitlement;
4) the type of scheme, for example, occupational or personal, final salary, money purchase, additional state pension, PPF or other;
5) the date of calculation for the CE or of the valuation of the PPF compensation entitlement or the additional state pension rights (i.e. SERPS or S2P);
6) a statement of whether the pension scheme is in drawdown or not;
7) if the arrangement is an occupational pension arrangement which is paying reduced CEs, what the CE would have been if it had not been reduced or, at least, the fact that it is a reduced CE; and
8) whether or not the PPF compensation entitlement is capped.

Further information: Pension Inquiry Forms (Form P) or Actuary's Report?

4–008   If more detailed information is sought by the parties or the court then a court may make a direction against the member spouse to complete all or part of the Pension Inquiry Form P[36] or, if necessary (for example where the member spouse is being

---

[32] i.e. a valuation complying with The Pensions on Divorce (Provision of Information) Regulations 2000 (SI 2000/1048) reg.2(2): see Family Procedure Rules 2010 r.9.30(1).
[33] See Form E para.2.13 Practice Direction 5A.
[34] The Pensions on Divorce etc. (Provision of Information) Regulations 2000 (SI 2000/1048) reg.2(5)(b).
[35] Family Procedure Rules 2010 r.9.30(3).
[36] Family Procedure Rules 2010 r.9.15(7)(c) and see Form P contained in Practice Direction 5A. Note that Thorpe L.J. in *Martin-Dye v Martin-Dye* [2006] EWCA Civ 681, at para.68, suggested that Form P should be completed "in every case where a pension is significant and where a pension sharing order might be made". In practice, directions requiring Form P are much rarer than this. It is arguable that in cases where there is to be an expert's report by a pensions' actuary then requiring a Form P might be a duplication of effort, but this is not always the case. The body of the pension sharing annex Form P1 used to suggest that (save for consent orders) a Form P was an essential pre-requisite for the making of an order and had to be annexed to the order, although this was habitually over-looked in

uncooperative), an order against the pension provider.[37] The information supplied in Form P will include many more relevant details about the pension scheme,[38] including the charges involved with implementing a Pension Sharing Order, whether or not an internal transfer is available and/or compulsory, whether or not the pension scheme is subject to any other order and whether there are any health issues involved. Such information may be very important to the court's decision as to what order should or could be made. In practice where pension issues are significant and not straightforward then it is more likely to be appropriate to seek a direction at the First Appointment for the commissioning of a pension actuary's report and this may well lessen or eliminate the need for a Form P. Before seeking such a direction, practitioners will need to consider the requirements of Family Procedure Rules 2010 Practice Direction 25D. Such reports will ordinarily be on a single joint expert basis and early thought, that is well before the First Appointment, will need to be given to the issues which are to be addressed with preliminary enquiries made of the proposed expert to establish, amongst other things, the timescales and costs involved. The letter of instruction will be an important document which can be settled by the court in the absence of the agreement of the parties.[39]

Making an order

Having obtained all necessary information the parties and, ultimately, the court will then consider whether or not one or more Pension Sharing Orders should be made. This may, of course, be by consent or on a contested basis. If an order is made by the court which includes a Pension Sharing Order then the body of the order must state that there is to be provision by way of pension sharing in accordance with the annex or annexes to the order.[40] The order must then be accompanied by an annex in Form P1.[41] There should be one annex per pension scheme affected.[42] Where a Pension Sharing Order is made against an AVC scheme then a separate annex is required.

4–009

The Form P1 pension sharing annex should provide a comprehensive record of all details which the pension provider will need to implement the order. This will include basic information such as the names, addresses, dates of birth and National Insurance numbers of the parties and enough information to identify clearly the pension scheme to be shared. Crucially it will specify the percentage of the value of the pension rights which is to be applied to the value on valuation day. It will also specify what portion of the pension sharing charges each party

---

practice and the anomaly was eliminated by the new Form P1 introduced by Family Procedure (Amendment) Rules 2012. The anomaly remains in the PPF1.

[37] The Pensions on Divorce etc. (Provision of Information) Regulations 2000 (SI 2000/1048) regs 2(1)(c) and 2(4).

[38] Including the matters referred to in The Pensions on Divorce etc. (Provision of Information) Regulations 2000 (SI 2000/1048) reg.4.

[39] See some sample letters of instruction in Section D below.

[40] Family Procedure Rules 2010 r.9.35(a).

[41] Family Procedure Rules 2010 r.9.35(b). Form P1 is contained in Practice Direction 5A.

[42] Family Procedure Rules 2010 r.9.35(b).

LAW AND PROCEDURE IN RELATION TO PENSION SHARING ORDERS

will be responsible for meeting[43] and if this is not specified then the default position is that the member spouse should pay these charges.[44]

If the order is not a consent order then the face of the Form P1 requires the parties to certify that[45]:

1) they have received the information required by Regulation 4 of the Pensions on Divorce etc (Provisions of Information) Regulations 2000; and
2) it appears from that information that there is power to make an order including provision under s.24B of the Matrimonial Causes Act 1973.

4–010   If the order is a consent order then the statement of information form introduced by Family Procedure Rules 2010 (Form D81) (as amended by Family Procedure (Amendment) Rules 2012 and in contrast to the pre-2012 version) require the parties to certify that requisite information has been supplied by the pension provider and that the court has power to make a Pension Sharing Order. In the event that the non-member spouse has a choice between an internal and an external transfer, the Form P1 should include a note of that preference. It can also include the details of the destination pension scheme in the event of an external transfer, but this is not compulsory. The Form P1 may draw attention to unusual features such as the member spouse's ill health or the pension scheme being wound up.

The pension sharing annex will specify a date upon which the order will "take effect". In the post-2000 draft (recommended, but not compulsory) pension sharing annexes the impression was given that the parties could select this date and it was arguable (but controversial) that the regulations[46] did not prevent the use of this mechanism to effect a deferred Pension Sharing Order.[47] Later (compulsory prescribed) versions of Form P1 [48] provided no scope for selecting a date. This is likely to continue to be the position under Form P1 under Practice Direction 5A, but it is just about possible that Family Procedure Rules 2010 r.5.1 gives some scope for re-opening this argument. Ordinarily at least, the "taking effect" date will be fixed as Decree Absolute or 28 days (i.e. the appeal period

---

[43] Note that the pension provider is entitled to demand payment of pension charges in real money prior to implementation: see The Pensions on Divorce etc. (Charging) Regulations 2000 (SI 2000/1049) reg.9. The authors' impression is that this is happening more often than formerly and charges can be unexpectedly expensive (for example, the NHS Pension Scheme charges £2,904 for implementing a Pension Sharing Order). In situations where there is little available money and/or where one party or the other may be awkward about producing the required amount the question of precisely how the charges are to be paid may need to be addressed at the time the Pension Sharing Order is made. This should not be a problem where the pension provider adopts the alternative measure of making a deduction of an appropriate amount from the pension credit received by the non-member spouse and/or from the member spouse's remaining pension rights. If the implementation becomes extended the pension provider in some circumstances may raise additional charges: above, reg.6.

[44] Welfare Reform and Pensions Act 1999 s.41(3)(b).

[45] Note the amendments to Form P1 introduced by Family Procedure (Amendment) Rules 2012.

[46] Matrimonial Causes Act 1973 s.24C(1) and The Divorce etc (Pensions) Regulations 2000 (SI 2000/1123) reg.9(1).

[47] This, in certain circumstances, could be a useful device to avoid the difficulty created by the "income gap" where, for example, a pension already in payment to a 65 year old member spouse would cease to be in payment to a 45 year old non-member spouse: see the discussion in Ch.10 below.

[48] Introduced by The Family Proceedings (Amendment (No.5)) Rules 2005.

plus 7 days[49]) after the Pension Sharing Order is made, whichever is the later; but this can be postponed if an appeal is issued within the period.[50]

Implementing the order

Within 7 days of Decree Absolute or the date of the order (whichever is later) the court should send (or direct a party to send) to the pension provider a copy of the Decree Absolute and the relevant financial order and pension sharing annex.[51] This should give the pension provider the information necessary to implement the order.[52] Allowing for hard pressed court staff, it may be prudent for the party who would be adversely affected by any delay to send a copy of these documents to the pension provider in any event. For example, the Principal Registry of the Family Division has adopted a policy of routinely requiring the non-member spouse to serve the pension sharing annex on the pension provider.

4–011

A Pension Sharing Order should be implemented during the "implementation period". This is defined as the period of four months beginning with the day the order takes effect or (if later) the first day on which the pension provider is given certain necessary information.[53] In certain circumstances this period can be extended by an application by the pension provider to the Occupational Pensions Regulation Authority, failing which the pension provider might be subjected to a financial penalty.[54] If, however, the pension provider unnecessarily delays the implementation within the four month period and losses arise as a result then the victim of the losses may have a remedy for maladministration on application to the Pensions Ombudsman: see *Boughton v Punter Southall & the Trustees of the Bell Clements Group Pension* (2009) ref 74851/1.

The amount transferred on implementation will be the specified percentage of the CE on the "valuation day"[55] of the rights that existed at "transfer day", i.e. the day the order takes effect.[56] The valuation day will usually[57] not be the day the order takes effect, but will be a day selected by the pension provider within the four month implementation period.[58] These distinctions are unlikely to make much difference in most cases, but might do so, for example, in the event of a significant change in market conditions or valuation methodology in the course of the process of making and implementing a Pension Sharing Order.[59]

---

[49] The Divorce etc (Pensions) Regulations 2000 (SI 2000/1123) reg.9(1).
[50] The Divorce etc (Pensions) Regulations 2000 (SI 2000/1123) reg.9(2).
[51] Family Procedure Rules 2010 r.9.36.
[52] The Pensions on Divorce etc. (Provision of Information) Regulations 2000 (SI 2000/1048).
[53] Welfare Reform and Pensions Act 1999 s.34(1). This information is that required by The Pensions on Divorce etc. (Provision of Information) Regulations 2000 (SI 2000/1048) para.5; but this information should be contained in a properly completed Form P1.
[54] The Pension Sharing (Implementation and Discharge of Liability) Regulations 2000 (SI 2000/1053) regs 3 and 5.
[55] Welfare Reform and Pensions Act 1999 s.49.
[56] See discussion in para.4–010 above.
[57] There are exceptions to this. For example, it is the normal practice of the Armed Forces Pension Scheme to use valuations of benefits as at the date the order takes effect.
[58] Welfare Reform and Pensions Act 1999 s.29(7).
[59] See Ch.10 in which various "implementation issues" are discussed in detail.

Pension credits

4–012   The amount transferred will be by way of pension credit to the non-member spouse either by way of internal transfer to create fresh, but independent, pension rights within the member spouse's pension scheme or to create fresh pension rights in a different pension scheme known as the "destination arrangement".[60] Some pension schemes (for example, unfunded public sector pension schemes, SERPS and S2P) only permit internal transfers. Some pension schemes will only permit external transfers and, where this is the case, they must provide this information in Form P.[61] Some pension schemes will give the option to the non-member spouse.[62] The non-member spouse may have additional rights of selection where the scheme is an underfunded occupational pension scheme.[63] Before any Pension Sharing Order is made the information as to which category the particular scheme falls should be available to the court and to the parties by virtue of the completion of Form P. If the transfer is to be an external transfer and the Form P1 has identified the destination arrangement then this is where the pension credit will be transferred.[64] This information may be supplied later by the non-member spouse to the pension provider (perhaps after taking proper financial advice after a financial order has been made as different destination arrangements may have very different investment performances and/or rules such as on the date when pension benefits can be taken). If the non-member spouse fails to supply this information to the pension provider or if the proposed destination arrangement does not qualify as a valid pension scheme then the pension providers may make their own choice, or possibly just defer the implementation period indefinitely.[65] A prudent non-member spouse will accordingly give careful thought to this issue in good time. If the pension providers are late in making the pension credit available (i.e. ordinarily, after the implementation period) then they have to compensate the non-member spouse by commensurately increasing the amount of the pension credit offered.[66]

---

[60] There can only be one tax-free lump sum so that if the member spouse has taken it then the non-member spouse will not have this advantage in the fresh pension scheme created: see Inland Revenue Personal Pension Schemes (Guidance Notes) IR76 (2000) and Occupational Pension Schemes (Practice Notes) IR12 (2001).
[61] The Pensions on Divorce etc. (Provision of Information) Regulations 2000 (SI 2000/1048) reg.2(3)(d) and (e) and Form P Pt B4.
[62] Hence para.F of Form P1.
[63] Welfare Reform and Pensions Act 1999 Sch.5 and The Pension Sharing (Implementation and Discharge of Liability) Regulations 2000 (SI 2000/1053) reg.16 and the discussion in para.7–010 below.
[64] The Pension Sharing (Implementation and Discharge of Liability) Regulations 2000 (SI 2000/1053) regs 11 to 15 for guidance on what schemes might qualify and what schemes might not qualify as a destination arrangement.
[65] Welfare Reform and Pensions Act 1999 s.35(1) and Sch.5 and The Pension Sharing (Implementation and Discharge of Liability) Regulations 2000 (SI 2000/1053).
[66] Welfare Reform and Pensions Act 1999 Sch.5 para.10 and The Pension Sharing (Implementation and Discharge of Liability) Regulations 2000 (SI 2000/1053) reg.18.

APPEALS AND APPLICATIONS TO SET ASIDE OR VARY AN ORDER

Completing the process

If the pension providers takes the view that insufficient information has been provided they will serve written notice on both spouses explaining either what further information is required or that all is in order and that they intend to proceed to implementation.[67] Once the pension providers have implemented the Pension Sharing Order they will serve written notice to both spouses confirming that this has taken place.[68]

4–013

APPEALS AND APPLICATIONS TO SET ASIDE OR VARY AN ORDER

Appeals

The normal time limit for issuing an appeal against a financial order is 21 days from the date of the decision or such different period as may be directed.[69] If an appeal is issued within 28 days of the date of the financial order (i.e. the appeal period plus 7 days) then a Pension Sharing Order will automatically not take effect, and accordingly will not be implemented, until the appeal has been dealt with.[70] In relation to appeals outside this time period the court could still exercise a discretionary power to stay implementation in appropriate circumstances.[71]

4–014

An appeal against a Pension Sharing Order issued inside the initial 28 day time period can result in a variation or setting aside of the original order. An appeal issued outside the initial 28 day period can have the same result if the Pension Sharing Order has not already been implemented. Even if the appeal is dealt with after the Pension Sharing Order has been implemented then it can still, in appropriate circumstances, be successful; but the remedy will not be an interference with the Pension Sharing Order itself if the pension provider has acted to his detriment in any way which is not insignificant in reliance on the taking effect of the order.[72] The remedy might, in such circumstances, be some other provision not amounting to interference with the implemented Pension Sharing Order, but which has the effect of putting the parties into what the court considers is an appropriate position.[73]

---

[67] The Pensions on Divorce etc. (Provision of Information) Regulations 2000 (SI 2000/1048) reg.7.
[68] The Pensions on Divorce etc. (Provision of Information) Regulations 2000 (SI 2000/1048) reg.8.
[69] Family Procedure Rules 2010 r.30.4.
[70] The Divorce etc. (Pensions) Regulations 2000 (SI 2000/1123) reg.9(2).
[71] Family Procedure Rules 2010 r.30.8.
[72] Matrimonial Causes Act 1973 s.40A(2) to (4).
[73] Matrimonial Causes Act 1973 s.40A(5).

Applications to vary

4–015 Pension sharing issues can arise in a number of ways on variation applications under the Matrimonial Causes Act 1973 s.31. A court can capitalise a periodical payments order by making, in its lieu, a Pension Sharing Order; but only where the periodical payments order being capitalised was made in divorce proceedings commenced after December 1, 2000.[74]

A Pension Sharing Order can also be varied by the court of first instance under the Matrimonial Causes Act 1973 s.31; but only where the application is made before it has taken effect[75] and where the original order and the application are made before Decree Absolute.[76]

DOUBLE ORDERS

Earlier Pension Attachment Order

4–016 Where there is a pre-existing Pension Attachment Order against a particular pension scheme in favour of an earlier non-member spouse and, under this Pension Attachment Order, benefits are either currently being paid or may in the future be paid to the earlier non-member spouse then the court cannot make a Pension Sharing Order against that pension scheme.[77] It follows that this would not prevent a Pension Sharing Order in circumstances where the particular pension scheme had been subject to a Pension Attachment Order, but this had ceased to be operative, for example, because it was for income only and the non-member spouse had re-married.

Earlier Pension Sharing Order

4–017 Where there has been a Pension Sharing Order in relation to a particular scheme the court cannot in the same divorce proceedings, or (curiously) in later divorce proceedings between the same spouses (if, for example, they re-marry and then re-divorce), make a further Pension Sharing Order against the same pension scheme.[78] It is not entirely clear whether these provisions prevent the court making a Pension Sharing Order on a capitalisation under the Matrimonial Causes Act 1973 s.31(7B)(ba) in relation to a pension scheme which has already been subjected to a Pension Sharing Order under the Matrimonial Causes Act 1973 s.24B in the original proceedings. It may be that the use of the expression "under this section" in the Matrimonial Causes Act 1973 s.24B(3) does permit such a later order under s.31(7B)(ba).

---

[74] Matrimonial Causes Act 1973 s.31(7B)(ba) and Welfare Reform and Pensions Act 1999 s.85(3)(b).
[75] Matrimonial Causes Act 1973 s.31(4A)(a)(i).
[76] Matrimonial Causes Act 1973 s.31(2)(g) and 31(4A)(a)(ii).
[77] Matrimonial Causes Act 1973 s.24B(5).
[78] Matrimonial Causes Act 1973 ss.24B(3), 25B(7B) and 25C(4).

There is nothing, however, to prevent a pension scheme which was subjected to a Pension Sharing Order in divorce proceedings being subjected to a further Pension Sharing Order between different parties in different divorce proceedings.[79]

More than one Pension Sharing Order in one divorce

The court may, on one occasion, make more than one Pension Sharing Order, i.e. intervene and redistribute rights in more than one pension scheme. In some circumstances this could involve the making of one Pension Sharing Order against one spouse and another against the other spouse.   4–018

It may be reasonable to assume that the law applicable to lump sums and property adjustment orders to the effect that (save for maintenance capitalisations under the Matrimonial Causes Act 1973 s.31) once one capital order is obtained no further application may be made also applies, by analogy, in relation to Pension Sharing Orders[80]; but this is by no means a universal view[81] and, for avoidance of doubt, a prudent litigant might insist on a clear statement to this effect in any order.

PRE-LEGISLATION DIVORCES

Some cases might still arise where there was a divorce petition in existence before December 1, 2000, but one or both spouses wish there now to be a Pension Sharing Order. Can this be done? This was quite common in the early years of the pension sharing legislation. It rarely arises now; but could in theory arise, for example, where a divorce petition was long ago issued, but the parties attempted to reconcile before concluding all the formalities of their divorce.   4–019

If the divorce has proceeded to Decree Absolute, even where no financial order has been made and where parties would like a Pension Sharing Order, then nothing can be done,[82] short possibly of the rather drastic step of re-marrying in order to re-divorce.

If the divorce has, for whatever reason, reached Decree Nisi, but not Decree Absolute, and both parties consent to a Pension Sharing Order, then there should be no difficulty in rescinding the Decree Nisi, issuing a fresh petition and proceeding to a Pension Sharing Order.[83] If one party objects, however, the court will probably not allow such an approach.[84]

If there is no Decree Nisi the most likely answer is that a court will allow either party (even against the wishes of the other) to issue a fresh petition and

---

[79] i.e. most obviously, where the member spouse re-marries a different spouse and then is divorced from the new spouse.
[80] See *Minton v Minton* [1979] A.C. 593 HL and *Sandford v Sandford* [1986] 1 F.L.R. 412.
[81] See, for example, the notes to the Matrimonial Causes Act 1973 s.24B in The Family Court Practice which states that "provided orders at different points in time relate to different schemes, the court, having made one pension sharing order, can subsequently make another in the absence of an appropriate dismissal".
[82] Welfare Reform and Pension Act 1999 s.85(3).
[83] *S v S (Rescission of Decree Nisi: Pension Sharing Provision)* [2002] 1 F.L.R. 457.
[84] *H v H (Pension Sharing: Rescission of Decree Nisi)* [2002] 2 F.L.R. 116.

allow the suits to be heard together so that pension sharing is an available remedy in financial order proceedings consequent upon Decree Nisi.[85]

PENSIONS AND THE STATUTORY CHARGE

4–020   If a party who has public funding is successful in being awarded a Pension Sharing Order then, on the face of it, that would be "property recovered" and thus subject to the statutory charge, unless exempt.[86]

The current view of the Legal Services Commission (as advised by leading counsel) is that awards of Pension Sharing Orders are exempt.[87]

ORDERS UNDER THE MATRIMONIAL CAUSES ACT 1973 S.37

4–021   Applications for Pension Sharing Orders are expressly included as within the meaning of a "claim" for "financial relief" for the purposes of the Matrimonial Causes Act 1973 s.37.[88] Accordingly, a transaction by a member spouse having the effect of impeding the non-member spouse's ability to pursue a Pension Sharing Order could be prevented or, once completed, set aside.

Such action might be necessary if, for example, the member spouse was preparing to transfer rights from a pension scheme which could be subjected to a Pension Sharing Order to a pension scheme which could not or might not be so subjected, for example because it was an overseas scheme or because it was already subjected to a Pension Attachment Order. If the interests of a pension provider might be adversely affected by such action then the court would expect the pension provider to be served and have the opportunity to make representations before any decisions were made.

In most procedural areas amendments to statutes and regulations have been implemented to ensure that the procedures utilised for Pension Compensation Sharing Orders (introduced by the Pensions Act 2008) are similar to those utilised by Pension Sharing Orders. One exception to this general approach is in the area of orders under the Matrimonial Causes Act 1973 s.37. Unlike Pension Sharing Orders, Pension Compensation Sharing Orders have not been included in the list of "financial relief" defined in the Matrimonial Causes Act 1973 s.37(1). The Pensions Act 2008 introduced many amendments to the Matrimonial Causes Act 1973, but did not amend s.37 at all. Accordingly, a s.37 freezing order will not be available to protect a claim for a Pension Compensation Sharing Order. This may have little impact in practice because PPF rights cannot readily be transferred, but it is a curious omission from the legislation.

---

[85] See the discussions on this in December [2000] Fam Law 914 and September [2001] Fam Law 691.
[86] i.e. "Exempt" within the meaning of The Community Legal Services (Financial) Regulations 2000 reg.44.
[87] See Legal Services Commission "Focus" Journal, Issue 39 for July 2002.
[88] Matrimonial Causes Act 1973 s.37(1) as inserted by Welfare Reform and Pensions Act 1999 Sch.3 para.9.

ORDERS UNDER THE MATRIMONIAL CAUSES ACT 1973 S.37

Summary of pension sharing order procedure

1) The petitioner can include an application prayer for a Pension Sharing Order in the divorce petition.
2) Either party applying for a Pension Sharing Order should issue a Form A including an application for a Pension Sharing Order.
3) Either party applying for a Pension Sharing Order should send a copy of the Form A to any pension provider in relation to which a Pension Sharing Order may be sought, either at the time of issue or as soon as possible thereafter.
4) As soon as possible after issue of Form A both parties should obtain the basic valuation of any pension rights in their own name.
5) Both parties should complete para.2.13 of Form E, giving the basic valuation of any pension rights in their own name. This should include any SERPS or S2P pension rights and any PPF compensation entitlements.
6) At the First Appointment, where a Pension Sharing Order might be made and where pensions are a significant element in the case, the parties should invite the court to make a direction for the completion of a Form P (pension inquiry form) in relation to any relevant pension. Careful consideration should be given at this stage to the issue of whether a report from an actuarial expert is necessary or appropriate.
7) If a Pension Sharing Order is to be made by consent then a Form D81 (statement of information) should be completed. Note the obligations in Family Procedure Rules 2010 r.9.32(2) if the pension provider has not been served.
8) Any draft order incorporating a Pension Sharing Order shall state in the body of the order that a Pension Sharing Order is to be made in the form of the annex and a pension sharing annex (Form P1) should be completed in full and attached to the order for each pension being subjected to the order.
9) The Form P1 must specify a percentage figure for the pension share and not a particular sum of money or formula.
10) Within 7 days after the order is made (or Decree Absolute, if later) the court should send to any relevant pension provider (or ask one of the parties to send) a copy of the Decree Absolute, the order and the pension sharing annex.
11) The recipient of the pension sharing order may need to select a destination pension fund and this may involve taking independent financial advice. The choice of destination pension fund should be given to the pension provider at the earliest opportunity.
12) The Pension Sharing Order should be implemented within four months of the requisite information being served on the pension provider.
13) Once the Pension Sharing Order has been implemented the pension provider will serve written notice on both parties.
14) The Pension Sharing Order will not take effect if an Appeal is issued within 28 days of the original order of the court.

CHAPTER 5

Law and Procedure in Relation to Pension Attachment Orders

LAW

Statutory framework

Just as with pension sharing, a practitioner dealing with a financial order case involving the possibility of a Pension Attachment Order needs to have some familiarity with a core number of provisions to be found in various statutes and statutory instruments, some of which are necessarily highly technical. The appendices to be found at the end of this book provide full extracts of most relevant materials likely to be encountered by the practitioner in this area. This chapter attempts to summarise the significance of the more important of these provisions to assist the digestibility of a more detailed reading of the extracts.

5–001

The main statutory provisions in relation to Pension Attachment Orders were introduced by the Pensions Act 1995 s.166, which had the effect of amending important parts of the Matrimonial Causes Act 1973 Pt II and it is again appropriate in this context to refer to the amended sections of the Matrimonial Causes Act 1973.

Definition of a Pension Attachment Order

In appropriate circumstances a court may decide to make a Pension Attachment Order. The effect of this will be to leave intact the pension scheme held by the member spouse (accordingly for tax purposes the income derived is that of the member spouse and there is also the danger that the member spouse's death will intervene to affect expected receipts from the pension). The order will require the pension providers to divert a percentage of any receivable monies to the non-member spouse, as and when monies are payable to the member spouse, and also make orders which prescribe how the benefits to be paid under that pension scheme will be taken. These powers apply to almost all pension schemes, but not to shareable state scheme rights.[1]

5–002

In its most straightforward form a Pension Attachment Order will require the pension providers to divert a specified percentage[2] of the income or lump sum[3]

---

[1] Matrimonial Causes Act 1973 ss.25B(3) and 25D(3).
[2] It must be a percentage of the sum due and not a fixed sum: see Matrimonial Causes Act 1973 s.25B(5) and the pension attachment annex Form P2 to be found in Family Procedure Rules 2010 Practice Direction 5A.

due from the pension scheme so that it is paid to the non-member spouse rather than to the member spouse. Further, a Pension Attachment Order may require the pension providers to divert death benefits accruing under a pension scheme to the non-member spouse and may require the member spouse to make specific nominations in favour of the non-member spouse (but not to the children of the family or anybody else)[4] and may require the member spouse to exercise rights of commutation under the pension scheme.[5]

Nature of a Pension Attachment Order

5–003 In each case the orders are, in effect, an enforcement mechanism and are derivative of standard periodical payments and lump sum orders under the Matrimonial Causes Act 1973 s.23.[6] Accordingly, unlike Pension Sharing Orders, they can be made in cases of judicial separation as well as those of divorce and nullity.

The fact that a Pension Attachment Order is a derivative order may have significant implications for the working of the order. Any income rights under a Pension Attachment Order will terminate on the death of either spouse or the re-marriage of the non-member spouse and are variable in the ordinary way,[7] for example where the circumstances of the non-member spouse have improved. Lump sum orders made by way of Pension Attachment Order are, unlike the standard version, also variable.[8]

Subsidiary powers

5–004 The subsidiary pension attachment powers enable the court to control certain matters which the member spouse might otherwise be able to manipulate to the detriment of the non-member spouse. Accordingly, if the pension scheme rules allow commutation, the court can specifically require the member spouse to commute a particular portion of the pension income to produce a lump sum.[9] Further, whatever mechanism exists within the pension scheme for determining who may nominate the recipient of any lump sum death benefits may be over-ridden by the terms of a Pension Attachment Order.[10] This power does not extend to death-related income benefits, nor does it allow the court to require payments to be diverted in favour of the children of the parties, although similar results might be achieved (in the event of consent) through a court undertaking, but query how enforceable they would be.[11] There are no powers for the court to

---

[3] Matrimonial Causes Act 1973 s.25B(4).
[4] Matrimonial Causes Act 1973 s.25C.
[5] Matrimonial Causes Act 1973 s.25B(7).
[6] Matrimonial Causes Act 1973 s.25B(3).
[7] Matrimonial Causes Act 1973 s.31(2)(b).
[8] Matrimonial Causes Act 1973 s.31(2)(dd); but this is unlikely to be appropriate in very many circumstances: see *Westbury v Sampson* [2002] 1 F.L.R. 166. A lump sum arising on the death of the member spouse is not, however, variable after the death of either spouse: Matrimonial Causes Act 1973 s.31(2B).
[9] Matrimonial Causes Act 1973 s.25B(7).
[10] Matrimonial Causes Act 1973 s.25C(2).
[11] See *Morton v MJF Associates Private Pension Scheme* (2010) 4 July, ref 77828/2, Pensions Ombudsman.

require the member spouse to retire and take pension payments at any particular time or to continue making contributions to the scheme.

PROCEDURE

Statutory Framework

Since April 6, 2011 the framework for pension attachment order procedures has been largely governed by the Family Procedure Rules 2010 Pt 9 Ch.8.[12]

These rules, via Practice Direction 5A, provide guidance on the pension parts of Form E (Statement of Means) and also Forms P (Pension Inquiry Form) and P2 (Pension Attachment Annex).

5–005

Commencing an application

The divorce petition (in Form D8) can contain an application for a Pension Attachment Order if it is to be sought.[13] Alternatively, either party can make a later free-standing application for a financial order, including a Pension Attachment Order (in Form A),[14] in the same court as the one in which the divorce is proceeding.[15] Unlike the position in relation to Pension Sharing Orders such an application cannot be made after the applicant has re-married.[16]

If Form A contains an application for a Pension Attachment Order (or if it is added later) then a copy of the Form A must be sent by the applicant to the pension provider for the pension scheme concerned together with the non-member spouse's address and bank account details of the account into which any sum paid as a result of the Pension Attachment Order should be paid.[17] This rule, on its face, requires this step to be taken at the time that Form A is issued (or amended). In practice, the non-member spouse may not, at that time, know the details necessary to comply with this rule. It will probably suffice to carry out the service as soon as these details are known and as far as possible in advance of any court date where the making of a Pension Attachment Order might occur. A sensible hedge against the possible costs consequences of not complying with this rule would be to put the other side on specific written notice that more details are required to permit compliance with this rule. In practice pension providers rarely do anything other than acknowledge receipt of the Form A so complying with this requirement later rather than earlier usually causes no great problem; but the step is a necessary pre-requisite for obtaining a Pension Attachment Order and a practitioner who fails to execute a timely service of the Form A might regret the omission in the event that there is a particular previously undiscovered problem with the pension scheme involved.

5–006

---

[12] SI 2010/2955.The procedural framework in fact largely follows the rules introduced by The Family Proceedings (Amendment) (No.5) Rules 2005 (SI 2005/2922).
[13] Family Procedure Rules 2010 r.9.4(a).
[14] Family Procedure Rules 2010 r.9.4(b).
[15] Family Procedure Rules 2010 r.9.5.
[16] Matrimonial Causes Act 1973 s.28(3).
[17] Family Procedure Rules 2010 r.9.33(1).

PENSION ATTACHMENT ORDERS

5–007   Failure to comply with this rule has implications for the parties if they later wish to present a consent order to the court at a court hearing or otherwise. The court should not make such a consent order unless the pension provider has been sent a copy of the order in draft form and been given 21 days to make objections to it, which the court must consider.[18]

In relation to applications for Pension Attachment Orders the pension provider, once served, is given certain specific rights, including a right to demand to see the member spouse's Form E,[19] the right to comment on the proposal[20] and the right to appear or be represented at the first appointment and other hearings where the court permits it.[21] In practice, pension providers rarely do anything other than acknowledge receipt of the Form A; but it should not be assumed that this will be the case.

Gathering valuation information

5–008   The procedure for gathering information for the purposes of considering a Pension Attachment Order is the same as that for pension sharing (see Chapter 4 above).

Form P is designed to include information useful for the court's consideration of a Pension Attachment Order as well as information on pension sharing. If not all the information in Form P is thought necessary (because only a Pension Attachment Order is sought) then the court can order that part of Form P is completed.[22]

Making an order

5–009   Having obtained all necessary information the parties and, ultimately, the court will then consider whether or not one or more Pension Attachment Orders should be made. This may, of course, be by consent or on a contested basis. If an order is made by the court which includes a Pension Attachment Order then the body of the order must state that there is to be provision by way of pension attachment in accordance with the annex or annexes to the order.[23] The order must then be accompanied by an annex in Form P2.[24] There should be one annex per pension scheme affected.[25] Where a Pension Attachment Order is made against an AVC scheme then a separate annex is required.

The Form P2 should provide a comprehensive record of all details which the pension provider will need to implement the order. This will include basic information such as the names of the parties, the National Insurance number of the member spouse, the address and bank account details of the non-member spouse and enough information to identify clearly the pension scheme which is to be subject to attachment. Crucially it will specify the percentage of the lump sum

---

[18] Family Procedure Rules 2010 r.9.34.
[19] Family Procedure Rules 2010 r.9.33(2).
[20] Family Procedure Rules 2010 r.9.33(5).
[21] Family Procedure Rules 2010 r.9.33(6).
[22] Family Procedure Rules 2010 r.9.15(7)(c).
[23] Family Procedure Rules 2010 r.9.35(a).
[24] Family Procedure Rules 2010 r.9.35(b). Form P2 is contained in Practice Direction 5A.
[25] Family Procedure Rules 2010 r.9.35(b).

or income benefits to be diverted to the non-member spouse and any other subsidiary details on commutation or death benefit nomination which form part of the order. Where the financial order is a consent order then the court should also confirm on the face of Form P2 that Form A has been served on the pension providers and either that no objection has been received or that the court has considered any objection received.

Implementing an order

Within 7 days of Decree Absolute or the date of the order (whichever is later) the court should send (or direct a party to send) to the pension provider a copy of the Decree Absolute and the relevant financial order and annex. This should give the pension provider the information necessary to implement the order.[26] Allowing for hard pressed court staff, it may be prudent for the party who would be adversely affected by any delay to send a copy of these documents to the pension provider in any event.

It may, of course, be some time before the Pension Attachment Order is implemented. It may in any event await decisions in relation to the taking of the pension by the member spouse which may be many years in the future at the time the order is made. The non-member spouse may move address in the meantime and/or may lose touch with the member spouse's intentions in this regard. It may, therefore, be sensible for the non-member spouse to check from time to time with the pension provider that correct details are held and that they are aware of their obligations under the Pension Attachment Order.

5–010

APPEALS AND APPLICATIONS TO SET ASIDE OR VARY AN ORDER

Appeals and applications to set aside

The normal time limit for issuing an appeal against a financial order, including a Pension Attachment Order, is 21 days from the date of the decision or such different period as may be directed.[27]

5–011

Applications to vary

Pension issues can arise in a number of ways on variation applications under the Matrimonial Causes Act 1973 s.31. A court can capitalise a periodical payments order by making, in its lieu, a Pension Attachment Order for a lump sum, it being a derivative species of the standard lump sum order.[28] A Pension Attachment Order for income, being one variety of periodical payments order, can be varied

5–012

---

[26] Family Procedure Rules 2010 r.9.36.
[27] Family Procedure Rules 2010 r.30.4.
[28] Matrimonial Causes Act 1973 s.31(7B)(a).

just like any other periodical payments order. A Pension Attachment Order for a lump sum is, unlike the standard version, also variable.[29]

DOUBLE ORDERS

Earlier Pension Sharing Order

5–013 Where there has been a Pension Sharing Order in relation to a particular scheme the court cannot in the same divorce proceedings, or (curiously) in later divorce proceedings between the same spouses (if, for example, they re-marry and then re-divorce), make a Pension Attachment Order against the same pension scheme.[30]

There is nothing, however, to prevent a pension scheme which was subjected to a Pension Sharing Order in divorce proceedings being subjected to a later Pension Attachment Order between different parties in different divorce proceedings.[31]

PRE-LEGISLATION DIVORCES

5–014 It is just about conceivable that a case could arise where there was a divorce petition in existence before July 1, 1996, but one or both spouses wish there now to be a Pension Attachment Order. Similar considerations would arise to those discussed in relation to pension sharing in Chapter 4 above.

PENSIONS AND THE STATUTORY CHARGE

5–015 If a party who has public funding is successful in being awarded a Pension Attachment Order then, on the face of it, that would be "property recovered" and thus subject to the statutory charge, unless exempt.[32]

The current view of the Legal Services Commission (as advised by leading counsel) is that all awards of income under Pension Attachment Orders are exempt, but that lump sums paid under Pension Attachment Orders are not exempt.[33]

---

[29] Matrimonial Causes Act 1973 s.31(2)(dd); but this is unlikely to be appropriate in very many circumstances: see *Westbury v Sampson* [2002] 1 F.L.R. 166.
[30] Matrimonial Causes Act 1973 ss.25B(7B) and 25C(4).
[31] i.e. most obviously, where the member spouse re-marries a different spouse and then is divorced from the new spouse.
[32] i.e. "Exempt" within the meaning of The Community Legal Services (Financial) Regulations 2000 reg.44.
[33] See Legal Services Commission "Focus" Journal, Issue 39 for July 2002.

ORDERS UNDER MATRIMONIAL CAUSES ACT 1973 S.37

A transaction by a member spouse having the effect of impeding the non-member spouse's ability to pursue a Pension Attachment Order could be prevented or, once completed, set aside.[34]

5–016

Once a Pension Attachment Order has been made it is open to the member spouse to transfer the pension rights to a different scheme; but in this instance an application under the Matrimonial Causes Act 1973 s.37 should not be necessary because the Pension Attachment Order will attach to the new scheme as long as the new pension provider has had notice.[35]

Summary of pension attachment order procedure

1) Either party applying for a Pension Attachment Order should issue a Form A including an application for a Pension Attachment Order.
2) Either party applying for a Pension Attachment Order should send to the pension provider (of the pension scheme for which a Pension Attachment Order may be sought), either at the time of issue or as soon as possible thereafter, a copy of the Form A, the applying party's address and the bank account details for an account to receive any pension attachment benefits.
3) The pension provider may make representations to the court or appear at the First Appointment.
4) As soon as possible after issue of Form A both parties should obtain the basic valuation of any pension rights in their own name and give the information to the other.
5) Both parties should complete paragraph 2.13 of Form E, giving the basic valuation of any pension rights in their own name. This should include any SERPS or S2P pension rights and PPF compensation entitlement.
6) At the First Appointment, where a pension attachment order might be made and where pensions are a significant element in the case, the parties should invite the court to make a direction for the completion of a Form P (pension inquiry form) in relation to any relevant pension.
7) If a Pension Attachment Order is to be made by consent then, if the Form A has not already been served, a copy of the draft order must be sent to the pension provider 21 days before an order is to be made so that they have the opportunity to object.
8) Any draft order incorporating a Pension Attachment Order shall state in the body of the order that a Pension Attachment Order is to be made in the form of the annex and a pension attachment annex (Form P2) should be completed in full and attached to the order for each pension being subjected to the order.
9) The Form P2 must specify comprehensively the information which the pension provider needs to implement the order.
10) Within 7 days after the order is made or Decree Absolute (if later) the court should send to any relevant pension provider (or ask one of the parties to send) a copy of the Decree Absolute, the order and the pension attachment annex.

---

[34] For a case in which an order may have assisted the non-member spouse see *Kemp v Axle Group Holdings Limited Directors and Executives Pension Scheme* (2010) 1 September, ref 76194/1.
[35] Matrimonial Causes Act 1973 s.25D(1).

PENSION ATTACHMENT ORDERS

11) The recipient of the Pension Attachment Order may from time to time update the pension provider with any changes in address or banking details, particularly if there is a long time between the date of the order and the taking of pension benefits by the member spouse.

CHAPTER 6

International Issues

PENSION SHARING AND ATTACHMENT ACROSS BORDERS WITHIN THE UNITED KINGDOM

Although the pension sharing and attachment legislation considered in this book relates to England and Wales, parallel systems exist in Scotland and Northern Ireland and there is rarely any difficulty in enforcing a Pension Sharing Order or Pension Attachment Order made in England and Wales in either Scotland or Northern Ireland or vice-versa.[1] It is of interest to note that in Scotland divorcing couples can execute an agreement to share their pensions which, if certain conditions are met, can be implemented without a court order.[2]

6–001

PENSION SHARING AND ATTACHMENT ACROSS BORDERS BETWEEN THE UNITED KINGDOM AND OTHER COUNTRIES

The problem

The growth of a global economy in recent decades means that, perhaps more than ever before, individuals and families move around the world to live and work. It is not uncommon for United Kingdom citizens to accrue rights in pension schemes constituted overseas when living or working away. Equally, it is not uncommon for overseas citizens to live and work in the United Kingdom and thus to accrue rights in pension schemes constituted in the United Kingdom. When these individuals are involved in a divorce then the international nature of the family can create its own problems. This chapter seeks to address these problems.

6–002

Before addressing some of the issues arising it is important to identify that the finer details of exactly how pensions are provided can vary significantly across the world. For example, a private pension in the United Kingdom typically incorporates substantial restrictions on the freedom of the owner of the pension rights in terms of when the monies tied up in the pension scheme can be accessed and in what manner. Although there is now greater freedom to take drawdown income rather than annuity income than there was in the past, United Kingdom pensions can almost never be surrendered for cash. In return, tax advantages are given by the Government in relation to the contributions to the scheme and /or the

---

[1] See, for example, Welfare Reform and Pensions Act 1999 s.28.
[2] The Pensions on Divorce etc. (Pension Sharing) (Scotland) Regulations 2000 (SI 2000/1051).

return on investments within the scheme. In many other countries, for example in the United States of America, private pensions can quite often be surrendered for cash, although there can be a financial penalty for doing this. Furthermore, the state pension scheme in the United Kingdom is different to and less generous than schemes available in other economically comparable countries. For example, a detailed analysis of European countries in 2009[3] put the United Kingdom at the bottom of the European league for generosity in state pensions. The countries at the top of the league (Austria, Spain and Germany) paid more than five times as much to pensioners through their state pension system. Probably because of this, private pensions in those countries are less utilised and dividing pensions on divorce is more akin to the division of state benefits than it is to the redistribution of capital.

6–003   Partly, at least, as a result of these differences there is no widely accepted international methodology for dividing pensions on divorce and there is no real prospect of the United Kingdom system of pension sharing being adopted universally or even widely. This means that enforcement across international borders is not common or easy.

For couples divorcing in England and Wales and wishing to divide a pension constituted overseas it is worth first asking the overseas pension provider whether they would honour a Pension Sharing Order or a Pension Attachment Order made in England and Wales and/or seeking local legal advice as to whether a court would enforce such an order.[4] In most cases the pension providers' answer and the local legal advice will be negative in relation to pension sharing. Pension attachment (more akin to a cross border enforcement mechanism) may be recognised in more cases.

Likewise, for couples divorcing overseas and wishing to divide a pension constituted in England and Wales it is worth first asking the pension providers whether they would honour an overseas pensions order. Again, the answer may depend on the nature of the order, but it is usually not possible for a United Kingdom pension provider to honour an overseas order purporting to redistribute a pension fund.

How then, should divorcing couples, receiving negative answers to the above questions, go about seeking a satisfactory resolution to the problem they face?

POSSIBLE SOLUTIONS

Exporting or importing the pension rights

6–004   It is sometimes possible to export pension rights from pension schemes in the United Kingdom to pension schemes in other countries. This is only possible if the recipient pension scheme is a Qualifying Recognised Overseas Pension Scheme (QROPS). This scheme is specifically designed to assist overseas citizens returning to a country of origin or United Kingdom citizens emigrating

---

[3] The Aon Consulting European Business Leaders Survey, June 2009.
[4] A court in England and Wales would be unlikely to exercise its discretion to make an order which was not going to be enforced overseas: see *Hamlin v Hamlin* [1986] 1 F.L.R. 61.

POSSIBLE SOLUTIONS

overseas. The pension schemes qualifying as QROPS are listed on an HMRC website at *www.hmrc.gov.uk/pensionschemes/qrops-list.htm*.

Any decision to use the QROPS route needs to be taken with the benefit of careful legal and financial advice as there may well be significant downsides to taking this step. There are likely to be penalty costs raised by the pension scheme in moving the pension rights. Also, there is the potential for future United Kingdom tax liabilities. For example, QROPS schemes have to report to the HMRC[5] payments made to individuals who are either resident in the United Kingdom in the year of payment or who were resident in one of the previous five tax years. In some circumstances the recipient may be liable for United Kingdom tax.

Once pension rights have been exported then ordinarily the United Kingdom system of pension intervention on divorce would give way to that of the country to which the rights have been exported.

It may be possible, on a similar basis, to transfer pension rights into the United Kingdom so making available United Kingdom pension sharing legislation. This will depend on the law of the particular country where the pension scheme is constituted and advice will need to be taken on a case by case basis in that country.

Plainly, this way forward will only be helpful if the member spouse agrees to the transfer. It is accordingly unlikely to help situations where the parties are in disagreement as to the way forward.

Securing a commitment by way of undertaking in a United Kingdom court order to the obtaining of an equivalent pension order in an overseas country

It may be possible to include within a United Kingdom order an undertaking to take steps in an overseas jurisdiction to secure an order which is the local equivalent of a Pension Sharing Order or Pension Attachment Order.   6–005

Before such a step is taken it is important to seek local legal advice in the country in which the pension is constituted to ensure that there is a local equivalent which is an available remedy to parties divorcing in the United Kingdom, to ascertain what precise steps are needed to secure the local order and to analyse the costs of any tax or penalty liabilities which might arise in the process.

An example of one country where this step is usually available is the United States of America where the local equivalent of a Pension Sharing Order is the "Qualified Domestic Relations Order" (QDRO).

Again, this way forward is likely only to be helpful where the member spouse consents to the approach and is willing to give an appropriate undertaking; but it may be possible for the court to secure the consent by inviting the member spouse to give the undertaking or face some other off-setting remedy which might be less attractive.

---

[5] The Pension Schemes (Information Requirements—Qualifying Overseas Pension Schemes, Qualifying Recognised Overseas Pensions Schemes and Corresponding Relief) Regulations 2006 (SI 2006/208).

INTERNATIONAL ISSUES

Applications under Matrimonial and Family Proceedings Act 1984

6–006 If the spouses have divorced overseas[6] then one of them may, if certain conditions are established linking the parties to England and Wales,[7] apply for a Pension Sharing Order, a Pension Attachment Order, a Pension Compensation Sharing Order or a Pension Compensation Attachment Order in the jurisdiction of England and Wales.[8] These remedies are not available if the applicant has re-married before any application is made.[9]

It should be noted that having an interest in a pension scheme constituted in England and Wales is not, on its own, sufficient to give jurisdiction for the making of a Pension Sharing Order or a Pension Compensation Sharing Order, although this is a lacuna in the legislation which many commentators in this area consider should be addressed. It should be further noted that if the link with England and Wales is based only on the existence of an interest in a matrimonial home in England and Wales this will not be sufficient to form the jurisdictional basis for the making of a Pension Sharing Order or a Pension Compensation Sharing Order.[10]

Leave of the court will be required before any application under this legislation can be pursued. Leave will only be granted if the court considers there is a "substantial ground for the making of an application".[11] Substantial means "solid". It is a higher test than "serious issue to be tried" or "good arguable case" found in other contexts; but it is a lower test than "the probability that the applicant will achieve a substantive order were the matter to be tried is 'greater than or equal to 50 per cent'".[12]

6–007 Once leave is granted and, before making any order, it will be necessary to establish that "it would be appropriate for such an order to be made by a court in England and Wales", having regard to certain specified criteria.[13] Amongst these criteria will be the extent to which remedies have been or could be pursued in another country. The court will "not lightly characterise foreign law, or the order of a foreign court, as unjust".[14]

In cases where parties divorcing overseas have a dispute over a pension constituted in the United Kingdom which is a clear free-standing dispute and the other country has identified the limits of its jurisdiction and expressly or impliedly opened the door to a separate application under the Matrimonial and

---

[6] This will only apply if the overseas divorce is based upon a marriage which is recognised in English law as a valid or void marriage: *Sharbatly v Shagroon* [2012] EWCA Civ 1507.
[7] Matrimonial and Family Proceedings Act 1984 s.15. These requirements (which are in the alternative) relate to domicile, habitual residence and the possession of an interest in a matrimonial home in England and Wales.
[8] Matrimonial and Family Proceedings Act 1984 s.17(1)(b) and (c) and 21(1)(bd) and (bg).
[9] Matrimonial and Family Proceedings Act 1984 see s.12(2). Note that the exemption of Pension Sharing Orders from a similar provision which applies within divorce proceedings in England and Wales—see Matrimonial Causes Act 1973 s.28(3) does not apply to applications under Matrimonial and Family Proceedings Act 1984.
[10] Matrimonial and Family Proceedings Act 1984 s.20.
[11] Matrimonial and Family Proceedings Act 1984 s.13.
[12] See *Agbaje v Agbaje* [2010] 1 F.L.R. 1813 and *Traversa v Freddi* [2011] EWCA Civ 81.
[13] Matrimonial and Family Proceedings Act 1984 s.16.
[14] See *Agbaje v Agbaje* [2010] 1 F.L.R. 1813.

POSSIBLE SOLUTIONS

Family Proceedings Act 1984 in the United Kingdom to deal with that pension then a court order in England and Wales is very likely to be appropriate.[15] In the words of Thorpe L.J.[16]:

> "It does seem to me very important that, where a pension is rooted and funded within jurisdiction A and where the divorce is to be pronounced in jurisdiction B, with all ancillary issues decided according to the law of State B, it is very important that there should be judicial collaboration to ensure that the applicant in State B is not deprived of her entitlement to share in the pension rooted and funded in State A."

It remains to be seen whether the implementation of "the Maintenance Regulation"[17] with effect from June 18, 2011 will cause practical difficulties for the approach advocated here by Thorpe L.J. in relation to EU cases. Some commentators have suggested that the pursuit of a Pension Sharing Order is the pursuit of maintenance within the meaning of the regulation such that the court first seized of maintenance jurisdiction has exclusive jurisdiction such that a subsequent application under the 1984 Act, even where a bifurcation of powers seems sensible, cannot be entertained.[18]

Any such leave application must be issued out of the Principal Registry of the Family Division,[19] following the Part 18 procedure.[20] This should initially be done on a without notice basis.[21] A High Court Judge granting leave may direct that the application should be heard by a District Judge of the Principal Registry of the Family Division.[22]

---

[15] See *Schofield v Schofield* [2011] 1 F.L.R. 2129.
[16] See *Schofield v Schofield* [2011] 1 F.L.R. 2129 at p.2133.
[17] Council Regulation (EC) 4/2009.
[18] "Scuppering Schofield? The impact of the EU Maintenance Regulation on claims for pension sharing" [2012] Fam Law 191.
[19] Family Procedure Rules 2010 r.8.24(1).
[20] Family Procedure Rules 2010 r.8.24(3).
[21] See Munby L.J. in *Traversa v Freddi* [2011] EWCA Civ 81 for an explanation as to how the application should or should not progress to an inter partes hearing.
[22] Family Procedure Rules r.8.28.

CHAPTER 7

Pensions on Divorce and Insolvency

The purpose of this chapter is to address aspects of insolvency that may arise where a practitioner is considering a Pension Sharing Order or a Pension Attachment Order. There will be cases where an individual is bankrupt or where there is a real risk they may become bankrupt. There will also be cases where doubts exist over the present or future financial position of the member spouse's occupational pension scheme. This might be because the pension scheme is underfunded (i.e. the assets in the scheme are not sufficient to pay the full amount of the CE in respect of all the members of the scheme[1]) or it may be because the employer to which the pension scheme relates has suffered an insolvency event[2] or it may be that the pension scheme is being wound up.[3] This chapter also refers to Market Value Reductions ("MVR") in money purchase schemes. These schemes are not insolvent but as MVR can be confused with underfunding it is dealt with briefly in para.7–011 below.

7–001

INDIVIDUAL INSOLVENCY

Property Adjustment or lump sum orders

Insolvency or the risk of insolvency is an important consideration in financial order proceedings. Lump sum orders and property adjustment orders will not generally be available to a spouse after the bankruptcy order is made because the assets no longer belong to the husband (for exceptions to this outcome see *Hellyer v Hellyer*[4] and *Re G*[5]). It follows that if bankruptcy is anticipated time may be of the essence. In *Mountney v Treharne*[6] the Wife had obtained an ancillary relief order providing for the transfer of the matrimonial home to her. The Husband was to execute the transfer documents within 14 days and in default the District Judge had power to execute them. On July 13, 2000 the Wife obtained Decree Absolute. On July 14, 2000 the Husband was declared bankrupt on his

7–002

---

[1] The Occupational Pension Schemes (Transfer Values) Regulations 1996 (SI 1996/1847) regs 8(4) and 8(4A), as amended by The Occupational Pension Schemes (Transfer Values and Miscellaneous Amendments) Regulations 2003 (SI 2003/1727) reg.2.
[2] Pensions Act 2004 s.127. For a full definition of what is meant by an "insolvency event" see Pensions Act 2004 s.121.
[3] Pensions Act 1995 ss.73 to 77.
[4] [1997] B.P.I.R. 85.
[5] [1996] 2 F.L.R. 171.
[6] [2002] 2 F.L.R. 930.

own petition. The transfer documents had not been executed by the date of the bankruptcy. It was held by the Court of Appeal that the bankrupt's estate did not include the matrimonial home as an equitable interest in favour of the Wife had been created when the order took effect (on Decree Absolute) and that the trustee took the Estate subject to the Wife's equitable rights. The manner in which an order is drafted may affect the Wife's position. The practitioner should ensure that the order provides for the transfer of all or part of the Husband's interest rather than an order for sale and a lump sum order for a distribution of the proceeds. The former will transfer the Husband's interest and the latter will not.[7] The position will be different if the petition pre-dates the financial relief order. Section 284 of the Insolvency Act 1986 provides that any disposition of property by the bankrupt between the date of the presentation of the position and the vesting of the bankrupt's estate in the trustee is void.

7–003   Even if the order is made in time it may be a "transaction at an undervalue".[8] In *Haines v Hill & Another*[9] the court had made an ancillary relief order providing for the transfer of the matrimonial home to the Wife and nominal periodical payments. The court also preserved the Wife's lump sum claims for the specific reason that bankruptcy was anticipated and the court wished to protect the Wife's position if the trustee sought to impugn the property transfer. The trustee applied to set aside the transfer as a transaction at an undervalue. The District Judge refused the application. On appeal to the Circuit Judge the trustee's application was allowed. On appeal to the Court of Appeal the District Judge's order was restored. The Court held that the determination of the parties' claims by the exercise of judicial discretion meant that the Wife had given consideration in money or money's worth for the transfer. It is essential though that the decision should be one made on its merits by the application of s.25 of the Matrimonial Causes Act 1973. An order obtained by collusion to defeat creditors will be susceptible to challenge as a transaction at an undervalue. See *Ball v Jones*[10] for an example of a case in which collusion was alleged but not found (H had received 90 per cent of the assets to enable him to remain in the home with the children).

A lump sum order made before the bankruptcy is a debt provable in the bankruptcy.[11] The balance of the debt may be recoverable after discharge subject to the order of the bankruptcy court.[12]

Income Payment Orders

7–004   Where an individual is adjudged bankrupt the bankruptcy court can make an Income Payments Order[13] ("IPO") against the bankrupt. This cannot be for a greater sum than that which will permit the bankrupt to provide for "the reasonable domestic needs" of the bankrupt and his family.[14] It is also open to the

---

[7] *Warwick v Yarwood* [2010] EWHC 2272 (Ch).
[8] Insolvency Act 1986 s.339.
[9] [2007] B.P.I.R. 1280.
[10] [2008] B.P.I.R. 1051.
[11] Insolvency Rules 1986 r.12.3 as amended by Insolvency Amendment Rules 2005 r.44.
[12] Insolvency Act 1989 s.281(5).
[13] Insolvency Act 1986 s.310.
[14] Family is defined as those living with the bankrupt; Insolvency Act 1986 s.385.

bankrupt to enter into an Income Payments Agreement[15] ("IPA"). Where a pension comes into payment during the currency of the bankruptcy the annuity and the lump sum may be the subject of an IPO or an IPA.[16] Where the bankrupt is or becomes entitled to his pension during the bankruptcy but has elected not to draw it the trustee can obtain an IPO against the pension.[17] Again this will include any lump sum that can be commuted. An IPO or IPA can last beyond discharge of the bankrupt but cannot extend for more than 3 years after the IPO or IPA is made.[18]

Pensions

In the event of bankruptcy, Pension Sharing Orders and Pension Attachment Orders are still available to the non-member spouse. This is because pensions are treated differently from other types of asset. Although the bankrupt's estate comprises "all property belonging to or vested in the bankrupt at the commencement of the bankruptcy"[19] HMRC approved pension schemes are expressly excluded by operation of the provisions of s.11 of the Welfare Reform and Pensions Act 1999.[20] The bankrupt may also come to an arrangement with the trustee or apply to the Court to exclude unapproved schemes from the estate.[21] The court may therefore make a Pension Sharing Order against a bankrupt's pension and the pension credit (save where there have been excessive contributions: see paragraph 7–006 below) cannot be challenged by the trustee. (If the bankrupt has reached pensionable age the trustee may be able to claim the lump sum and the annuity during the period of the bankruptcy: see paragraph 7–004 above). The court could also make a Pension Attachment Order against any lump sum that was likely to be received after discharge from bankruptcy and a Pension Attachment Order against future income.

7–005

Excessive contributions—recovery by trustee

If the member spouse is thought to have made "excessive" pension contributions with a view to putting money beyond the reach of creditors then the trustee in bankruptcy may apply to the bankruptcy court to claw back these contributions from the member spouse's pension scheme[22] and the court has power in those circumstances to direct that the pension provider make a payment to the trustee and to reduce the member's pension rights in the scheme. In considering whether the contributions are excessive the court must consider whether they were made with the object of defeating the creditors and whether they were of an amount "which is excessive in view of the individual's circumstances when they were made".[23]

7–006

---

[15] Insolvency Act 1986 s.310A.
[16] Insolvency Act 1986 s.310(7), *Kilvert v Flackett and another* [1998] 2 F.L.R. 806.
[17] *Raithatha v Williamson* [2012] EWHC 909 (Ch).
[18] Insolvency Act 1986 s.310(6).
[19] Insolvency Act 1986 s.283.
[20] Welfare Reform and Pensions Act s.11(2) for a summary of approved schemes.
[21] Welfare Reform and Pensions Act s.12.
[22] Welfare Reform and Pensions Act 1999 s.15, amending Insolvency Act 1986 s.342A to C.
[23] Welfare Reform and Pensions Act 1999 s.15(6).

Excessive contributions—setting aside of Pension Sharing Order

7–007 The trustee could also seek to recover excessive contributions that have been transferred to a non-member spouse by means of a Pension Sharing Order. The trustee's application will be to set aside the court order which included the Pension Sharing Order on the basis that it was a transaction at an undervalue.[24] Following *Haines*[25] and *Ball*[26] however the trustee's application is unlikely to succeed unless there has been collusion between the parties.

UNDERFUNDED OCCUPATIONAL PENSION SCHEMES

7–008 A pension is underfunded if it has insufficient funds to meet in full its obligation to all members of the scheme.[27] The fact that a particular pension scheme is underfunded should emerge from the basic information provided in the body of the Form E.[28] It is a requirement of Family Procedure Rules 2010 r.9.30 that any person with pension rights must apply for a CE within 7 days of notice of the First Appointment (unless there is a CE in existence dated not earlier than 12 months before the First Appointment). The member spouse must also serve the pension provider[29] who has 21 days from service to provide the prescribed information.[30] In any case in which a Pension Sharing Order or Pension Attachment Order is sought the court may at the First Appointment direct a party to file a Form P in full or in part as the court may direct.[31] In any case in which an issue arises as to underfunding the court can expressly require that part of Form P relating to reduced CE to be completed.

If the scheme is underfunded the member spouse retains the right to transfer out of the scheme,[32] but on such a transfer the CE will be subject to a reduction proportionate to the level of underfunding in the scheme.[33] Form E should contain both the CE at full value and the reduced CE.[34] The trustees of the scheme are not obliged to reduce CEs where the scheme is underfunded—they will also consider issues such as the level of underfunding, the strength of employer's covenants and any recovery plans that may be in place. Where the trustees have produced a reduced CE the parties and the court should treat this as an important indication that the underfunding issues are serious.

---

[24] Insolvency Act 1986 ss.339 and 340.
[25] [2007] B.P.I.R. 1280.
[26] [2008] B.P.I.R. 1051.
[27] Occupational Pension Schemes (Transfer Value) Regulations 1996 reg.8 and Schs 1 and 1A as substituted by Occupational Pension Schemes (Transfer Value) (Amendment) Regulations 2008 reg.4 and Sch.1.
[28] One of the boxes in the Form E requires the person completing it to state whether or not the pension provider is "paying reduced CEs". As set out above this is one of the features of an underfunded pension scheme.
[29] Family Procedure Rules 2010 r.9.31.
[30] Pensions on Divorce etc (Provision of Information) Regulations 2000 reg.2(7) and 4.
[31] Family Procedure Rules 2010 r.9(7)(c).
[32] Although an internal share must also be offered—see para.7–010.
[33] Welfare Reform and Pensions Act 1999 Sch.5 para.8 and The Pension Sharing (Implementation and Discharge of Liability) Regulations 2000 (SI 2000/1053) reg.16.
[34] See above: para.7–008.

In contrast to most other situations, the pension provider cannot insist on an external transfer if the pension credit offered is based on a reduced CE. The pension provider must first offer the non-member spouse an internal transfer using the full value of the member spouse's CE (i.e. without applying any reduction of the member spouse's CE attributable to the underfunding).[35] In many cases this will be the solution preferred by the non-member spouse; but if, having received this offer, the non-member spouse would prefer an external transfer then, provided a full explanation is given by the pension provider as to the reasons for the underfunding and of the likely timescale for the elimination of the underfunding, the pension provider may offer an external transfer on the basis that the member spouse's CE used in the calculation will be reduced proportionately with the extent of the underfunding.[36] The percentage pension share will be implemented against a reduced CE (to give a simple example: if the original CE is £200,000 and the reduced CE is £120,000 a 50 per cent external pension share will result in a transfer of £60,000).

7–010

A decision will have to be made by the parties or by the court as to whether it is appropriate to make a Pension Sharing Order against the underfunded pension scheme. This decision may turn on factors such as the actuarial predictions as to the likely future of the underfunded pension scheme, the willingness of the non-member spouse to take a risk with an underfunded scheme and on what other pension schemes or assets are available. If, after due consideration, the decision is made to make a Pension Sharing Order against the underfunded pension scheme then the percentage of CE selected for the Pension Sharing Order should take into account the chosen method of implementation (internal or external).

MARKET VALUE REDUCTIONS

A Market Value Adjustment Factor ("MVAF") is sometimes seen on the document containing the CE of a pension scheme, most often in relation to money purchase schemes such as "with profits" schemes. (It is possible to see an MVAF on a CE of a defined benefit scheme. In these cases, this is part of the basis of the calculations and should not unduly concern the divorce practitioner). The MVAF does not indicate that there is any insolvency within the scheme. This is not an insolvency issue. However MVAFs can be confused with underfunding in occupational schemes and therefore the issue is considered here.

7–011

The purpose of with profits schemes is that they are designed to provide a good rate of return similar to that available from equities but yet to provide rather less volatility by averaging the returns over different generations of scheme holders. A member whose scheme matures when the market is very high will receive less than if the money in the scheme had been invested directly in an equity fund and, commensurately, those whose schemes mature when the market is low will receive more than if the money in the scheme had been invested directly in an equity fund. This is achieved by the "smoothing" of the final return.

---

[35] Practitioners should be aware that some pension providers do not readily comply with this obligation.
[36] Welfare Reform and Pensions Act 1999 Sch.5 para.8 and The Pension Sharing (Implementation and Discharge of Liability) Regulations 2000 (SI 2000/1053) reg.16.

The provider has to protect itself against the possibility of all of the investors wanting to take their money out of the fund when the market is at a low level and the value of the investments is therefore low. The provider does this by stating that any individual who wants to transfer out of the fund other than at the maturity date may have their CE value reduced at the time.

Commonly therefore the document setting out the benefits will set out the CE value and then a second CE reduced by the MVAF. A Pension Sharing Order will be implemented against the reduced CE. In the majority of cases this will be an inevitable outcome. The practitioner though should be careful where the party with pension rights is close to retirement because the CE will recover in full when the scheme matures. Some examples of the consequences of various orders are set out in Chapter 14.

THE PENSION PROTECTION FUND

Notification of an Insolvency Event

7–012 The value of a pension fund will be affected if the scheme provider has suffered an insolvency event.[37] There is a duty on the pension provider to give this information to all members of the scheme within 28 days of notification of the insolvency event.[38] There is a duty on the member spouse to pass on information to the non-member spouse within 7 days of its being received.[39] The pension scheme itself, when served with Form A, may alert the non-member spouse to the existence of these features. Alternatively, the information should be apparent from Form P[40]. In these circumstances the practitioner will need to consider the situation as affected by the involvement of the Pension Protection Fund.

Introduction of the Pension Protection Fund

7–013 Before the advent of the Pensions Act 2004 pension rights might have been significantly diminished or lost altogether by insolvency; but where the insolvency event took place after April 6, 2005 the effects of insolvency will be ameliorated by the existence of a safety net introduced by the Pensions Act 2004 known as the Pension Protection Fund ("PPF").[41] The aim of the Fund was described as "to provide increased protection for members of defined benefit and hybrid schemes by paying compensation should the employer become insolvent and the pension scheme is underfunded". Details of schemes that have transferred to the PPF can be found at *www.pensionprotectionfund.org.uk/ TransferredSchemes/pages/transferred-Schemes.aspx*.

---

[37] Pensions Act 2004 s.121 defines the expression "insolvency event".
[38] The Pension Protection Fund (Provision of Information) Regulations 2005 (SI 2005/674) reg.4 and Sch.2.
[39] Family Procedure Rules 2010 r.9.37(3).
[40] Form P is reproduced in Section D below. Part C2 of Form P specifically deals with pension schemes being wound up. Part C3 of Form P specifically deals with reduced CEs.
[41] Pensions Act 2004 Pt 2 (ss.107–220) and Schs 5–9.

THE PENSION PROTECTION FUND

Funding

The Board of the Pension Protection Fund holds and administers two funds; the PPF and (since September 1, 2005) the Fraud Compensation Fund ("FCF"). The assets of the PPF and the FCF are raised by the imposition of a levy on eligible pension schemes.[42] The FCF is considered further below in paragraph 7–026.

7–014

Eligibility and assessment period

For the purpose of the PPF, eligible schemes are defined by the Pensions Act 2004 s.126. Essentially the PPF protects defined benefit schemes and hybrid schemes (schemes that have an element of defined benefit and an element of money purchase). "Insolvency events" and "insolvency practitioners" are defined by the Pensions Act 2004 s.121. Where an insolvency event occurs the insolvency practitioner must issue a "scheme failure notice".[43] The insolvency practitioner must give such notice to the pension trustees, the Regulator and the Board of the PPF.[44] Once an insolvency event occurs the pension scheme will enter an "assessment period"[45] during which a valuation will be undertaken by the Pension Protection Fund to determine the value of assets in the scheme against the members' protected liabilities and an assessment will be made as to whether a scheme rescue can be carried out, for example by extracting assets from the employer. The assessment period begins with an assessment date (the date of the qualifying insolvency event) and ends when either the Board ceases to be involved with the scheme (because rescue in some form has occurred),[46] the Board issues a "transfer notice" (takes responsibility for the Scheme)[47] or the board determines that there are sufficient assets in the Scheme to meet the PPF level of compensation.[48] In the latter case the pension scheme reverts to being under the control of the pension providers as normal, but may still be in the "underfunded" category and may have to be wound up outside the Pension Protection Fund.

7–015

Transfer Notice, Compensation

If at the end of the assessment period a transfer notice is issued the liabilities of the pension scheme are converted into obligations to pay "compensation" to the scheme members. The Pensions Act 2004 Sch.7 sets out detailed provisions in relation to compensation. The following is a summary of some common situations and is not a comprehensive guide to the compensation provisions:

7–016

---

[42] Pensions Act 2004 ss.175 and 189.
[43] Pensions Act 2004 s.122(2).
[44] Pensions Act 2004 s.122(6).
[45] Pensions Act 2004 s.132.
[46] Pensions Act 2004 s.132(2)(b)(i) and s.149.
[47] Pensions Act 2004 s.132(2)(b)(ii) and s.160.
[48] Pensions Act 2004 s.132(2)(b)(ii) and s.154(2).

1) Where a pension is in payment at the assessment date (the date the assessment period commenced) 100 per cent of the pension will continue to be paid.[49] This compensation is not subject to the PPF compensation cap (see below).
2) Where at the assessment date the drawing of the pension has been postponed beyond the normal retirement date the member will receive 100 per cent of their entitlement and may commute a part of the pension for a lump sum.[50]
3) Where an active member has achieved Normal Retirement Date ("NRD") at the assessment date 100 per cent of the pension will be paid.[51]
4) Where the scheme member has not achieved NRD at the assessment date (whether he is an active member or the pension is deferred) the level of compensation is 90 per cent of the entitlement subject to the compensation cap. The cap for 2013/14 is £34,867.04 and the maximum that will be paid is 90 per cent of the cap i.e. £31,380.34.[52]
5) Where the scheme member becomes entitled to compensation a commuted lump sum up to 25 per cent of the value of the pension may be paid although this is subject to the cap where applicable.[53]
6) Survivor's benefits will be paid where provision was made for those benefits under the scheme rules.[54]
7) Pensions in payment derived from pensionable service on or after April 6, 1997 are increased in line with RPI or 2.5 per cent per annum if less. Pension in deferment will be revalued in line with RPI or 5 per cent per annum if less.
8) PPF compensation does not include death in service lump sums.

Matrimonial Causes Act 1973 s.25E and Family Procedure Rules 2010 rr.9.37–9.45

7–017   The Matrimonial Causes Act 1973 s.25E (as amended by The Pensions Act 2004 s.319(1) and Sch.12) provides that the court should take into account any PPF compensation to which a party is entitled or is likely to become entitled. The relevant procedural rules are the Family Procedure Rules 2010 rr.9.37–9.45.

Pre-existing Pension Sharing Orders

7–018   If an internal Pension Sharing Order has been implemented against the scheme before the insolvency event then it will be honoured by the PPF subject to the compensation cap.[55] If a Pension Sharing Order has already been made but has not taken effect or been implemented before the insolvency event then it will be implemented by the PPF.[56] This is likely to be implemented by an internal

---

[49] Pensions Act 2004 Sch.7 para.3.
[50] Pensions Act 2004 Sch.7 para.5.
[51] Pensions Act 2004 Sch.7 para.8.
[52] Pensions Act 2004 Sch.7 paras 11, 15 and 26 (and see SI 2013/105).
[53] Pensions Act 2004 Sch.7 para.24.
[54] Pension Act 2004 Sch.7 paras 4, 6, 9, 13 and 18.
[55] Pensions Act 2004 Sch.7 para.21.
[56] The Pension Protection Fund (Pension Sharing Regulations) 2006 (SI 2006/1690) reg.2.

transfer.[57] The CE used for this purpose "shall be calculated and verified in such manner as may be approved by the PPF".[58] If valuation day[59] occurs after the insolvency event then the CE will be calculated in such a way as to reflect the PPF compensation limits (which also apply during the assessment period: see below[60]).

Pension sharing in the assessment period

A Pension Sharing Order can be made during the assessment period. The court is specifically required to take into account likely future compensation payments from the PPF.[61] During an assessment period no new members may be admitted to the scheme, no further contributions may be made and no further benefits may accrue.[62] Benefits payable to members are reduced to the extent necessary to ensure they do not exceed compensation levels[63] (in practice this will not affect pensions in payment where the compensation level is 100 per cent). Valuation methodology is prescribed by The Pension Protection Fund (Pension Sharing) Regulations 2006 r.2(2)(b) (i.e. "calculated and verified by the Board"). The order will be implemented by the PPF during the assessment period, by the PPF if a transfer notice is issued before implementation (see below) and by the pension scheme if the scheme can be rescued.

7–019

Pension Compensation Sharing Orders

When the PPF provisions were originally introduced it was impossible to make a pension related order against a pension that had been transferred to the administration of the PPF (as it was no longer a pension). The position was altered by the Pensions Act 2008 ss.107–123 and Schs 5 and 6. These provisions came into force on April 6, 2011. The Matrimonial Causes Act 1973 s.21B creates the new "Pension Compensation Sharing Order". This enables the court to share the member spouse's pension compensation rights.

7–020

Where the PPF is involved or likely to become involved with a scheme, practitioners need to consider the Family Procedure Rules 2010 rr.9.37–9.45. Where, in the course of proceedings the member spouse receives notification that there is an assessment period or that the fund has been transferred to the PPF he must send that information to the other party.[64] Where a party to proceedings has an entitlement to PPF compensation he must request the Board to provide information about the value of his entitlement.[65] Where notification of transfer is received during the course of proceedings the party with compensation rights must within 7 days of receipt of notification of transfer write to the PPF Board

---

[57] Pensions Act 2004 s.133(8).
[58] The Pension Protection Fund (Pension Sharing Regulations) 2006 (SI 2006/1690) reg.2.
[59] See para.4–011 above.
[60] Pensions Act 2004 s.138(2).
[61] Matrimonial Causes Act 1973 s.25E, as inserted by Pensions Act 2004.
[62] Pensions Act 2004 s.133.
[63] Pensions Act 2004 s.138.
[64] Family Procedure Rules 2010 r.9.37.
[65] Family Procedure Rules 2010 r.9.39.

asking for a forecast of pension entitlement.[66] Any application for a Pension Compensation Sharing Order must be served on the Board.[67] The order for pension compensation sharing is made pursuant to the Matrimonial Causes Act 1973 s.24E and is defined by s.21B. Pension Compensation Sharing Orders may not be made against pensions that are the subject of pension attachment or pension sharing between the parties to the marriage (or compensation attachment or compensation sharing).[68] Where a Pension Compensation Sharing Order is made the court order must have attached to it a PPF Sharing Annex in Form PPF1.

Pre-existing Pension Attachment Orders

7–021 A Pension Attachment Order made before a transfer notice is served will bind the PPF who will step into the shoes of the trustees of the scheme: Matrimonial Causes Act 1973 s.25E. This applies to pension annuity attachment orders, to lump sum orders and requirements to commute. The PPF will not pay death in service lump sums as there is no compensation requirement in relation to death in service. If a death in service lump sum becomes payable during the assessment period it will not be paid. If the scheme is rescued, i.e. no transfer notice is served, then the lump sum will be paid by the trustees when the PPF withdraws.

Pension Attachment Orders against PPF compensation rights

7–022 Where a party to proceedings has PPF compensation rights the court may make a Pension Compensation Attachment Order against the PPF.[69] Such orders can be made against annuities and commuted lump sums but not against death in service lump sums and have the effect of re-directing compensation sums due from the member spouse to the non-member spouse. Where a Pension Compensation Attachment Order is made the court order must have attached to it a PPF Attachment Annex in Form PPF2. Where the member spouse's entitlements are limited by the compensation cap then so, commensurately, will the non-member spouse's portion. Like Pension Attachment Orders, Pension Compensation Attachment Orders are derivative of standard income and capital payment orders so will be affected by, for example, the re-marriage of the non-member spouse.[70]

Pension Protection Fund Charges

7–023 The PPF website contains a full list of applicable charges for Pension Compensation Sharing Orders and Pension Compensation Attachment Orders. These can be surprisingly expensive. For example the PPF charge £1,000 plus VAT for a CE quotation and £3,000 plus VAT to implement a Pension Compensation Sharing Order.

---

[66] Family Procedure Rules 2010 r.9.37(5)(a).
[67] Family Procedure Rules 2010 r.9.40.
[68] Matrimonial Causes Act 1973 s.24E(3).
[69] Matrimonial Causes Act 1973 s.25F.
[70] See Ch.5.

CIVIL PARTNERSHIP

The provisions applicable in relation to the dissolution of civil partnerships are identical to those on divorce. For ease of reference the civil partnership provisions are set out in Chapter 11. The Dissolution etc (Pension Protection fund) Regulations 2006 (SI 2006/1934) is the counterpart of the provisions of The Divorce etc. (Pension Protection Fund) Regulations 2006 (SI 2006/1932).

7–024

PENSION SCHEMES BEING WOUND UP

If a pension scheme is being wound up then the pension provider will be considering how to discharge its liabilities. The options open to the pension provider include transferring the pension interests to a different pension scheme or schemes, purchasing annuities or, in some small cases, paying a lump sum to the member.[71] If the pension scheme being wound up is underfunded then the rights being transferred elsewhere will be reduced in the ways discussed above. The non-member spouse will need to make enquiries of the pension provider to establish what method of discharge is being contemplated. The non-member spouse will need to express a preference as to how any pension sharing order should be dealt with, in particular whether an external or internal transfer is requested.[72]

7–025

FRAUD COMPENSATION

The fraud compensation provisions of the Pensions Act 2004 essentially provide that where an act of fraud has occurred, the Board may make a payment to the trustees of the scheme (or to the PPF if the PPF has taken over the scheme[73]). The Board must maintain a separate fund for fraud compensation payments and this is levied against schemes eligible for fraud compensation. These provisions only have effect upon Pension Attachment Orders and Pension Sharing Orders to the extent that they may improve the viability of a scheme and the potential for rescue.

7–026

---

[71] Pensions Act 1995 s.74. Note also the provisions of The Occupational Pension Schemes (Winding Up) Regulations 1996 (SI 1996/3126), The Occupational Pension Schemes (Winding Up etc.) Regulations 2005 (SI 2005/706) and The Occupational Pension Schemes (Winding Up etc.) Regulations 2007 (SI 2007/1930).
[72] See part H of the Form P1 (which is reproduced in Section D below).
[73] Pensions Act 2004 s.187.

CHAPTER 8

Solutions for Cases in which Pension Sharing Orders are Not Appropriate

There will be cases in which, for one reason or another, the parties will wish to avoid sharing pensions. The decision to avoid a Pension Sharing Order may be driven by the parties: one or other of them may be attached to or dependent upon a certain asset (pension or other property) and wish to retain it. There will be other situations in which, for one reason or another, pension sharing is inadvisable. In these circumstances the practitioner will wish to consider whether a Pension Sharing Order can be avoided whilst at the same time devising a solution that is fair between the parties and will meet the approval of the court. This chapter attempts to identify common situations in which pension sharing may be inappropriate and to propose potential orders in cases where pension sharing is not employed.

8–001

SMALL SELF-ADMINISTERED PENSION SCHEMES ("SSASS")

SSASs can be very difficult to share. The nature of the schemes is described in Chapter 1. In summary SSASs tend to be schemes set up for one or more senior employees of a small company. It is quite common for money to be invested in commercial property with the intention that the property will be sold to provide pension at a later date. Where there is more than one member of the SSAS it is a requirement that all members should be trustees of the scheme or that all members should be directors of a company that is trustee of the scheme. All decisions must be unanimous unless there is a professionally appointed trustee.[1]

8–002

Pension Sharing Orders (either external or internal) can be made against SSASs. Where there is only one member of the scheme, pension sharing may be relatively unproblematic. If the transfer is external funds may need to be raised by mortgage or sale. If the transfer is internal the spouses will have to be joint trustees of the scheme so such orders are likely to work only if the spouses are on reasonably good terms.

Even where there is only one member of the scheme pension sharing may present difficulties. It may well be that the SSAS investment is integral to the success or efficiency of the company and therefore the member spouse may be

---

[1] Occupational Pension Schemes (Investment of Scheme Resources) Regulations 1992 (SI 1991/246) now revoked and replaced by Occupational Pension Schemes (Investment) Regulations 2005 (SI 2005/3378).

reluctant to entertain an external pension share. If the spouses do not have a cooperative relationship an internal transfer will be problematic.

Pension sharing may also be difficult (but not impossible) where the scheme already has more than one member. In such a case, even if there is liquidity in the scheme, it is quite possible that the other members will refuse (as trustees) to allow an external transfer as this will reduce the liquidity of the scheme. An internal transfer may present difficulties as the non-member spouse may not trust the other trustees to deal with matters fairly in the future. The authors have recently come across such a scheme in respect of which a Pension Sharing Order was proposed and agreed. The trustees, however, were only prepared to implement a scheme for a capital sum and not a percentage of CE. The reason for this was understandable: the trustees were unwilling to embark upon the risk, uncertainty and expense of revaluation of assets; but the law is clear that Pension Sharing Orders have to be expressed by way of percentage.[2] In some cases there may be ways around this, for example by the non-member spouse giving an undertaking to reimburse the member spouse in cash in the event that a revaluation produces an unexpectedly high pension credit (or vice-versa). It is schemes of this type that are likely to encounter most difficulty in implementing percentage orders.

SELF-INVESTED PERSONAL PENSION SCHEMES

8–003 SIPPs are in some ways similar to SSASs save that they are personal pension plans in which the single member's pension is invested in a more liberal manner than other types of pension scheme. It is again very common for SIPP funds to be invested in commercial premises. A transfer from a SIPP must be external as this is necessary to separate it from the fund of the member (although if the fund is a group SIPP a separate personal fund may be created in the same SIPP wrapper). The fund can be liquidated by sale and thereby a pension credit could be paid. However in the majority of cases it is likely that the SIPP will be an integral part of an income producing business and the member spouse will be very resistant to a pension share. As with a SSAS if this is the case other options must be considered.

UNAPPROVED RETIREMENT BENEFIT SCHEMES (FUNDED AND UNFUNDED)

8–004 The nature of UURBS and FURBS is explained in Chapter 1. These schemes can be the subject of Pension Sharing Orders, but such orders may carry unacceptable risks as benefits may be subject to conditions or may have to be retained in the scheme and there may be tax implications. The authors are aware of at least one of these schemes where the pension was forfeited if the member left the company to work for a competitor. If a pension share in such a scheme is considered the

---

[2] *H v H* [2010] 2 F.L.R. 173.

PENSION SHARING RESULTING IN DIMINUTION OF ASSETS

Transfer out of defined benefit schemes with disadvantageous CEs

There are situations in which a pension share will diminish assets. This will sometimes happen where the pension is transferred out of a defined benefit scheme. An example is given in Chapter 14 (para.14.34) of a member spouse aged 64 with a pension of £50,000 per annum, inflation linked for life. The non-member spouse in the example is 60 and has pension income of £30,000 per annum, inflation linked for life. If a Pension Sharing Order is implemented to create equality of income both spouses will receive £36,300 per annum, inflation linked. Clearly this represents a loss to the parties during joint lives of £7,400 per annum. It may be that the parties in such a case will be willing to accept such a loss in order to have a "fair" order. However there will be cases where the loss is unacceptable on the facts.

8–005

Guaranteed Annuities

Another situation in which sharing may diminish assets is where one of the parties has the benefit of guaranteed annuity rates. A pension fund that has guaranteed annuity rates is more valuable than its CE would suggest. This is because the pension income is guaranteed at a higher rate than would be achievable if current annuity rates were applied. In some of these funds £100,000 will buy an annuity of £10,000. At current rates a fund of £155,000 would be required to buy an annuity of £10,000. If the pension is moved out of a guaranteed annuity scheme via an external transfer the pension credit can only be transferred to a conventional money purchase scheme which will not enjoy a guaranteed annuity rate. This is another situation in which it may be in the interests of the parties to preserve the pension, at least until retirement when the CE will increase to reflect the guarantee.

8–006

INCOME GAP

This difficulty arises where the member spouse in some public unfunded schemes can take retirement early and the non-member spouse (who is required to take an internal transfer and is therefore bound by the scheme rules) cannot retire until 60 or 65. The pension debit takes effect immediately thus reducing the member's pension and the credit does not result in any payment to the non-member spouse until the Normal Retirement Date for the scheme.

8–007

PENSION PROTECTION FUND

8–008 It was initially the case that pension related orders could not be made against the PPF. The position was altered by the Pensions Act 2008 (ss.107–123 and Schs 5 and 6). These provisions came into force on April 6, 2011. Matrimonial Causes Act 1973 s.21B creates the new "Pension Compensation Sharing Order".

OTHER CASES

8–009 Other situations in which pension sharing may be inadvisable are where the charges are high relative to the value of the pensions, where a petition is issued before 2000 (although this predicament can be circumvented by an agreement to issue a fresh petition[3]) or where the pension scheme is an overseas pension.[4]

SOLUTIONS IN CASES WHERE PENSION SHARING IS NOT APPROPRIATE

Deferring pension sharing

8–010 One way to avoid some of the difficulties described above is to defer Pension Sharing Orders until both parties are closer to retirement or have retired. In the early days of pension sharing, orders were made which requested pension providers to implement orders at a distant date. This is no longer (assuming it ever was) permissible.[5] The only way therefore to make a defined deferred pension share is for the parties to agree (say in a side letter or in a preamble) that they will seek to implement a certain pension share at a certain future date. Such an approach is perfectly feasible although there are potential problems that should not be overlooked. For instance the parties' circumstances may change and one or other spouse may seek to argue that the agreement should not be implemented.[6] In addition the order cannot be made if the member spouse dies (although this problem could be addressed through life insurance and/or a Pension Attachment Order against a death in service lump sum[7]). The remarriage of the non-member spouse would not prevent the order being made both because the application will have been made before remarriage and because it would seem that applications for Pension Sharing Orders can be made after remarriage.[8] It may be a risk if the member spouse is devious because a Pension Attachment Order made to a subsequent spouse could prevent the order being made and a pension share to a subsequent spouse might reduce the asset. It is also the case that the order will

---

[3] See Ch.4.
[4] See Ch.6.
[5] See para.4–010.
[6] This would presumably turn on *Edgar v Edgar* (1981) 2 F.L.R. 19 principles.
[7] See para.8–013 below for the inter-relation between sharing and attachment.
[8] Matrimonial Causes Act s.28(3). See para.4–006.

SOLUTIONS WHERE PENSION SHARING NOT APPROPRIATE

have to take effect at date some distance from the original order. It will therefore have to be sent to the court and approved by the court separately from the original order.

It is also possible simply to leave pension claims open. This could be done by dismissing other claims save pensions sharing. See also para.8–014 below for consideration of the option of dismissing capital claims but making a joint lives maintenance order which may at a future stage be capitalised pursuant to the provisions of Matrimonial Causes Act 1973 s.31.

Any deferral should probably be accompanied by a life insurance policy to preserve the position of the spouse without pension rights in the event of death.

Offsetting

In practice offsetting is likely to be the most popular means of avoiding pension sharing where it is necessary or convenient to do so. There is also the possibility of orders which combine offsetting with a smaller pension share than would otherwise be appropriate. Offsetting is considered in Chapter 13.

8–011

Lump sums in instalments/series of lump sums

Where there is insufficient capital to offset, consideration could be given to a series of lump sum orders or a lump sum in instalments. Only one lump sum order can be made on the application of a party to a marriage.[9] However the lump sum can be paid in several tranches or can be paid in instalments.[10] Care should be taken when drafting as to which form of order is sought as a lump sum expressed to be payable by instalments is variable.[11] The power to make a series of lump sum orders could be used (as could periodical payments) to permit the non-member spouse to make payments into a pension fund. The amount that can be paid into a pension fund in any one tax year is the Annual Limit, which is the amount of an individual's salary or £50,000 if lower.[12]

8–012

Pension attachment

Pension Attachment Orders could also be considered. It should be remembered that Pension Attachment Orders made against annuities are periodical payments orders. They therefore do not survive the remarriage of the non-member spouse. In addition orders made pursuant to Matrimonial Causes Act 1973 s.25B(4) (orders in relation to commuted lump sums) and s.25C (lump sums of death in service) are variable.[13] In the latter case (death in service lump sums) the orders are only variable prior to the death of either party.[14] Practitioners should consider drafting orders so as to take effect only if the non-member spouse does not pre-decease the member spouse. Pension Attachment Orders (save death in

8–013

---

[9] *Coleman v Coleman* [1973] Fam 10.
[10] *Hamilton v Hamilton* [2013] EWCA Civ 13.
[11] Matrimonial Causes Act 1973 s.31(2)(d). *Hamilton v Hamilton* [2013] EWCA Civ 13.
[12] £40,000 from April 2014.
[13] Matrimonial Causes Act 1973 s.31(2)(dd).
[14] Matrimonial Causes Act 1973 s.31(2B).

service orders) will normally not survive the death of the member spouse. A further matter always to be borne in mind is that the income from the pension scheme, even if it is diverted by way of a Pension Attachment Order to the non-member spouse remains taxable in the hands of the member spouse. This may be an important consideration, for example where one party is a higher rate tax payer and the other is not.

The power to order the payment of a death in service lump sum is an often forgotten tool. In many cases it will be the best means of protecting a periodical payments order in the event of the death of the payer. Caution must be exercised however as the same scheme cannot be the subject of both a Pension Sharing Order and a Pension Attachment Order.[15] It follows that these orders are likely to be most useful where (say) the pension assets have been offset or where there is more than one pension. It is important also to remember that such orders are variable during the lifetime of the parties.[16]

Joint lives maintenance orders

8–014 Before the introduction of pension sharing by the Welfare Reform and Pensions Act 1999 it was reasonably common for joint lives maintenance orders to be made to preserve the right of the non-member spouse to share in the income from pensions. In cases where the parties wish or need to avoid pension sharing and where offset is not possible the preservation of income claims during joint lives may well be the simplest approach.

If such an approach is adopted the parties may want to ensure that the life of the member spouse is insured and/or that a pension attachment order is made against any death in service lump sum. The parties will also want to bear in mind the capitalisation provisions in Matrimonial Causes Act 1973 s.31. These provide that if the court at any stage discharges a maintenance order or limits its term it can also make provision by way of payment of a lump sum, property adjustment orders or one or more Pension Sharing Orders. The practitioner will recall that a Pension Sharing Order cannot be made against a pension that has been the subject of Pension Attachment Order where the latter is currently being paid or may yet be paid.[17] It follows that death in service provision could be the subject of a Pension Attachment Order at the time of an original order and thereafter (after retirement) a Pension Sharing Order could be made against the same scheme in capitalisation proceedings under Matrimonial Causes Act 1973 s.31.

If this is an avenue to be considered by the parties then consideration must be given to the quantum of the claim. This is because the level of periodical payments tends to be assessed differently from the level of pension share income. It is very common for the party earning income to have a higher income than the party receiving periodical payments. This is because periodical payments are based upon reasonable needs (generously interpreted) rather than an equal division of income; it also reflects the fact that one party is working to earn the income whilst the other is not. The situation is different insofar as pension sharing is concerned; the court tends to take the view (certainly after a long

---

[15] See Ch.4 for a full discussion of "double orders".
[16] Matrimonial Causes Act 1973 s.31(2)(dd) and 31(2B).
[17] Matrimonial Causes Act 1973 s.24B(5).

SOLUTIONS WHERE PENSION SHARING NOT APPROPRIATE

marriage) that the pension is a capital asset that has been earned by both parties. Where income claims are capitalised the capitalisation will be based upon a Duxbury type[18] calculation with the multiplicand is the quantum of periodical payments considered to be appropriate.[19] There is a degree of flexibility in the calculation[20] and it may be prudent where this approach is adopted for the original order to record that a Pension Sharing Order was not made for whatever reason and for the order to record the division of capital and pension at the date of the order.

Imaginative Actuarial Solution

In a situation where the parties are able to cooperate and where they are concerned to maximise their income a further possibility is to defer pension sharing but in the meantime implement an agreement that the party with substantial income pay significant funds into a pension scheme. These funds will attract tax relief and will therefore be augmented significantly. After a given number of years a pension sharing order could be made transferring the pension to the non-member spouse. The advantages of this approach could be the avoidance of lost income from a fund that would lose value on sharing and the tax benefits enhancing the value of the new fund. The disadvantages will be obvious to any practitioner and a good level of trust between spouses is likely to be necessary to make this work.

8–015

---

[18] The Duxbury model itself is no longer always considered to be appropriate as the predicated investment returns are very optimistic.
[19] *Pearce v Pearce* [2003] 2 F.L.R. 1144 CA.
[20] See *Pearce v Pearce* [2003] 2 F.L.R. 1144 CA and *Lauder v Lauder* [2007] 2 F.L.R. 802.

CHAPTER 9

The Work of the Pensions Ombudsman

STATUS OF THE PENSIONS OMBUDSMAN

The Pensions Ombudsman is constituted under the Pensions Schemes Act 1993 Pt 10. His terms of reference require him to perform the following tasks: **9–001**

1) The Pensions Ombudsman may investigate and determine any complaint made to him in writing by or on behalf of an authorised complainant who alleges that he has sustained injustice in consequence of maladministration in connection with any act or omission of the trustees or managers of an occupational pension scheme or personal pension scheme.
2) The Pensions Ombudsman may also investigate and determine any dispute of fact or law which arises in relation to such a scheme between:
   (a) the trustees or managers of the scheme;
   (b) an authorised complainant; and
   (c) which is referred to him in writing by or on behalf of the authorised complainant.

The Pensions Ombudsman also operates as the Pensions Protection Fund Ombudsman (constituted under the Finance Act 2004) which gives him a similar role in relation to issues relating to the Pensions Protection Fund.

The Pensions Ombudsman investigates nearly 1,000 complaints per year, making detailed findings which are publicised and which are open to appeal to a High Court Judge. The Pensions Ombudsman's website (*www.pensions-ombudsman.org.uk*) exhibits full transcripts of all these decisions.

RELEVANCE TO A DIVORCE PRACTITIONER

Some of these decisions are relevant to the practitioner dealing with pensions on divorce and a prudent practitioner will keep one eye on the work of the Pensions Ombudsman. Cases may arise where the Pensions Ombudsman can provide a more suitable remedy than any which the court can offer. **9–002**

The following cases of fairly recent provenance are examples of the Pensions Ombudsman grappling with issues relevant to the pensions on divorce practitioner:

- *Shepherd v Trustees of the Air Products Pension Plan* (2006) 21 September, ref Q00278

The Ombudsman's ruling established that where a pension is in payment and a Pension Sharing Order is made then the member spouse's reduced entitlements will be effective from the date that the Pension Sharing Order takes effect. Because it can take a number of months beyond that point to implement the pension sharing order the member spouse may (for those months) continue to receive a monthly sum which has not been subjected to the appropriate reduction. The member spouse may therefore be subjected to a recoupment, which can be a significant sum. If the member spouse has been paying periodical payments in the meantime to the non-member spouse he may feel that he has ended up paying the same money twice over, once to the non-member spouse and then again back to the pension provider. This is an example of the **clawback** problem discussed in para.10–011 et seq. below. Unless the financial order contains a provision to enable the member spouse to recover a contribution to the recoupment from the non-member spouse then the member spouse may have no remedy (save possibly against his lawyers).

- *Pike v Teachers Pension Scheme* (2008) 26 March, ref 26355

This is another **clawback** case and the essential facts were similar to those in *Shepherd* above. The husband argued that because the pension providers had, by indicating that the draft consent order was "acceptable" to them, effectively made a representation to him which meant he could raise a defence of estoppel against their claim for a recoupment. It was alleged that the pension providers induced the husband reasonably to believe by written representation that the scheme knew and accepted that he would be paying the wife maintenance payments and that the scheme should have made it clear that they would not be able to comply with the consent order and that the payments under the pension sharing order would be backdated. The Ombudsman rejected the estoppel defence determining that in his view the husband could not reasonably have relied on the statement that the documents were "acceptable" to mean that he could proceed without risk of something going wrong in the way that it did. "He could reasonably have assumed the Teachers' Pension thought that the documents, if finalised in the same form, would give them what they needed to carry out the split. He should not have taken it to mean that he should regard it as acceptable to him".

- *Crabtree v BAE Systems Executive Pension Scheme* (2008) 19 May, ref S00522

The CE of an occupational pension scheme fell dramatically between the date of the Pension Sharing Order taking effect and the date of implementation and the non-member spouse sought compensation for the fact that the amount of the pension credit received by her was consequently much smaller than she had anticipated at the time of the order. Had the pension sharing order been implemented very quickly after it took effect then this dramatic fall (largely caused by a change in CE valuation methodology) might have been avoided; but the implementation was delayed longer than should normally have been the case, but this was because of acts and omissions of the non-member spouse and not the pension providers. The Ombudsman ruled that the non-member spouse

should receive no compensation for her loss. This is an example of **moving target syndrome** discussed in para.10–009 et seq. below.
- *Kerbel v Southwark Council* (2009) 26 January, ref 725771
Shortly before the Pension Sharing Order was made the pension providers informed the non-member spouse that she would begin receiving payments arising from an internally transferred pension credit from age 60. She relied on this information in her negotiations with the member spouse which led to a pension sharing order. On implementation of the Pension Sharing Order the pension providers indicated that their previous statement had been made in error and the non-member spouse would in fact only begin receiving payments from age 65. The Ombudsman accepted that this amounted to maladministration by the pension providers. He declined, however, to order that the non-member spouse receive payments from age 60 and instead awarded her £800 for her distress and disappointment. He justified this by reference to the facts that by commencing payments later the non-member spouse would receive a greater monthly amount over a shorter period (and thus had not suffered a long term loss) and that the negotiated Pension Sharing Order would not necessarily have been different if the true facts had been known. This is a practical illustration of the **income gap** problem discussed in para.10–012 et seq. below.
- *Boughton v Punter Southall and the Trustees of the Bell and Clements Group Pension* (2009) 22 September, ref 74851/1
In this case the Pension Sharing Order was implemented within the four month **implementation period** (see discussion in para.4–004 above), but could reasonably have been implemented more quickly than it was. The delay was the fault of the pension provider. It was not open to the pension provider to say that any implementation within the four month period was adequate and they were required to pay compensation to the non-member spouse for the delay within the four month period.
- *Morton v MJF Associates Private Pension Scheme* (2010) 4 July, ref 77828/2
The divorce in this case pre-dated the introduction of **Pension Attachment Orders** (the use of which should have prevented the problem arising here, for which see the discussion in para.5–007 above). By a consent order made in divorce proceedings on May 31, 1995 the member spouse undertook to direct his pension providers to nominate his first wife as the beneficiary of the lump sum payable on his death, notwithstanding any subsequent remarriage of either party. He remarried in 1998 and in 2006 made a Will which, inter alia, specified that his second wife should receive his pension benefits. He then died in 2009. The pension providers applied to the Pensions Ombudsman for a determination as to how to proceed. The Ombudsman found that the pension providers had a discretion and that the consent order did not directly bind them nor did it give the first wife an entitlement to any payment, in particular since they had not been made aware of the terms of the consent order at the time of its making. The later nomination of the second wife in the Will did not automatically supersede the earlier one which followed the consent order. The pension provider was entitled to regard both the consent order and the Will as containing

nominations and the weight which the trustee ultimately attributes to either nomination was a matter for his discretion.

- *Kemp v Axle Group Holdings Limited Directors and Executives Pension Scheme* (2010) 1 September, ref 76194/1

  The member spouse separated from his wife and conducted negotiations with her preceding their anticipated divorce which included offers by him to utilise his entitlement to a lump sum death benefit under his pension scheme as security for some of the payment obligations he expected to incur to his financially dependent wife by way of an appropriately drafted **Pension Attachment Order.**[1] Before the negotiations were concluded the member spouse died. It emerged that prior to his death he had made an express nomination of his pension death benefits in favour of his sister. The pension providers were minded to honour the nomination in favour of his sister. The Pensions Ombudsman held that the pension providers should not in the circumstances be bound by the express nomination; but should instead ask themselves the following question: "Who were the legitimate potential beneficiaries for the lump sum death benefit and how should the death benefit be distributed amongst them?" In exercising their discretion the pension providers were entitled to take into account the life-time views of the member spouse, but this was not the only factor which they should have taken into account. The matter was duly remitted to the pension providers for reconsideration. It is worth noting that the non-member spouse might have been able to prevent the uncertainty which arose here by seeking an order under Matrimonial Causes Act 1973 s.37, to prevent the member spouse making nominations adverse to her interests.[2]

- *Symons v Astra Zeneca Pension Trustees Limited* (2011) 15 July, ref 83880/2

  Following a divorce from his first wife the member spouse had made a nomination of his pension death benefits in favour of the children from that marriage. Some years later he married his second wife. The member spouse re-wrote his will after the second marriage, a fact which appeared to demonstrate that he had given thought to the competing interests of his first and second families, but he did not make any fresh nomination of his death benefits. On his death the two families disagreed about who should receive the death benefits. The pension providers looked carefully at all the circumstances and were able to establish that they had given proper thought to the merits of the competing claims. Their conclusion was that that the life-time expression of wishes by the member spouse should, in the circumstances, be honoured. The second wife complained to the Pensions Ombudsman that this should not be the case, in particular because it had been made before the second marriage. The Pensions Ombudsman rejected the complaint and upheld the decision of the pension providers. It is interesting to note that the first wife could not have obtained a **Pension**

---

[1] For a discussion of Pension Attachment Orders in relation to lump sum death benefits see para.5–004 above.

[2] See para.5–016 above.

RELEVANCE TO A DIVORCE PRACTITIONER

Attachment Order securing the pension death benefits in favour of her children because no jurisdiction exists for such an order.[3]

- *Davis v Windsor Life Assurance Company* (2012) 6 March, ref 80998/1
  As the parties negotiated their divorce the husband obtained a CE of his Windsor Life pension dated November 2007 at £91,908 which was in drawdown. A consent order was made on January 28, 2008 which included a 100 per cent Pension Sharing Order. This order took effect when Decree Absolute was ordered on March 11, 2008. The four month implementation period ran from March 31, 2008 to July 31, 2008. The implementation did not in fact take place until October 2008, but this was because the wife had failed to complete a form in good time and was not the fault of the pension trustees. From March to September 2008 the husband continued to receive income of £725 pcm from the pension trustees, less than half of which he passed on to the wife. By October 2008 the CE of the fund had gone down to about £55,000. The Deputy Pensions Ombudsman decided that, in relation to drawdown/unsecured pensions the making of a Pension Sharing Order should have triggered a review of how much the member spouse receive from the fund pursuant to (HMRC Guidance Note RPSM09102480). Where the Pension Sharing Order was for 100 per cent this should have caused a suspension of drawdown payments to the husband. The pension trustees were therefore guilty of maladministration and should reimburse the wife with the payments taken by the husband, save where he passed the payments on to the wife. The report does not reveal whether these sums were recollected from the husband by way of **clawback.**

- *Hendry v The Tarmac UK Pension Scheme* (2012) 6 March, ref 85218/1
  Mr Hendry worked for Tarmac. He had separated from his wife in 2004 and divorce proceedings were in progress. He had a relationship with Mrs S, the nature of which was in dispute—on one version he supported her financially and wanted to marry her as soon as he could, on another version he was not supporting her, had ended their relationship and was contemplating a reconciliation with his wife. On July 14, 2009 Mr and Mrs Hendry agreed (in correspondence) a clean break in life and death. On July 30, 2009 there was a Decree Nisi of divorce. On July 31, 2009 Mr Hendry was killed in an accident. Mrs Hendry received, as of right, the widow's income benefit under the Tarmac pension, notwithstanding the apparently imminent divorce. A dispute arose as to whether Mrs Henry or Mrs S should receive the **discretionary lump sum death benefit** under the Tarmac pension scheme. The pension trustees, believing their task of deciding which version of the facts was correct would be "practically difficult" and "personally intrusive" decided to pay the lump sum to Mrs S after only a fairly peremptory investigation. The Deputy Pensions Ombudsman considered their investigation to be inadequate and directed them to carry it out afresh, obtaining appropriate documentary evidence to enable them to assess the rival positions.

- *Staley v Marlborough Investment Management Limited Retirement Scheme* (2012) 31 July, ref 81482/2

---

[3] See para.5–004 above.

Mr Staley had rights in the Marlborough Retirement Scheme. He was also a pension trustee, although no decisions could be taken without the consent of the professional trustee, namely Scottish Widows. The pension scheme owned a commercial property which was leased by a company over which Mr Staley exercised control. Mr and Mrs Staley were divorcing and their financial order proceedings were heard by a judge, who was supplied with CE figures for Mr Staley's interest in the pension scheme. At the end of the hearing on July 28, 2008 the judge reserved his judgment. On October 24, 2008 the judge released his written judgment by which he announced that he would be making a 75 per cent Pension Sharing Order against Mr Staley's rights in the pension scheme. On October 27, 2008 the pension trustees (including the professional trustee) paid £343,406 towards the cost of refurbishing the commercial property. The Pension Sharing Order was formally approved on November 20, 2008. When the Pension Sharing Order came to be implemented it emerged that, as a result of the payment towards the refurbishment works, the value of the assets to be received by Mrs Staley under the Pension Sharing Order had fallen substantially. The Pensions Ombudsman, partly relying upon the involvement of the professional trustee, accepted that the decision to make the payment of £343,406 was a bona fide decision within the scheme rules and declined to find that the pension trustees had a duty to inform the court about the payment before the Pension Sharing Order was made. He was not, in any event, satisfied that the court would have made any different Pension Sharing Order if the fact of the payment had been drawn to the judge's attention between October 27, 2008 and November 20, 2008. Mrs Staley's complaint was dismissed. This is a good illustration of **moving target syndrome** in action.

- *Culverwell v Teachers' Pension Scheme* (2012) 13 November, ref 82981/3
Mr Culverwell was a teacher. He reached his normal pension age on July 31, 2008 but continued working until December 31, 2008 and, even then, did not complete the necessary forms to activate his pension. He and his wife were going through a divorce and, on February 20, 2009, a CE of £500,234 was obtained. On December 17, 2009 the court approved a consent order, including a 41.8 per cent Pension Sharing Order in relation to Mr Culverwell's rights under the scheme. The consent order included a provision which committed Mr Culverwell to "delaying his retirement" until after the Pension Sharing Order was implemented, which he thought he was entitled to do. It had been specifically envisaged that Mrs Culverwell would be entitled to a tax-free cash sum from her share of the pension, which had been calculated at £25,350, and she needed this to fund her housing. Teachers' Pension, however, decided that, on a proper application of their rules, the pension should be deemed to have been taken on January 1, 2009, the day after Mr Culverwell stopped work, and, since this pre-dated the Pension Sharing Order, the lump sum should be taken in its entirety by Mr Culverwell and the CE taken for implementation purposes calculated after the payment of the lump sum, which was commensurately and significantly less than that anticipated. The Deputy Pension Ombudsman's decision was that Teachers' Pension's interpretation

of their rules was correct, but that by producing the CE on February 20, 2009 which gave a contrary impression Teachers' Pension were at fault and should pay some compensation. Mrs Culverwell would not receive full compensation, however, since she should have submitted the draft consent order to Teachers' Pension before it was approved by the court, such practice being (in the view of the Deputy Pension Ombudsman) "standard industry practice". The authors are not convinced that this is in fact standard industry practice, but the problems here illustrate the importance of proceeding with care where a normal pension age occurs at about the same time as the Pension Sharing Order. It may be that Mrs Culverwell also had a remedy against Mr Culverwell for setting aside the consent order on the grounds of mutual mistake.

- *Cleworth v Teachers' Pension Scheme* (2012) 21 December 2012, ref 87725/2

Mr Cleworth was a teacher and his rights under the Teachers' Pension Scheme had a CE of £514,664. On March 20, 2008 a Pension Sharing Order of 51.4 per cent was made against Mr Cleworth. Mr Cleworth failed to pay his portion of the pension sharing charges until July 2009 (he said he had not been asked to pay and the pension trustees said they had asked him to pay in March 2008 and had a policy of not sending reminders). The Pension Sharing Order was finally implemented on July 31, 2009. By this time Mr Cleworth had received overpayments of £22,613 and the pension trustees demanded this money back by way of **clawback**. The Deputy Pensions Ombudsman decided that the policy of not sending reminders amounted to maladministration (for which they should pay Mr Cleworth £200 to compensate him for inconvenience and distress), but this did not remove his responsibility to make the clawback payment.

CHAPTER 10

Implementation Issues

UNEXPECTED DEATH

Basis of Pension Sharing Orders

Pension Sharing Orders are made on the assumption that the member spouse and the non-member spouse have a normal life expectancy in front of them (or at least on the basis that any variation from a normal life expectancy has been considered prior to the selection of an appropriate pension sharing percentage). In some, hopefully rare, instances one or other party will die unexpectedly, soon after the order has been made. Depending on which party dies and precisely when this occurs, this can have an impact on the implementation of the Pension Sharing Order.

10–001

Death by either party before Decree Absolute

If either party dies before Decree Absolute then none of the provisions for lump sum orders, periodical payments orders and property adjustment orders will take effect and they will not be enforceable.[1] The position is the same in relation to Pension Sharing Orders. They cannot take effect before Decree Absolute.[2] The surviving spouse, as a widow or widower of the deceased, may be left with death benefits under the rules of the pension scheme and or any monies due under the deceased's will or intestacy. If this is inadequate the surviving spouse may have a claim under Inheritance (Provision for Family and Dependants) Act 1975, but this cannot give rise to any Pension Sharing Order.

10–002

Barder appeals

As a matter of general law, if both parties survive to Decree Absolute, but one party dies fairly soon thereafter in circumstances where the death fundamentally undermines the assumptions upon which the order was based then a *Barder* appeal of the entire order may be an appropriate way forward for the surviving

10–003

---

[1] Matrimonial Causes Act 1973 s.23(5), 24(3) and 24A(3). For a practical illustration of an unexpected death occurring after Decree Nisi and after the making of a Xydhias agreement over finances see *Hendry v The Tarmac UK Pension Scheme* (2012) 6 March, ref 85218/1, which is referred to in para.9–002 above.

[2] Family Procedure Rules 2010 Practice Direction 5A, Form P1.

spouse.[3] If no *Barder* appeal is pursued in such circumstances then the position in relation to Pension Sharing Orders will be as set out below. If a legitimate *Barder* appeal is issued and pursued after the Pension Sharing Order has been implemented then the pension provider may, with justification, be resistant to unravelling the order.[4]

Death of either party after Decree Absolute but before order has taken effect

10–004 Unlike other orders, a Pension Sharing Order will not necessarily come into effect upon Decree Absolute. A Pension Sharing Order cannot take effect until 28 days after it has been made.[5] The Decree Absolute may have been made prior to the financial order or within a few (less than 28) days after the financial order. It follows that there may be a short period of time after Decree Absolute is made when the rest of the order has taken effect, but the Pension Sharing Order has not taken effect. If either spouse dies during this period then the Pension Sharing Order will not be enforceable,[6] but the remainder of the order will be enforceable.

If it is the non-member spouse who has died then the pension scheme will simply remain the property of the member spouse. Nobody will have suffered any injustice.

If it is the member spouse who has died then injustices might arise. The non-member spouse may well be left in a difficult position, for there will be no widow's/widower's rights, no Pension Sharing Order and quite possibly no claim under Inheritance (Provision for Family and Dependants) Act 1975. If the Pension Sharing Order was to be a significant portion of the provision made for the non-member spouse then this will be an unattractive position for the non-member spouse. A prudent non-member spouse should, therefore, insist that any consent to a dismissal of claims, including those under Inheritance (Provision for Family and Dependants) Act 1975, is deferred until such time as a Pension Sharing Order has been fully implemented and/or insist that Decree Absolute takes place at least 28 days after the financial order is made.

Death of non-member spouse after order has taken effect, but before implementation

10–005 If the non-member spouse dies after a Pension Sharing Order has taken effect, but before it has been implemented, then the pension provider should, if the rules of the pension scheme so permit, make some equivalent financial provision to "one or more persons".[7] Logically, this should be the beneficiaries of the non-member spouse's will or intestacy; but the regulation does not actually specify this and there appears to be nothing to prevent such provision being made to anybody

---

[3] See *Barder v Barder (Caluori intervening)* [1988] A.C. 20 and note Ch.4 above on Appeals.
[4] See the discussion in Ch.4 on Appeals.
[5] See Divorce etc. (Pensions) Regulations 2000 reg.9(1) and Family Procedure Rules 2010 r.30.4(2)(b).
[6] Welfare Reform and Pensions Act 1999 s.28(1)(a) and 29(1).
[7] Welfare Reform and Pensions Act 1999 s.35(2)(b) and The Pension Sharing (Implementation and Discharge of Liability) Regulations 2000 (SI 2000/1053) reg.6, as amended by The Pension Sharing (Consequential and Miscellaneous Amendments) Regulations 2000 (SI 2000/2691).

else, possibly the member spouse. Further, in some circumstances the pension credit may, rather unfairly, be retained by the scheme itself.[8] In such circumstances, a *Barder* appeal by the member spouse may be an attractive option for the court. Indeed, to deal with this problem, it is quite common to see a provision in a Pension Sharing Order committing the non-member spouse's personal representatives to consent to a *Barder* appeal by the member spouse in the event of the non-member spouse's death in these circumstances. Another common way of dealing with this problem is for the Pension Sharing Order to provide that its implementation is conditional upon the non-member spouse being alive at the time of implementation.

Death of member spouse after order has taken effect, but before implementation

If the member spouse dies after a Pension Sharing Order has taken effect, but before it has been implemented, then the death will not have a significant effect on the process because the benefits to be valued are those the member spouse had at the date the Pension Sharing Order took effect when the member spouse was (ex hypothesi) still alive.[9]

10–006

Death of either party after implementation of Pension Sharing Order

Once the Pension Sharing Order has been implemented then the two pension schemes (i.e. the depleted original one held by the member spouse and the fresh one created for the non-member spouse with the pension credit) will operate separately and the death of either party will have the ordinary implications applicable under the rules of the relevant scheme.

10–007

Effect of death on a Pension Attachment Order

A Pension Attachment Order for income or a lump sum will not be enforceable if either spouse dies after the order is made but before Decree Absolute.[10] A death of either spouse after Decree Absolute (and the re-marriage of the non-member spouse) will bring an immediate end to a Pension Attachment Order for income.[11] The death of the non-member spouse will not (subject to any variation application) affect a Pension Attachment Order for a lump sum and the future benefits will accrue to the non-member spouse's estate. The death of the member spouse will, of course, trigger any Pension Attachment Order for a lump sum where provision for a portion of a death benefit has been made.[12]

10–008

---

[8] The Pension Sharing (Implementation and Discharge of Liability) Regulations 2000 (SI 2000/1053) reg.6(4), as amended by The Pension Sharing (Consequential and Miscellaneous Amendments) Regulations 2000 (SI 2000/2691).
[9] Welfare Reform and Pensions Act 1999 s.29. This day is called "Transfer Day", which is not the same day as "Valuation Day".
[10] Matrimonial Causes Act 1973 s.23(5).
[11] Matrimonial Causes Act 1973 s.28(1)(a).
[12] Matrimonial Causes Act 1973 s.25C.

MOVING TARGET SYNDROME AND CLAWBACK

CE valuation changes between the Pension Sharing Order and Valuation Day—Moving Target Syndrome

10–009 Once a Pension Sharing Order is made, its implementation will in due course take place by reference to the percentage identified in the order. The percentage will not be applied against the CE valuation figure which the court will have had before it on the day the order was made, but instead of a fresh CE valuation figure of the shareable rights. This fresh valuation will be made as at "the valuation day".[13] The valuation day will ordinarily be some months after the court hearing and will be a date selected by the pension provider within a four month implementation period.[14]

This leads to the difficulty which has been identified as "Moving Target Syndrome". The valuation of the pension against which the Pension Sharing Order is to be enforced may be quite different at the time of implementation from the valuation identified by the parties and the judge at trial. Commensurately, the level of the pension credit may also be quite different.

Often this will not matter very much as the use of a percentage figure in the order will ensure that both parties will share proportionately in any increase or decrease in the value. If the percentage of the Pension Sharing Order to be executed is not very far away from 50 per cent and the movements in value are relatively modest market fluctuations then little injustice will be done by the moving target, a fact observed by Baron J in *H v H* (Financial Relief: Pensions) [2010] 2 F.L.R. 173 on the facts of that case.

10–010 There may, however, be cases where significant injustice might be done by a moving target. It may be that some event, such as a pay rise or fall, or a decision to retire, between the date of the valuation and the date of the court hearing which undermines the reliability of the CE used at court.[15] The problem is the same for events which occur between the date of a hearing and the date an order is approved if, for example, the judge reserves judgment for a period.[16] In some cases changes occurring between the date of the order taking effect and its implementation can also cause a similar difficulty; but it should be remembered

---

[13] Welfare Reform and Pensions Act 1999 s.29(2).
[14] Welfare Reform and Pensions Act 1999 ss.29(7) and 34.
[15] See *Culverwell v Teachers' Pension Scheme* (2012) 13 November, ref 82981/3, the facts of which are set out in para.9–002 above. Further, the authors were all involved (Edward Hess and Fiona Hay as Counsel representing the wife and David Lockett as the wife's expert actuary) in a civil case against the wife's former Barrister (whom we choose not to name) seeking damages for negligence arising out of a compromise reached at an FDR negotiated by the former Barrister. He advised the wife to accept a Pension Sharing Order drafted as a fixed sum which represented 50 per cent of the CE of the husband's NHS pension which was before the court. The Pension Sharing Order was duly made. The NHS agreed to implement the order, despite the way it was worded. Since that particular CE had been produced the husband had received a substantial increase in remuneration and the CE therefore substantially under-represented the true value of the pension. In February 2012 the BMIF agreed to pay damages to the wife in the sum of £167,500. By doing so they accepted that the Barrister involved should have appreciated that the CE he was using was badly misleading and he was negligent not to do so.
[16] See, for example, *Staley v Marlborough Investment Management Limited Retirement Scheme* (2012) 31 July, ref 81482/2, the facts of which are set out in para.9–002 above.

that the rights which are valued are those which the member spouse has at the date the order "takes effect",[17] also known as "transfer day"[18] so changes occurring at this point are less likely to make a significant difference. There are cases, however, where there might be significant differences. For example, there might be a significant change in market conditions or valuation methodology[19] in the course of the process of making and implementing a Pension Sharing Order. If the member spouse may have some influence in investment decisions or valuation methodology then particular care may need to be taken.

Depending on the mathematics used to calculate the pension sharing percentage one party or the other may make an unfair gain or loss. If the parties have sufficient concern and/or foresight at the time the Pension Sharing Order is drafted then there are ways of dealing with the problem. In some circumstances it may be possible for funds to be moved, by agreement and pending implementation of the Pension Sharing Order, into a specific investment fund in relation to which both parties are comfortable with the level of investment risk. Alternatively, it could be agreed that the expected level of pension credit to be derived from the Pension Sharing Order is a particular figure and it could be provided, by way of undertakings given by each party to the court, that in the event of the actual pension credit being larger or smaller than the expected amount, then the gaining party will reimburse the losing party with a compensatory lump sum. It is suggested that the wording of such undertakings would have to be carefully considered on a case by case basis and also that such provisions are unnecessary in the majority of cases; but they are available and permissible in the right case. It is possible that, even absent agreement, a court could make a lump sum order framed along these lines, but some judges might regard this as an unnecessary complication in the absence of agreement.

Clawback

Another similar implementation problem is known as "clawback". This problem arises most commonly in a situation where, at the time of the Pension Sharing Order, a pension is in payment and a periodical payments order is in force. The parties may intend that the benefits received by the non-member spouse from the pension credit received under the Pension Sharing Order will be not dissimilar to and will in due course replace the monies received under the periodical payments order. At first glance an order terminating the periodical payments upon implementation of the Pension Sharing Order will bring about the desired result.

There can, however, be a catch for the member spouse. The pension provider is entitled to identify that between the date the Pension Sharing Order took effect and the date of implementation the member spouse has been receiving all the income from the pension scheme. Now that a pension debit is to be deducted with effect from the date the order took effect the pension provider will identify that the member spouse has been overpaid and can seek to recoup the overpayments

10–011

---

[17] See *Slattery v Cabinet Office (Civil Service Pensions) and Another* [2009] 1 F.L.R. 1365.
[18] Welfare Reform and Pensions Act 1999 ss.29(4), 29(5) and 29(8).
[19] See, for example, *Crabtree v BAE Systems Executive Pension Scheme* (2008) 19 May, ref S00522, and *Culverwell v Teachers' Pension Scheme* (2012) 13 November, ref 82981/3, the facts of which are set out in para.9–002 above.

from the member spouse by way of a recoupment or clawback demand. From the perspective of the member spouse it can appear that he has ended up paying what seems to be the same money twice over, once to the non-member spouse and then again back to the pension provider.[20]

Again, if this is likely to be a problem, and the parties have sufficient concern and/or foresight at the time the Pension Sharing Order is drafted, then there are ways of dealing with the problem. For example, the financial order could include an appropriate undertaking which ensures that the member spouse is properly compensated by the non-member spouse by a reimbursement of the clawback amount or some agreed portion of it. Again, a court might be persuaded to impose a lump sum order against the non-member spouse along these lines in the right case, but an agreed clause is likely to be the better course.

INCOME GAP

10–012   A problem which has often arisen in pension sharing cases is sometimes referred to as the "Income Gap". This arises most acutely where the pension is a significant part of the parties' current income and the intention of the order is to allow both parties access to the income. The ages of the parties may be such that the non-member spouse cannot draw pension income until a later date than the member spouse draws pension income. This can lead to a significant cash flow issue for parties.

An example of this might be where the member spouse is a Head Teacher age 58 and the non-member spouse does not work and is aged 50. If a Pension Sharing Order is used, the non-member spouse cannot receive the benefits of the "pension credit" until age 55. The member spouse may be willing and able to pay maintenance whilst still earning (i.e. until retirement at age 60) but may not be in a position, if pension sharing is implemented now, to continue such payments after this point from the reduced pension fund. This leaves a three year Income Gap for the non-member spouse, who will be without maintenance from the husband and unable to access any pension income until age 55.[21]

The problem is not as acute as it used to be because the Pensions Act 2008 and The Pensions Act (Abolition of Safeguarded Rights)(Consequential) Order 2009, with effect from April 6, 2009, permitted trustees of public sector schemes to pay out to internal transferees at a much earlier date. The Armed Forces Pension Scheme, the NHS Pension Scheme and the Teachers Pension Scheme have responded by changing their policy to allow internal transferees to take benefits (actuarially reduced) from age 55 and not age 60 or 65, as was previously the

---

[20] See, for example, a number of Pensions Ombudsman's decisions on this subject: *Shepherd v Trustees of Air Products Pension Plan* (2006) 21 September, ref Q00278; *Pike v Teachers Pension Scheme* (2008) 26 March, ref 26355; *Davis v Windsor Life Assurance Company* (2012) 6 March, ref 80998/1; *Cleworth v Teachers' Pension Scheme* (2012) 21 December, ref 87725/2. The facts of all these cases are set out in para.9–002 above.
[21] Attempts to argue that such differences are discriminatory have failed: see *Smith v Secretary of State for Defence* [2005] 1 F.L.R. 97 and *Thomas v Secretary of State for Defence* [2008] 2 F.L.R. 1385.

case. The Police Pension Scheme and the Firefighters Pension Scheme, on the other hand, both decline to allow recipients of pension credits to receive any benefits until age 60 or 65.

One way used to solve this problem has been for the parties to agree that there will be a Pension Sharing Order, but postpone making the Pension Sharing Order until the point when the non-member spouse can take the benefits as income. In this scenario, the full pension is paid to the member spouse until the non-member spouse can receive the benefits. Thus the member spouse has the full pension from which to make maintenance payments and the member spouse's pension income is only reduced at the point when the benefits from the "pension credit" can be actually payable to the non-member spouse as income. It is generally accepted that Pension Sharing Orders cannot be made now to be implemented at a date in the distant future[22]; but as long as the application for a Pension Sharing Order has been made and remains live, there is nothing to prevent the Pension Sharing Order itself being adjourned for a number of years after the remainder of the order has been made. This solution is, however, far from ideal. Difficulties might very well arise if, in the postponement period, something significant happens—for example the death of the member spouse or a substantial reduction in the value of the pension. In this scenario the non-member spouse is undoubtedly exposed to risk; but it may be, on the facts of a particular case, that this risk is not as disadvantageous as suffering from the loss of income caused by the Income Gap.

10–013

---

[22] Subject to the possibility raised (with a degree of timid caution) in Ch.4 above.

CHAPTER 11

Pension Sharing and Attachment on Dissolution of Civil Partnership

CIVIL PARTNERSHIPS

The Statutory provisions

Civil partnerships were created by the Civil Partnership Act 2004. The regulations for dissolution of civil partnerships are contained in the Civil Partnership Act Pt 2. Proceedings for Financial Relief are regulated by the Civil Partnership Act 2004 Sch.5. **11–001**

Entitlement to pension provision on death of the other civil partner

It is a requirement of a civil partnership (Civil Partnership Act 2004 s.3) that the partners should be of the same sex. The debate continues as to whether it is discriminatory for same sex partners to be unable to marry and for partners of the opposite sex to be prevented from entering into a civil partnership. Argument in relation to the former point has largely been laid to rest by the Marriage (Same Sex Couples) Bill 2012/2103. Further controversy has arisen because trustees of occupational pension schemes are permitted[1] to treat civil partners differently from spouses in relation to death in service benefits. In effect death benefits need not be paid in relation to contributions made prior to the coming into force of the 2004 Act.[2] **11–002**

Pension sharing and attachment in civil partnership dissolution—provisions and regulations

There are some distinctions between the treatment of civil partners and spouses; a difference in the treatment of pensions on dissolution is not however among them. The attachment and sharing provisions on the breakdown of civil partnership are identical to those in the Matrimonial Causes Act 1973.The mirror provisions in the Civil Partnership Act 2004 are Sch.5 Pt 4 ss.16–19 (sharing) and Pt 4A ss.19A–19F (pension compensation sharing), Pt 6 ss.24–29 (attachment) and Pt 7 (pension compensation attachment). **11–003**

---

[1] Equality Act 2010 Sch.9 s.18(1).
[2] Although some think this may be discriminatory and subject to challenge.

PENSION SHARING AND ATTACHMENT ON DISSOLUTION OF CIVIL PARTNERSHIP

In the event of a breakdown of a civil partnership the Applicant will issue Form A and Family Procedure Rules 2010 will apply to the application just as they apply to divorce proceedings. Where the PPF is not involved the provisions are set out in Family Procedure Rules 2010 Pt 9. Family Procedure Rules 2010 r.9.29(2)(b) provides that in proceedings under the Civil Partnership Act 2004 that the "party with pension rights" has the meaning given to the "civil partner with pension rights" in the Civil Partnership Act 2004 Sch.5.

Where the application is for a Pension Sharing Order the relevant rules are Family Procedure Rules 2010 rr.9.31 to 32. For Pension Attachment Orders the relevant rules are 9.33 and 9.34. There are further rules (9.35 and 9.36) about the drafting of orders and the service of them on pension providers.

The Dissolution etc (Pension) Regulations 2005 provide effectively that the Pensions on Divorce) Provision of Information Regulations 2000 shall apply to applications for orders under Sch.5 and provide for the provision of information to pension providers in the event of civil partnership attachment. In addition reg.9 provides that—as with spousal orders—the pension share cannot take effect until seven days after the expiry of the time for lodging an appeal.

Pension Sharing Orders after remarriage/new civil partnership

11-004   It was a feature of the Matrimonial Causes Act 1973 that whilst a right to other forms of financial provision is lost on remarriage[3] the right to a pension share is not sacrificed. This anomaly is recreated in the civil partnership legislation lending force to the argument that it is an intentional omission.

THE PPF AND PENSION SHARING IN CIVIL PARTNERSHIP PROCEEDINGS

11-005   Rights to compensation from the PPF are not pension rights and cannot be subject to Pension Sharing Orders. This created a problem until Pensions Act 2008 (see ss.107–123 and Schs 5 and 6) which created, with effect from April 6, 2011, a new section in the Matrimonial Causes Act 1973, namely s.21B, and a new form of order called the "Pension Compensation Sharing Order". These provisions are mirrored in the Civil Partnership Act 2004 Sch.5 para.4A.

Pre-existing orders

11-006   The reader is referred to chapter 7 for a full account of the situation where there are pre-existing orders. However, in summary, if a civil partner has a pre-existing internal pension share (i.e. one made against a fund that seemed at the time solvent) that order will be honoured by the PPF[4] subject to the compensation cap.[5] If a Pension Sharing Order has already been made but not implemented at the date of the insolvency event it will be implemented by the PPF.[6] The share

---

[3] Matrimonial Causes Act 1973 s.28(3).
[4] Pensions Act 2004 Sch.7 para.21.
[5] £34,049.84 per annum in 2012/13. See Ch.7 para.7–014 for a summary of PPF compensation rules.
[6] The Pension Protection Fund (Pension Sharing) Regulations 2006 reg.2 (SI 2006/1690).

will be by way of internal transfer. If valuation day occurs after the insolvency event the CE will be calculated in such a way as to reflect the PPF compensation limits.[7]

Pension Sharing Orders can be made during the assessment period. The CE will be calculated by reference to the PPF compensation levels.[8] The order will be implemented by the PPF during the assessment period or on transfer and by the scheme if it is rescued.

The PPF and Pension Compensation Attachment Orders in civil partnership proceedings

Pension Compensation Attachment Orders may be made against the PPF. The provisions are found in the Civil Partnership Act 2004 Sch.5 para.7. The relevant rules are to be found in Family Procedure Rules 2010 r.9.38 onwards. 11–007

The PPF and pre-existing Pension Attachment Orders

Where there is a pre-existing Pension Attachment Order the PPF will step into the shoes of the trustees of the scheme and will meet the obligations.[9] This will not apply to death in service lump sums as these are not payable by the PPF. If a death in service lump sum becomes payable during the assessment period it will not be paid. If the scheme is rescued then the lump sum will be paid by the trustees after the PPF withdraws. 11–008

Pension Attachment Orders may be made in the assessment period. This applies to annuity orders and lump sum/commutation orders. No order may be made in relation to death in service benefits.

---

[7] Pensions Act 2004 s.138(2) and para.7–017.
[8] Valuation methodology is prescribed by The Pension Protection Fund (Pension Sharing) Regulations 2006 reg.2(2)(b).
[9] Pensions Act 2004 Sch.5 para.31.

CHAPTER 12

The Section 25 Factors, Fairness and Equality in Relation to Pensions

In determining an application for a financial order by a party to a marriage the court must have regard to the Matrimonial Causes Act 1973 s.25. This chapter attempts to analyse how the courts deal with pension CEs and to examine the approach of the courts in relation to issues of fairness and equality,[1] the s.25 factors and their influence on the size of Pension Sharing Order which the court is likely to make. The reader's attention is drawn to areas where actuarial assistance may be helpful but these areas are dealt with in more detail in Chapter 14.

12–001

FORESEEABLE FUTURE

The Matrimonial Causes Act 1973 s.25(2)(a) refers to assets that a party may have "in the foreseeable future". The phrase "in the foreseeable future" is expressly deleted in relation to pension assets.[2] It follows that all pension rights, however remote their receipt, may be relevant to the court's deliberations in an application for a financial order.

12–002

THE RELEVANT S.25 FACTORS

In relation to pensions there are some s.25 factors which are likely to be of relevance more often than others. These are:

12–003

- the quantification of the asset (ss.25(2)(a) and 25B(1)(a));
- the financial needs and obligations of the parties (s.25(2)(b));
- the age of the parties and the duration of the marriage (s.25(2)d));
- the health of the parties (s.25(2)(e));
- contributions (s.25(2)(f));
- The court is also specifically enjoined to have regard to the value of any benefit that a party may lose by virtue of the dissolution of the marriage including any benefits under a pension arrangement that the party may lose a chance of acquiring (ss.25(2)(h) and 25B(1)(b)).

---

[1] See the discussion in "Pensions and Equality" [2007] Fam Law 310 and "Pensions: equality of income or equality of capital?" [2009] Fam Law 525.
[2] Matrimonial Causes Act 1973 s.25B(1) as inserted by Pensions Act 1995 s.166.

SECTION 25 FACTORS

These particular factors are considered below in the context of pension sharing and attachment. Specific consideration is given to issues of off-setting in Chapter 13.

QUANTIFICATION OF THE ASSET

12–004   In the context of the quantification of pension assets the court will be considering the pension benefits which either spouse has or is likely to have in the future, whether the distant future or the foreseeable future.[3] The court will also be considering what benefits in these categories either spouse will lose the chance of acquiring once a divorce takes place.[4] To obtain a full picture of such benefits the practitioner should consider all types of pension provision including state pension provision (basic,[5] additional and graduated) and pensions with former employers. The pension provider will provide a Cash Equivalent figure. This is a notional capital value representing the potential value of future benefits. The CE may be misleading and may significantly undervalue or overvalue pension rights. This is highly significant in the context of pension sharing because any order must be expressed as a percentage of the CE calculated by the pension provider on valuation day.[6]

Consideration should always be given in a case in which pensions are a significant issue to the question of whether an actuary's report is necessary either in relation to the CE or in relation to projected income or both. Although CEs are the prescribed currency for determination of pension issues in financial order proceedings,[7] further evidence is admissible and the introduction of Form P[8] for applications issued after December 5, 2006 is a clear indication that the inadequacy (in some cases) of the CE is recognised. Furthermore, Thorpe L.J. in *Martin-Dye v Martin-Dye*[9] expressly held that "where proportionate" the court will require a bespoke valuation and that the appropriate procedure will usually be the instruction of a joint expert.[10]

12–005   The actuary's report—if it is required—should be sought at the First Appointment. A full analysis of the actuarial issues that may arise on valuation is to be found in Chapter 14. Below are some examples of situations in which the practitioner should consider the instruction of an expert.

(i)   The CE may be misleading. This is particularly likely to be the case if the pension is a "shorter career" public sector pension (see Chapter 15), but this

---

[3] Matrimonial Causes Act 1973 s.25(B)(1).
[4] Most obviously widow or widower's benefits.
[5] Basic State Pensions cannot be shared. On divorce or the breakdown of a civil partnership one party can substitute the other's contributions for their own to give a greater basic state pension (Social Security Contributions and Benefits Act 1992 s.48) so the basic pension is likely to be approximately equivalent. However the date at which the pension is payable may be relevant. See Ch.1 for an analysis of likely changes in the State Pension system to be brought into force in April 2016.
[6] See the discussion in Ch.4 and *H v H* [2010] 2 F.L.R. 173.
[7] Divorce etc. (Pensions) Regulations 2000 (SI 2000/1123) and the Pensions on Divorce etc (Provision of Information) Regulations 2000 (SI 2000/1048).
[8] See para.4–008. Form P is reproduced in Section D.
[9] [2006] 2 F.L.R. 901, [2006] EWCA Civ 681.
[10] [2006] 1 F.L.R. 901, EWCA Civ 681 para.70.

may also apply to other public sector schemes. The CE may also be misleading if the pension is underfunded or in the process of being wound up.

(ii) Some private sector schemes may have discretionary benefits (i.e. benefits that may be paid at the discretion of the trustees). It is permissible for the CE to exclude discretionary benefits.

(iii) The current economic climate and demographic changes have created deficits in many company pension schemes (i.e. the assets held by the pension trustees are insufficient to meet the pension promises made by the scheme). In some cases these schemes may quite legitimately provide low CEs.

(iv) An independent valuation may also be necessary where the scheme is complex, such as a SSAS or SSIP in which valuation of company assets or commercial real property is required to arrive at a conclusion as to the value of the pension. In these cases the underlying assets will need to be valued before the actuary can calculate the CE.

(v) There may be a risk that the value of the pension itself may be affected by sharing. This may be the case where the CE is distorted (reduced or inflated) or in a final salary scheme (where the non-member spouse must take an external transfer).[11]

(vi) Some older schemes offer guaranteed annuities. These guarantees will be lost on transfer. Actuarial evidence may be necessary to advise as to the extent of any potential loss.

(vii) There may be a need for more detailed evidence in relation to income in retirement. The CE will give no real information in relation to the projected level of income at retirement. Even if the pension is in payment it may be unsafe to attempt without expert assistance to predict the likely level of annuity payments after a pension share. Whilst there is no clear authority as to whether the court should endeavour to equalise (if it is a case of equal division) CE or pension income[12] the court in most cases should still have income projections available to it.[13] This may be even more important in a case in which there is an age difference between the parties or where parties are nearing retirement.

(viii) If there are several pensions, advice may be needed as to which pension or pensions should be shared to maximise the parties' respective incomes.

(ix) If the non-member spouse has a choice between an internal and an external transfer then advice may be needed as to which option is preferable.

(x) There may be a gap in the date of receipt. If the member spouse in, for instance, the Armed Forces has taken early retirement, he may be receiving pension income from aged 40 whereas a non-member spouse receiving a

---

[11] In the case described by Mary Banham-Hall in her article at [2008] Fam Law January 2008, a wife required 66% of the pension pot on an external transfer to achieve equality of income whereas she would have required 47.2% if an internal transfer had been achievable. This demonstrates the vast loss of asset value that can result where pension assets are transferred out of final salary schemes. Offsetting and even attachment could be considered in these circumstances.
[12] See discussion on this topic below.
[13] *B v B* [2012] 2 F.L.R. 22.

pension credit will not be able to draw pension until age 55.[14] The Court may therefore need expert advice as to the effect of a Pension Sharing Order on the member spouse's income during working life and projections in relation to the parties' respective incomes at retirement.

(xi) It used to be the case that women would receive a lower annuity than men for an investment of the same amount of capital. This is no longer the case. The European Court ruling in *Association Belge des Consummation Test-Achats*[15] led to the introduction (on December 21, 2012) of unisex annuity rates.

Widow's/ Widower's pensions

12–006 The CE of a pension scheme may (depending upon the scheme's rules) include survivor's rights. The importance of these rights in relation to pension sharing (as opposed to off-setting in which this issue is also of importance but for different reasons[16]) is that they may affect the CE. This is a further reason why it may be of assistance to have actuarial evidence of projected income. A scheme with very generous survivor's rights may have a CE reflecting that fact. However the non-member may be content to invest in a scheme that has no survivor's benefits (thereby increasing both the member's and the non-member's income in retirement). Actuarial evidence will be necessary to determine what share is required to give each party a specified income given the differing nature of their respective schemes.

FINANCIAL NEEDS AND OBLIGATIONS

Equalisation of CE or of income?

12–007 The difficulty in characterising pension schemes as having either a capital or an income nature creates the consequential difficulty of deciding the general approach which the court should take towards considering questions of equality. Since *White v White*[17] the courts have been enjoined to consider any suggested order against the yardstick of equality. Should the court endeavour to equalise (in an appropriate case) the parties' pension respective CE's or the income which they will each derive from such CE?

Given that equal division of CE will in most cases not create equal income[18] this is a moot and difficult issue. Where the parties have been married for many years and their contributions are adjudged to be equal it could certainly be strongly argued that the requirements of equality and fairness could not be met save by an order for division of CE which equalised retirement income. Coleridge

---

[14] Occupational Personal and Stakeholder Pensions (Miscellaneous Amendments) Regulations 2009 (SI 2009/615). Prior to these regulations being adopted by the Armed Forces the income gap was greater than this—the pension credit could not be received until 65. This is still the case in (for instance) the fire fighters scheme.
[15] ECT case C-236/09.
[16] See Ch.13 below.
[17] [2000] 2 F.L.R. 981.
[18] See Ch.14.

J's decision in the case of *RP v RP*[19] is an example of a case in which such an approach was adopted seemingly as a matter of course. In that case an actuary was employed to advise the court of the pension share necessary to provide both parties with equivalent commuted lump sums and income at 60 on the basis of the pension rights earned by the date of the hearing. The necessary pension share was 54.4 per cent of one of the husband's funds with each party retaining other smaller funds.[20] There is no doubt that it has become common practice for actuaries to be asked to advise the courts as to the level of pension share necessary to provide the parties with equivalent income in retirement. This approach was given some judicial approval by David Salter sitting as a Deputy High Court Judge in *B v B*.[21]

> "If a court is to make a pension sharing order, it must be provided with the valuation evidence required by reg.3. As Thorpe LJ observed in *Martin-Dye v Martin-Dye* [2006] EWCA Civ 681, [2006] 1 WLR 3448, [2006] 2 F.L.R. 901 at para [70], actuarial advice on a single joint expert basis will be appropriate where proportionate. This will be particularly important where the argument is to be advanced that a pension sharing order should be made by reference to equality of projected income rather than equality of capital values, as might well have been appropriate in the present instance. Such evidence of projected income would have been of particular importance here because of the disparity in ages between the parties, where the wife would require a lower percentage to achieve equality of income at, say, age 65".

On the other hand it might be argued that the equalisation of income is not considered as being imperative in relation to present and future earned income.[22] (See though the observations of Wilson LJ in *Vaughan v Vaughan*[23] "unlike any attempted capitalisation of earning capacity, it [pension] does not depend on the application of future effort but, subject only to market and other vagaries, it is in the bag"). In addition there is anecdotal evidence that the courts are reluctant to make pension sharing orders that award a non-member significantly more than 50 per cent of the pension CE. *S v S (Ancillary Relief after Lengthy Separation)*[24] is an example of a case in which CEs were equalised—although in that case the other assets were divided unequally because of the length of separation and the build up of assets since separation and furthermore the scale of the pension funds in that case (£2.1 million) may have meant that less attention had to be paid to precise levels of income in retirement. *Martin-Dye v Martin-Dye*[25] is a further example of a case in which emphasis was placed on the CE value and little or no attention was paid to the parties' respective incomes at retirement.[26]

12–008

---

[19] [2006] EWHC 3409 pp.44 and 70, [2007] 1 F.L.R. 2105.
[20] The authors are grateful to Christopher Sharp QC for clarifying the basis of the order in *RP v RP*, which is not clear from the transcript of the judgment.
[21] [2012] 2 F.L.R. 222.
[22] See "Assessing the Quantum of Periodical Payments after McFarlane" [2006] Fam Law 780 and *H v H* [2007] EWHC 459.
[23] [2008] 1 F.L.R. 1108 and [25].
[24] [2006] EWHC 233.
[25] [2006] 2 F.L.R. 901, [2006] EWCA Civ 681.
[26] For a further example of equalisation of CE in a "big money" case, see *H v H* [2007] EWHC 459 para.18.

In cases where pensions are small or—conversely—very large it may well be that equalisation of CE is a simpler and more proportionate approach. In addition division of CE may be more proportionate approach where retirement is a distant prospect; actuarial calculations of predicted income stretching into the future are based upon assumptions any of which may turn out to be inaccurate and therefore an order that may appear to create equality in 2013 may turn out in 2033 to have created a significant inequality.[27]

Maintaining the value of the pension

12–009   It is possible that dividing a pension to create equal income (or in any significant manner) may depress the value of the pension asset.[28] If this is the case the court then the parties may have to find another solution. There may be cases in which pension attachment orders or joint lives maintenance (combined with insurance) may provide a better solution and there may be cases in which some pension sharing can be combined with off-set to produce a more financially satisfactory but equitable outcome.[29]

HEALTH

12–010   The health of the parties may be relevant where one or other party has a reduced life expectancy.[30] It will be a matter for the pension scheme rules as to whether the CE is reduced because of the ill-health of the member spouse. Some schemes will drastically reduce CE and others will not alter the CE at all. Form P has a specific box for the pension provider to complete in the event that they will require information about the health of the member spouse before implementation. If the CE is not affected then the parties may wish to consider a significant pension share to the non-member spouse possibly with some reverse periodical payments. Similarly if the non-member spouse has a reduced life-expectancy it may be sensible to avoid a pension share altogether and to utilise periodical payment orders or attachment orders.

Another consideration in relation to life expectancy relates to the death of a member or non-member during the implementation period. This issue is dealt with in chapter 10. The most important practical consideration for practitioners is the protection of the transferee spouse against the possibility of the member spouse dying between Decree Absolute and the taking effect of the pension share. The life and death clean break provisions in any such order should not take effect until after the pension share has come into effect.[31]

If ill-health is likely to lead to early retirement of the member spouse (but does not affect life-expectancy) the pension CE may be increased—to take account of the extra years of payment. In these circumstances the parties and the court will

---

[27] See "Pensions: Equality of Income or Equality of Capital" [2009] Fam Law 525 for a useful discussion of this issue.
[28] For example, where there is a Guaranteed Annuity Rate: see Ch.14 below.
[29] See Ch.8 for a discussion about the use of orders other than pension sharing and Ch.13 for a discussion of offsetting.
[30] Also see Ch.14 below.
[31] See Ch.10.

need to consider whether and to what extent the member spouse affected by ill-health should retain that part of the pension attributable to the years during which the member spouse is unable to earn.

MATRIMONIAL ACQUEST/CONTRIBUTIONS

12–011

The Matrimonial Causes Act 1973 s.25(2)(f) provides that the contributions of the parties are relevant to the determination of an application for ancillary relief. It is arguable that since *Miller, McFarlane*[32] this factor (certainly in larger money cases) has become more formulaic. In many cases the court will be invited first to identify the "matrimonial assets" and then to consider appropriate division both of matrimonial and non-matrimonial assets.

The debate as to the correct approach in relation to the identification and division of extra marital assets has continued to exercise the higher courts. See for instance *Robson v Robson*,[33] *Jones v Jones*,[34] *N v F*,[35] *Whaley v Whaley*,[36] *K v L*[37] and *AR v AR*.[38]

The above are all "high net worth" cases and none of them concern pensions. It might be thought that this issue would only rarely concern the practitioner attempting to resolve cases in which there are fewer assets. In fact the question of non-marital contribution is one which tends to arise in relation to pension assets very frequently. It is of course in the very nature of the pension asset that as a general rule it will not be integrated with other matrimonial property or "mingled".[39]

Different principles apply to contributions that are pre-marital, post-separation and post-trial or settlement. These aspects of contribution are considered separately below.

PRE-MARITAL CONTRIBUTIONS

H v H

In *H v H*[40] Thorpe J. (as he then was) considered the husband's pension contributions before the marriage and during it and also considered, on the invitation of the wife's counsel, the likely increase in the husband's pension between the date of the trial and his retirement. Thorpe J. observed that of the husband's 13 years of pension accrual "only 7 of them are years of cohabitation". He further said that:

12–012

---

[32] [2006] 1 F.L.R. 1186, [2006] UKHL 24.
[33] [2010] EWCA Civ 1171.
[34] [2011] EWCA Civ 41.
[35] [2011] EWHC 586 (Fam).
[36] [2011] EWCA 617.
[37] [2011] EWCA Civ 550.
[38] [2011] EWHC 2717 (Fam).
[39] See Mostyn J.'s use of this phrase in *N v F* [2011] EWHC 586. For a rare example of a "mingled" pension see *S v S* [2006] EWHC 2793.
[40] [1993] 2 F.L.R. 335.

"I think that in deciding what weight to attach to pension rights it is more important in this case to look to the value of what has been earned during cohabitation than to look to the prospective value of what may be earned over the course of the 25 or 30 years between separation and retirement age."

The outcome in *H v H* was that each party retained their capital assets (£277,000 for the husband and £227,000 for the wife), no orders were made in relation to the husband's pension and a nominal joint lives periodical payments order was made. Thorpe J. took the view that there was no rationale for capital adjustment and that the discretionary powers of the court to adjust capital shares between spouses "should not be exercised unless there is a manifest need for intervention". Consequently there was no need for any order in relation to pensions.

H v H is frequently cited in support of the contention that only pension contributions made during marriage (including seamless pre-marital cohabitation) should be taken into account by the court. One might speculate that Thorpe L.J. would be rather surprised to discover that his judgment—delivered in 1993—is still so frequently relied upon to exclude all pre-marital and post-separation contributions from the "matrimonial pot".[41] After all *H v H* was decided before *White v White*[42] and before the widespread use of CE figures. Furthermore the pension in *H v H* was valued at the date of the trial at £3,200 per annum, together with a lump sum of the order of £9,000 (which figures can be compared to the husband's income in that case of £18,000 per annum). Given that Thorpe J. (as he then was) took the view that approximately half of the pension was not a relevant asset it may well be that the size of the pension even now would not justify intervention given that the parties were so far from retirement.

Harris v Harris

12–013 In the unreported case of *Harris v Harris*[43] Thorpe L.J. gave judgment in an appeal (primarily concerning the application of the Matrimonial Causes Act 1973 s.31(7)(A)) in which a point arose about pre-marital pension contributions. In rejecting the argument that the capitalised award (which represented periodical payments paid from pension income and was to be paid from the pension fund which was an overseas fund and not subject to annuity limits) should be "cross-checked" against the proportion of pension earned during the marriage Thorpe L.J. said "I do not myself find the argument on proportionality to the pension earned during the marriage to be an attractive one. It seems to me that it is an ingenious submission but one that, if followed with any sort of confidence might well lead to unrealistic results".[44] Plainly the situation in *Harris* was very different to that in most cases—the parties' capital claims had earlier been compromised and Thorpe L.J. was dealing only with periodical payments— however the whole of the pension was clearly treated by Thorpe L.J. as an asset available to satisfy the award made.

---

[41] See "Pensions and Equality" [2007] Fam Law 310.
[42] [2000] 2 F.L.R. 981.
[43] The authors are grateful to Christopher Hall of Crosse, Crosse solicitors for drawing their attention to this case.
[44] *Harris v Harris*, 23 November 2000, unreported, para.26 of the Court of Appeal transcript.

The straight-line discount

12–014 One other interesting aspect of the judgment in *H v H*[45] is Thorpe J.'s use (or rather mention) of the straight line discount (length of cohabitation divided by number of years' contribution to the pension fund[46]) to assess the marital proportion of the pension. Although Thorpe J. did not in fact employ such a discount (no order in relation to the pension was made) his simple observation is also often relied upon to support the employment of a straight line discount. Anecdotal evidence suggests that the straight line discount is a very common approach to the assessment of the pension related "matrimonial property". In a simple case (such as *H v H*) where pensions are not significant this may be a reasonable approach. However in many cases it may not be equitable.[47]

White v White, Miller, McFarlane, Charman and *N v F*—cases involving pre-marital contributions

12–015 Practitioners will be familiar with the dicta of Lord Nicholls in *White v White*[48] in relation to the treatment by the courts of inherited and pre-owned property:

> "Plainly, when present, this factor is one of the circumstances of the case. It represents a contribution made to the welfare of the family by one of the parties to the marriage. The judge should take it into account. He should decide how important it is in the particular case. The nature and value of the property, and the time when and circumstances in which the property was acquired, are among the relevant matters to be considered. However, in the ordinary course, this factor can be expected to carry little weight, if any, in a case where the claimant's financial needs cannot be met without recourse to this property". The issue (in relation to types of property other than pensions) was also considered in *Miller v Miller, McFarlane v McFarlane*[49] and in *Charman v Charman*[50] in which it was held that the "sharing principle" applies to all the parties' property but "to the extent that the property is non-matrimonial, there is likely to be better reason for departure from equality".[51]

In *N v F*[52] Mostyn J. considered relevant authority including the Court of Appeal decisions in *Robson v Robson*[53] and *Jones v Jones*[54] and offered the following guidance:

---

[45] [1993] 2 F.L.R. 335.
[46] The 7/13ths referred by Thorpe J. Note also paras 14–033 to 14–039 below.
[47] In many cases accrual will have been very much higher towards the end of the marriage. In addition it is likely that the asset will have increased in value during the marriage not just because of further contributions but also due to inflationary factors and/or growth on the earlier investment. The straight line discount approach will not reflect these factors.
[48] [2000] 2 F.L.R. 981.
[49] [2006] 1 F.L.R. 1186, [2006] UKHL 24.
[50] [2007] EWCA Civ 503, [2007] 1 F.L.R. 593.
[51] Above paras 65 and 66.
[52] [2011] EWHC 586 Fam.
[53] [2010] EWCA Civ 1171.
[54] [2011] EWCA Civ 41.

"I adhere to my view that the two step approach is the right one, generally speaking. It is precisely what Wilson LJ did in Jones. It seems to me that the process should be as follows:

i) Whether the existence of pre-marital property should be reflected at all. This depends on questions of duration and mingling.
ii) If it does decide that reflection is fair and just, the court should then decide how much of the pre-marital property should be excluded. Should it be the actual historic sum? Or less, if there has been much mingling? Or more, to reflect a springboard and passive growth, as happened in Jones?
iii) The remaining matrimonial property should then normally be divided equally.
iv) The fairness of the award should then be tested by the overall percentage technique.

Of course all of this is subject to the question of need. As Lord Nicholls said in White 'however, in the ordinary course, this factor can be expected to carry little weight, if any, in a case where the claimant's financial needs cannot be met without recourse to this property'".

Pre-marital contributions—cases involving pensions

12–016 The analysis of the House of Lords in *Miller, McFarlane* was fully considered by Burton J. in *S v S*,[55] a case in which there was considerable debate about the extent of "matrimonial property", particularly relating to the pension fund. The husband had brought £435,000 pension assets to the marriage. He liquidated these pension assets and bought with the proceeds (as a Self-Invested Pension Fund) commercial properties that were very successful, increasing the value of the pension assets over a 7 year marriage to £3.6 million. Burton J. concluded that the alteration of the funds in this way converted them to "matrimonial property" whereas had they been left untouched they might well have remained "non-matrimonial" property.[56]

In *B v B*[57] David Salter sitting as a Deputy High Court Judge was invited to find that the Husband's pension was acquired before the marriage and that it should therefore be excluded from the "matrimonial assets". He considered that the Husband had not discharged the requisite burden of proof:

"Whilst I note the husband's assertion that the whole of his pension rights now transferred into his Standard Life SIPP has been acquired prior to the commencement of cohabitation, I have no means of assessing the value of such rights as at 1993 and have, therefore, ignored this, as the husband has not discharged the onus of proof upon him."

King J in *GS v L*[58] took the view that the pension should be excluded:

---

[55] [2006] EWHC 2793.
[56] para.34.
[57] [2012] 2 F.L.R. 22. The pension formed a small part of the assets and although David Salter sitting as a Deputy High Court Judge divided the assets in accordance with the Vaughan approach he calculated the percentage treating the pensions as an asset equivalent to capital.
[58] [2013] 1 F.L.R. 300.

"So far as the pension is concerned, it can and should, in my judgment, properly be excluded from the division of the assets, a position effectively, although not absolutely, conceded by the wife. The pension cannot be drawn down for many years and was accrued in its entirety before the marriage; the fund cannot be used to provide for the wife's needs in either the short or medium term. Given the benefit of the capital with which she will leave the marriage and a working life of 25 years ahead of her, fairness in my judgment requires that the husband should retain his pension fund absolutely."

Summary of the position where pension assets are "pre-marital property"

Pension assets acquired before the marriage are almost by definition "non-matrimonial" (unless they have been significantly altered during the marriage).[59] It follows that the "yardstick of equality" may not so forcefully apply to them.[60] As has been mentioned above anecdotal evidence suggests that pre-marital pension contributions are routinely excluded by the court (often on a straight-line discount basis[61]) before the assets are assessed and divided. The authors would suggest that, while this approach may be justified in some cases, the authorities do not support that approach as a matter of course. In cases where the pre-marital assets are required to meet the parties' needs or to compensate for relationship generated disadvantage[62] they may be taken fully into account. Furthermore the straight-line discount may also (in some cases) be a flawed approach to the calculation of pre-marital pension assets.

12–017

CONTRIBUTIONS BETWEEN SEPARATION AND FINAL HEARING

Whereas pre-marital contributions may be characterised (in almost all cases) as "non-matrimonial" the position is not nearly so clear in relation to accruals between separation and final hearing.

12–018

N v N, Cowan v Cowan

In *N v N* the husband was expressly given some credit for the increase in turnover of his company since separation,[63] although Coleridge J. also observed that in "most cases" the date of the hearing would be the appropriate date for valuation.

In *Cowan v Cowan*[64] Thorpe L.J. held that:

"The third [submission] namely that much of the husband's fortune was generated in the six years post separation, receives no reflection because in my opinion it is

12–019

---

[59] *S v S* [2006] EWHC 2793.
[60] See *Charman v Charman* [2007] EWCA Civ 503 at para.66 where Sir Mark Potter P giving the judgment of the Court of Appeal held that the principle of (equal) sharing applies to all property but in relation to non-matrimonial property there is likely to be a better reason for departure from equality.
[61] See the discussion in para.12–014 above.
[62] *Miller, McFarlane* per Lord Nicholls at para.13 and Baroness Hale para.140.
[63] *N v N* [2001] 2 F.L.R. 69 p.78 B.
[64] (2001) EWCA Civ 679, [2001] 2 F.L.R. 192.

inherently fallacious. The assessment of assets must be at the date of trial or appeal. The language of the statute requires that. Exceptions to that rule are rare and probably confined to cases where one party has deliberately or recklessly wasted assets";

and further

"If this factor has any relevance it is within the evaluation of the husband's exceptional contribution".[65]

Mance L.J.[66] agreed that the submission was inconsistent with the wording of s.25 of the MCA[67] and suggested that if there was any relevance in the increase in assets since separation it would be because:

"...one party's special skill in accumulating assets will achieve some added weight as a factor if it occurs after separation, but before any divorce or financial hearing".

Mance L.J.[68] suggested that the judgment of Coleridge J. in $N \ v \ N$[69] was an application of this principle.

Miller, McFarlane

12–020 In *Miller, McFarlane*[70] Mance L.J. returned to the issue in relation to the growth in value of the Mr. Miller's shares since separation. He held[71] that the determining factor was the degree of marital contribution and that in the *Miller* case Mrs. Miller had made no contribution (she had no entitlement to the shares and had remained in the £2.3 million matrimonial home) and that therefore the shares should be valued at the date of separation. Mance L.J. considered the situation in *Miller* to be comparable to that in $N \ v \ N$[72] in which (as he had suggested in *Cowan v Cowan*[73]) the husband's contribution was beyond the ordinary.

Rossi v Rossi

12–021 The above authorities were considered by Nicholas Mostyn QC (as he then was) in *Rossi v Rossi*.[74] He drew a distinction between capital accrual after separation and income accrual after separation. He suggested that the following principles can be deduced:

---

[65] para.70.
[66] [2001] 2 F.L.R. 236 para.131–136.
[67] "the income, earning capacity, property or other financial resources which each of the parties to the marriage has or is likely to have in the foreseeable future".
[68] *Cowan v Cowan* para.135.
[69] [2001] 2 F.L.R. 69.
[70] [2006] UKHL 24, [2006] 1 F.L.R. 1186.
[71] per Mance L.J. para.174.
[72] [2001] 2 F.L.R. 69.
[73] [2001] 2 F.L.R. 192, (2001) EWCA Civ 679.
[74] [2006] EWHC 1482, [2007] 1 F.L.R. 790.

CONTRIBUTIONS BETWEEN SEPARATION AND FINAL HEARING

1) The statute requires all assets to be valued at the date of trial.
2) In determining the extent of matrimonial property ("to which the yardstick of equality will forcefully apply") assets that are brought into the marriage as gifts or inheritance (other than the matrimonial home) should be excluded.[75]
3) Assets acquired after (or during a period of) separation may be non-matrimonial assets if the property was acquired by virtue of that party's "personal industry".
4) In relation to income there may be grounds for asserting that bonuses or other income received after separation are "non-matrimonial" assets but this will depend upon the continuing contributions of the other spouse and the length of time elapsing. (Nicholas Mostyn QC (as he then was)—whilst conceding that a time frame was arbitrary—suggested that he would be unlikely to consider any bonus acquired within 12 months of separation as non-matrimonial property. He also observed that the wife would at the same time be making her contributions which would not be generating wealth and that consideration should be given to that).
5) Matrimonial property will in all likelihood be divided equally although there may be departure from equality if the marriage is short and part of the assets are business assets earned by one party or the other and/or the parties are both economically productive and have separated their finances during marriage.[76]
5) Non-matrimonial property represents an "unmatched contribution". The court will decide how it should be treated. The length of the marriage will be a relevant factor.
7) In relation to post-separation accrual, the court will consider delay, the manner in which assets have been managed by the parties since separation and the capacity of the party who has accrued the asset to continue to accrue the asset and the rights of the other party to share in that future income or gain.

Mostyn QC (as he then was) therefore drew a distinction between capital (which must be accrued by "personal industry") and bonuses or income where other considerations may apply.

The Court of Appeal in *Charman v Charman*[77] was asked by the husband to consider this issue in relation to a £1million bonus acquired by the husband since separation. Sir Mark Potter P described the issue as a "grey area" and declined in the light of the size of the assets in the case to consider the issue.[78]

12–022

The observations of Mostyn QC (as he then was) in *Rossi v Rossi*[79] were quoted with approval and adopted by Singer J. in *S v S (Ancillary Relief after Lengthy Separation).*[80] In that case Singer J. found himself "unable to categorise"

---
[75] In accordance with *Miller, McFarlane* pre-owned property would fall into this category also.
[76] This conclusion is based upon Baroness Hale's analysis in *Miller, McFarlane* at paras 150 and 151 and the observations of Mance L.J. at para.170. See also *Charman v Charman* [2007] EWCA Civ 503 paras 83–85.
[77] [2007] EWCA 503, [2007] 1 F.L.R. 593.
[78] Above paras 103 and 104.
[79] [2006] EWHC 1482, [2007] 1 F.L.R. 790.
[80] [2006] EWHC 233.

SECTION 25 FACTORS

the growth that had occurred (in the husband's company—which was worth very little at separation and between £3.75 and £27.2 million at trial[81]) "as a financial fruit of the matrimonial partnership". *S v S* was a very unusual case on its facts. The parties were married in 1977 and separated in 1996. Financial proceedings were initiated in 2003. The capital assets in the case (less the business) amounted to some £1.9 million. The pensions were worth £2.1 million. These pensions were shared equally notwithstanding that a very significant proportion of the pension was built up after separation. Although there was no dispute about this provision which had been agreed by the parties Singer J. took it into account when determining the wife's entitlement to a share in the future profitability of the husband's business.[82]

H v H[83] was a case about post separation bonuses. Charles J. took the view that the date for assessing marital property was the date at which "mutual support ends"[84] and therefore (in that case) the date of separation. This can be contrasted with the view of Baron J. in *M v M*[85] in which she took the view that the bonuses accrued since separation fell to be considered because there had been delay in the litigation, the parties had been financially interlinked throughout and the Husband had not made adequate interim provision.

12–023
P v P[86] and *B v B*[87] are both decisions of Moylan J. In *P v P* the Husband who was a stockbroker had accrued wealth since separation. On the other hand he had a significantly greater earning capacity than that of the Wife. Moylan J. held that the court did not need to conduct a detailed forensic examination of the accrual of post separation assets. He considered that it was a fair exercise of his discretion considering post separation accrual and earning capacity to divide the assets approximately equally. In *B v B* the parties' wealth was almost all attributable to the vast bonuses the Husband had earned in the latter years of marriage and after separation. These were payable in arrears on various terms. Moylan J. at [48] said as follows:

> "Mr. Dyer's broad submission is that, in general, absent needs and/or compensation, sharing ends at the end of the marital partnership is based on the passages in the speech of Baroness Hale in *Miller, McFarlane*. I accept this proposition in general terms. However as Mr. Dyer accepts the sharing principle is not confined to "matrimonial property" but applies to all the parties' resources. The search is for 'the division of property which best achieves the fair overall outcome'...: para [67] *Charman v Charman* 'the requirements of fairness in a particular case': para [9] *Miller/McFarlane*."

In *B v B* the wife received more than half of the then available assets, marginally less than half (7/15) of the assets that were likely to be paid up to and including the year of trial. She also received 15 per cent of the future bonuses that had been earned in the period of separation but were not due until after the year of trial.

---

[81] The accountants being some way apart.
[82] Above para.75.
[83] [2007] EWHC 459.
[84] Above para.116.
[85] [2004] 2 F.L.R. 236.
[86] [2008] 2 F.L.R. 1135.
[87] [2010] 2 F.L.R. 1214.

Summary of the position in relation to post separation accrual

As with pre-marital accrual the practitioner must be guided by cases involving other assets and by the guidance offered in "high net worth" cases in which the facts are very different from those encountered in many cases. The "outstanding contribution" argument which reached its zenith in *Cowan*[88] was disapproved (save for the most exceptional cases) in *Lambert v Lambert*.[89] One analysis of the above cases[90] is that whilst "outstanding contribution" is no longer relevant (save in the exceptional case) to contributions made during cohabitation that it may re-emerge as a factor where the contribution is "unmatched" by the other spouse because the parties are no longer living together. However there is scope for argument (see *Rossi v Rossi*[91]) that post separation accruals can be excluded where they are due merely to "personal industry".[92] This may be more arguable still where assets are accrued in the form of income rather than capital (see *Rossi v Rossi*,[93] *H v H*,[94] *P v P*[95] or *B v B*[96]).

12–024

Much will depend upon whether a true construction of the authorities[97] requires the post-separation accrual to be unusual or outstanding. If it must be characterised as such then it may be that it will be relatively difficult to argue that pension contributions qualify as they will tend—in the vast majority of cases—to be related to the continued unexceptional earnings of the pension member. If on the other hand (as seems to be the import of the cases involving continued bonuses/earnings) any degree of post-separation contribution attributable to personal industry after a reasonable length of separation may be treated as "non-matrimonial" then many cases will fall into this category. As with pre-acquired assets the characterisation of the asset as "non-matrimonial" means merely that the "yardstick of equality" does not forcefully apply; if the parties' needs (or requirement for compensation) require utilisation of the asset then it may be divided as the court considers just and equitable.

Where this issue arises in relation to pension assets the first task will be to identify the value of the asset at settlement/hearing (as is required) and then to calculate the accrual since separation. In a simple case it may be reasonable to do this by a straight line discount.[98] If, however, the member spouse is advancing an argument that post-separation accrual is unusual an actuary may be required to determine what proportion of the pension CE is related to post-separation accrual.[99]

---

[88] [2001] 2 F.L.R. 192.
[89] Although note a re-emergence in *S v S* [2006] EWHC 2793 in which the husband received 60% of the assets on the basis of "substantial financial contribution": para.66.
[90] In particular *Cowan v Cowan* [2001] 2 F.L.R. 192 and *Miller, Mcfarlane* [2006] 1 F.L.R. 1186.
[91] [2006] EWHC 1482, [2007] 1 F.L.R. 790.
[92] *Rossi v Rossi* [2007] 1 F.L.R. 790.
[93] [2006] EWHC 1482, [2007] 1 F.L.R. 790.
[94] [2007] EWHC 459.
[95] [2008].
[96] [2010] 2 F.L.R. 1214.
[97] See discussion above.
[98] See the discussion at 12–014 above.
[99] See discussion below.

SECTION 25 FACTORS

Delay

12–025 Delay is a different issue. Notwithstanding the observations of Thorpe L.J. in *Cowan*[100] excessive delay has often been held to justify a reduced award to the spouse seeking relief.[101] It would certainly seem to be a good reason for arguing that post separation accrual should be excluded from the assets to be divided. A useful summary of the position in relation to delay can be found in *Rossi v Rossi*.[102]

FUTURE ACCRUAL

12–026 In *Miller, McFarlane*[103] the House of Lords introduced the concept of compensation for the wife (or husband as it may be) who had suffered economic disadvantage as a direct result of the manner in which the parties' had organised their affairs.[104] This concept has particular relevance to pensions because it is very often the case that the non-member spouse will have less opportunity than the member spouse to make pension contributions after settlement. In many cases one party may belong to (say) a good occupational final salary scheme. In such a situation the non-member spouse who in all likelihood will be investing pension contributions in a private scheme is very unlikely to be able to accrue pension benefits to anything like the same degree as the member spouse after separation. In some cases (where there are sufficient funds) a term periodical payments order may permit the non-member to make comparable pension contributions. However the parties may desire or the court may wish to implement a clean break. It is certainly arguable in these circumstances that the pension sharing provision might be adjusted so as to give the parties equal income at retirement taking into account future contributions. On the face of it there would seem to be a tension between the approach taken in cases such as *H v H*,[105] *P v P*[106] and *B v B*[107] and the argument that there should be an adjustment to take account of future contributions. The answer to the tension lies, the authors would suggest, in the concepts of "needs" and "compensation" which may justify such an approach whereas "sharing" would not. In addition the party trying to achieve a higher award to take account of future contributions will face the argument that future contributions are related to the member spouse's continuing capacity to work. There may also be issues between the parties about the likelihood of ill-health or redundancy and about likely dates of retirement.

---

[100] "Exceptions to the rule are rare and are probably confined to cases where one party has deliberately or recklessly wasted assets".
[101] See *Twiname v Twiname* [1992] 1 F.L.R. 29, *S v S* [1990] 2 F.L.R. 252.
[102] [2007] 1 F.L.R. 790 paras 25–32.
[103] [2006] UKHL 24, [2006] 2 W.L.R. 1283.
[104] Although Coleridge J. in *RP v RP* suggested that the concept of "compensation" may not add anything to MCA 1973 s.25(2)(b) and that the House of Lords had perhaps usefully highlighted an issue that "was not new".
[105] [2007] EWHC 459. See the discussion in relation to these cases at para.12–024 above.
[106] [2008] 2 F.L.R. 1135.
[107] [2010] 2 F.L.R. 1214.

AGE AND DURATION OF THE MARRIAGE

Where the parties have many years to go until retirement and pensions are a small proportion of the assets they can usually be dealt with by off-setting (see Chapter 13) or by equalising CE's. Similarly the shorter the marriage the less vexing pension issues are likely to be. Where there is significant pension accrual over the period of a short marriage the Court is likely to apply the approach in *Miller v Miller*[108] and will calculate the level of the marital acquest and divide it accordingly. In such a case it is unlikely that the straight line discount approach will be appropriate and actuarial evidence may be required to calculate the level of the marital acquest and to determine the appropriate pension share to divide that acquest equally.

12–027

More complex issues arise where there is a significant age difference between the parties, where the parties have accrued pension benefits before the marriage and where they have accrued pension benefits after the separation or have the capacity to accrue pension benefits after settlement. The majority of these issues are dealt with in the section on contributions above. Insofar as age disparity is concerned this is an area in which analysis of pension income is likely to be invaluable. It is also likely that in the majority of cases involving significant age disparity a reasonable proportion of the pension will have built up outside the marriage. Where this is not the case there will still be grounds for awarding the older partner more pension assets as the younger partner will have further years for accrual and because their pension fund can remain invested for longer.

There may also be cases in which there is an income gap. This may arise because of age difference or because of the nature of some early retirement pension schemes. A pension credit taken from an occupational or money purchase scheme and placed (as is inevitable) in a money purchase pension scheme can be drawn from 55. However, where the pension is drawn from 55 this will reduce the level of income (as against a pension drawn from (say) 65) considerably. It may be that the answer in such a case is to have an order for periodical payments for a term.

Members of the "shorter career" public sector schemes can (and almost invariably do) retire early. Full details of these schemes are considered in Chapter 15. By way of example a police officer can retire at 50 after 25 years' service or immediately on completion of 30 years' service. A pension credit taken against this scheme cannot be drawn until the spouse is 60, although the reduction will apply to the member's scheme immediately. Hence there is both a loss to the family and an income gap. If one of the spouses is much younger than the other this will either eradicate the problem or make it worse. The Occupational Personal and Stakeholder Pensions (Miscellaneous Amendments) Regulations 2009[109] permitted schemes to amend their rules in such a way that pension credits could be accessed at 55. This is now the case with the NHS Pension Scheme, the Principal Civil Service Pension Scheme and the Armed Forces Pension Scheme, but not the case with the Police Pension Scheme or the Firefighters' Pension Scheme.

---

[108] [2006] 1 F.L.R. 1186, [2006] UKHL 24.
[109] SI 2009/615 reg.15.

Pension Sharing Orders and continuing periodical payments

12–028   There are many cases in which a Pension Sharing Order will need to be made alongside an order for continuing periodical payments. In such circumstances consideration will need to be given to the question of a deferred clean break.[110] The appropriate date for such a clean break has up to now typically been the 60th or 65th birthday of, more often, the paying spouse. As State Pension Age moves towards 68 (and upwards) there are good arguments for moving the date of deferred clean break. There may also be circumstances in which a different date is appropriate because of the parties' particular circumstances. In any case in which the issue of a deferred clean break arises the court will also be considering the appropriateness or otherwise of an order pursuant to s.28(1)(A) of the Matrimonial Causes Act 1973. The practitioner will be aware that such an order (or "bar" as it is commonly called) prevents any application to extend the term of the deferred order.

There may also be cases in which periodical payments will continue beyond the date of receipt of a pension share. Such orders may be appropriate where the pensions are small compared to income and/or the paying spouse has a capacity to generate significant income beyond the usual retirement age perhaps from a small company or some other similar vehicle.

Re-building

12–029   The tax treatment of pensions changed on April 6, 2006—"A Day". An individual can now accrue a lifetime allowance (currently £1.5 million[111]). Accrual above the lifetime allowance is subject to a penal tax charge.[112] If a scheme member loses part of their pension through a pension share they may re-build the pension up to the lifetime allowance with no penalty. Conversely the pension share will be added to the non-member spouse's existing pension provision in the calculation of their lifetime allowance.

---

[110] See in particular *D v D* [2004] 1 F.L.R. 988 where Coleridge J. expressed the view that a continuing periodical payments claim might in these circumstances be described as "rampant".

[111] The lifetime allowance will reduce to £1.25 million from April 2014.

[112] There are exceptions for members with schemes that were worth more than the lifetime allowance at A Day.

CHAPTER 13

OFF-SETTING

CIRCUMSTANCES IN WHICH OFF-SETTING MAY BE APPROPRIATE

In spite of the availability of the remedy of pension sharing there will still be cases in which the parties or the court will wish to offset all or part of a pension. This may be the case where:

1) One party wishes to retain a capital asset (such as the matrimonial home) the value of which exceeds half the capital assets.
2) The value of the pension is reduced by sharing.
3) One party wishes to retain a pension, perhaps because it is invested in commercial property or because that party is close to retirement or for some other reason.
4) The cost of pension sharing is excessive given the value of the pensions.
5) The relevant pensions are overseas pensions or are not capable of being shared for other reasons.
6) The divorce petition was issued before December 2000.

13–001

THE COURTS' APPROACH TO OFFSETTING

Maskell v Maskell: pension CE cannot be treated as equivalent to a realisable asset

There are many cases in which assets are limited where off-setting is the only sensible approach to pension discrepancy. The most common situation in which this arises is that contemplated in 13–001 1) above where (say) a wife's case may be that she needs to stay in the matrimonial home and there are insufficient realisable matrimonial assets for the husband to recover a similar level of capital award. In *Maskell v Maskell*[1] Thorpe L.J. expressed the view that a pension CE should not generally be treated as equivalent to realisable capital. In that case the District Judge had awarded the wife the house and an endowment policy (worth £32,000) and the husband his pension (worth £40,000 at CE) and an endowment policy. The husband was to take responsibility for some debt so—the argument

13–002

---

[1] [2003] 1 F.L.R. 1138, [2001] EWCA Civ 858.

went—there was approximate equivalence. The Circuit Judge upheld the decision on the basis that the order was "conventional". Of that observation Thorpe L.J. had this to say:

> "....for the judge is making the seemingly elementary mistake of confusing present capital with a right to financial benefits on retirement, only 25 per cent of which maximum could be taken in capital terms, the other 75 per cent being taken as an annuity stream".

The case was remitted for re-hearing. *Maskell* has generally been considered authority that, for most purposes, the aggregation of pension and non-pension assets was not good practice. An obvious way forward in cases of this type is for the pensions to be divided by way of a Pension Sharing Order and for the realisable assets to be separately divided. If this prevents immediate housing needs being met, for example where there are children to be considered, then a Mesher order may be a way forward, although in many cases that will still be an unsatisfactory solution.

Norris v Norris, *GW v GW* and *S v S*

13–003   *Maskell v Maskell* was distinguished at first instance by Bennett J. in *Norris v Norris*.[2] In *Norris* the husband proposed that his pension CE (£733,000) should be discounted to £500,000. The basis of this suggested discount was that the pension should be treated as having a Duxbury value based upon the annuity together with the 25 per cent tax-free commuted sum. Bennett J. took the view that the husband (aged 60) in *Norris* was much closer than Mr. Maskell to receipt of benefits and that it would not be "unfair"[3] therefore to include the whole of the CE. This finding was not challenged at the appeal of the case,[4] which turned on costs issues. In *GW v RW*[5] Nicholas Mostyn QC, as he then was, preferred the *Norris* approach and declined to discount the value of a US pension scheme to reflect the fact that tax would be payable if the husband were to withdraw the pension fund.

The distinction between *Maskell* on the one hand and *Norris* and *GW v RW* on the other might be that the assets in *Maskell* were very limited and that therefore the husband's award would be comprised almost entirely of pension.

S v S[6] is another case in which CE was aggregated with capital. In *S v S* Burton J. treated a pension portfolio that was comprised largely of commercial property as, in effect, realisable capital.[7] In *S v S* the net assets were assessed by the judge to be worth £7 million of which £6 million was assessed to be matrimonial property.[8] The net effect of the order awarding the wife 40 per cent of the matrimonial assets was that the wife received £2.4 million in realisable assets and the husband received £3.4 million pension assets together with realisable capital

---

[2] [2003] 1 F.L.R. 1142, [2002] EWHC 2996 (Fam).
[3] *Norris v Norris* para.72.
[4] *Norris v Norris*, *Haskins v Haskins* [2003] EWCA Civ 1084, [2003] 2 F.L.R. 1124.
[5] [2003] 2 F.L.R. 118; at para.20.
[6] [2006] EWHC 2793, [2007] 1 F.L.R. 1496.
[7] para.16, 19(iv) and 70 of the judgment.
[8] As described by the House of Lords in *Miller v Miller, McFarlane v McFarlane* [2006] 1 F.L.R. 1186, [2006] UKHL 24.

of £1.2 million. It is worth noting however that the husband received almost all his proportion of the matrimonial assets in pension assets. *S v S* is an unusual case on its facts given the size and nature of the pension. In addition it was not the husband's case that the pension assets should be treated differently or discounted.

Martin-Dye

Martin Dye v Martin-Dye[9] is the only reported Court of Appeal case in which pension sharing has been a substantive issue. The progress of the case was complicated by the fact that neither party, for their own different reasons, wished the court to deal with the case by way of a Pension Sharing Order.[10]

13–004

In *Martin-Dye* the parties had assets of £6.3 million including pensions valued at just over £1 million. The husband's British Airways pension was valued at £940,000 and was therefore by far the larger of the pensions. There was considerable uncertainty (until after the hearing in the Court of Appeal) in relation to the basis of the valuation of the pension.[11] The uncertainty arose because British Airways had provided a CEB figure but had erroneously referred to it as a CETV.[12] The issue was only resolved after the draft judgment had been circulated to the parties. At first instance the District Judge had divided the assets including the pensions (incorporated in the schedule of capital assets at their CEB value) as to 57 per cent to the wife and 43 per cent to the husband.[13] The District Judge had treated the husband's pension CEB as part of his assets and accordingly he received only such balancing capital payment as was necessary to make up 43 per cent of the total assets. The order was upheld at first appeal. Thorpe L.J., giving judgment in the Court of Appeal, concluded that that was the wrong approach:

> "Pensions in payment, being different in kind to other available assets, should have been apportioned by means of a pension sharing order".[14]

Accordingly the Court of Appeal re-drew the order so as to award the wife 57 per cent of the capital and 57 per cent of the pensions by way of pension share.

There is room for debate about the extent to which the approach of the Court of Appeal in *Martin-Dye* can be extrapolated to apply to deferred pensions, i.e. those not yet in payment. Thorpe L.J. took trouble to restrict his observations, at least expressly, to pensions in payment:

13–005

> "The arguments in support are self-evident. A pension in payment is no more than a whole life income stream akin to an annuity. It cannot be sold, commuted for cash or offered as security for borrowings. It has no capacity for capital appreciation. The benefit does not survive the death of the scheme member and thus cannot form part

---

[9] [2006] 2 F.L.R. 901.
[10] Although the husband's counsel did address the District Judge on the issue as an alternative to the set-off proposed.
[11] This problem would not now arise as pension valuations (whether the pension is in payment or not) are universally referred to as Cash Equivalents.
[12] This is not an issue that need any longer trouble the practitioner—Form E, Form P and Form P1 now all refer to the universal CE.
[13] The departure from equality reflected the parties' differing initial contributions.
[14] Thorpe L.J. at para.47.

of his estate[15]...In the present appeal we are not dealing with deferred pensions and CETV. Our focus is upon pensions in payment".[16]

Yet, it could be argued that the observations about pensions in payment apply almost as strongly to deferred pensions.

The judgment of Dyson L.J. in *Martin-Dye* suggested that it may still sometimes be appropriate to aggregate pensions with other assets:

> "...I do not read Lord Justice Thorpe as saying that, as a matter of law, it is never open to the court to aggregate the value of pensions with that of other assets and distribute the resultant total value between the parties. Examples of where such an approach might be appropriate could be where the parties have pensions in payment that are of approximately equal value and/or where the value of the pensions is small in comparison with that of the other assets".[17]

Added to these examples might also be the situation which existed in *S v S*,[18] where the assets in the pension scheme are commercial properties and the member spouse has substantial control over the way in which the asset, or income from it, is realised.

Vaughan v Vaughan

13–006 More recently in *Vaughan v Vaughan*[19] Wilson L.J. suggested that a net effect schedule should have the capitalised values of the pensions (adjusted in accordance with any proposed pension order) represented:

> "so in my view the convenient practice, which respects the difference in kind to which I have referred [liquid/illiquid capital], is that, underneath the total value of other capital, the balance sheet should present the capital value of pension rights and then arrive at a grand total".

Wilson L.J. also said as follows[20]:

> "We can now see from the calculation in para [46] above that the updated effect of the district judge's order remains one of departure from the principle of equality. If adopted, it would result in an award to the wife 62 per cent of the assets or (as I consider to be the more relevant percentage, at any rate when the court intends to impose a clean break with the result that neither spouse can later benefit from the other's pension rights through periodical payments) 57 per cent of the assets".

The more relevant percentage was that calculated including the pensions. These calculations are now routinely used in financial relief cases and tend to be referred to as "Vaughan" calculations—the previous practice having been to discourage calculations that amalgamated capital and pensions. The authors

---

[15] Thorpe L.J. at para.48.
[16] per Thorpe L.J. at para.61.
[17] per Dyson L.J. at para.86.
[18] [2006] EWHC 2793, [2007] 1 F.L.R. 1496.
[19] [2008] 1 F.L.R. 1116.
[20] para.49.

would suggest that whilst a Vaughan calculation is a useful tool it is exactly that and the practitioner must always take care to ensure that the nature of assets is carefully considered.

In *J v J*[21] Moylan J. having awarded the Wife 46 per cent of the assets was addressed after his judgment on the question of whether the Wife's award should include a pension share (presumably a 46 per cent share) in relation to the Husband's £500,000 pension. He concluded that it should not. It would appear that until after judgment the pension had simply been aggregated with the other assets. Moylan J. did not consider that approach to be inappropriate:

> "This issue did not receive much attention during the course of the hearing, understandably given that it is a relatively minor having regard to the amount involved."

Summary of position in relation to Courts' approach to offsetting

It is not a universal rule that pensions may not be amalgamated with capital and treated as equivalent. This approach will be entirely reasonable where the assets are small compared with other assets, where the parties' pensions are similar in value or (possibly) where the nature of the asset is such that the member spouse has control over its use and income drawn from it. However where amalgamation will produce the result that one party's award is disproportionately comprised of pension then amalgamation is likely to produce an unfair result. Identifying this issue is only the first part of the problem. Where a pension share can resolve the issue (as in *Martin-Dye*[22]) the problem is relatively easily resolved. If a pension share is not feasible the court will be considering offset. How will the offset be valued?

13–007

VALUATION OF THE SET OFF

Utilising CE and cases in which that may be appropriate

There may be any number of reasons why the court or the parties may be considering set off rather than pension share. Whatever category of case the court is dealing with there will almost always be debate about the valuation of the set-off. There are many ways of calculating set off. Some of the most common are considered below. It is right to say, however, that none of them has been adopted by the courts as a universal or even a favoured approach. The authors would suggest that the reason for this is that the value of the set-off will change depending upon the nature of the case and the reason for it. Consequently a rigid approach would prevent the court from utilising its full discretionary powers in accordance with the requirements of the Matrimonial Causes Act 1973 s.25.

13–008

---

[21] [2011] EWHC 1010 (Fam), [2011] 2 F.L.R. 1280.
[22] [2006] 2 F.L.R. 901.

OFFSET WITHOUT EXPERT EVIDENCE

Offset based on the Cash Equivalent

13–009   The simplest approach to calculating offset (and one which may or may not require an actuary) is to adjust the CE provided. The adjustment will take account of issues such as tax and the perceived preference to hold realisable capital. Whilst this is a perfectly acceptable approach in some cases caution is required as the same pension rights have different cash equivalents in different schemes. It is therefore not a consistent approach and for instance will undervalue the offset if the CE calculated is less than the true value as it is in some cases.

There are however cases where this will be the appropriate method and then there is a necessity to decide what adjustment to make. The adjustment is effectively for tax (pension income is taxed as earned income and not available immediately as a single sum to spend) and "utility". In simple cases (see the example below in para.13–010 below) the parties may not think it proportionate to instruct an actuary. In other cases it may be useful to have an actuary consider tax issues; the court and the parties will have to decide upon any utility deduction.

It is probably right that the deduction should be less if there is still a tax-free cash lump sum to be paid from the pension rights as both the tax and utility are diluted (the member pays less tax and has 25 per cent of the fund in realisable capital). If a lump sum is available immediately or in the near future; it might even be argued that you take the value of the lump sum and then adjust a reduced CE based on the remaining fund.

Simple cases

13–010   In the vast majority of cases of set off the court will exercise its discretion utilising the CE. Where the assets are small or large, where pensions are not a significant proportion of the assets of where the parties are a distance from retirement the court will in all likelihood carry out an exercise pursuant to the Matrimonial Causes Act 1973 s.25 which will probably not be capable of challenge. The exercise will almost always[23] reflect a reduction in CE to reflect taxation and the "utility" of realisable assets. The reduction is usually not more than 40 per cent and not less than 20 per cent (there is no authority for this proposition; it merely reflects the authors' experience and anecdotal reports). The following discussion is based upon an assumption that in the case under consideration equal division of capital and pension is the desired outcome. There are of course many cases in which that outcome is not appropriate.

There are two approaches to the mathematical calculation of offset; either the pension is taken off the top of the assets i.e. deductions are made before assets are divided or there is an adjustment at the end to reflect the fact that one party has retained pension. In the former case the non-member will receive a sum

---

[23] See paras 13–003—13–006 above for a discussion of authorities in which no deduction was made.

equivalent to the reduced CE. In the latter case the member will pay the non-member a sum equivalent to half the adjusted CE. An example may be useful:

Assume that the parties have realisable assets of £2,000,000 and the husband has a pension with CE of £200,000 which the parties wish to offset for one reason or another. The parties are content with the CE and do not wish to commission actuarial evidence. If the pension is aggregated with assets on a pound for pound basis the asset table looks as follows:

Asset Type	Husband	Wife	Joint	Total
Realisable Assets			£2,000,000	£2,000,000
Pension	£200,000			£200,000
Total	£200,000		£2,000,000	£2,200,000

Assume that the court decides that the pension is not to be treated as equivalent to realisable assets and that it discounts the pension by 25 per cent. The court therefore treats the husband as having an asset worth £150,000. If the pension is dealt with first the Wife will need £150,000 from the capital pot to compensate for the pension and the remaining capital (£1,850,000) will be divided in half. The Vaughan table looks as follows:

Asset Type	Husband	Wife	Joint	Total
Realisable Assets	£925,000	£1,075,000		£2,000,000
Pension	£200,000	nil		£200,000
Total	£1,125,000	£1,075,000		£2,200,000
%	51%	49%		

The husband receives slightly more than 50 per cent when the pension CE is the currency but this reflects the fact that the CE is being treated as overvalued for offsetting purposes.

If the pensions are adjusted after distribution of assets then each party will have £1,000,000 and the husband will then need to pay the wife half of the notional CE figure (£75,000) from his share of the capital. The outcome is the same.

ACTUARIALLY CALCULATED OFFSET

It will not always be adequate to take the broad brush approach described above. In particular if pension offset is imposed upon the parties at the wish of the scheme member or because the pension cannot be shared the non-member may wish to argue that they should have a fund of equivalent value to that of the member spouse. The value of the fund benefits can be calculated actuarially in a number or ways. A variety of ways are set out below, they range from the highest

13–011

value to the lowest. The calculation of the equivalent value of the fund to the non-member will often be quite different from the CE; it may even be more than the CE.

Full Replacement Value

13–012 The full replacement value is the amount that is required in a personal pension policy at the date of the order (subject to various assumptions) to provide the non-member with equivalent benefits. In effect the actuary will calculate what fund is required to enable the non-member to have a lump sum and buy an annuity equivalent to that of the non-member. This will involve the actuary estimating annuity rates at retirement and investment returns until then. The annual allowance for pension contributions has been reduced to £50,000 in the tax year 2012/2013.[24] Consideration will also therefore have to be given to the manner of investment in pension funds over time. There may be many variations on this theme. For instance the member spouse may be contemplating placing funds in drawdown[25] and the non-member spouse may wish to have the same facility.

Net Full Replacement Value

13–013 It may be reasonable for the Full Replacement Value to be reduced to reflect tax considerations. For example if the individual is working (and therefore paying tax) and has some years to go until retirement it may be that the funds can be invested to gain tax relief and that that gain to the non-member should be reflected in the Replacement Value. Another approach that may reflect tax treatment is to assume that the fund will be used to buy a Purchased Life Annuity[26] and therefore that the tax treatment of the annuity will be favourable.

Fund Account Value

13–014 The Fund account Value is arrived at by:

1) Calculating the net amount to be received over retirement, and
2) Estimating the capital sum needed at the date of the order to be invested so that the non-member can meet all those payments allowing for a reasonable and achievable rate of return so that the fund is extinguished at death.

The Replacement Value methods are based upon the purchase of annuities. The fund account value method is based upon a diminishing capital fund. The drawback is that the fund is extinguished at the expected date of death leaving the party without any income should they survive to and beyond that projected date of death. It is stating the obvious to say that if you use average life expectancy approximately half of the people will live beyond that age and date. This may not

---

[24] It was £225,000 in the year 2010/2011 and will be £40,000 in the tax year 2014/15.
[25] See Ch.1.
[26] When a Purchased Life Annuity is in payment the payment comprises capital and investment return. The capital element is not taxed.

be a bar to the use of the Fund Account Value method in the matrimonial court as the Duxbury calculations (based upon the same principle of diminishing capital funds) are still often used.

The Net Actuarial Value

13–015 The Net Actuarial Value involves calculating the expected future payments from the pension to the member after deduction of any tax that would be payable and placing an actuarial value (discounted value of those payments) on the net future payments taking into account mortality figures and discount rates. The net actuarial value tends to be significantly lower than the fund value or the replacement value. (A table is produced in para.13–018 below illustrating the difference between the various methods set out in this chapter).

Replacement of pension sharing value

13–016 Another approach is to calculate the value that replaces a postulated Pension Sharing Order. To do this, the amount to be transferred if pension sharing is used is calculated. The lump sum required now to compensate for this is then calculated. If it is appropriate in any case this sum can be reduced to allow for tax relief. This approach has a logical attraction as it recreates the result that would have been achieved had the court been able to make a Pension Sharing Order.

Duxbury value

13–017 A variation on the fund account value approach is the Duxbury Value. Whereas the fund account value is predicated on a reasonable and achievable rate of return that will be estimated by the actuary the Duxbury method has a prescribed rate of return of 3.75 per cent. For example, if inflation were to average 4 per cent over the term of the investment then the rate of return on the investment would have to average 9 per cent (allowing for tax) for the fund to fit the Duxbury model and extend for the lifetime of the non-member spouse. It is for this reason that the Duxbury value is the lowest of the figures in the table below.

Comparison of the approaches

13–018 Consider the example of two 55 year olds and one pension promising £40,000 per annum (RPI linked) to the member at age 65 with a CE of £800,000. The values calculated under the above bases are:

Replacement Value	£966,360
Net Replacement Value	£773,090
Fund account	£629,470
Net Actuarial Value	£511,070
PSO Replacement	£700,280
Adjusted Cash Equivalent	£800,000 x whatever percentage is chosen

| Duxbury Value | £472,210 |

Conclusion

13-019 The authors would suggest that there can be no "one size fits all" solution to the offsetting problem. The fair and equitable offset will depend upon a number of features that will vary from case to case. There may be cases where the offset value should be assessed as very close to the replacement value. On the other hand where parties are some distance from retirement or where one party retains fewer liquid assets than the other it is possible that a significant discount will be made. There may also be variations to reflect the fact that one party or the other has sought an offset rather than a share. In smaller money cases the value of the offset may simply be determined by the assets available.

CAPITALISATION OF PERIODICAL PAYMENTS AFTER OFFSET

13-020 In accordance with the Matrimonial Causes Act 1973 s.31(7B)(ba) the court may make a Pension Sharing Order at the same time as it discharges or varies (so as to limit in time) a periodical payments order. A party against whom such an order is sought may find that a pension share is being sought against the very asset that he (or she) retained in exchange for an additional capital payment to the other party. If it is intended that the pension should not be susceptible to a future Pension Sharing Order it is probably advisable for the parties to record that intention in a preamble to the original order.

PART B
ACTUARIAL SECTION

CHAPTER 14

Actuarial Issues Arising from the use of CEs

There are a number of issues which need to be considered when using a CE in considering the value of the assets on divorce. 14–001

THE NATURE OF THE CE AS A METHOD OF VALUATION

CEs were introduced for the purpose of a scheme member transferring benefits from one scheme to another. Therefore the value used was the expected cost to the scheme of providing the benefits. Under this approach, allowance is made in the discount rate for the expected investment return from the assets held by the scheme. In addition, the value represents the value of the gross (with tax) payments that will be made by the scheme. 14–002

CEs had been available for many years in relation to schemes which chose to allow members to transfer out their rights. Only later, when the option to transfer out became a compulsory right for all scheme members, were CEs available from all schemes. In their earliest form, therefore, CEs were only available to members who had the choice to leave their benefits in the scheme or to transfer them out to another pension arrangement.

Accordingly, it was often argued that if the CE on offer was very low compared to the value of the benefits, this would not be particularly important as the member also had the option to retain the benefits in the scheme and receive the full value of the promised benefits at retirement. It was against this background that CEs developed.

A further influence on the development of CE calculations was that they have always been carried out on non-member specific assumptions. Accordingly, the calculations assume that each member is in average health for a person of their age and has a probability of being married at the time of their death in line with a population average and, again in line with the national average, a man will usually be assumed to have a spouse three years younger than him and a woman has a spouse three years older than her. Members who were unmarried would have included in their CE the value of a widow's or widower's pension that might never be paid. Members who had lower life expectancy than the average or with a family history of poor health or alternatively smokers (who have lower life expectancy than non-smokers) would all have included in their CE calculation the value of benefits in excess of the amount they could expect to receive. If the CE was a true representation of the value of the benefit based on population averages, the CE for members with the potential health problems described above, or who were unmarried, would be higher than the real value of their likely benefits or the likely cost to the scheme of providing the benefits. Potentially, those members could select against the scheme by taking a transfer to an alternative provider prepared to offer higher benefits on the basis that these factors were taken into account.

14–003   Thus, there was a further influence to provide CEs lower than the true value of the benefits.

Whilst it is arguable that a low CE produced to a member in the context of a decision whether or not to transfer benefits to a different scheme does not unduly penalise the member as there is always the option to remain in the scheme and retain the full value of the benefits in that scheme, this does create a difficulty in the context of pension sharing orders. Schemes in the private sector are entitled to insist that if there is a Pension Sharing Order, the non-member spouse has to transfer the benefits out of the scheme to another pension provider of their choice, which will usually be a personal pension or stakeholder pension. Since the CE is used in these circumstances as the basis of the transfer, if the CE is lower than the true value of the benefits, it is the proportion of that lower value that is transferred out. This seems unfair and has acted as a further catalyst to the initiatives to revise CEs in recent years.

In the context of a divorce the CE will be provided as the first step in the normal disclosure of assets. The starting point is that the court will assume that the CE represents the true value of the pension asset, but there are many situations when this is a dangerous assumption as the CE does not necessarily represent the true value. We discuss later in this book some very specific features and special cases, however, even as a general proposition it can be stated that the court is often not helped by the way that CEs are calculated.

If we consider the example of a CE calculated for a member spouse of age 60 who has a right to a pension of £10,000 per annum inflation linked for life, the CE can be very different depending on the scheme:

- If the member spouse is a member of the Principal Civil Service Pension Scheme, then the CE will be £201,200 (April 2012).
- If the member spouse has funds in Drawdown and is about to convert them to an annuity, then the CE is £368,000; however if the member spouse is to provide a 50 per cent pension for a spouse three years younger on death (as is provided for in the above schemes) then the CE is £405,000 and if the spouse is 10 years younger it becomes £447,000.
- Exactly the same pension benefits to the same person can have a CE ranging between £201,200 and £447,000 and indeed they can be even outside this range.

14–004   The above illustration demonstrates why it is so difficult to compare pension values with the values of other assets and why the presentation of a CE should not be regarded as a reliable representation of the value of pension rights under any particular scheme.

Another example of how the divorce court can be misled by a CE is the position of the member of a defined benefit scheme which includes amongst its benefits a widow's or widower's pension. The value of this will be included in the calculation of the CE and yet the member spouse will never receive any personal benefit from it and may never re-marry and have a spouse who benefits from it. The spouse's pension on the member's death is a benefit that will possibly be received by a future spouse of the member should that spouse be the survivor of that future marriage. It seems legitimate to question where the value of this potential benefit should fall in the context of the divorce court's consideration of pension issues.

The inescapable conclusion is that the CE has many drawbacks in its use in the context of divorce proceedings although it is the valuation method and value that the pension provider must use in implementing a pension sharing order.

SECURITY OF BENEFITS IN A FINAL SALARY SCHEME

Some high profile cases in recent years have raised the issue of the security of a member's benefits in an occupational final salary pension scheme where the sponsoring employer is not a public sector employer, i.e. the private sector schemes. 14–005

In divorce cases, two extreme positions are occasionally put forward. At one extreme, it is argued that defined benefit schemes are so unsafe that they should be treated on a par with a money purchase scheme with the same CE. This approach suggests that the sponsoring employer's commitments are worthless. The other extreme argues that the benefits are cast iron guaranteed to the extent that they can only be compared with government gilt edge stock as that is the only comparable asset with a similar level of risk.

The two arguments above are both incorrect. The member's benefits in a defined benefit pension scheme are like any financial contract. They depend on the ability of the party or parties liable to make the payments to be able to do so. The benefits from a company defined benefit pension scheme have several layers of security and therefore the benefits do carry more security than many financial contracts.

The top level of security for these benefits is the ongoing solvency of the company. The scheme has to pay the promised benefits when they become due to the member. The rules of the scheme will always require it to have sufficient funds invested to meet future liabilities and therefore it is unlikely that the scheme will be unable to meet liabilities which fall due in the short term, but in the event that, for whatever reason, the scheme does not have sufficient funds then the company has to put funds into the scheme. It follows that, providing the company remains solvent, the expected payments will be paid from the scheme's funds when they fall due.

The second layer of security is the assets of the scheme. Private sector pension schemes have to have funds invested to meet future liabilities in order to obtain all the tax benefits that are attached to full HMRC approval of the scheme. Typically, the scheme will have to commission an actuarial valuation every three years. This valuation compares the value of the liabilities; the promises of future benefits (accrued benefits to members and their dependants) that it has made with the funds it has invested in the scheme. On the basis of this value, the actuary will 14–006 recommend the contributions which need to be made to the scheme in future so that the value of the benefits that will become due will be met by the funds invested in the Scheme.

The scheme will therefore have a fund of assets in the event of the employer becoming insolvent. In the event that a company does become insolvent, then as long as the scheme assets are sufficient to meet the future benefits that have accrued to the members, then all benefits will be paid.

The third level of security is the company's assets. This means that if the company ceases trading and the scheme's assets are insufficient to meet the future payments, the shortfall of funds in the pension scheme becomes a creditor of the company assets and ranks quite highly on the list of creditors. Accordingly, if the employer is a company which has considerable assets which can be realised when it becomes insolvent, the scheme may be able to make up any deficit from the company assets. This does not, of course, assist where the employer is a company which does not have available assets and there are examples of companies seeking to avoid the liabilities to their pension schemes by re-structuring and selling a part of the business to a different company on the basis that the different company would then become the sponsoring company for the pension scheme and its liabilities.

14–007 The fourth level of security is the PPF. This has been set up to protect individuals who have pension rights in defined benefit schemes where the scheme is unable to pay those benefits and the employer is no longer trading. The PPF will only accept the schemes after all the other levels of security have been examined and there is still a shortfall. The PPF will work by taking all of the funds that are left in a company's pension fund and also taking on the liabilities, or promises made, by the company to its pension fund members.

The liabilities will not be met in full. Members who are already past the scheme's Normal Retirement Date will receive 100 per cent of their pension. This will usually be the pension that is in payment but will occasionally be the pension that would be payable if the member chose to put it into payment. This meets the full liability initially, but future increases to pensions in payment will be limited to a maximum of 2.5 per cent per annum (applicable only to accrual after April 1997) and also limited by the scheme rules. Many schemes offer increases in payment in line with inflation up to 5 per cent per annum and for any year that inflation is more than 2.5 per cent per annum the member will receive a lower increase as a result of the upper limit in the PPF.

Discretionary benefits will not be paid. Discretionary benefits are not guaranteed by a scheme, but are awarded by the Trustees. One example of this with significant effects might be where inflationary increases are paid at the Trustees' discretion. The PPF will not give inflationary increases if they are discretionary rather than promised under the scheme rules.

14–008 Members who have benefits deferred in the scheme as they are below the scheme's Normal Retirement Age have their entitlement from the PPF limited to a maximum of 90 per cent of their deferred benefit (and lower at younger ages). This is then subject to a cap of £31,380.34 per annum for 2013/2014 after the reduction to 90 per cent. High earners who have been in the original employer's scheme for a long time will therefore find their benefits considerably reduced. Modest earners will have most of their benefits paid but once again the revaluation until retirement is limited to 5 per cent per annum and pension increases when the pension is in payment again limited to the increase that is promised by the scheme rules up to a maximum of 2.5 per cent per annum (applicable only to accrual after April 1997).

The PPF was originally set up with a fund supplied by the Government, but this is supplemented by all schemes paying an annual levy. The levy is set so that the more secure a scheme can demonstrate itself to be, the lower the levy will be. This provides an incentive to sponsoring employers to improve the level of funding of their scheme in the expectation of paying a lower levy and it is hoped that this will serve to improve funding levels and therefore reduce the potential future liabilities of the PPF as fewer schemes will be unable to meet their liabilities.

It is, however, possible that in time the employers who have to meet this levy each year (through their pension schemes) will try to find ways not to do this. The PPF is in its early years and it is yet to be seen whether it will continue in existence in the long term.

It can be seen that, for most purposes, defined benefit schemes enjoy substantial security. Plainly, though, there are no absolute guarantees and individual cases will slip through all levels of safeguard and many have suffered as a result of problems in recent years with companies such as Equitable Life, BCCI and Barings Bank.

In early 2007, the Government announced further funding for the Financial Assistance Scheme (a scheme set up to provide assistance for those who lost pension rights as a result of company insolvencies before April 6, 2005 which was the eligibility date for the PPF).

THE CE AND THE EXTERNAL OPTION

One typical issue that can arise and does arise very frequently is in relation to defined benefit final salary schemes in the private sector. These schemes are permitted to insist that the non-member spouse transfers any "pension credit" received as a result of a pension sharing order out of the scheme and to a different pension provider. The amount received will be the percentage stated in the order of the CE (re-calculated at the time that the order is implemented). **14–009**

Typically, the amount of pension income that the non-member spouse will receive from the "pension credit" will be considerably less than the amount that the member spouse gives up and therefore a 50 per cent Pension Sharing Order will mean that the member spouse will frequently have a considerably higher pension from these rights less the "pension debit" than the non-member spouse will receive from the "pension credit". There are a number of reasons for this:

- The non-member spouse has to take the "pension credit" out of the scheme and purchase a pension on the open market. This will incur both explicit and implicit costs before and at retirement and therefore there is a loss in value of pension rights through doing this.
- The non-member spouse will usually have to purchase an annuity at retirement and annuity rates contain margins in them so that if the

provider's experience is worse than expected (for example, if all the annuitants live longer than expected and therefore they have to pay more than expected) they do not make a loss due to the contingencies in the rates for such eventualities.
- Women have longer life expectancies than men and in the great majority of cases it is the wife who is the non-member spouse.[1]
- The CE often does not represent the true value of the benefits promised to the member spouse. There are a number of reasons for this. A CE is a discounted value of future expected payments. However, many schemes' CEs are calculated on a basis that leads to low values. This will be because either the scheme basis does not fully reflect recently recorded improvements in life expectancies (which lead to pensions being paid for longer and therefore being worth more) or because the scheme is optimistic about the rate of investment return that it will achieve on invested pension assets and therefore discounts the future payments at a higher rate.

14–010 Accordingly, it is not untypical to have a scenario where the member spouse has accrued pension rights of, say, £20,000 per annum and where a 50 per cent Pension Sharing Order is made, the member spouse will retain pension rights of £10,000 per annum but the non-member spouse will only receive approximately £7,000–£8,000 per annum from the "pension credit".

Legislation does not prescribe how to deal with this situation but many Courts have decided that pensions are there to provide retirement income and the correct solution is equality of income and equality can only be achieved in retirement by a higher percentage than 50 per cent in the Pension Sharing Order. A typical example involves a husband member spouse and a wife non-member spouse of the same age.

Example 1

14–011 The member spouse is the husband who has accrued pension rights payable at age 60. He is currently age 59 and the expected pension is £40,000 per annum, inflation-linked for life. The CE is £880,000. The non-member spouse is the wife who is also 59.

The required pension sharing order to achieve equality of income assuming both start to receive benefits at age 60 is 56 per cent and this will provide each with an income of approximately £17,600 per annum, inflation-linked for life.

It should be noted that in the above example, the member spouse has pension rights that include a pension payable to a future spouse on death should they re-marry in future. No spouse's pension is assumed payable on the non-member's spouse's benefits.

If equality of income is sought, then the issue of the attaching spouse's pension is one that cannot be resolved in a completely satisfactory way. It would be possible to increase the percentage so that the non-member spouse has sufficient "pension credit" to receive the income and in addition purchase a

---

[1] Although unisex annuity rates were introduced in December 2012, it remains the case that the factors for calculating CEs are still likely to be based on gender. Thus a male life expectancy will be used for a CE and a unisex life expectancy for the annuity.

pension for a future spouse. However in such a case, the member spouse can argue that in practice, the non-member spouse could use the additional funds to purchase additional pension. Furthermore, the Court may be reluctant to use marital assets to purchase benefits (effectively) for a third party.

The member spouse is unlikely to be able to give up the spouse's benefits on a final salary pension scheme pension.

Example 2

One spouse has accrued pension rights payable at age 65 and is aged 39. The rights have a CE of £110,000. The other spouse is aged 37 and has pension rights with a CE of £40,000, again payable at age 65. **14–012**

Although the same conditions could be applied and a calculation done to confirm the amount required to achieve equality of potential income, the calculations are dependent on variables over a period of nearly 30 years to retirement.

The Court would have to consider this carefully. It is possible that whilst recognising the non-member spouse's need to receive more, this would be done on a broad brush adjustment rather than by actuarial calculation.

Example 3

The member spouse is the husband who has a pension in payment. He is currently age 64 and the pension is £50,000 per annum, inflation-linked for life. The CE is £650,000. **14–013**

The non-member spouse is the wife who is 60. She has pension rights with a pension income of £30,000 per annum, again inflation-linked for life with a CE of £500,000.

The same issue as in Example 1 could be resolved by pension sharing and the required Pension Sharing Order to achieve equality of income assuming both start to receive benefits immediately is 27.4 per cent and this will provide each with an income of approximately £36,300 per annum, inflation-linked for life.

In this case however, the parties could consider other options. The wife's pension may be considered sufficient to provide financial security in retirement and therefore instead of pension sharing, the parties might consider a Pension Attachment Order for, say, 20 per cent thus providing the net equivalent of £40,000 per annum during joint lives. The wife has an income of £30,000 if she outlives the husband.

One significant difficulty with this solution is that if the wife re-marries then the Pension Attachment Orders cease.

Example 4

The member spouse is the husband who has accrued pension rights payable at age 65. He is currently age 56 and the accrued pension is £50,000 per annum, inflation-linked for life. The CE is £600,000. The non-member spouse is the wife who is also 56. The member spouse has an income of £140,000 per annum. **14–014**

The required Pension Sharing Order to achieve equality of income assuming both start to receive benefits at age 65 is 64 per cent and this will provide each with an income of approximately £17,880 per annum, inflation-linked for life.

The difficulty with the above solution is that the Pension Sharing Order itself leads to a considerable loss of value in the pension rights (the combined income of £50,000 per annum becoming £35,760 per annum).

One option the parties could consider as an alternative would be to keep the financial claims open (with a suitable life insurance policy to protect the non-member spouse) for a number of years on the basis of the husband paying approximately £48,000 per annum gross into a personal pension policy in his own name for a period of 7 years. This would provide approximately the same benefit for the wife. Tax relief would mean the actual cost to the husband would be £28,800 per annum for seven years. In return for this he would retain £32,120 per annum gross of additional pension in retirement.

It is worth considering whether this is a preferable solution to the loss of pension rights caused by a Pension Sharing Order.

GUARANTEED ANNUITY RATES

14–015 The issue of guaranteed annuity rates or guaranteed annuity options hit the headlines in 2000. A House of Lords ruling against the Equitable Life Assurance Society in July 2000 required Equitable Life to honour the rates payable to its policyholders who had the option of these rates on their with profits policies. (It was probably not consistent with the nature of with profits business that these options should be available on the schemes; but they did exist.)

This fact is well known; but it is less widely known that many other companies offered schemes with guaranteed annuity options during the latter half of the 1980s and the 1990s.

Guaranteed annuity rates are very valuable. This can probably be inferred from the fact that the above ruling led to the Equitable Life closing to new business on December 8, 2000.[2]

Guaranteed annuity options offer the scheme holder the option when they reach the maturity date of the policy, which might be at a particular age or might be available at a range of ages, to convert their pension to an annuity at a rate pre-defined in the policy contract.

A typical such rate for a male policyholder would be that, at age 60, the scheme holder would be able to purchase an annuity of £100 per annum from a fund of £1,000, payable once a year at the end of the year. Thus a scheme with a fund value of £100,000 which had these guaranteed annuity options could be used to buy a pension of £10,000 per annum. A scheme with a fund value of £155,000 would be needed to purchase this level of pension currently if there were no guaranteed annuity options available. The options are very valuable.

14–016 The authors are not aware of any guaranteed annuity options that can be retained if a policy is transferred out of the pension scheme at the request of a

---

[2] The operating assets and the economic interest in much of the non-profit business was sold to Halifax Plc in February 2001. From March 2001 Equitable Life continued as an independent company with services provided under contract by Halifax Plc.

member spouse. Likewise if a scheme is the subject of a Pension Sharing Order, the rates will be retained on that part of the policy which the member spouse retains. The rates will not be available on the funds that are transferred to the non-member spouse.

Two important points arise for divorce cases. The first point is that details of the guaranteed annuity options will not necessarily be included in the standard disclosure of policy details. This should always be checked. The member spouse may well not remember, nor possibly ever have realised, that the rates exist on the policy.

The second point is that if a Pension Sharing Order is being considered, the schemes carrying these rates should be retained by the member spouse to maintain the guaranteed annuity rates. It might be reasonable in this context to consider the policies as having a higher value than the face value. It could be argued that a scheme with a CE of £100,000 with the qualities described in the above example should be deemed to have a value of £155,000 when being compared to other money purchase pensions.

The value to be placed on a policy with guaranteed annuity rates has to be considered in the light of the period until the benefits become payable. The longer the period until this becomes payable, the more time there is for annuity rates in the market to change and therefore there is less certainty about the additional value provided by the rates.

In deciding what value to place on the scheme, it could also be considered that the guaranteed annuity rates are only available in a prescribed format. To consider the value as £155,000 in the above example might be considered wrong as the scheme may not have the flexibility in terms of the benefits that could be provided by another scheme with a fund value of £155,000. There is therefore some room for debate on the proper valuation, but on any view the scheme with guaranteed annuity rates fixed in the 1980's is worth significantly more than a scheme with the same face value without those rates. 14–017

One other matter of which practitioners need to be aware occurs when the scheme is about to reach maturity. A scheme valued at £100,000, as above, immediately prior to maturity would be valued at £155,000 immediately after maturity as long as the guaranteed annuity options were selected. Therefore if it is necessary to use a Pension Sharing Order on such a policy it may be better for all parties to delay the Pension Sharing Order until after the policy has matured when the CE may be higher.

MARKET VALUE ADJUSTMENT FACTORS

A Market Value Adjustment Factor ("MVAF") is sometimes seen on the document containing the CE of a pension scheme, most often in relation to money purchase schemes such as "with profits" schemes. (It is possible to see an MVAF on a CE of a defined benefit scheme. In these cases, this is part of the basis of the calculations and should not unduly concern the divorce practitioner.) 14–018

The purpose of with profits policies is that they are designed to provide a good rate of return similar to that available from equities but yet to provide rather less volatility by averaging the returns over different generations of scheme holders. A member whose scheme matures when the market is very high will receive less than if the money in the scheme had been invested directly in an equity fund and, commensurately, those whose schemes mature when the market is low will receive more than if the money in the scheme had been invested directly in an equity fund. This is achieved by the "smoothing" of the final return.

The most common scheme currently available that has these properties is the "unitised with profit" scheme. A unit-linked scheme is one where the investor purchases a number of units in a fund and the fund invests this along with all its other funds. The value of a unit will typically be the value of the investments in the fund divided by the number of units in that fund. Unitised with profit schemes will usually have a feature whereby the value of the units can only increase with time. As explained above, the principle is that those whose schemes mature when the market is high effectively "subsidise" those whose schemes mature when the market is low so that the provider of the funds does not make a loss.

The provider has to protect itself against the possibility of all of the investors wanting to take their money out of the fund when the market is at a low level and the value of the investments is therefore low. The provider does this by stating that any individual who wants to transfer out of the fund other than at the maturity date may have their CE value reduced at the time.

14–019 The effects of this can be illustrated by considering, by way of example, three different policy holders all of whom have investments in the same fund, this being a unitised with profits fund. In this example all are assumed to have 10,000 units in the fund with a maturity date of age 60. The first is assumed to be aged 60 now, the second assumed to be aged 59 years and three months and the third assumed to be aged 42 years. The units have a nominal value of £11.40 each but the market is at a very low level.

The first investor has reached maturity age and can therefore receive the full value of £114,000.

The second and third investors are told that there is an MVAF that will apply to their CEs due to the fact that the market level is low. Both are given a CE which states the same thing:

Current Value of the Funds	=	£114,000
less		
Market Value Adjustment	=	£41,000
equals		
CE	=	£73,000

In the case of the second investor, it is only nine months until the age of 60 is reached when the full value of the interest without an MVAF can be obtained. The true value of this policy is therefore very close to £114,000 and the policy should not be subjected to a Pension Sharing Order at this time as only the adjusted CE will be used.

This is not true for the third investor. The third investor will not reach maturity age for eighteen years. During those eighteen years, if investments returns are reasonable, then the increase in the value of the units will be less than the investment return and effectively the CE now will represent a value close to the value of that policy to the investor.

The divorce practitioner should be wary where there is an MVAF and should ensure that the workings of these MVAF's are fully understood.

THE INCOME GAP AND ADJOURNMENT

The "Income Gap" is a well known problem where the non-member spouse cannot draw pension income until a later date than the member spouse draws pension income. This can lead to a significant cash flow issue for parties. **14–020**

A simple situation where this arises might be, for example, where the member spouse is a Head Teacher age 58 and the non-member spouse does not work and is aged 55. If a Pension Sharing Order is used, the non-member spouse cannot receive the benefits of the "pension credit" until age 60. The member spouse may be willing and able to pay maintenance whilst still earning (i.e. until retirement at age 60) but may not be in a position, if pension sharing is implemented now, to continue such payments after this point from the reduced pension fund. This leaves a three year Income Gap for the non-member spouse.

Situations arise in the uniformed services which are more significant. A member of the Police Pension Scheme can retire at age 48 on completion of 30 years' service and yet the non-member spouse has to wait until age 60 to receive the benefits of the "pension credit". In the Armed Forces Pension Scheme, a member of officer rank may be able to take benefits at age 37 (on completion of 16 years' service) but the non-member spouse will not receive the benefits of a "pension credit" until age 65.

One way of solving this problem is to postpone making the Pension Sharing Order. This would usually be until the point when the non-member spouse can take the benefits. In principle, this can be helpful as the full pension is paid until the non-member spouse can receive the benefits and therefore the member spouse has the full pension from which to make maintenance payments and the pension is only reduced at the point where the payments cease and the benefits from the "pension credit" becomes payable. **14–021**

Occupational Pension Schemes should not accept an order made now to be implemented at a date in the future,[3] but as long as the application for a Pension Sharing Order has been made and remains live, there is nothing to prevent the Pension Sharing Order itself being made some time after the final hearing or Decree Absolute and indeed the authors are aware of cases where agreements have been made to adjourn the application for a Pension Sharing Order by as much as ten years after the divorce. It is likely that agreement of both parties will be necessary to adopt this option.

There are however a number of potential pitfalls to avoid and a number of issues that can arise of which practitioners need to be aware.

---

[3] Note, however, para.4–010 above.

Pitfall A

14-022 In principle, if there is no change in the scheme's actuarial basis for the calculations of the CE, then once the pension comes into payment, the CE will reduce at least in real terms. This is because life expectancies reduce as people get older and a CE is a prospective value of a series of future payments. These payments will gradually be expected to be made over a shorter period and therefore the value will be less and the CE will reduce, reducing the amount available to the non-member spouse. Therefore, the benefits available after sharing are likely to be less the later that it is done (at least in principle).

Example (the effect of inflation is stripped out to ease understanding):

The member spouse is aged 60 and retiring as a member of the Teachers' Pension Scheme with a pension of £30,000 per annum. The non-member spouse is aged 55 with no pension rights. They have agreed that they should receive equality of income. If a Pension Sharing Order for 49.9 per cent is made now then the member spouse will receive £15,015 from the date of implementation and the non-member spouse will receive £15,015 per annum in five years time at age 60.

If the Pension Sharing Order is delayed for five years then the member spouse will receive the full £30,000 per annum for the first five years. The Pension Sharing Order at that time to achieve equality of income would be for 57.6 per cent and the member spouse and non-member spouse would each receive £12,725 per annum after the Pension Sharing Order is implemented.

Accordingly, the effect of deferring making the Pension Sharing Order is that the parties will have received (in terms of combined income) an additional £14,985 per annum for the first five years against a reduction in the combined income of £4,550 per annum thereafter for the remainder of the parties' lives. It is plain that this is a solution which, while increasing the short term cash flow, ultimately reduces the income received (depending, of course, on the longevity of the parties).

Pitfall B

14-023 There is additional administration cost in that the Pension Sharing Order has to be made at a date in future and therefore costs will be incurred in presenting the case to the court at the later date.

Pitfall C

14-024 The court has to agree to do this and may decide that it is not willing to make an order which requires the court to make a Pension Sharing Order at a future date.

Pitfall D

14-025 The Pension Sharing Order will only be able to be made if the member is still alive at that time. Therefore the issue of the member's death before the Pension Sharing Order is made needs to be considered. One option would be to consider taking life insurance on the member spouse's life to provide a lump sum to purchase benefits equivalent to the amount that the nonmember would have received from the Pension Sharing Order had it been possible for it to be implemented.

It might be preferable for the policy to belong to the non-member spouse but on the member spouse's life. This way the non-member spouse who is beneficiary can ensure that the premiums are paid.

Further issues surround the possibility of a policy paying out. At one extreme, the member spouse's health or occupation may be such that they will not be able to obtain life insurance. This would be a significant problem. Additionally, there are issues about whether the policy pays out on death. Many policies have exclusion clauses for suicide in the early years, death from the pursuit of dangerous pastimes and death through the pursuit of certain vocations (such as a courier to a country at war or a mercenary). The non-member spouse might also be at risk if the member spouse failed to disclose a medical condition on the application form. The non-member spouse needs to take steps to limit any of the possibilities and in any event claims under Inheritance (Provision for Family and Dependants) Act 1975 should be left open in this process.

Pitfall E

The rules of the scheme could change. This has happened with many of the postponed orders proposed on the Armed Forces Pension Scheme between 2000 and 2005. In April 2006, the scheme increased the age at which the non-member spouse could receive the "pension credit" pension rights from age 60 to age 65. It is now 55—see para.10–012 above. Although this has not removed the possibility of this solution, it has served to alter the plans of the parties.

14–026

Pitfall F

The member spouse could, even though having agreed to this solution in the first instance, oppose it at the time when the Pension Sharing Order is due to be made, perhaps on the grounds that circumstances have changed in the meantime (for example, if the non-member spouse's financial circumstances have changed for the better). The court will always retain the discretion not to make an order.

14–027

Pitfall G

The ability of the court to make Pension Sharing Orders could disappear as a result of future legislation. This is unlikely and it is likely a replacement solution would be available, but it is a possibility.

14–028

Pitfall H

There is the possibility that the sponsoring employer and scheme will run into difficulties and fold in which case it will only be the compensation package or reduced benefit that will be available. This circumstance is likely to be an issue for both parties.

14–029

Pitfall I

14-030 Defined Benefit pension schemes are allowed to take into account a member's health when implementing a Pension Sharing Order. Therefore, if at the time that the pension sharing order is due to be implemented the member is in poor health then, depending on whether the Scheme does take health into account, the CE could be reduced making pension sharing a poor solution. This concept is discussed further below. The solution to this may be to ensure the life insurance policy is "renewable" so that it can be continued along with the maintenance in these circumstances.

Pitfall J

14-031 The statutory provisions prevent a Pension Sharing Order being made where there already exists a Pension Attachment Order in relation to the same pension.[4] If the member spouse wished to prevent a Pension Sharing Order being made, then one way of doing this would be to consent to a Pension Attachment Order in favour of a subsequent spouse. It may be that an undertaking by the member spouse not to do this would render it quite unlikely.

14-032 In situations where the member spouse is in active service or the pension is in payment, a further calculation may be needed at the time of the Pension Sharing Order being made. It would usually be preferable to agree the formula in advance at the time that the postponement is agreed.

Whilst these pitfalls do exist, this approach remains a viable solution for some types of cases.

There are also cases where CEs are very low and there are many years until retirement where it might be worth considering postponing the order. This would be the case if the scheme insisted on the external option and the non-member spouse has to transfer out of the scheme. A Pension Sharing Order crystallises the poor value of the CE and the parties could wait until the CE rose before making any Pension Sharing Order.

APPORTIONING PENSION RIGHTS

14-033 It is sometimes argued, more so in relation to short marriages, that in deciding what Pension Sharing Orders to make, the courts should consider only those rights accrued during the marriage.[5]

If this is to be properly considered by the court then some analysis over and above a straight line discount may be necessary and appropriate. This presents some considerable difficulties. There can often be some debate about when the period to be considered should be deemed to commence and when it should be deemed to stop. Starting points can be the date of co-habitation or the date of marriage and end points can be the date of separation or the date of divorce. For a fuller discussion of these issues see Chapter 12. This chapter deals with the method of apportionment.

---

[4] See para.4-016 above.
[5] See Ch.12 above.

PENSION RIGHTS AT DIFFERENT DATES

In Scotland, the issue is very precisely defined. The period runs from the date of marriage to the date of separation and the apportionment is automatic in every case. The apportionment is defined as the length of the period of marriage (ending on the date of separation) divided by the total period of service in the Scheme and then this is multiplied by the CE at the date of separation. This is described as the "straight line method" of apportionment or "Uniform Accrual".

English courts have not defined how the apportionment should be calculated and there are a number of different methods that have been proposed. It is probably best to consider this by looking at a straightforward example.

In this example, it is assumed that the member spouse is male, joined the Principal Civil Service Pension Scheme on June 1, 1987, aged 35. The start of the period of accrual within the relationship is June 1, 1997 and the end of the period is June 1, 2007, when any Pension Sharing Order is deemed to take place. The pensionable salary in 1987 is assumed to be £20,000 per annum, in 1997 to be £40,000 per annum and in 2007 to be £100,000 per annum.

14–034

The provisions of the Pension Schemes Act 1993[6] set out that:

> "so far as any short service benefit is not required to be computed in accordance with subsection (1), it must be computed on the basis of uniform accrual, so that at the time when pensionable service is terminated, it bears the same proportion to long service benefit as the period of that service bears to the period from the beginning of that service to the time when the member would attain normal pension age or such lower age as may be prescribed."

This is known as the principle of "Uniform Accrual". The Act only refers to how an Occupational Pension Scheme should calculate pensions for members not completing full service and therefore does not have to apply in other circumstances.

Under the principle of Uniform Accrual in our example, 50 per cent of the pension rights (10 years divided by 20 years) would be deemed to be attributable to the period of marriage.

Though mathematically simpler, it is debatable however, whether this is method is fair in apportioning these rights. There are other methods to consider as well. It is best to consider the pension accrued at each of the dates and the CE at the two dates to show the difference:

PENSION RIGHTS AT DIFFERENT DATES

Date	Accrued Pension at that date	CE at that date
June 1, 1997	£5,000 per annum	£49,330
June 1, 2007	£25,000 per annum	£497,570

14–035

(A tax-free cash lump sum of three times the pension IS also payable at retirement.)

---

[6] Pension Schemes Act 1993 Pt IV s.74(6).

ACTUARIAL ISSUES ARISING FROM THE USE OF CES

The CE is more than 10 times what it was at the earlier date. The CE has increased for a number of reasons:

- The member spouse has accrued an additional 10 years service since the date of the start of the accrual period.
- The member spouse's pensionable salary has increased considerably. This is a final salary pension scheme and if the pensionable salary were to double then all the pension rights accrued also double during that period.
- The "unravelling" of the basis. The CE discounts all future payments to be made. All of the future payments are 10 years closer to being paid at the second date than they were at the first date and therefore they are discounted by 10 fewer years and as a consequence their value is much greater.
- The basis of the calculations has changed to reflect, amongst other points, current views on mortality. The value of a pension payable for life is clearly dependent on the period over which that pension will be paid and if it is assumed that the pension will be paid over a longer period then clearly the value will be greater.

14-036 Therefore a number of different methods could be postulated for apportioning the pension rights over the period of service if it is decided to exclude those rights which accrued prior to the starting point.

Method I

14-037 The Uniform Accrual Method is as described above. In this example, 50 per cent of the pension rights would be deemed to be attributable to the period of marriage.

Method II

14-038 Using CEs. This does seem to be at the extreme. This involves simply dividing the CE at the starting point by the CE at the end point. In this example, the CE at the first point is only 9.9 per cent of the CE at the second point.

Method III

14-039 Another method would be to consider what the pension and CE would be now had the member left at the starting point. If the member had left service the accrued pension would be increased in line with inflation (up to a cumulative maximum of 5 per cent per annum). The effect of this is as follows:

Period of Service	Accrued Pension revalued to June 1, 2007	CE at that date
June 1, 1987 to June 1, 1997	£6,505 per annum	£129,470 (26.0% of CE)
June 1, 1997 to June 1, 2007	£12,500 per annum	£248,785 (50% of CE)

June 1, 1987 to June 1, 2007	£25,000 per annum	£497,570

These figures can be used in one of two ways. It might be argued that the CE accumulated before the marriage (£129,470) should be excluded and that a pension sharing order should be made only in relation to the balance of the CE (£497,570 less £129,470). On the other hand it could be argued that the court should consider only the CE that would have accumulated during the marriage if there had been no accumulation of pension prior to the marriage (£248,785).[7]

The calculations become more complicated still if it is decided to exclude both rights accrued prior to the marriage/co-habitation and those accrued post separation. The principles of the calculation do however remain the same.

HEALTH ISSUES

There are a number of issues that need to be considered if one of the parties is in poor health. 14–040

A CE is calculated by estimating the value based on average life expectancies. A CE for a man aged 60 might be based on a life expectancy of 25 years and would therefore assume that the pension is paid for 25 years. If the individual's life expectancy is less than the average for a person of their age in normal health, then their pension will be paid for a shorter period than is anticipated in the CE calculation and therefore the real value will be less. In the above example if the man has a life expectancy of 10 to 12 years, the true value may be only approximately half of the CE.

This issue can be important if the pension is being retained and the true value is being used for offsetting. The true value of the pension rights will be lower to a member spouse who has a shorter period of life expectancy than is assumed in the calculations. In principle, if it were accepted that the member spouse was likely to live longer than average, it would be possible to argue for a higher value to be used. It is very unlikely, however, in practice that unusually long potential longevity (for example, on the basis of an established family history of long life expectancy) would be taken into account in calculating CEs or annuities.

The issue is more important if pension sharing is being considered. It is important to note that pension schemes have the right to request information about the health of the member when implementing a pension sharing order. Some schemes do take the member's health into account and some do not. The impact of this can best be seen by using an example. If we consider that the member spouse is aged 60 and has retired on an inflation linked pension of £20,000 per annum. A CE calculated ignoring health issues might be in the region of £400,000. In the example, it is assumed that the member spouse is suffering from an illness giving a life expectancy of just one year. 14–041

If the Scheme does not take health into account when implementing a Pension Sharing Order, then the CE of £400,000 will be available for pension sharing purposes.

---

[7] See Ch.12 for a discussion on the legal aspects of the issue of pre-separation acquisition of pension.

- If no pension sharing takes place, the member spouse retains all of the pension rights and therefore the pension of £20,000 which is expected to be paid for a year. Thus the value is approximately £20,000.
- If there is a 50 per cent Pension Sharing Order, then the non-member spouse receives a "pension credit" for £200,000 and the member spouse's pension rights reduce to £10,000 per annum and have a value of approximately £10,000. Therefore the value of the combined pension rights is approximately £210,000.
- If there is a 100 per cent Pension Sharing Order, then the non-member spouse receives a "pension credit" for £400,000 and the member spouse's pension rights are extinguished. Therefore the value of the combined pension rights is approximately £400,000.

If, however the scheme does take health into account, then the value available for pension sharing is likely to be only £20,000.

14–042 From the above example, if the member spouse is in poor health and the scheme does not take health into account, then it will be better, from an overall financial point of view, if pension sharing is implemented to the maximum.

Practitioners should also be wary that although the above may be an opportunity to obtain an improved overall settlement, they should also be alert, when representing the non-member spouse, to ascertain clearly either that health will not be taken into account or that the member is in good health. Otherwise the non-member spouse could receive less than expected. Practitioners should also be aware when considering non-member spouses in poor health that if pension sharing is used then the benefits of the "pension credit" die with the non-member spouse. Income from pension attachment orders reverts back to the member spouse on the death of the non-member spouse.

In any case in which Form P is completed this issue will be addressed. Question 8 of Section C of the Form requires the pension provider to indicate whether they will require information about the member's health before implementing a pension sharing order.

When dealing with money purchase pension policies or alternatively "pension credits" where only the external option is available, practitioners should be aware that individuals in poor health can often obtain enhanced annuity rates when purchasing a pension. Therefore, if the solution is to be based on expected incomes in retirement, then the income may need to be based on a rate that is better than the average. It is of course the health at the time of taking the annuity that is important so if this date is some time in the future, current health may not be relevant.

CHAPTER 15

The Shorter Career Public Sector Pension Schemes

ARMED FORCES PENSION SCHEME 1975 (AFPS 1975)—NON-OFFICERS SECTION

Contact details

Administrators' Address	Pensions Division, Service Personnel and Veterans Agency, Mail Point 480, Kentigern House, 65, Brown Street, Glasgow G2 8EX	15–001
Contact Telephone Number	0800 085 3600	
Contact E-mail address	JPAC@spva.mod.uk	
Website	*www.afpaainfocentre.dii.r.mil.uk*	

Eligibility

Provision made for ordinary ranks under the AFPS 1975 is different from the provision made for officers. 15–002

All non-officer ranks serving in the Armed Forces prior to April 6, 2005, were automatically enrolled in the AFPS 1975; but those commencing their service from April 6, 2005 onwards are not eligible for this scheme and they will instead join the Armed Forces Pension Scheme 2005 (AFPS 2005), which makes no distinction between officers and other ranks.

Members of the AFPS 1975 were given a one off opportunity to transfer to the AFPS 2005 at the commencement of the new scheme, so that some pre-2005 members are not now members of the AFPS 1975. Most such non-officer ranks, however, will be.

Main features of the scheme

Benefits accrue during "reckonable service" which is in essence all service in the Armed Forces from age 18 onwards for a maximum of 37 years. 15–003

THE SHORTER CAREER PUBLIC SECTOR PENSION SCHEMES

The scheme member will accrue benefits calculated by reference to a combination of length of "reckonable service" and "representative pay", i.e. the typical pay for the relevant rank rather than the actual pensionable salary of the member.

Members who retire from the Armed Forces after 22 years or more of reckonable service are eligible to receive their pension income straight away since they will have reached the "Immediate Pension Point". Retirement at age 40 with a pension paid straight away at 31.833 per cent of final salary is therefore possible in some cases. When this occurs the amount received is not subject to inflationary increases until the recipient reaches the age of 55, at which time the amount received is enhanced by inflationary increases backdated to the time of the initial receipt of payments.

Non officer ranks who retire from the Armed Forces after less than 22 years of reckonable service will be eligible for a deferred benefit.

All benefits which accrued prior to April 6, 2006 accrued by reference to a retirement age of 60; but all benefits which accrued from April 6, 2006 onwards accrued by reference to a retirement age of 65. Any member with service before and after April 6, 2006 will thus have two sets of benefits, one payable at age 60 and one payable at age 65.

15–004 Benefits under AFPS 1975 accrue as an amount of pension payable per annum plus a tax-free cash lump sum of three times that pension. It is possible to take a further lump sum if retirement is before age 55 (known as "Re-Settlement Commutation" or a "Re-Settlement Grant") and this reduces the pension paid until age 55, but not beyond.

Historically, it was also possible to exchange some of the pension for a further lump sum (known as "Lifetime Commutation") but this was removed for future accrual many years ago and therefore is unlikely to be possible in most cases now.

One half of the accrued pension is payable to a spouse or civil partner on the death of the scheme member, provided the marriage or civil partnership took place prior to the scheme member leaving service in the Armed Forces.

The scheme is contracted out of the Additional State Pension or State Second Pension. Accordingly, a member who has worked in the Armed Forces throughout his working life will not have any income at State Pension Age from the Additional State Pension or State Second Pension.

Cash Equivalents

15–005 Cash Equivalents (CEs) of the member's rights in the scheme for pension sharing purposes will be calculated on the assumption that the member in service will leave service on the date of the calculation. This can have a significant distorting effect in the context of the AFPS 1975.

This is best illustrated by an extreme example. A calculation carried out for an officer with 21 years and 364 days reckonable service will assume that his entitlements will be deferred to age 60 or 65. A calculation for the same officer just two days later, at 22 years and 1 day, will assume that he has immediate entitlements. The resulting CE will be dramatically different. For example, if the

AFPS 1975 – NON-OFFICERS SECTION

member in this illustration is, at the date of the notional calculations a Private, then the CE at 21 years and 364 days will be £119,480 and the CE at 22 years and 1 day will be £269,400.

Accordingly CEs in cases involving AFPS 1975 need to be treated with particular care.

Pension sharing

When subjected to a Pension Sharing Order, rights under the AFPS 1975 provide only pension credits by way of internal transfer. The non-member spouse will accordingly accrue rights within the scheme to the value of the pension credit.   15–006

Pension sharing charges made by AFPS 1975 are currently £300 plus VAT for implementation and £10 plus VAT per annum for paying the pension credit member's pension.

The rights accruing to a non-member spouse under a pension credit are calculated by reference to a retirement age of 65. Until 2006 these benefits could not be taken until age 60, which was increased to 65 from 2006 until 2009 and this led to "Income Gap" issues (see, for example, *R (Thomas) v Ministry of Defence*[1] and *R (Smith) v Secretary of State for Defence*[2]). Since April 6, 2009, however, the non-member spouse has been able to take benefits at age 55. Again, these will be subjected to an actuarial reduction. The earlier the benefits are taken the larger the reduction.

Equal income calculations for pension sharing within the AFPS 1975

The practical consequences of some of the matters referred to above can be surprising in the context of an attempt by the court to leave the parties with an equal level of income at retirement after a pension sharing order. Particular care must be taken to identify what assumptions are going to be made as to the expected retirement date of the member spouse. This is best illustrated by a number of case studies.   15–007

Case study one

A Private in the Army is age 35, having started his service at age 18 so that he has 17 years of reckonable service. He expects to retire from service on completion of 22 years of reckonable service in 5 years' time. His CE is £81,010. His wife is also age 35. The Private should receive his pension immediately on his retirement in five years' time. It is assumed that his wife will take her benefits at her age 55. The court decides that it is appropriate to calculate a pension sharing order so as to create equality of pension income at mutual age 55 based on those rights accrued to date. The appropriate Pension Sharing Order required is for 94.0 per cent. This will provide pension income of £4,695 per annum gross for both the Private and his wife in today's terms at mutual age 55. In the period between the Private's age 40 and his age 55 he will receive an income and his wife will receive no income. The Private will also receive benefits accrued in the future.

15–008

---

[1] [2008] 2 F.L.R. 1385.
[2] [2004] EWHC 1797.

THE SHORTER CAREER PUBLIC SECTOR PENSION SCHEMES

Case study two

15–009 | A Private in the Army is age 35, having started his service at age 18 so that he has 17 years of reckonable service. Although he could retire from service on completion of 22 years of reckonable service in 5 years' time, he states (and this is accepted) that he wishes to remain in the Armed Forces until age 55. His CE is £81,010. His wife is also age 35. It is assumed that both parties will take their benefits at age 55. The court decides that it is appropriate to calculate a pension sharing order so as to create equality of pension income at mutual age 55 based on those rights accrued to date. The appropriate Pension Sharing Order required is for 72.8 per cent. This will provide pension income of £3,635 per annum gross for both the Private and his wife in today's terms at mutual age 55. The Private will also receive pension benefits accrued in future.

Case study three

15–010 | A Private in the Army is age 41, having started his service at age 18 so that he has 23 years of reckonable service. He expects to retire from service on completion of 37 years of reckonable service in 14 years' time. His CE is £281,400. His wife is also age 41. It is assumed that the Private's wife will take her benefits at her age 55 at the same time as the Private's retirement. The court decides that it is appropriate to calculate a pension sharing order so as to create equality of pension income at mutual age 55 based on those rights accrued to date. The appropriate Pension Sharing Order required is for 27.3 per cent. This will provide pension income of £7,270 per annum gross for both the Private and his wife in today's terms at mutual age 55.

15–011 It can be seen from these illustrations that the assumption that a 50 per cent Pension Sharing Order will provide an equal level of income on retirement is, certainly in the context of the AFPS 1975, a dangerous one. Indeed, counter-intuitively, there are cases where a 100 per cent Pension Sharing Order will produce an equal level of incomes on retirement.

Miscellaneous other matters

15–012 There are a number of other matters which sometimes arise in relation to the AFPS 1975 and of which practitioners ought to be aware.

There are a number of benefits payable to injured members which are not subject to a pension sharing order. These include benefits under the Armed Forces Attributable Benefits, the Armed Forces Compensation Scheme and the Service Invaliding Pension.

The final report of the Independent Public Service Pensions Commission, published on March 10, 2011, the "Hutton Report", recommended that the uniformed services, including members of the armed forces, should be treated differently from other public servants for pension purposes, but recommended increasing the normal retirement age from 55 to 60.[3]

---

[3] See para.1–027 above.

ARMED FORCES PENSION SCHEME 1975 (AFPS 1975)—OFFICERS SECTION

Contact details

Administrators' Address	Pensions Division, Service Personnel and Veterans Agency, Mail Point 480, Kentigern House, 65, Brown Street, Glasgow G2 8EX	15–013
Contact Telephone Number	0800 085 3600	
Contact E-mail address	JPAC@spva.mod.uk	
Website	*www.afpaainfocentre.dii.r.mil.uk*	

Eligibility

Provision made for officers under the AFPS 1975 is different from the provision made for other ranks.   15–014

All officers serving in the Armed Forces prior to April 6, 2005, including those promoted from non-officer ranks, were automatically enrolled in the AFPS 1975; but officers commencing their service from April 6, 2005 onwards are not eligible for this scheme and they will instead join the Armed Forces Pension Scheme 2005 (AFPS 2005), which makes no distinction between officers and other ranks.

Members of the AFPS 1975 were given a once off opportunity to transfer to the AFPS 2005 at the commencement of the new scheme so that some pre-2005 officers are not now members of the AFPS 1975. Most such officers, however, will be.

Main features of the scheme

Benefits accrue during "reckonable service" which is in essence all service in the Armed Forces from age 21 onwards for a maximum of 34 years.   15–015

The scheme member will accrue benefits calculated by reference to a combination of length of "reckonable service" and (save for very senior officers) "representative pay", i.e. the typical pay for the relevant rank rather than the actual pensionable salary of the member.

Officers who retire from the Armed Forces after 16 years or more of reckonable service are eligible to receive their pension income straight away since they will have reached the "Immediate Pension Point". Retirement at age 37 with a pension paid straight away at 28.5 per cent of final salary is therefore possible in some cases. When this occurs the amount received is not subject to inflationary increases until the recipient reaches the age of 55, at which time the amount received is enhanced by inflationary increases backdated to the time of the initial receipt of payments.

Officers who retire from the Armed Forces after less than 16 years of reckonable service will be eligible for a deferred benefit.

THE SHORTER CAREER PUBLIC SECTOR PENSION SCHEMES

15–016 All benefits which accrued prior to April 6, 2006 accrued by reference to a retirement age of 60; but all benefits which accrued from April 6, 2006 onwards accrued by reference to a retirement age of 65. Any officer with service before and after April 6, 2006 will thus have two sets of benefits, one payable at age 60 and one payable at age 65.

Benefits under AFPS 1975 accrue as an amount of pension payable per annum plus a tax-free cash lump sum of three times that pension. It is possible to take a further lump sum if retirement is before age 55 (known as "Re-Settlement Commutation" or a "Re-Settlement Grant") and this reduces the pension paid until age 55, but not beyond.

Historically, it was also possible to exchange some of the pension for a further lump sum (known as "Lifetime Commutation") but this was removed for future accrual many years ago and therefore is unlikely to be possible in most cases now.

One half of the accrued pension is payable to a spouse or civil partner on the death of the scheme member provided the marriage or civil partnership took place prior to the scheme member leaving service in the Armed Forces.

The scheme is contracted out of the Additional State Pension or State Second Pension. Accordingly, a member who has worked in the Armed Forces throughout his working life will not have any income at State Pension Age from the Additional State Pension or State Second Pension.

Cash Equivalents

15–017 Cash Equivalents (CEs) of the member's rights in the scheme for pension sharing purposes will be calculated on the assumption that the member in service will leave service on the date of the calculation. This can have a significant distorting effect in the context of the AFPS 1975.

This is best illustrated by an extreme example. A calculation carried out for an officer with 15 years and 364 days reckonable service will assume that his entitlements will be deferred to age 60 or 65. A calculation for the same officer just two days later, at 16 years and 1 day, will assume that he has immediate entitlements. The resulting CE will be dramatically different. For example, if the officer in this illustration is, at the date of the notional calculations a Commander in the Royal Navy then the CE at 15 years and 364 days will be £161,000 and the CE at 16 years and 1 day will be £401,000.

Accordingly CEs in cases involving AFPS 1975 need to be treated with particular care.

Pension sharing

15–018 When subjected to a pension sharing order, rights under the AFPS 1975 provide only pension credits by way of internal transfer. The non-member spouse will accordingly accrue rights within the scheme to the value of the pension credit.

Pension sharing charges made by AFPS 1975 are currently £300 plus VAT for implementation and £10 plus VAT per annum for paying the pension credit member's pension.

The rights accruing to a non-member spouse under a pension credit are calculated by reference to a retirement age of 65. Until 2006 these benefits could not be taken until age 60, which was increased to 65 from 2006 until 2009 and this led to "Income Gap" issues (see, for example, *R (Thomas) v Ministry of Defence*[4] and *R (Smith) v Secretary of State for Defence*[5]). Since April 6, 2009, however, the non-member spouse has been able to take benefits at age 55. Again, these will be subjected to an actuarial reduction. The earlier the benefits are taken the larger the reduction.

Equal income calculations for pension sharing within the AFPS 1975

The practical consequences of some of the matters referred to above can be surprising in the context of an attempt by the court to leave the parties with an equal level of income at retirement after a pension sharing order. Particular care must be taken to identify what assumptions are going to be made as to the expected retirement date of the member spouse. This is best illustrated by a number of case studies.

15–019

Case study one

A Major in the Army is age 35, having started his service at age 21 so that he has 14 years of reckonable service. He expects to retire from service on completion of 16 years of reckonable service in 2 years' time. His CE is £136,880. His wife is also age 35. The Major should receive his pension immediately on his retirement in two years' time. It is assumed that his wife will take her benefits at her age 55. The court decides that it is appropriate to calculate a pension sharing order so as to create equality of pension income at mutual age 55 based on those rights accrued to date. The appropriate Pension Sharing Order required is for 97.4 per cent. This will provide pension income of £8,215 per annum gross for both the Major and his wife in today's terms at mutual age 55. In the period between the Major's age 37 and his age 55 he will receive an income and his wife will receive no income.

15–020

Case study two

A Major in the Army is age 35, having started his service at age 21 so that he has 14 years of reckonable service. Although he could retire from service on completion of 16 years of reckonable service in 2 years' time, he states (and this is accepted) that he wishes to remain in the Armed Forces until age 55. His CE is £136,880. His wife is also age 35. It is assumed that both parties will take their benefits at age 55. The court decides that it is appropriate to calculate a pension sharing order so as to create equality of pension income at mutual age 55 based on those rights accrued to date. The appropriate Pension Sharing Order required is for 72.8 per cent. This will provide pension income of £6,140 per annum gross for both the Major and his wife in today's terms at mutual age 55.

15–021

---

[4] [2008] 2 F.L.R. 1385.
[5] [2004] EWHC 1797.

Case study three

15–022

> A Major in the Army is age 38, having started his service at age 21 so that he has 17 years of reckonable service. He expects to retire from service on completion of 34 years of reckonable service in 17 years' time. His CE is £422,100. His wife is also age 38. It is assumed that the Major's wife will take her benefits at her age 55 at the same time as the Major's retirement. The court decides that it is appropriate to calculate a pension sharing order so as to create equality of pension income at mutual age 55 based on those rights accrued to date. The appropriate Pension Sharing Order required is for 35.6 per cent. This will provide pension income of £9,665 per annum gross for both the Major and his wife in today's terms at mutual age 55.

15–023 It can be seen from these illustrations that the assumption that a 50 per cent Pension Sharing Order will provide an equal level of income on retirement is, certainly in the context of the AFPS 1975, a dangerous one. Indeed, counter-intuitively, there are cases where a 100 per cent Pension Sharing Order will produce an equal level of incomes on retirement.

Miscellaneous other matters

15–024 There are a number of other matters which sometimes arise in relation to the AFPS 1975 and of which practitioners ought to be aware.

There are a number of benefits payable to injured officers which are not subject to a pension sharing orders. These include benefits under the Armed Forces Attributable Benefits, the Armed Forces Compensation Scheme and the Service Invaliding Pension.

The final report of the Independent Public Service Pensions Commission, published on March 10, 2011, the "Hutton Report", recommended that the uniformed services, including members of the armed forces, should be treated differently from other public servants for pension purposes, but recommended increasing the normal retirement age from 55 to 60.[6] In fact, except where there has been a career break, all officers in the Armed Forces Pension Scheme 1975 will have been within 10 years of retirement age in April 2012, and therefore will all retain the benefits as promised at the commencement of service in the Armed Forces and therefore their right to retire at 16 years' service without pension reduction.

---

[6] See para.1.69 above.

ARMED FORCES PENSION SCHEME 2005 (AFPS 2005)

Contact details

Administrators' Address	Pensions Division, Service Personnel and Veterans Agency, Mail Point 480, Kentigern House, 65, Brown Street, Glasgow G2 8EX
Contact Telephone Number	0800 085 3600
Contact E-mail address	JPAC@spva.mod.uk
Website	*www.afpaainfocentre.dii.r.mil.uk*

15–025

Eligibility

Provision made for officers under the AFPS 2005 is the same as for other ranks.

15–026

All officers serving in the Armed Forces prior to April 6, 2005 were automatically enrolled in the AFPS 1975; but officers commencing their service from April 6, 2005 onwards are not eligible for this scheme and they will instead join the Armed Forces Pension Scheme 2005 (AFPS 2005).

Members of the AFPS 1975 were given a once off opportunity to transfer to the AFPS 2005 at the commencement of the new scheme so that some pre-2005 officers are now members of the AFPS 2005.

Main features of the scheme

Benefits accrue during "reckonable service" which is in essence all service in the Armed Forces. Those who transferred from AFPS 1975 could count service with the Forces prior to their eligibility for AFPS 1975.

15–027

The scheme member will accrue benefits calculated by reference to a combination of length of "reckonable service" and "pensionable pay".

The Scheme has a peculiar feature, being the existence of non pension "Early Departure Payments".

Benefits accrue in the Scheme being payable at age 65. The pension accrues as a pension plus a lump sum of three times the pension.

The pension rights can be paid immediately from age 55 if the member remains in service until that age.

If the member leaves service between 40 and 55 and has sufficient accrued service, then the pension is deferred to be payable at 65 but the member can receive an Early Departure Lump Sum and Early Departure Payments until age 65. The Early Departure Lump Sum is the same as the retirement Lump Sum and the Early Departure Payments are a proportion of the retirement pension income.

15–28

The Early Departure Payments are not pension and cannot be the subject of a Pension Sharing Order.

One half of the accrued pension is payable to a spouse or civil partner on the death of the scheme member provided the marriage or civil partnership took place prior to the scheme member leaving service in the Armed Forces.

The scheme is contracted out of the Additional State Pension or State Second Pension. Accordingly, a member who has worked in the Armed Forces throughout his working life will not have any income at State Pension Age from the Additional State Pension or State Second Pension.

Cash Equivalents

15–029 Cash Equivalents (CEs) of the member's rights in the scheme for pension sharing purposes will be calculated on the assumption that the member in service will leave service on the date of the calculation. This can have a significant distorting effect in the context of the AFPS 2005.

This is best illustrated by an extreme example. A calculation carried out for a member of age 54 years and 364 days reckonable service will assume that his entitlements will be deferred to age 65. A calculation for the same officer just two days later, at age 55 years and 1 day, will assume that the pension is paid immediately. The resulting CE will be dramatically different. For example, if the officer in this illustration is, at the date of the notional calculations a Commander in the Royal Navy then the CE at age 54 years and 364 days will be £642,000 and the CE at age 55 years and 1 day will be £1,012,000.

Accordingly CEs in cases involving AFPS 2005 need to be treated with particular care.

Pension sharing

15–030 When subjected to a pension sharing order, rights under the AFPS 2005 provide only pension credits by way of internal transfer. The non-member spouse will accordingly accrue rights within the scheme to the value of the pension credit.

Pension sharing charges made by AFPS 2005 are currently £300 plus VAT for implementation and £10 plus VAT per annum for paying the pension credit member's pension.

The rights accruing to a non-member spouse under a pension credit are calculated by reference to a retirement age of 65. Until 2006 these benefits could not be taken until age 60, which was increased to 65 from 2006 until 2009 and this led to "Income Gap" issues (see, for example, *R(Thomas) v Ministry of Defence*[7] and *R (Smith) v Secretary of State for Defence*[8]). Since April 6, 2009, however, the non-member spouse has been able to take benefits at age 55. Again, these will be subjected to an actuarial reduction. The earlier the benefits are taken the larger the reduction.

---

[7] [2008] 2 F.L.R. 1385.
[8] [2004] EWHC 1797.

AFPS 2005

Equal income calculations for pension sharing within the AFPS 2005

The practical consequences of some of the matters referred to above can be surprising in the context of an attempt by the court to leave the parties with an equal level of income at retirement after a pension sharing order. Particular care must be taken to identify what assumptions are going to be made as to the expected retirement date of the member spouse. This is best illustrated by a number of case studies.

15–031

Case study one

> A Major in the Army is age 53, having started his service at age 17. If he leaves before age 55, Early Departure Payments of £30,950 per annum until 65 (plus lump sum of £123,800) followed by a pension at 65 of £41,266 per annum plus a lump sum of £123,800 at 65.
> If he leaves at 55, an immediate pension of £41,266 per annum plus a lump sum of £123,800.
> He expects to retire from service on completion at age 54 in one year's time. His CE is £624,800. His wife is also age 53. The Major should receive his pension at age 65 but will receive Early Departure Payments until that time from leaving. It is assumed that his wife will take her benefits at her age 55. The court decides that it is appropriate to calculate a pension sharing order so as to create equality of pension income at mutual age 65 based on those rights accrued to date. The appropriate Pension Sharing Order required is for 48.0 per cent. This will provide pension income of £20,815 per annum gross for both the Major and his wife in today's terms at mutual age 65. In the period between the Major's age 54 and his age 65 he will receive an income of £30,950 plus a lump sum at age 54 and another lump sum at age 65. The wife will receive her income between 55 and 65 and her lump sum at 55 as well as the incomes from 65.

15–032

Case study two

> A Major in the Army is age 53, having started his service at age 17. If he leaves before age 55, Early Departure Payments of £30,950 per annum until 65 (plus lump sum of £123,800) followed by a pension at 65 of £41,266 per annum plus a lump sum of £123,800 at 65.
> If he leaves at 55, an immediate pension of £41,266 per annum plus a lump sum of £123,800.
> He expects to retire from service on completion at age 55 in two years' time. His CE is £624,800. His wife is also age 53. The Major should receive his pension at age 55. It is assumed that his wife will take her benefits at her age 55. The court decides that it is appropriate to calculate a pension sharing order so as to create equality of pension income at mutual age 55 based on those rights accrued to date. The appropriate Pension Sharing Order required is for 82.5 per cent. This will provide pension income of £20,825 per annum gross for both the Major and his wife in today's terms at mutual age 55.

15–033

It can be seen from these illustrations that the assumption that a 50 per cent Pension Sharing Order will provide an equal level of income on retirement is,

15–034

THE SHORTER CAREER PUBLIC SECTOR PENSION SCHEMES

certainly in the context of the AFPS 2005, a dangerous one. In addition, the effect of making an Order based on one of the above assumptions will distort the result if the other proves to be true.

Miscellaneous other matters

15–35 There are a number of other matters which sometimes arise in relation to the AFPS 2005 and of which practitioners ought to be aware.

There are a number of benefits payable to injured officers which are not subject to a pension sharing orders. These include benefits under the Armed Forces Attributable Benefits, the Armed Forces Compensation Scheme and the Service Invaliding Pension.

Even for members will relatively small amounts of service, the Early Departure Payments can be valuable and will not be able to be shared and will need to be dealt with through another Order in the settlement.

The final report of the Independent Public Service Pensions Commission, published on March 10, 2011, the "Hutton Report", recommended that the uniformed services, including members of the armed forces, should be treated differently from other public servants for pension purposes, but recommended increasing the normal retirement age from 55 to 60.[9]

POLICE PENSION SCHEME 1987

Contact details

15–036

Administrators' Address	Each Force has its choice of administrator. Some use the central administrators such as Xafinity or Capita whereas others administer it in house.

Eligibility

15–037 All officers serving prior to April 6, 2006 were automatically enrolled in the Police Pension Scheme 1987; but officers commencing their service from April 6, 2006 onwards are not eligible for this scheme and they will instead join the New Police Pension Scheme.

Main features of the scheme

15–038 Benefits accrue during "reckonable service" which is in essence all service in the Police from age 18 onwards for a maximum of 30 years.

The scheme member will accrue benefits calculated by reference to a combination of length of "reckonable service" and "pensionable pay".

The set up of the scheme is described so that one-sixtieth of final pensionable salary accrues in the first 20 years and two-sixtieths in the final ten years. However in most cases, this is misleading. The potential accrual (usually

---

[9] See para.1.69 above.

forty-sixtieths) is calculated on joining and then the benefits are deemed to accrue evenly over the first 30 years of service. The only exception is where the member takes retirement benefits in their 50s with less than 30 years' service. This point is often the subject of mistakes.

Officers who retire from the Police after 30 years or more of reckonable service are eligible to receive their pension income straight away. Retirement at age 48 with a pension paid straight away at 66.67 per cent of final salary is therefore possible in many cases. When this occurs the amount received is not subject to inflationary increases until the recipient reaches the age of 55, at which time the amount received is enhanced by inflationary increases backdated to the time of the initial receipt of payments.

Officers who retire from the Force after less than 25 years of reckonable service will be eligible for a deferred benefit payable at age 60.

15–39

Officers who leave service with more than 25 years' service but less than 30 years' service can start to receive benefits from age 50 or a later date of leaving.

Benefits under Police Pension Scheme 1987 accrue as an amount of pension payable per annum. It is possible to take a lump sum at retirement by exchanging some of the pension for a lump sum ("Commutation").

One half of the pension before commutation is payable to a spouse or civil partner on the death of the scheme member.

The scheme is contracted out of the Additional State Pension or State Second Pension. Accordingly, a member will not have any income at State Pension Age from the Additional State Pension or State Second Pension in respect of their period of service in the Police Pension Scheme.

Cash Equivalents

Cash Equivalents (CEs) of the member's rights in the scheme for pension sharing purposes will be calculated on the assumption that the member in service will leave service on the date of the calculation. This can have a significant distorting effect in the context of the Police Pension Scheme 1987.

15–040

This is best illustrated by an example. A calculation carried out for an officer with 24 years and 364 days reckonable service will assume that his entitlements will be deferred to age 60. A calculation for the same officer just two days later, at 25 years and 1 day, will assume that the pension is payable at age 50. The resulting CE will be dramatically different. For example, the CE at 24 years and 364 days will be £225,070 and the CE at 25 years and 1 day will be £310,720.

Accordingly CEs in cases involving the Police Pension Scheme 1987 need to be treated with particular care.

Pension sharing

When subjected to a pension sharing order, rights under the Police Pension Scheme 1987 provide only pension credits by way of internal transfer. The non-member spouse will accordingly receive rights within the scheme to the value of the pension credit.

15–41

Pension sharing charges made by Police Pension Scheme 1987 vary according to the administrator.

The rights accruing to a non-member spouse under a pension credit are calculated by reference to a retirement age of 60. This can lead to "Income Gap" issues. At the time of writing, the pension credit benefits cannot be taken early subject to actuarial reduction.

Equal income calculations for pension sharing within the Police Pension Scheme 1987

15–042 The practical consequences of some of the matters referred to above can be surprising in the context of an attempt by the court to leave the parties with an equal level of income at retirement after a pension sharing order. Particular care must be taken to identify what assumptions are going to be made as to the expected retirement date of the member spouse. This is best illustrated by a number of case studies.

Case study one

15–043 A Police Officer is age 40, having started his service at age 18 so that he has 22 years of reckonable service. He expects to retire from service on completion of 30 years of reckonable service in 8 years' time. His CE is £187,420. His wife is also age 40. The Officer should receive his pension immediately on his retirement in eight years' time. It is assumed that his wife will take her benefits at her age 60. The court decides that it is appropriate to calculate a pension sharing order so as to create equality of pension income at mutual age 60 based on those rights accrued to date. The appropriate Pension Sharing Order required is for 61.1 per cent. This will provide pension income of £10,330 per annum gross for both the Officer and the non-member spouse in today's terms at mutual age 60 and the officer will also receive the future accrual whilst remaining an active member of the scheme up to 30 years' service. In the period between the Officer's age 48 and age 60 the Officer will receive an income and the non-member spouse will receive no income. The Court would have to consider whether it is also appropriate to make periodical payments for this period.

Case study two

15–044 An Officer is age 44, having started his service at age 18 so that he has 26 years of reckonable service. He expects to retire from service on completion of 30 years of reckonable service in 4 years' time. His CE is £342,020. His wife is also age 44. It is assumed that the Officer's wife will take her benefits at her age 60. The court decides that it is appropriate to calculate a pension sharing order so as to create equality of pension income at mutual age 60 based on those rights accrued to date. The appropriate Pension Sharing Order required is for 39.9 per cent. This will provide pension income of £10,785 per annum gross for both the Officer and the non-member spouse in today's terms at mutual age 60 and the officer will also receive the future accrual whilst remaining an active member of the scheme up to 30 years' service. In the period between the Officer's age 48 and age 60 the Officer will receive an income and the non-member spouse will receive no income. The Court would have to consider whether it is also appropriate to make periodical payments for this period.

It can be seen from these illustrations that the assumption that a 50 per cent Pension Sharing Order will provide an equal level of income on retirement is, certainly in the context of the Police Pension Scheme 1987, a dangerous one. Indeed, counter-intuitively, there are cases where an 80 per cent Pension Sharing Order will produce equal level of incomes on retirement.

15–045

Miscellaneous other matters

There are a number of other matters which sometimes arise in relation to the Police Pension Scheme 1987 and of which practitioners ought to be aware.

15–046

There are a number of benefits payable to injured officers which are not subject to a pension sharing orders. These include benefits described as Injury pensions which are not part of the pension scheme.

An improvement to commutation factors in 2011 means that those retiring at ages 48 to 53 could find that if they commute the maximum lump sum, they will incur tax on a portion of the lump sum

The final report of the Independent Public Service Pensions Commission, published on March 10, 2011, the "Hutton Report", recommended that the uniformed services, including members of the armed forces, should be treated differently from other public servants for pension purposes, but recommended increasing the normal retirement age from 55 to 60.[10] It is proposed that the right to take accrued benefits unreduced on completion of thirty years' service will start to be phased out in respect of service after April 2015 for those who were not within 10 years' of retirement in April 2012. Thus joiners before April 1992 will retain the original benefit structure but those who joined after April 1992 but before April 2006 are likely to find a reduction, even if quite a small reduction, in their total pension if they retire after 30 years' service.

POLICE PENSION SCHEME 2008

Contact details

Administrators' Address	Each Force has its choice of administrator. Some use the central administrators such as Xafinity or Capita whereas others administer it in house.	15–047

Eligibility

This Scheme is for those who joined service on or after April 6, 2006.

15–048

Main features of the scheme

Benefits accrue during "reckonable service" which is in essence all service in the Police Pension Scheme from joining until retirement or completion of 35 years.

15–049

---

[10] See para.1.69 above.

THE SHORTER CAREER PUBLIC SECTOR PENSION SCHEMES

The scheme member will accrue benefits calculated by reference to a combination of length of "reckonable service" and "pensionable pay".

The retirement age is 65; however, the accrued pension will be payable immediately at age 55 if the member remains in service until that date.

The set up of the scheme is described so that one-seventieth of final pensionable salary for each year of service. Tax-free cash of four times the pension is payable in addition.

Officers who retire from the Force before age 55 will be eligible for a deferred benefit payable at age 65.

15–050 One half of the pension is payable to a spouse or civil partner on the death of the scheme member.

The scheme is contracted out of the Additional State Pension or State Second Pension. Accordingly, a member will not have any income at State Pension Age from the Additional State Pension or State Second Pension in respect of their period for service in the Police Pension Scheme.

Cash Equivalents

15–051 Cash Equivalents (CEs) of the member's rights in the scheme for pension sharing purposes will be calculated on the assumption that the member in service will leave service on the date of the calculation. This can have a significant distorting effect in the context of the Police Pension Scheme 2008.

This is best illustrated by an example. A calculation carried out for an officer at age 54 years and 364 days reckonable service will assume that his entitlements will be deferred to age 65. A calculation for the same officer just two days later, at age 55 years and 1 day, will assume that the pension is payable immediately. The resulting CE will be dramatically different. For example, if the member had joined at age 23, the CE at age 54 years and 364 days will be £202,310 and the CE at age 55 years and 1 day will be £326,290.

Accordingly CEs in cases involving the Police Pension Scheme 2008 need to be treated with particular care.

Pension sharing

15–052 When subjected to a pension sharing order, rights under the Police Pension Scheme 2008 provide only pension credits by way of internal transfer. The non-member spouse will accordingly receive rights within the scheme to the value of the pension credit.

Pension sharing charges made by Police Pension Scheme 2008 vary according to the administrator.

The rights accruing to a non-member spouse under a pension credit are calculated by reference to a retirement age of 65. This can lead to "Income Gap" issues. At the time of writing, the pension credit benefits cannot be taken early subject to actuarial reduction.

Equal income calculations for pension sharing within the Police Pension Scheme 2008

The practical consequences of some of the matters referred to above can be surprising in the context of an attempt by the court to leave the parties with an equal level of income at retirement after a pension sharing order. Particular care must be taken to identify what assumptions are going to be made as to the expected retirement date of the member spouse. This is best illustrated by a number of case studies.

15–053

Case study one

A Police Officer is age 50, having started his service at age 18 so that he has 32 years of reckonable service. He expects to retire from service at age 55 in 5 years' time. His CE is £181,470. His wife is also age 50. The Officer should receive his pension immediately on his retirement in five years' time. It is assumed that his wife will take her benefits at her age 65. The court decides that it is appropriate to calculate a pension sharing order so as to create equality of pension income at mutual age 65 based on those rights accrued to date. The appropriate Pension Sharing Order required is for 60.5 per cent. This will provide pension income of £9,480 per annum gross for both the Officer and his wife in today's terms at mutual age 65. The Officer will however receive the income as well between 55 and 65 and will also receive anything that they accrue in future.

15–054

It can be seen from these illustrations that the assumption that a 50 per cent Pension Sharing Order will provide an equal level of income on retirement is, certainly in the context of the Police Pension Scheme 2008, a dangerous one. Indeed, counter-intuitively, there are cases where an 80 per cent Pension Sharing Order will produce equal level of incomes on retirement.

15–055

Miscellaneous other matters

There are a number of other matters which sometimes arise in relation to the Police Pension Scheme 2008 and of which practitioners ought to be aware.

There are a number of benefits payable to injured officers which are not subject to a pension sharing orders. These include benefits described as Injury Pensions which are not part of the pension scheme.

15–056

FIREFIGHTERS' PENSION SCHEME

Contact details

Administrators' Address	Each Force has its choice of administrator. Some use the central administrators such as Capita whereas others administer it in house.

15–057

THE SHORTER CAREER PUBLIC SECTOR PENSION SCHEMES

Eligibility

15–058 All Members serving prior to April 6, 2006 were automatically enrolled in the Firefighters' Pension Scheme 1992; but Members commencing their service from April 6, 2006 onwards are not eligible for this scheme and they will instead join the New Firefighters' Pension Scheme.

Main features of the scheme

15–059 Benefits accrue during "reckonable service" which is in essence all service as a firefighter from age 18 onwards for a maximum of 30 years.

The scheme member will accrue benefits calculated by reference to a combination of length of "reckonable service" and "pensionable pay".

The set up of the scheme is described so that one-sixtieth of final pensionable salary accrues in the first 20 years and two-sixtieths in the final ten years. However in most cases, this is misleading. The potential accrual (usually forty-sixtieths) is calculated on joining and then the benefits are deemed to accrue evenly over the first 30 years of service. The only exception is where the member takes retirement benefits in their 50s with less than 30 years' service. This point is often the subject of mistakes.

15–060 Members who retire from the Fire Service after 30 years or more of reckonable service are eligible to receive their pension income straight away if they are 50 or over. Retirement at age 50 with a pension paid straight away at 66.67 per cent of final salary is therefore possible in many cases. When this occurs the amount received is not subject to inflationary increases until the recipient reaches the age of 55, at which time the amount received is enhanced by inflationary increases backdated to the time of the initial receipt of payments.

Members who retire from the Service after less than 25 years of reckonable service or before age 50 will be eligible for a deferred benefit payable at age 60.

Members who leave service with more than 25 years' service and over age 50 can receive immediate benefits but at less than the maximum accrual.

Benefits under Firefighters' Pension Scheme 1992 accrue as an amount of pension payable per annum. It is possible to take a lump sum at retirement by exchanging some of the pension for a lump sum ("Commutation").

15–061 One half of the pension before commutation is payable to a spouse or civil partner on the death of the scheme member.

The scheme is contracted out of the Additional State Pension or State Second Pension. Accordingly, a member will not have any income at State Pension Age from the Additional State Pension or State Second Pension in respect of their period of service in the Firefighters' Pension Scheme.

Cash Equivalents

15–062 Cash Equivalents (CEs) of the member's rights in the scheme for pension sharing purposes will be calculated on the assumption that the member in service will leave service on the date of the calculation. This can have a significant distorting effect in the context of the Firefighters' Pension Scheme 1992.

FIREFIGHTERS' PENSION SCHEME

This is best illustrated by an example. A calculation carried out for an officer with 24 years and 364 days reckonable service and age 49 years and 364 days will assume that his entitlements will be deferred to age 60. A calculation for the same officer just two days later, at 25 years and 1 day and age 50 years and 1 day, will assume that the pension is payable immediately. The resulting CE will be dramatically different. For example, the CE at 24 years and 364 days will be £291,840 and the CE at 25 years and 1 day will be £451,910.

Accordingly CEs in cases involving the Firefighters' Pension Scheme 1992 need to be treated with particular care.

Pension sharing

When subjected to a pension sharing order, rights under the Firefighters' Pension Scheme 1992 provide only pension credits by way of internal transfer. The non-member spouse will accordingly receive rights within the scheme to the value of the pension credit. 15–063

Pension sharing charges made by Firefighters' Pension Scheme 1992 vary according to the administrator.

The rights accruing to a non-member spouse under a pension credit are calculated by reference to a retirement age of 60. This can lead to "Income Gap" issues. At the time of writing, the pension credit benefits cannot be taken early subject to actuarial reduction.

Equal income calculations for pension sharing within the Firefighters' pension Scheme

The practical consequences of some of the matters referred to above can be surprising in the context of an attempt by the court to leave the parties with an equal level of income at retirement after a pension sharing order. Particular care must be taken to identify what assumptions are going to be made as to the expected retirement date of the member spouse. This is best illustrated by a number of case studies. 15–064

Case study one

A Fire Service Officer is age 44, having started his service at age 22 so that he has 22 years of reckonable service. He expects to retire from service on completion of 30 years of reckonable service in 8 years' time. His CE is £254,030. His wife is also age 44. The Officer should receive his pension immediately on his retirement in eight years' time. It is assumed that his wife will take her benefits at her age 60. The court decides that it is appropriate to calculate a pension sharing order so as to create equality of pension income at mutual age 60 based on those rights accrued to date. The appropriate Pension Sharing Order required is for 59.3 per cent. This will provide pension income of £11,920 per annum gross for both the Officer and his wife in today's terms at mutual age 60 and the Officer will also receive any rights accrued in future. In the period between the Officer's age 52 and his age 60 he will receive an income and his wife will receive no income.

15–065

Case study two

15-066

> An Officer is age 50, having started his service at age 22 so that he has 28 years of reckonable service. He expects to retire from service on completion of 30 years of reckonable service in 2 years' time. His CE is £485,210. His wife is also age 50. It is assumed that the Officer's wife will take her benefits at her age 60. The court decides that it is appropriate to calculate a pension sharing order so as to create equality of pension income at mutual age 60 based on those rights accrued to date. The appropriate Pension Sharing Order required is for 37.4 per cent. This will provide pension income of £12,110 per annum gross for both the Officer and his wife in today's terms at mutual age 60 and the Officer will also receive any rights accrued in future. However, the Officer will still receive a pension between age 52 and age 60.

15-067 It can be seen from these illustrations that the assumption that a 50 per cent Pension Sharing Order will provide an equal level of income on retirement is, certainly in the context of the Firefighters' Pension Scheme 1992, a dangerous one. Indeed, counter-intuitively, there are cases where an 80 per cent Pension Sharing Order will produce equal level of incomes on retirement.

Miscellaneous other matters

15-068 There are a number of other matters which sometimes arise in relation to the Firefighters' Pension Scheme 1992 and of which practitioners ought to be aware.

There are a number of benefits payable to injured Members which are not subject to a pension sharing orders. These include benefits described as Injury pensions which are not part of the pension scheme.

The final report of the Independent Public Service Pensions Commission, published on March 10, 2011, the "Hutton Report", recommended that the uniformed services, including members of the armed forces, should be treated differently from other public servants for pension purposes, but recommended increasing the normal retirement age from 55 to 60.[11]

FIREFIGHTERS' PENSION SCHEME 2006

Contact details

15-069

Administrators' Address	Each Force has its choice of administrator. Some use the central administrators such as Xafinity or Capita whereas others administer it in house.

Eligibility

15-070 This Scheme is for those who joined service on or after April 6, 2006.

---

[11] See para.1.69 above.

FIREFIGHTERS' PENSION SCHEME 2006

Main features of the scheme

Benefits accrue during "reckonable service" which is in essence all service in the Firefighters' Pension Scheme from joining until retirement or completion of 40 years. **15–071**

The scheme member will accrue benefits calculated by reference to a combination of length of "reckonable service" and "pensionable pay".

The retirement age is 65; however, the accrued pension will be payable immediately at age 60 without reduction if the member remains in service until that date.

The set up of the scheme is described so that one-sixtieth of final pensionable salary for each year of service. Tax-free cash is payable by reducing the pension payable.

Officers who retire from the Force before age 60 will be eligible for a deferred benefit payable at age 65. It is possible for them to take reduced benefits on retirement at 55 or unreduced benefits if the employer agrees that it is in the interests of the management of the service. **15–072**

One half of the pension before commutation is payable to a spouse or civil partner on the death of the scheme member.

The scheme is contracted out of the Additional State Pension or State Second Pension. Accordingly, a member will not have any income at State Pension Age from the Additional State Pension or State Second Pension in respect of their period of service in the Firefighters' Pension Scheme.

Cash Equivalents

Cash Equivalents (CEs) of the member's rights in the scheme for pension sharing purposes will be calculated on the assumption that the member in service will leave service on the date of the calculation. This can have a significant distorting effect in the context of the Firefighters' Pension Scheme 2006. **15–073**

This is best illustrated by an example. A calculation carried out for an officer at age 59 years and 364 days reckonable service will assume that his entitlements will be deferred to age 65. A calculation for the same officer just two days later, at age 60 years and 1 day, will assume that the pension is payable immediately. The resulting CE will be dramatically different. For example, the CE at age 59 years and 364 days will be £402,420 and the CE at age 60 years and 1 day will be £517,810.

Accordingly CEs in cases involving the Firefighters' Pension Scheme 2006 need to be treated with particular care.

Pension sharing

When subjected to a pension sharing order, rights under the Firefighters' Pension Scheme 2006 provide only pension credits by way of internal transfer. The non-member spouse will accordingly receive rights within the scheme to the value of the pension credit. **15–074**

Pension sharing charges made by Firefighters' Pension Scheme 2006 vary according to the administrator.

The rights accruing to a non-member spouse under a pension credit are calculated by reference to a retirement age of 65. This can lead to "Income Gap" issues. At the time of writing, the pension credit benefits cannot be taken early subject to actuarial reduction.

Equal income calculations for pension sharing within the Firefighters' Pension Scheme 2006

15–075 The practical consequences of some of the matters referred to above can be surprising in the context of an attempt by the court to leave the parties with an equal level of income at retirement after a pension sharing order. Particular care must be taken to identify what assumptions are going to be made as to the expected retirement date of the member spouse. This is best illustrated by a number of case studies.

Case study one

15–076
> A Firefighter is age 50, having started his service at age 18 so that he has 32 years of reckonable service. He expects to retire from service at age 60 in 10 years' time. His CE is £251,410. His wife is also age 50. The Officer should receive his pension immediately on his retirement in ten years' time. It is assumed that his wife will take her benefits at her age 65. The court decides that it is appropriate to calculate a pension sharing order so as to create equality of pension income at mutual age 65 based on those rights accrued to date. The appropriate Pension Sharing Order required is for 54.9 per cent. This will provide pension income of £11,915 per annum gross for both the Officer and his wife in today's terms at mutual age 65.

15–077 It can be seen from these illustrations that the assumption that a 50 per cent Pension Sharing Order will provide an equal level of income on retirement is, certainly in the context of the Firefighters' Pension Scheme 2006, a dangerous one. Indeed, counter-intuitively, there are cases where a 70 per cent Pension Sharing Order will produce equal level of incomes on retirement.

Miscellaneous other matters

15–078 There are a number of other matters which sometimes arise in relation to the Firefighters' Pension Scheme 2006 and of which practitioners ought to be aware.

There are a number of benefits payable to injured officers which are not subject to a pension sharing orders. These include benefits described as Injury pensions which are not part of the pension scheme.

CHAPTER 16

Some "Longer Career" Public Sector Schemes

LOCAL GOVERNMENT PENSION SCHEME

Contact Details

Administrators' Address	There are various administrators depending on where the member is employed.	16–001

Eligibility

There are many different sections of the Local Government Pension Scheme, most of which are with the various Councils. Employees of the relevant authority are eligible to join. The Local Authorities have sometimes offered membership to outside bodies; often local charities who can participate in the Scheme.

16–002

Main Features of the scheme

Benefits accrue during "reckonable service" which is in essence all service in the Local Government Pension Scheme from joining onwards for a maximum of 40 years up to age 60 although they can accrue up to 45 years if they work past age 60.

16–003

The scheme member will accrue benefits calculated by reference to a combination of length of "reckonable service" and "pensionable pay".

The retirement age is 65; however, older members who have sufficient service may be eligible to retire from age 60 with unreduced benefits.

Benefits accrued prior to April 1, 2008 accrue as one eightieth of final salary per annum for each year of service plus a tax-free cash lump sum of three times that pension; benefits accrued since that time accrue as a pension only but the accrual is one sixtieth of final salary per annum for each year of service.

Early retirement from age 55 is possible subject to actuarial reduction.

16–004

A pension is payable to a spouse or civil partner on the death of the scheme member provided the marriage or civil partnership took place prior to the scheme member leaving service. For service pre 2008, this is usually half of the pension and three eighths for service since that date.

The scheme is contracted out of the Additional State Pension or State Second Pension. Accordingly, a member who has been in the Scheme throughout their working life will not have any income at State Pension Age from the Additional State Pension or State Second Pension.

Cash Equivalents

16–005 Cash Equivalents (CEs) of the member's rights in the scheme for pension sharing purposes will be calculated on the assumption that the member in service will leave service on the date of the calculation.

There are circumstances where the member is able to take benefits at age 60 but the pension is not enhanced if the member works after age 60 and therefore this can lead to the cash equivalent being higher than the true value for an active member.

This would lead to the need for a Pension Sharing Order of a lower percentage than expected for a member in this position where you try to equate incomes assuming the parties work until and take benefits at age 65.

Pension sharing

16–006 When subjected to a pension sharing order, the Scheme will provide either pension credits by way of internal transfer payable at age 65 (with the option to take a reduced pension from age 60) or the external transfer to a provider of their choice.

Under the internal option, the pension credit benefits will have an automatic lump sum of three times the pension although that is expected to be removed at some stage in the future when the lump sum from the pension credit will be payable by commutation.

Pension sharing charges made by the Local Government Pension Scheme depend on the status of the member and on the administrator concerned.

Under the internal option, the rights accruing to a non-member spouse under a pension credit are calculated by reference to a retirement age of 65. The pension credit member is able to take benefits at age 60. These will be subjected to an actuarial reduction. The earlier the benefits are taken the larger the reduction.

Miscellaneous other matters

16–007 There are a number of benefits payable to members who retire early through ill health and these can be non shareable. Often there are redundancy enhancements and sometimes these are deemed to be non shareable.

TEACHERS' PENSION SCHEME (SECTION FOR MEMBERS IN SERVICE BEFORE JANUARY 1, 2007)

Contact Details

Administrators' Address	Teachers' Pensions, Capita Mowden Hall Darlington DL3 9EE
Contact Telephone Number	0845 606 6166
Website	*www.teacherspensions.co.uk*

16–008

Eligibility

There are now two types of members in the Teachers' Pension Scheme. If you were already a member of the Teachers' Pension Scheme on or before December 31, 2006, you have one set of benefits. Those who joined later have different benefits.

16–009

Main Features of the scheme

Benefits accrue during "reckonable service" which is in essence all service in the Teachers' Pension Scheme from joining until retirement or completion of 45 years.

16–010

The scheme member will accrue benefits calculated by reference to a combination of length of "reckonable service" and "pensionable pay".

The retirement age is 60; however, the accrued pension will not be actuarially enhanced if the member works on past 60 although they can accrue further benefits.

Benefits accrue as an amount of pension payable per annum plus a tax-free cash lump sum of three times that pension.

Early retirement from age 55 is possible subject to actuarial reduction.

16–011

One half of the accrued pension is payable to a spouse or civil partner on the death of the scheme member provided the marriage or civil partnership took place prior to the scheme member leaving service.

The scheme is contracted out of the Additional State Pension or State Second Pension. Accordingly, a member who has been in the Scheme throughout their working life will not have any income at State Pension Age from the Additional State Pension or State Second Pension.

Cash Equivalents

Cash Equivalents (CEs) of the member's rights in the scheme for pension sharing purposes will be calculated on the assumption that the member in service will leave service on the date of the calculation.

16–012

SOME "LONGER CAREER" PUBLIC SECTOR SCHEMES

There are no particular issues about the CE except that if a member remains in service after age 60, the CE is calculated based on immediate retirement.

Pension sharing

16–013 When subjected to a pension sharing order, rights under the Scheme only provide pension credits by way of internal transfer. The non-member spouse will accordingly accrue rights within the scheme to the value of the pension credit.

Pension sharing charges made by Teachers' Pension Scheme are currently £920 plus VAT for implementation.

The rights accruing to a non-member spouse under a pension credit are calculated by reference to a retirement age of 60. The pension credit member is able to take benefits at age 55. These will be subjected to an actuarial reduction. The earlier the benefits are taken the larger the reduction.

Miscellaneous other matters

16–014 There are a number of other matters which sometimes arise in relation to the Teachers' Pension Scheme and of which practitioners ought to be aware.

There are a number of benefits payable to members who retire early through ill health and these can be non shareable. Occasionally there are also redundancy enhancements and sometimes these are deemed to be non shareable.

NATIONAL HEALTH SERVICE PENSION SCHEME (1995 SECTION)

Contact Details

16–015

Administrators' Address	Hesketh House, 200-220 Broadway, Fleetwood Lancashire FY7 8LG
Contact Telephone Number	0845 421 4000
Website	www.nhspa.gov.uk

Eligibility

16–016 There are now two sections to the NHS Pension Scheme. Members serving in the NHS Pension Scheme prior to April 1, 2008 were automatically enrolled in the NHS Pension Scheme (1995 Section); but those commencing their service from April 1, 2008 onwards are not eligible for this Section and they will instead join the 2008 Section.

Members of the 1995 Section were given an opportunity to transfer to the 2008 Section and the opportunity was staggered between the different members

NHS PENSION SCHEME (1995 SECTION)

so that some pre-2008 members are not now members of the 1995 Section but the 2008 Section. Most pre 2008 members, however, will be members of the 1995 section.

In March 2012, proposals were released that members of this section would have their benefits changed so that from a date in the future the benefits would accrue with a retirement age of 65 and at a different rate of accrual. This would only happen for those more than 10 years from their retirement age and would be from April 2015 for those more than 13 years and 5 months from retirement age. For those between 10 years and 13 years 5 months from retirement age at April 2012, the date of change would be after April 2015 according to how far they are from retirement age.

Main Features of the scheme

Benefits accrue during "reckonable service" which is in essence all service in the NHS Pension Scheme from joining onwards for a maximum of 40 years up to age 60 although they can accrue up to 45 years if they work past age 60. **16–017**

The scheme member will accrue benefits calculated by reference to a combination of length of "reckonable service" and "pensionable pay".

The retirement age is 60; however, the accrued pension will not be actuarially enhanced if the member works on past 60 although they can accrue further benefits.

There are however, some roles that allow retirement at age 55 if the previous 5 years has been in that role. These are known as the "Special Classes".

Within the Special Classes there are a number of occupations that also accrue benefits at double the rate between 50 and 55.

However it should be noted that again, there is no actuarial enhancement if retirement is after age 55.

Benefits under 1995 Section accrue as an amount of pension payable per annum plus a tax-free cash lump sum of three times that pension up to the date of change as detailed in 16.4.4 and as pension only from that date. **16–018**

Early retirement from age 55 is possible subject to actuarial reduction if the member is not in a Special Class.

One half of the accrued pension is payable to a spouse or civil partner on the death of the scheme member provided the marriage or civil partnership took place prior to the scheme member leaving service.

The scheme is contracted out of the Additional State Pension or State Second Pension. Accordingly, a member who has worked in the NHS throughout their working life will not have any income at State Pension Age from the Additional State Pension or State Second Pension.

Cash Equivalents

Cash Equivalents (CEs) of the member's rights in the scheme for pension sharing purposes will be calculated on the assumption that the member in service will leave service on the date of the calculation. This can have a significant distorting effect if the member is a member of a Special Class, close to age 55 and intends **16–019** to retire at age 55. In addition, if the member is a member of a Special Class and is over age 55, then the calculation may assume immediate retirement.

This is best illustrated by examples. A calculation carried out for a member of a Special Class with 30 years reckonable service at age 54 years and 364 days will assume that his entitlements will be deferred to age 60. A calculation for the same member just two days later, at age 55 years and 1 day, will assume that they have immediate entitlements.

The resulting CE will be dramatically different. For example, if the member in this illustration is, at the date of the notional calculations a Mental Health Officer with a pensionable salary of £80,000 per annum then the CE at 54 years and 364 days will be £707,350 and the CE at 55 years and 1 day will be £885,700.

Accordingly CEs in cases involving Special Classes need to be treated with particular care.

Pension sharing

16–020 When subjected to a pension sharing order, rights under the 1995 Section provide only pension credits by way of internal transfer. The non-member spouse will accordingly accrue rights within the scheme to the value of the pension credit.

Pension sharing charges made by the NHS Pension Scheme are currently £2,904 for implementation and £126 (set up) and £49 per annum for paying the pension credit member's pension.

The rights accruing to a non-member spouse under a pension credit are calculated by reference to a retirement age of 60. The pension credit member is able to take benefits at age 55. These will be subjected to an actuarial reduction. The earlier the benefits are taken the larger the reduction.

Equal income calculations for pension sharing within the NHS Pension Scheme

16–021 The practical consequences for a member of a Special Class can be surprising in the context of an attempt by the court to leave the parties with an equal level of income at retirement after a pension sharing order. Particular care must be taken to identify what assumptions are going to be made as to the expected retirement date of the member spouse. This is best illustrated by two case studies.

Case Study One

16–022 A Mental Health Officer is age 53, having started his service at age 21 so that he has 32 actual years of reckonable service. He expects to retire from service on completion of 34 years of reckonable service in 2 years' time. His CE is £707,350. His wife is also age 53. The Officer should receive his pension immediately on his retirement in two years' time. It is assumed that his wife will take her benefits at her age 55. The court decides that it is appropriate to calculate a pension sharing order so as to create equality of pension income at mutual age 55 based on those rights accrued to date. The appropriate Pension Sharing Order required is for 54.2 per cent. This will provide pension income of £16,020 per annum gross for both the Officer and his wife in today's terms at mutual age 55.

Case Study Two

> A Doctor is age 53, having started his service at age 21 so that he has 32 actual years of reckonable service. He expects to retire from service on completion of 34 years of reckonable service in 2 years' time. His CE is £646,720. His wife is also age 53. The Doctor should receive his pension immediately on his retirement in two years' time. It is assumed that his wife will take her benefits at her age 55. The court decides that it is appropriate to calculate a pension sharing order so as to create equality of pension income at mutual age 55 based on those rights accrued to date. The appropriate Pension Sharing Order required is for 50.5 per cent. This will provide pension income of £13,640 per annum gross for both the Doctor and his wife in today's terms at mutual age 55.

16–023

Miscellaneous other matters

There are a number of other matters which sometimes arise in relation to the NHS Pension scheme and of which practitioners ought to be aware.

16–024

There are a number of benefits payable to members who retire early through ill health and these can be non shareable. Occasionally there are also redundancy enhancements and sometimes these are deemed to be non shareable.

The proposals are currently that those who at April 2012 were within 10 years' of retirement (so generally those aged 50 or over then, although age 45 for Special Classes) will retain their benefit structure, but those younger will have their pension age increased gradually for service after April 2015 so they will find a reduction in their benefits if they choose to retire at age 60.

NATIONAL HEALTH SERVICE PENSION SCHEME (2008 SECTION)

Contact Details

Administrators' Address	Hesketh House, 200-220 Broadway, Fleetwood Lancashire FY7 8LG
Contact Telephone Number	0845 421 4000
Website	www.nhspa.gov.uk

16–025

Eligibility

There are now two sections to the NHS Pension Scheme. If you were already a member of the NHS Pension Scheme on or before March 31, 2008, you are a member of what is called the 1995 Section (even if you joined before 1995). From April 1, 2008, new staff are only able to join the new 2008 section.

16–026

Members serving in the NHS Pension Scheme prior to April 1, 2008, were automatically enrolled in the NHS Pension Scheme (1995 Section); but those commencing their service from April 1, 2008 onwards are not eligible for this Section and they will instead join 2008 Section.

Members of the 1995 Section were given a once off opportunity to transfer to the 2008 Section and the opportunity was staggered between the different members so that some pre-2008 members are not now members of the 1995 Section but the 2008 Section. Most pre-2008 members, however, will be members of the 1995 section.

Main Features of the scheme

16–027 Benefits accrue during "reckonable service" which is in essence all service in the NHS Pension Scheme from joining onwards for a maximum of 40 years up to age 60 although they can accrue up to 45 years if they work past age 60.

The scheme member will accrue benefits calculated by reference to a combination of length of "reckonable service" and "pensionable pay".

The retirement age is 65.

Benefits under 2008 Section accrue as an amount of pension payable per annum; a tax-free cash lump sum is only available by reducing the pension.

Early retirement from age 55 is possible subject to actuarial reduction.

16–028 A pension is payable to a spouse or civil partner on the death of the scheme member provided the marriage or civil partnership took place prior to the scheme member leaving service.

The scheme is contracted out of the Additional State Pension or State Second Pension. Accordingly, a member who has worked in the NHS throughout their working life will not have any income at State Pension Age from the Additional State Pension or State Second Pension.

Cash Equivalents

16–029 Cash Equivalents (CEs) of the member's rights in the scheme for pension sharing purposes will be calculated on the assumption that the member in service will leave service on the date of the calculation.

There are no issues with this in this Scheme.

Pension sharing

16–030 When subjected to a pension sharing order, rights under the 2008 Section provide only pension credits by way of internal transfer. The non-member spouse will accordingly accrue rights within the scheme to the value of the pension credit.

Pension sharing charges made by NHS Pension Scheme are currently £2,904 for implementation and £126 (set up) and £49 per annum for paying the pension credit member's pension.

The rights accruing to a non-member spouse under a pension credit are calculated by reference to a retirement age of 65. The pension credit member is able to take benefits at age 55. These will be subjected to an actuarial reduction. The earlier the benefits are taken the larger the reduction.

Miscellaneous other matters

There are a number of other matters which sometimes arise in relation to the NHS Pension scheme and of which practitioners ought to be aware.   16–031

There are a number of benefits payable to members who retire early through ill health and these can be non shareable. Occasionally there are also redundancy enhancements and sometimes these are deemed to be non shareable.

PRINCIPAL CIVIL SERVICE PENSION SCHEME (CLASSIC PLUS SECTION)

Contact Details

Administrators' Address	There are various administrators depending on where the member is employed.	16–032
Website	*www.civilservice.gov.uk*	

Eligibility

There are now five sections to the Principal Civil Service Pension Scheme. Those who had joined the Principal Civil Service Pension Scheme on or before September 30, 2002 were a member of what is called the Classic Section. From October 1, 2002, new staff were only able to join one of three other sections.   16–033

Members serving in the Principal Civil Service Pension Scheme on October 1, 2002, had been automatically enrolled in the Principal Civil Service Pension Scheme—Classic Section; but those continuing their service from October 1, 2002 onwards were not eligible for this Section.

Members of the Classic Section were given a once off opportunity to transfer to this section whereby they retained their accrued rights in the classic Section but accrued future rights in the Premium Section and their benefits were a combination of the two.

Main Features of the scheme

Benefits accrue during "reckonable service" which is in essence all service in the Principal Civil Service Pension Scheme from joining onwards for a maximum of 40 years up to age 60 although they can accrue up to 45 years if they work past age 60.   16–034

The scheme member will accrue benefits calculated by reference to a combination of length of "reckonable service" and "pensionable pay".

The retirement age is 60; however, the accrued pension will not be actuarially enhanced if the member works on past 60 although they can accrue further benefits.

Benefits under Classic Section accrued as an amount of pension payable per annum plus a tax-free cash lump sum of three times that pension; benefits under   16–035 the premium section accrued as a pension only but accrual is at a higher rate of one sixtieth of the final pensionable salary.

Early retirement from age 55 is possible subject to actuarial reduction.

A pension is payable to a spouse or civil partner on the death of the scheme member provided the marriage or civil partnership took place prior to the scheme member leaving service.

The scheme is contracted out of the Additional State Pension or State Second Pension. Accordingly, a member who has been in the Scheme throughout their working life will not have any income at State Pension Age from the Additional State Pension or State Second Pension.

Cash Equivalents

16–036   Cash Equivalents (CEs) of the member's rights in the scheme for pension sharing purposes will be calculated on the assumption that the member in service will leave service on the date of the calculation.

Pension sharing

16–037   When subjected to a pension sharing order, rights under the Classic Plus Section provide only pension credits by way of internal transfer. The non-member spouse will accordingly accrue rights within the scheme to the value of the pension credit.

The pension credit benefits will have an automatic lump sum in the same proportion to the pension as the member's benefits. This is variable as it depends on the relative periods of service in the two parts of the scheme.

Pension sharing charges made by the Principal Civil Service Pension Scheme depend on the status of the member.

The rights accruing to a non-member spouse under a pension credit are calculated by reference to a retirement age of 60. The pension credit member is able to take benefits at age 55. These will be subjected to an actuarial reduction. The earlier the benefits are taken the larger the reduction.

Miscellaneous other matters

16–038   There are a number of other matters which sometimes arise in relation to the Principal Civil Service Pension Scheme and of which practitioners ought to be aware.

There are a number of benefits payable to members who retire early through ill health and these can be non shareable. Occasionally there are also redundancy enhancements and sometimes these are deemed to be non shareable.

There are circumstances where the member is made redundant and receives the lump sum before 60 but the pension is deferred to age 60 with compensation paid in the meantime so they have a deferred pension but no lump sum.

PRINCIPAL CIVIL SERVICE PENSION SCHEME (CLASSIC SECTION)

Contact Details

Administrators' Address	There are various administrators depending on where the member is employed.	16–039
Website	*www.civilservice.gov.uk*	

Eligibility

There are now five sections to the Principal Civil Service Pension Scheme. Those who had joined the Principal Civil Service Pension Scheme on or before September 30, 2002 were a member of what is called the Classic Section. From October 1, 2002, new staff were only able to join one of three other sections. 16–040

Members serving in the Principal Civil Service Pension Scheme on October 1, 2002, had been automatically enrolled in the Principal Civil Service Pension Scheme–Classic Section; but those continuing their service from October 1, 2002 had the option to transfer to another Scheme if they chose to.

Main Features of the scheme

Benefits accrue during "reckonable service" which is in essence all service in the Principal Civil Service Pension Scheme from joining onwards for a maximum of 40 years up to age 60 although they can accrue up to 45 years if they work past age 60. 16–041

The scheme member will accrue benefits calculated by reference to a combination of length of "reckonable service" and "pensionable pay".

The retirement age is 60; however, the accrued pension will not be actuarially enhanced if the member works on past 60 although they can accrue further benefits.

Benefits under Classic Section accrued as an amount of pension payable per annum calculated as one eightieth of final pensionable pay for each year of service plus a tax-free cash lump sum of three times that pension.

Early retirement from age 55 is possible subject to actuarial reduction if the member is eligible to retire at leaving on an unreduced pension.

A pension of one half of the member's pension is payable to a spouse or civil partner on the death of the scheme member provided the marriage or civil partnership took place prior to the scheme member leaving service. 16–042

Certain types of members, with long service, have better benefits. Prison Officers who have been in service long enough accrue benefits at double rate between 50 and 55 and then can retire immediately on an unreduced pension. If they do this and take the lump sum, they can re-commence service and continue to accrue pension and lump sum at double rate for a further two and a half years.

Historically, certain overseas postings, particularly for diplomats also accrued pension at double or one and a half times the normal rates.

SOME "LONGER CAREER" PUBLIC SECTOR SCHEMES

The scheme is contracted out of the Additional State Pension or State Second Pension. Accordingly, a member who has been in the Scheme throughout their working life will not have any income at State Pension Age from the Additional State Pension or State Second Pension.

Cash Equivalents

16–043 Cash Equivalents (CEs) of the member's rights in the scheme for pension sharing purposes will be calculated on the assumption that the member in service will leave service on the date of the calculation. This can have a significant distorting effect if the member is a Prison Officer, close to age 55 and intends to retire at age 55. In addition, if the member is a Prison Officer and is over age 55, then the calculation may assume immediate retirement.

This is best illustrated by examples. A calculation carried out for a Prison Officer with 30 years reckonable service at age 54 years and 364 days will assume that his entitlements will be deferred to age 60. A calculation for the same member just two days later, at age 55 years and 1 day, will assume that they have immediate entitlements.

The resulting CE will be dramatically different. For example, if the member in this illustration is, at the date of the notional calculations a Prison Officer with a pensionable salary of £40,000 per annum then the CE at 54 years and 364 days will be £775,800 and the CE at 55 years and 1 day will be £1,012,200.

Accordingly CEs in cases involving Prison Officers who have been serving a long time need to be treated with particular care.

Pension sharing

16–044 When subjected to a pension sharing order, rights under the Classic Section provide only pension credits by way of internal transfer. The non-member spouse will accordingly accrue rights within the scheme to the value of the pension credit.

The pension credit benefits will have an automatic lump sum of three times the pension.

Pension sharing charges made by the Principal Civil Service Pension Scheme depend on the status of the member.

The rights accruing to a non-member spouse under a pension credit are calculated by reference to a retirement age of 60. The pension credit member is able to take benefits at age 55. These will be subjected to an actuarial reduction. The earlier the benefits are taken the larger the reduction.

Equal income calculations for pension sharing within the Principal Civil Service Pension Scheme

16–045 The practical consequences for a Prison Officer can be surprising in the context of an attempt by the court to leave the parties with an equal level of income at retirement after a pension sharing order. Particular care must be taken to identify what assumptions are going to be made as to the expected retirement date of the member spouse. This is best illustrated by a case study.

Case Study One

A Prison Officer is age 53, having started his service at age 21 so that he has 32 actual years of reckonable service. He expects to retire from service on completion of 34 years of reckonable service in 2 years' time. His CE is £330,000. His wife is also age 53. The Officer should receive his pension immediately on his retirement in two years' time. It is assumed that his wife will take her benefits at her age 55. The court decides that it is appropriate to calculate a pension sharing order so as to create equality of pension income at mutual age 55 based on those rights accrued to the present date. The appropriate Pension Sharing Order required is for 56 per cent. This will provide pension income of £7,750 per annum gross for both the Officer and his wife in today's terms at mutual age 55.	16–046

Miscellaneous other matters

There are a number of other matters which sometimes arise in relation to the Principal Civil Service Pension Scheme and of which practitioners ought to be aware.   16–047

There are a number of benefits payable to members who retire early through ill health and these can be non shareable. Occasionally there are also redundancy enhancements and sometimes these are deemed to be non shareable.

There are circumstances where the member is made redundant and receives the lump sum before 60 but the pension is deferred to age 60 with compensation paid in the meantime so they have a deferred pension but no lump sum.

The benefits for Prison Officers can be unusual as they may have already taken the lump sum but still be in service.

PRINCIPAL CIVIL SERVICE PENSION SCHEME (NUVOS SECTION)

Contact Details

Administrators' Address	There are various administrators depending on where the member is employed.	16–048
Website	*www.civilservice.gov.uk*	

Eligibility

There are now five sections to the Principal Civil Service Pension Scheme. The Nuvos Section was introduced from July 30, 2007.   16–049

Main Features of the scheme

Benefits accrue during "reckonable service" which is in essence all service in the Principal Civil Service Pension Scheme from joining.   16–050

SOME "LONGER CAREER" PUBLIC SECTOR SCHEMES

16–051 The scheme is a Career Average Revalued Earnings Scheme. Members will accrue benefits at 2.3 per cent of pensionable salary each year and this will be revalued each year with the inflation index.

The retirement age is 65.

Benefits under Nuvos Section accrue as an amount of pension payable per annum with the option to commute some of the pension for a tax-free cash lump sum at retirement.

Early retirement from age 55 is possible subject to actuarial reduction if the member is eligible to retire at leaving on an unreduced pension.

A proportion of the accrued pension is payable to a spouse or civil partner on the death of the scheme member provided the marriage or civil partnership took place prior to the scheme member leaving service.

The scheme is contracted out of the Additional State Pension or State Second Pension. Accordingly, a member who has been in the Scheme throughout their working life will not have any income at State Pension Age from the Additional State Pension or State Second Pension.

Cash Equivalents

16–052 Cash Equivalents (CEs) of the member's rights in the scheme for pension sharing purposes will be calculated on the assumption that the member in service will leave service on the date of the calculation.

Pension sharing

16–053 When subjected to a pension sharing order, rights under the Nuvos Section provide only pension credits by way of internal transfer. The non-member spouse will accordingly accrue rights within the scheme to the value of the pension credit.

Pension sharing charges made by Principal Civil Service Pension Scheme depend on the status of the member.

The rights accruing to a non-member spouse under a pension credit are calculated by reference to a retirement age of 65. The pension credit member is able to take benefits at age 55. These will be subjected to an actuarial reduction. The earlier the benefits are taken the larger the reduction.

PRINCIPAL CIVIL SERVICE PENSION SCHEME (PREMIUM SECTION)

Contact Details

16–054

Administrators' Address	There are various administrators depending on where the member is employed.
Website	www.civilservice.gov.uk

PRINCIPAL CIVIL SERVICE (PREMIUM)

Eligibility

There are now five sections to the Principal Civil Service Pension Scheme (Classic, Classic Plus, Premium, Nuvos and Partnership). Those who had joined the Principal Civil Service Pension Scheme on or before September 30, 2002 were a member of what is called the Classic Section. From October 1, 2002 new staff were only able to join one of the last three mentioned sections.   16–055

Main Features of the scheme

Benefits accrue during "reckonable service" which is in essence all service in the Principal Civil Service Pension Scheme from joining onwards for a maximum of 40 years up to age 60 although they can accrue up to 45 years if they work past age 60.   16–056

The scheme member will accrue benefits calculated by reference to a combination of length of "reckonable service" and "pensionable pay".

The retirement age is 60; however, the accrued pension will not be actuarially enhanced if the member works on past 60 although they can accrue further benefits.

Benefits under the Premium Section accrue as an amount of pension payable per annum with the option to commute some of the pension for a tax-free cash lump sum at retirement.

Early retirement from age 55 is possible but will be subject to actuarial reduction unless the member is eligible to retire at leaving on an unreduced pension.   16–057

Three-eighths of the accrued pension is payable to a spouse or civil partner on the death of the scheme member provided the marriage or civil partnership took place prior to the scheme member leaving service.

The scheme is contracted out of the Additional State Pension or State Second Pension. Accordingly, a member who has been in the Scheme throughout their working life will not have any income at State Pension Age from the Additional State Pension or State Second Pension.

Cash Equivalents

Cash Equivalents (CEs) of the member's rights in the scheme for pension sharing purposes will be calculated on the assumption that the member in service will leave service on the date of the calculation.   16–058

Pension sharing

When subjected to a pension sharing order, rights under the Premium Section provide only pension credits by way of internal transfer. The non-member spouse will accordingly accrue rights within the scheme to the value of the pension credit.   16–059

Pension sharing charges made by Principal Civil Service Pension Scheme depend on the status of the member.

SOME "LONGER CAREER" PUBLIC SECTOR SCHEMES

The rights accruing to a non-member spouse under a pension credit are calculated by reference to a retirement age of 60. The pension credit member is able to take benefits at age 55. These will be subjected to an actuarial reduction. The earlier the benefits are taken the larger the reduction.

Miscellaneous other matters

16–060   There are a number of other matters which sometimes arise in relation to the Principal Civil Service Pension Scheme and of which practitioners ought to be aware.

There are a number of benefits payable to members who retire early through ill health and these can be non shareable. Occasionally there are also redundancy enhancements and sometimes these are deemed to be non shareable.

There are circumstances where the member is made redundant and receives the lump sum before 60 but the pension is deferred to age 60 with compensation paid in the meantime so they have a deferred pension but no lump sum.

CHAPTER 17

Some Private Sector Schemes

BRITISH AIRWAYS PENSION SCHEMES—AIRWAYS PENSION SCHEME

Contact Details

Administrators' Address	British Airways Pension Services Limited Whitelocke House 2–4 Lampton Road Hounslow Middlesex TW3 1HU	17–001
Contact Telephone Number	020 8538 2100	
Contact E-mail address	enquiries@bapensions.co.uk	
Website	*www.mybapension.com*	

Eligibility

Airways Pension Scheme (APS) was introduced in 1948 and closed on April 1, 1984 when the New Airways Pension Scheme (NAPS) was introduced. It is closed to new entrants since that date. 17–002

There are two separate defined benefit schemes, Airways Pension Scheme and New Airways Pension Scheme. The Airways Pension Scheme has 30,000 members, most of who are retired whilst the New Airways Pension Scheme has 70,000 of who approximately one half are current employees.

British Airways has not ruled out closing its final salary pension scheme to 100,000 existing members. Members joining since April 1, 2003 have joined the British Airways Money Purchase Scheme.

Main features of the scheme

This is a contributory final salary scheme arrangement. For Ground Staff, the benefits accrue as one fifty-sixths of final salary for each year of service and for Flying Staff, the benefits accrue at one fifty-second for each year of service. 17–003

Ground Staff pay contributions of 7.25 per cent of salary and Flying Staff 8.5 per cent of salary. Members can choose to pay 1.5 per cent less contributions and they will forfeit the Adult Dependant's pension.

SOME PRIVATE SECTOR SCHEMES

The scheme member will accrue benefits calculated by reference to a combination of length of service and pensionable salary of the member.

Before October 1, 2010 Active Members had the option to increase their pension build up rate for future service by paying higher contribution rates. Flexible pension build up is no longer available and any Active Members who had elected faster build up rates reverted back to standard pension build up (one fifty-sixths for Ground Staff or one fifty-second for Flying Staff) for service from October 1, 2010. The faster build up rates that were available until October 1, 2010 were:

- Ground Staff: one fifty-second or one fourty-ninth.
- Flying Staff: one fourty-eighth or one fourty-fifth.

17–004 In addition, an active member will receive life cover of three times final salary.

Retirement age is age 60 for Ground Staff and 55 for Flying Staff, unless otherwise stated in the member's contract of employment.

In fact any of these benefits can be taken from age 55, but these will be subjected to an actuarial reduction. The earlier the benefits are taken the larger the reduction.

The pension increases in line with CPI up to 5 per cent per annum in payment.

The standard pension package includes a pension for a spouse, Civil Partner or partner when you die. Members can choose to pay 1.5 per cent less than each of the contribution rates and opt-out of paying for this cover. If a member decides not to have Adult Survivor's Pension cover, they may still be entitled to a minimum amount required to be given by legislation.

17–005 If there is no Adult Survivor's Pension payable because the member is single at the date of death an additional lump sum will be payable equal to the member's own contributions to the Scheme, plus interest.

The Adult Survivor's pension is two-thirds of the member's pension and additionally for one child, a pension of one-sixth of your pension; for two children one-sixth of your pension each. If there are more, then generally a total of one-third of your pension divided between each eligible child.

The scheme is contracted out of the Additional State Pension or State Second Pension. Accordingly, a member who has been in the Scheme throughout his working life will not have any Additional State Pension or State Second Pension.

Cash Equivalents

17–006 Cash Equivalents (CEs) of the member's rights in the scheme for pension sharing purposes will be calculated on the assumption that the member in service will leave service on the date of the calculation. There are no issues with the calculations.

Pension sharing

17–007 When subjected to a pension sharing order, rights under the BA Pension Scheme provide pension credits only by way of external transfer. The non-member spouse will accordingly have to set up a personal arrangement to accept the credit.

The standard minimum charges applied in all cases are (2012):

- current member or member with a deferred pension: £1,350.00 plus VAT;
- retirement member with pension in payment: £1,600.00 plus VAT.

Miscellaneous

The Schemes have a large deficit. In March 2009, this was £3.7 billion, although reduced when increases to pensions in payment were reduced to be based on CPI.   17–008

BRITISH AIRWAYS PENSION SCHEMES—NEW AIRWAYS PENSION SCHEME

Contact Details

Administrators' Address	British Airways Pension Services Limited Whitelocke House 2–4 Lampton Road Hounslow Middlesex TW3 1HU
Contact Telephone Number	020 8538 2100
Contact E-mail address	enquiries@bapensions.co.uk
Website	*www.mybapension.com*

17–009

Eligibility

Staff who joined British Airways before April 1, 1984 became members of the Airways Pension Scheme (APS). Those who joined between April 1, 1984 and April 1, 2003 became members of the New Airways Pension Scheme (NAPS). The Schemes are closed to new entrants since that date. Members joining since April 1, 2003 have joined the British Airways Money Purchase Scheme.   17–010

There are two separate schemes, Airways Pension Scheme and New Airways Pension Scheme. The Airways Pension Scheme has 30,000 members, most of who are retired whilst the New Airways Pension Scheme has 70,000 members of whom approximately one half are current employees.

British Airways has not ruled out closing its final salary pension scheme to 100,000 existing members.

Main features of the scheme

This is a contributory final salary scheme arrangement. Accrual has varied throughout the life of the Plan.   17–011

In respect of service to April 1, 2007, then for Ground Staff, the benefits accrued as one fifty-sixth of final salary for each year of service with a retirement age of 60 and for Flying Staff, the benefits accrued at one fifty-second for each year of service with a retirement age of 55.

Between April 1, 2007 and September 30, 2010, pension built up with an accrual rate of one sixtieth and then from that date, pension built up with an accrual rate of one seventy-fifth payable at a retirement age of 65.

Despite the different retirement ages, all of the benefits have to be paid at the same date and benefits taken after the retirement age are enhanced for late payment and if taken before retirement age, they are reduced for early payment.

The standard pension arrangement in the Scheme is now called Plan 65 (named after the arrangement's current Normal Retirement Age). It is possible to increase the build up rate of Scheme benefit by paying higher contribution rates. Currently, there is a yearly opportunity, on October 1, to review the build up rate of future pension benefits from that date onwards:

Plan 65—increasing the build up rate

17–012 Instead of the standard one seventy-fifth build up rate the member can choose a build up rate of one sixty-seventh or one sixtieth.

In addition, prior to October 1, 2010, Active Members had the opportunity to pay higher contributions to accrue a pension at the build up rate of one fifty-sixth or one fifty-second.

It is also possible to build benefits with a Retirement Age of 60; this is called Plan 60. The standard Plan 60 formula is the same as that shown above except the date the pension becomes payable in full is age 60 instead of age 65. As in Plan 65 a reduced pension can be taken before age 60.

Just like in Plan 65, members can also choose to pay extra contributions within Plan 60 to increase the rate that the pension builds up each year. Instead of the standard one seventy-fifth build up rate members can choose a build up rate of one sixty-seventh or one-sixtieth.

Alternatively, if they are eligible members can choose to pay no contributions and reduce the rate at which your pension builds up each year to one one-hundred and thirty.

Those who joined Plan 60 and elected (before July 1, 2009) to pay higher contributions to allow future pension not to be reduced for early payment at age 55 (known as Option 55) are paying the extra contributions to buy-out the reduction which is usually applied when benefits are paid early. Option 55 operates on special discretionary terms laid down by the Company.

17–013 There is currently a yearly opportunity, on October 1, to review the build up rate of future pension benefits from that date onwards. There is also currently a yearly opportunity to reduce contributions by moving back to Plan 60. Option 55 is closed to new joiners, so those who are not already an Option 55 Member are no longer able to elect to become one. Similarly, an Option 55 Member who decides to move back to Plan 60 will not have another opportunity to become an Option 55 Member from a future date.

Some Active Members may anticipate receiving a step up in their pension value, following promotion for example, and may therefore be caught by the

Annual Allowance (AA) in that year. To assist those Active Members to manage any potential Annual Allowance tax charge the Company has introduced a lower pension build up rate.

The lower build up rate is available to Active Members whose Pensionable Pay is £60,000 a year or more. The lower build up rate is funded only by employer contributions meaning that members pay a zero rate of contribution whilst on the lower build up rate. The initial lower build up rate has been set at one one-hundred and thirtieth of pensionable pay for each future year of service in NAPS. The build up rate will be subject to review following future Scheme valuations and adjustments to the current level of employer pension contributions. The effective date of this option is initially April 1, 2012. Thereafter the option will be included alongside the range of NAPS pension options on October 1 each year.

To ensure that the Scheme can maintain its contracted-out status, which requires an individual's pension to build up at a minimum level each year, the lower build up rate can only be made available to members whose Pensionable Pay is £60,000 a year or more. To be eligible to switch to the lower build up rate, the Pensionable Pay must be, and remain above, £60,000. 17–014

Whilst a member may choose to move from Plan 65 to Plan 60, currently on October 1 of any year, they cannot move back to Plan 65 once they have moved to Plan 60. 17–015

Members need to consider carefully their retirement age as if they opt for benefits payable at an earlier age and then do not retire at that time, they have paid for a benefit they will not receive. This is a significant issue in divorce cases as their intentions may change as a result of the divorce.

The contributions payable from October 1, 2011 are:

	Plan 65	Plan 60
standard pension build up (1/75)	5.25%	8.50%
faster pension build up (1/67)	7.50%	10.75%
fastest pension build up (1/60)	9.75%	13.00%
slower accrual option (1/130)	0.00%	0.00%

17–016

Option 55

standard pension build up (1/75)	17.50%
faster pension build up (1/67)	19.75%
fastest pension build up (1/60)	22.00%

17–017

Since all options other than the standard arrangement are at the Company's discretion, the contribution levels quoted are correct as at April 2012 but are subject to future review and may potentially change. 17–018

The standard pension package includes a pension for a spouse, Civil Partner or partner when you die. Members can choose to pay 1.5 per cent less than each of the contribution rates and opt-out of paying for this cover. If a member decides not to have Adult Survivor's Pension cover, they may still be entitled to a minimum amount required to be given by legislation.

In addition, an active member will receive life cover of three times final salary on death in service. If there is no Adult Survivor's Pension payable because the member is single at the date of death an additional lump sum will be payable equal to the member's own contributions to the Scheme, plus interest.

The Adult Survivor's pension is two-thirds of the member's pension and additionally for one child, a pension of one-sixth of your pension; for two children one-sixth of your pension each. If there are more than generally a total of one-third of your pension divided between each eligible child.

The pension increases in line with CPI up to 5 per cent per annum in payment.

The scheme is contracted out of the Additional State Pension or State Second Pension. Accordingly, a member who has been in the Scheme throughout his working life will not have any Additional State Pension or State Second Pension.

Cash Equivalents

17–019 Cash Equivalents (CEs) of the member's rights in the scheme for pension sharing purposes will be calculated on the assumption that the member in service will leave service on the date of the calculation. There are no issues with the calculations.

Pension sharing

17–020 When subjected to a pension sharing order, rights under the BP Pension Scheme provide pension credits only by way of external transfer. The non-member spouse will accordingly have to set up a personal arrangement to accept the credit.

The standard minimum charges applied in all cases are (2012):

- current member or member with a deferred pension: £1,350 plus VAT;
- retirement member with pension in payment: £1,600 plus VAT.

Miscellaneous

17–021 The Schemes have a large deficit. In March 2009, this was £3.7billion, although reduced when increases to pensions in payment were reduced to be based on CPI.

BP PENSION SCHEME—FINAL SALARY SECTION

Contact Details

17–022

Administrators' Address	Chertsey Road Sunbury-on-Thames Middlesex TW16 7LN
Contact Telephone Number	BP Pension Fund: +44 (0) 845 602 1063 Burmah Castrol Pension Fund: +44 (0) 845 600 0295
Contact E-mail address	pensionlineuk@bp.com

BT – FINAL SALARY SECTION

Website	https://pensionline.bp.com

Eligibility

BP closed the final salary pension scheme to new entrants from April 2010 in an attempt to curb the growing cost of providing for its employees' retirement. Those already in the Scheme can continue to accrue benefits.

17–023

The Scheme has 69,000 members, of whom 39,000 are drawing their pensions, with another 18,000 who have left the company but have yet to start claiming any payout. The remainder, approximately three-quarters of BP's 16,000-strong workforce in the UK, are current employees.

The new defined contribution scheme will allow employees to pay between 5 per cent and 15 per cent of their base salary into their pension pot.

Main features of the scheme

This is a non-contributory final salary scheme arrangement within the BP Pension Scheme. It provides an annual pension based on one-sixtieth (1.66 per cent) of final salary for each year of pensionable service.

17–024

The scheme member will accrue benefits calculated by reference to a combination of length of service and pensionable salary of the member.

The scheme offers employees the option to accrue benefits at a faster rate if they are prepared to contribute. The figures below show the accrual rate and the contribution rate expressed as a percentage of basic salary.

Accrual rate	Contribution rate
60ths	0%
54ths	2%
51sts	3%
45ths	5%
40ths	10%
35ths	15%

17–025

In addition, an active member will receive life cover of three times final salary.

17–026

Retirement age is age 65, unless otherwise stated in the member's contract of employment.

In fact any of these benefits can be taken from age 55, but these will be subjected to an actuarial reduction. The earlier the benefits are taken the larger the reduction.

The pension increases in line with RPI up to 5 per cent per annum in payment and no change has been made to move it in line with CPI.

On death in service, a lump sum death benefit of three times annual salary will be paid (four times if at death the member is on one of the contributory options). If you leave a spouse/civil partner or dependant(s), a survivor's pension and/or children's pension will usually be payable as well.

17–027

SOME PRIVATE SECTOR SCHEMES

Approximately one half of the pension is payable to a spouse or civil partner on the death of the scheme member.

The scheme is contracted out of the Additional State Pension or State Second Pension. Accordingly, a member who has been in the Scheme throughout his working life will not have any Additional State Pension or State Second Pension.

Cash Equivalents

17–028　Cash Equivalents (CEs) of the member's rights in the scheme for pension sharing purposes will be calculated on the assumption that the member in service will leave service on the date of the calculation. There are no issues with the calculations.

Pension sharing

17–029　When subjected to a pension sharing order, rights under the BP Pension Scheme provide pension credits only by way of external transfer. The non-member spouse will accordingly have to set up a personal arrangement to accept the credit.

Pension sharing charges made by BP Pension Scheme are currently £1,760 (2012).

Miscellaneous

17–030　Unusually, the Scheme is currently in surplus.

BRITISH TELECOM PENSION SCHEMES—DEFINED BENEFIT SECTIONS

Contact Details

17–031

Administrators' Address	Administrators for the BTPS Accenture HR Services Ltd Venture House Venture Way Chesterfield S41 8NR
Contact Telephone Number	0800 731 4747
Contact E-mail address	Peopleline.pensions@accenture.com
Website	www.btpensions.net

Eligibility

17–032　There are three Sections for defined benefits. Section A is for members who were eligible to join before December 1, 1971. Section B is for members who last joined the Scheme between December 1, 1971 and March 31, 1986 (or Section A or B members who left BT and subsequently rejoined after March 31, 1986).

BT – DEFINED BENEFIT SECTIONS

Section C is for members who last joined the Scheme on or from April 1, 1986 but before the Scheme closed on March 31, 2001.

All sections are closed to new entrants.

Main features of the scheme

In Section A, benefits accrue as one eightieth of (94 per cent of final salary) for each year of service plus an additional tax-free cash lump sum of three times the pension.

17–033

In Section B, the pension benefit accrues at different rates for benefits before and after April 1, 2009. Benefits accrue as one eightieth of final salary for each year of service plus an additional tax-free cash lump sum of three times the pension. Pension benefits built up from April 1, 2009 will be on a Career Average Revalued Earnings (CARE) basis. For each year of Pensionable Service from April 1, 2009 the member builds up a block of pension equal to one eightieth of Pensionable Salary, plus a lump sum of three times that pension, payable at Normal Pension Age of 65. At the end of the following year and annually thereafter, each block is increased up to retirement, or leaving the BTPS if earlier, by the lower of:

- the change in the Retail Prices Index (RPI) (but never below zero); and
- any change in Pensionable Salary.

If there is no change in Pensionable Salary, the CARE blocks earned during previous years would not be revalued for that particular year. The blocks will all be added together to give a total CARE pension and lump sum.

As service from April 6, 2009 (or the date a Section A member elected to be subject to Section B terms) is not contracted out of the State Second Pension (S2P), there will be a S2P (State Second Pension) from the State for that period in addition to the BTPS pension. To allow for this, the BTPS pension will be reduced by the S2P pension accrued for that period.

In Section C, The pension built up before April 1, 2009 will build up at one sixtieth of final salary for each year of service. Pension benefits built up from April 1, 2009 will be on a Career Average Revalued Earnings (CARE) basis and will based on the value of the pension built up each year of membership from that date. Pension benefits built up from April 1, 2009 will be on a Career Average Revalued Earnings (CARE) basis. For each year of Pensionable Service from April 1, 2009 the member builds up a block of pension equal to one eightieth of Pensionable Salary, plus a lump sum of three times that pension, payable at Normal Pension Age of 65. At the end of the following year and annually thereafter, each block is increased up to retirement, or leaving the BTPS if earlier, by the lower of:

17–034

- the change in the Retail Prices Index (RPI) (but never below zero); and
- any change in Pensionable Salary.

SOME PRIVATE SECTOR SCHEMES

If there is no change in your Pensionable Salary, the CARE blocks earned during previous years would not be revalued for that particular year. The blocks will all be added together to give your total CARE pension and lump sum.

Contributions

17–035 In Section A, members pay contributions of 6 per cent of Pensionable Salary.

In Section B, then at January 1, in each year Pensionable Salary will be compared to the Contribution Earnings Threshold (CET) and the member will pay the contribution rate set out below from your next pay review date:

17–036

Pensionable Salary	Contribution rate
If earning below the CET (Contributions Earnings Threshold)	7%
If earning above the CET	8.5%

The CET for 2011/12 is £46,425, and will be reviewed annually.

In Section C, then at January 1, in each year Pensionable Salary will be compared to the Contribution Earnings Threshold (CET) and the member will pay the contribution rate set out below from your next pay review date:

17–037

Pensionable Salary	Contribution rate
If earning below the CET (Contributions Earnings Threshold)	6%
If earning above the CET	7%

The CET for 2011/12 is £46,425, and will be reviewed annually.

In addition, an active member will receive life cover of three times final salary.

17–038 In Section A, Normal Pension Age (NPA) is age 60. In Section B, Normal Pension Age (NPA) is age 65, although benefits built up before April 1, 2009 will be treated as if NPA was 60. Benefits built up before April 1, 2009 must be taken at the same time as benefits built up from April 1, 2009, and cannot be drawn at different times. In Section C, Normal Pension Age is 65.

Members can retire before NPA or after NPA. They can also, subject to HMRC regulations, and BT agreeing, receive your pension whilst still working for BT at any time from age 55.

The pensions in Sections A and B increase in line with CPI. The pension in Section C increases in line with RPI up to 5 per cent per annum.

17–039 The standard pension package includes a pension for a spouse, Civil Partner or partner when you die.

The Adult Survivor's pension is half of the member's pension and additionally for one child, a pension of one fourth of your pension; for two children one fourth of your pension each. If there are more then generally a total of half of your pension divided between each eligible child. These amounts are increased to one-third and two-thirds if there is no Adult Dependant.

The scheme was contracted out of the Additional State Pension or State Second Pension until April 2009.

Cash Equivalents

Cash Equivalents (CEs) of the member's rights in the scheme for pension sharing purposes will be calculated on the assumption that the member in service will leave service on the date of the calculation. There are no issues with the calculations.   17–040

Pension sharing

When subjected to a pension sharing order, rights under the BT Pension Scheme provide pension credits only by way of external transfer. The non-member spouse will accordingly have to set up a personal arrangement to accept the credit.   17–041

The standard maximum charges applied in all cases are (2012):

- current member or member with a deferred pension: £900 plus VAT;
- retired member: £800 plus VAT.

Miscellaneous

The Scheme currently has a deficit.   17–042

SHELL CONTRIBUTORY PENSION SCHEME

Contact Details

Administrators' Address	Trustee Services Unit (TSU), Pensions Trust Limited, Shell Centre, London, SE1 7NA
Contact Telephone Number	020 7934 1190
Contact E-mail address	pensions-administration-london-l@shell.com
Website	*www.shell.co.uk/home/content/pensions*

17–043

Eligibility

The Pre-2009 Section applies to existing SCPF members at December 31, 2008. New members and re-joiners cannot join this Section. The Post-2009 Section is open to new SCPF members who are eligible to join on or after January 1, 2009.   17–044

Main features of the scheme

This is a contributory final salary scheme arrangement within the Shell Pension Scheme. It provides an annual pension based on one fifty-fourth x Pensionable Service x Final Pensionable Salary in the Pre-2009 Section and one sixtieth x Pensionable Service x Final Pensionable Salary in the Post-2009 Section.   17–045

The scheme member will accrue benefits calculated by reference to a combination of length of service and pensionable salary of the member.

In both sections, contributions are 2 per cent of your Pensionable Salary up to £30,000 and 6 per cent of your Pensionable Salary over £30,000. Contributions cease after 36 years' Pensionable Service if you are in the Pre-2009 Section.

In addition, an active member will receive life cover of three times final salary.

Retirement age is age 60 for most Pre-2009 Section members and 65 for Post-2009 Section members.

17–046 In fact any of these benefits can be taken from age 55, but these will be subjected to an actuarial reduction. The earlier the benefits are taken the larger the reduction.

The pension increases in payment in line with RPI up to 7 per cent per annum for Pre-2009 members and in line with RPI up to 5 per cent per annum for Post-2009 Section members and no change has been made to move it in line with CPI.

In most cases, approximately 60 per cent of the pension (including prospective service to retirement age) is payable to a spouse or civil partner on the death of the scheme member. Children's pensions are 20 per cent for one child or a share of 40 per cent for more than one where there is a Qualifying Dependant and if there is no Qualifying Dependant, then 40 per cent for each if there are one or two children or a share of 100 per cent if there are more than two children.

The scheme is contracted out of the Additional State Pension or State Second Pension. Accordingly, a member who has been in the Scheme throughout his working life will not have any Additional State Pension or State Second Pension.

Cash Equivalents

17–047 Cash Equivalents (CEs) of the member's rights in the scheme for pension sharing purposes will be calculated on the assumption that the member in service will leave service on the date of the calculation. There are no issues with the calculations.

Pension sharing

17–048 When subjected to a pension sharing order, rights under the Shell Pension Scheme can provide pension credits in the Scheme (internal option) or be transferred out by way of external transfer. The non-member spouse will accordingly have to choose which option to take.

There are no Pension sharing charges made by Shell Pension Scheme at the time of writing.

Miscellaneous

17–049 Unusually, the Scheme is currently in surplus.

SHELL OVERSEAS CONTRIBUTORY PENSION SCHEME

Contact Details

Administrators' Address	Trustee Services Unit (TSU), Pensions Trust Limited, Shell Centre, London, SE1 7NA	17–050
Contact Telephone Number	020 7934 1190	
Contact E-mail address	pensions-administration-london-l@shell.com	
Website	*www.shell.co.uk/home/content/pensions*	

Eligibility

The Pre-2009 Section applies to existing SOCPF members at December 31, 2008. New members and re-joiners cannot join this Section. The Post-2009 Section is open to new SOCPF members who are eligible to join on or after January 1, 2009.   17–051

Main features of the scheme

This is a contributory final salary scheme arrangement within the Shell Pension Scheme. It provides an annual pension based on one fifty-fourth x Pensionable Service x Final Pensionable Salary in the Pre-2009 Section and one sixtieth x Pensionable Service x Final Pensionable Salary in the Post-2009 Section.   17–052

The scheme member will accrue benefits calculated by reference to a combination of length of service and pensionable salary of the member.

In both sections, contributions are 2 per cent of your Pensionable Salary up to £30,000 and 6 per cent of your Pensionable Salary over £30,000. Contributions cease after 36 years' Pensionable Service if you are in the Pre-2009 Section.

In addition, an active member will receive life cover of three times final salary.

Retirement age is age 60 for most Pre-2009 Section members and 65 for Post-2009 Section members.

In fact any of these benefits can be taken from age 55, but these will be subjected to an actuarial reduction. The earlier the benefits are taken the larger the reduction.   17–053

The pension increases in payment in line with RPI up to 7 per cent per annum for Pre-2009 members and in line with RPI up to 5per cent per annum for Post-2009 Section members and no change has been made to move it in line with CPI.

In most cases, approximately 60 per cent of the pension (including prospective service to retirement age) is payable to a spouse or civil partner on the death of the scheme member. Children's pensions are 20 per cent for one child or a share of 40 per cent for more than one where there is a Qualifying Dependant and if there is no Qualifying Dependant, then 40 per cent for each if there are one or two children or a share of 100 per cent if there are more than two children.

SOME PRIVATE SECTOR SCHEMES

The scheme is contracted out of the Additional State Pension or State Second Pension. Accordingly, a member who has been in the Scheme throughout his working life will not have any Additional State Pension or State Second Pension.

Cash Equivalents

17–054 Cash Equivalents (CEs) of the member's rights in the scheme for pension sharing purposes will be calculated on the assumption that the member in service will leave service on the date of the calculation. There are no issues with the calculations.

Pension sharing

17–055 It is not possible to make a Pension Sharing Order on these rights as the Fund is based in Bermuda. In exceptional circumstances, there is a method whereby the total benefit can be transferred into a personal pension in the UK and then be subject to a Pension Sharing order but this is complicated and would involve losing the defined benefit nature.

UNIVERSITIES SUPERANNUATION SCHEME—FINAL SALARY SECTION

Contact Details

17–056

Administrators' Address	Universities Superannuation Scheme Ltd Royal Liver Building Liverpool L3 1PY
Contact Telephone Number	0151 227 4711
Website	*www.uss.co.uk*

Eligibility

17–057 Eligibility was for anyone who joined a University or College in an eligible role and became a member before October 1, 2011. New joiners join a Career Revalued Average Earnings section. If a member has a break in eligible employment of less than 30 months they will remain a member of the Final Salary section if they rejoin USS. If the break is 30 months or more, or the member took a refund of contributions or transferred out benefits, the member will join the Career Revalued Benefits section of USS and the final salary benefits will be "deferred". The only exception to this is if the last employer confirmed a reasonable expectation of re-employment within five years of leaving. If this is the case and they confirmed this to USS at the time, the member may rejoin the Final Salary section.

UNIVERSITIES SUPERANNUATION SCHEME—FINAL SALARY

Main features of the scheme

Benefits accrue during "reckonable service" which is in essence all service in the Universities' Superannuation Scheme from joining onwards and there is no maximum service.

17–058

The scheme member will accrue benefits calculated by reference to a combination of length of service and final pensionable salary.

The normal pension age (NPA) in USS is currently 65. Members are automatically entitled the full pension at this age. The NPA in USS will increase in the future, broadly in line with increases to the state pension age for men and women.

Contributions are 7.5 per cent of pensionable salary.

Benefits accrue at one eightieth of final pensionable salary per annum for each year of service plus a tax-free cash lump sum of three times that pension.

Early retirement from age 55 is possible subject to actuarial reduction.

Pension increases for service built up after September 30, 2011 is CPI up to 5 per cent a year, however, if official pensions increase by more than 5 per cent (which would mean CPI was above 5 per cent) then USS will match half of the difference up to a maximum increase of 10 per cent. So, if CPI increased by 15 per cent, USS increases would be 10 per cent in that year. Benefits built up before October 1, 2011 will increase fully in line with CPI.

17–059

A pension is payable to a spouse or civil partner on the death of the scheme member provided the marriage or civil partnership took place prior to the scheme member leaving service. This will be 50 per cent of the member's pension including prospective service to age 65 if the member is in service below retirement age.

The scheme is contracted out of the Additional State Pension or State Second Pension. Accordingly, a member who has been in the Scheme throughout their working life will not have any income at State Pension Age from the Additional State Pension or State Second Pension.

Cash Equivalents

Cash Equivalents (CEs) of the member's rights in the scheme for pension sharing purposes will be calculated on the assumption that the member in service will leave service on the date of the calculation. There have been issues historically with the assumed retirement age. In addition, the basis used has been volatile and values can change quickly.

17–060

Pension sharing

When subjected to a pension sharing order, the Scheme will provide either pension credits by way of internal transfer payable at age 65 (with the option to take a reduced pension from age 55) or the external transfer to a provider of their choice.

17–061

SOME PRIVATE SECTOR SCHEMES

Under the internal option, the pension credit benefits will not have an automatic lump sum although if the member has not retired at the time of the implementation, there will be available a lump sum from the pension credit payable by commutation.

Pension sharing charges made by Universities' Superannuation Scheme are currently £705. The Scheme currently charges £352.50 for a sample calculation of what the non-member spouse might receive from a Pension Share.

PART C

RELEVANT LEGISLATION

Statutes and Statutory Instruments

Statutes

Matrimonial Causes Act 1973 ss.21A, 21B, 21C, 24B, 24C, 24D, 24E, 24F, 24G, 25, 25A, 25B, 25C, 25D, 25E, 25F, 25G, 28, 31, 37, 40A and 40B
Welfare Reform and Pensions Act 1999 ss.11, 23, 24, 26, 27, 28, 29, 31, 33, 34, 35, 41, 46, 47, 85(3) and Schs 5 and 6
Matrimonial and Family Proceedings Act 1984 ss.17, 18, 19, 20 and 21
Pension Schemes Act 1993 s.1
Pensions Act 2008 ss.107, 108, 109, 111,112, 116, 117, 118 and 120
Insolvency Act 1986 ss.342A, 342B and 342C

Statutory Instruments

Family Procedure Rules 2010 (SI 2010/2955) rr.9.3, 9.4, 9.14, 9.15 and 9.29 to 9.45
Pensions on Divorce etc (Provision of Information) Regulations 2000 (SI 2000/1048) regs 2-5 and 7-8
Pensions on Divorce (Charging) Regulations 2000 (SI 2000/1049) reg.9
Pension Sharing (Valuation) Regulations 2000 (SI 2000/1052) regs 1 and 2
Pension Sharing (Implementation and Discharge of Liability) Regulations 2000 (SI 2000/1053) regs 3 and 5–6
Divorce etc. (Pensions) Regulations 2000 (SI 2000/1123) regs 3 and 9
Sharing of State Scheme Rights (Provision of Information and Valuation) Regulations 2000 (SI 2000/2693) regs 1–4
Occupational Pension Schemes (Transfer Values) Regulations 1996 (SI 1996/1847) as amended by the **Occupational Pension Schemes (Transfer Values)(Amendment) Regulations 2008** (SI 2008/1050) reg.7
Personal Pension Schemes (Transfer Values) Regulations 1987 (SI 1987/1112) as amended by the **Occupational Pension Schemes (Transfer Values)(Amendment) Regulations 2008**(SI 2008/1050) and the **Occupational Pension Schemes (Transfer Values)(Amendment) Regulations 2008** (SI 2008/2450) reg.3

Statutes

MATRIMONIAL CAUSES ACT 1973

(Incorporating amendments made under Matrimonial and Family Proceedings Act 1984, Pensions Act 1995, Welfare Reform and Pensions Act 1999, Civil Partnership Act 2004, Pensions Act 2004 and Pensions Act 2008)

PENSIONS ON DIVORCE

Pension sharing orders

21A.—(1) For the purposes of this Act, a pension sharing order is an order which—
  (a) provides that one party's—
    (i) shareable rights under a specified pension arrangement, or
    (ii) shareable state scheme rights,
  be subject to pension sharing for the benefit of the other party, and
  (b) specifies the percentage value to be transferred.
(2) In subsection (1) above—
  (a) the reference to shareable rights under a pension arrangement is to rights in relation to which pension sharing is available under Chapter I of Part IV of the Welfare Reform and Pensions Act 1999, or under corresponding Northern Ireland legislation,
  (b) the reference to shareable state scheme rights is to rights in relation to which pension sharing is available under Chapter II of Part IV of the Welfare Reform and Pensions Act 1999, or under corresponding Northern Ireland legislation, and
  (c) "party" means a party to a marriage.

Pension compensation sharing orders

21B.—(1) For the purposes of this Act, a pension compensation sharing order is an order which—
  (a) provides that one party's shareable rights to PPF compensation that derive from rights under a specified pension scheme are to be subject to pension compensation sharing for the benefit of the other party, and
  (b) specifies the percentage value to be transferred.
(2) In subsection (1)—
  (a) the reference to shareable rights to PPF compensation is to rights in relation to which pension compensation sharing is available under Chapter 1 of Part 3 of the Pensions Act 2008 or under corresponding Northern Ireland legislation;
  (b) "party" means a party to a marriage;
  (c) "specified" means specified in the order.

Pension compensation: interpretation

21C In this Part—
- "PPF compensation" means compensation payable under the pension compensation provisions;
- "the pension compensation provisions" means—
  (a) Chapter 3 of Part 2 of the Pensions Act 2004 (pension protection) and any regulations or order made under it,
  (b) Chapter 1 of Part 3 of the Pensions Act 2008 (pension compensation on divorce etc) and any regulations or order made under it, and

Pension sharing orders in connection with divorce proceedings etc.

24B.—(1) On granting a decree of divorce or a decree of nullity of marriage or at any time thereafter (whether before or after the decree is made absolute), the court may, on an application made under this section, make one or more pension sharing orders in relation to the marriage.

(2) A pension sharing order under this section is not to take effect unless the decree on or after which it is made has been made absolute.

(3) A pension sharing order under this section may not be made in relation to a pension arrangement which—
   (a) is the subject of a pension sharing order in relation to the marriage, or
   (b) has been the subject of pension sharing between the parties to the marriage.

(4) A pension sharing order under this section may not be made in relation to shareable state scheme rights if—
   (a) such rights are the subject of a pension sharing order in relation to the marriage, or
   (b) such rights have been the subject of pension sharing between the parties to the marriage.

(5) A pension sharing order under this section may not be made in relation to the rights of a person under a pension arrangement if there is in force a requirement imposed by virtue of section 25B or 25C below which relates to benefits or future benefits to which he is entitled under the pension arrangement.

Pension sharing orders: duty to stay

24C.—(1) No pension sharing order may be made so as to take effect before the end of such period after the making of the order as may be prescribed by regulations made by the Lord Chancellor.

(2) The power to make regulations under this section shall be exercisable by statutory instrument which shall be subject to annulment in pursuance of a resolution of either House of Parliament.

Pension sharing orders: apportionment of charges

24D If a pension sharing order relates to rights under a pension arrangement, the court may include in the order provision about the apportionment between the parties of any charge under section 41 of the Welfare Reform and Pensions Act 1999 (charges in respect of pension sharing costs), or under corresponding Northern Ireland legislation.

PENSIONS ON DIVORCE

Pension compensation sharing orders in connection with divorce proceedings

24E.—(1) On granting a decree of divorce or a decree of nullity of marriage or at any time thereafter (whether before or after the decree is made absolute), the court may, on an application made under this section, make a pension compensation sharing order in relation to the marriage.

(2) A pension compensation sharing order under this section is not to take effect unless the decree on or after which it is made has been made absolute.

(3) A pension compensation sharing order under this section may not be made in relation to rights to PPF compensation that—
   (a) are the subject of pension attachment,
   (b) derive from rights under a pension scheme that were the subject of pension sharing between the parties to the marriage,
   (c) are the subject of pension compensation attachment, or
   (d) are or have been the subject of pension compensation sharing between the parties to the marriage.

(4) For the purposes of subsection (3)(a), rights to PPF compensation "are the subject of pension attachment" if any of the following three conditions is met.

(5) The first condition is that—
   (a) the rights derive from rights under a pension scheme in relation to which an order was made under section 23 imposing a requirement by virtue of section 25B(4), and
   (b) that order, as modified under section 25E(3), remains in force.

(6) The second condition is that—
   (a) the rights derive from rights under a pension scheme in relation to which an order was made under section 23 imposing a requirement by virtue of section 25B(7), and
   (b) that order—
      (i) has been complied with, or
      (ii) has not been complied with and, as modified under section 25E(5), remains in force.

(7) The third condition is that—
   (a) the rights derive from rights under a pension scheme in relation to which an order was made under section 23 imposing a requirement by virtue of section 25C, and
   (b) that order remains in force.

(8) For the purposes of subsection (3)(b), rights under a pension scheme "were the subject of pension sharing between the parties to the marriage" if the rights were at any time the subject of a pension sharing order in relation to the marriage or a previous marriage between the same parties.

(9) For the purposes of subsection (3)(c), rights to PPF compensation "are the subject of pension compensation attachment" if there is in force a requirement imposed by virtue of section 25F relating to them.

(10) For the purposes of subsection (3)(d), rights to PPF compensation "are or have been the subject of pension compensation sharing between the parties

to the marriage" if they are or have ever been the subject of a pension compensation sharing order in relation to the marriage or a previous marriage between the same parties.

Pension compensation sharing orders: duty to stay

24F.—(1) No pension compensation sharing order may be made so as to take effect before the end of such period after the making of the order as may be prescribed by regulations made by the Lord Chancellor.
(2) The power to make regulations under this section shall be exercisable by statutory instrument which shall be subject to annulment in pursuance of a resolution of either House of Parliament.

Pension compensation sharing orders: apportionment of charges

24G The court may include in a pension compensation sharing order provision about the apportionment between the parties of any charge under section 117 of the Pensions Act 2008 (charges in respect of pension compensation sharing costs), or under corresponding Northern Ireland legislation.

Matters to which court is to have regard in deciding how to exercise its powers under ss.23, 24, 24A, 24B and 24E

25.—(1) It shall be the duty of the court in deciding whether to exercise its powers under section 23, 24, 24A, 24B or 24E above and, if so, in what manner, to have regard to all the circumstances of the case, first consideration being given to the welfare while a minor of any child of the family who has not attained the age of eighteen.
(2) As regards the exercise of the powers of the court under section 23(1)(a), (b) or (c), 24, 24A, 24B or 24E above in relation to a party to the marriage, the court shall in particular have regard to the following matters—
  (a) the income, earning capacity, property and other financial resources which each of the parties to the marriage has or is likely to have in the foreseeable future, including in the case of earning capacity any increase in that capacity which it would in the opinion of the court be reasonable to expect a party to the marriage to take steps to acquire;
  (b) the financial needs, obligations and responsibilities which each of the parties to the marriage has or is likely to have in the foreseeable future;
  (c) the standard of living enjoyed by the family before the breakdown of the marriage;
  (d) the age of each party to the marriage and the duration of the marriage;
  (e) any physical or mental disability of either of the parties to the marriage;
  (f) the contributions which each of the parties has made or is likely in the foreseeable future to make to the welfare of the family, including any contribution by looking after the home or caring for the family;

(g) the conduct of each of the parties, if that conduct is such that it would in the opinion of the court be inequitable to disregard it;

(h) in the case of proceedings for divorce or nullity of marriage, the value to each of the parties to the marriage of any benefit [...] which, by reason of the dissolution or annulment of the marriage, that party will lose the chance of acquiring.

(3) As regards the exercise of the powers of the court under section 23(1)(d) or (e) or (f), (2) (4), 24 or 24A above in relation to a child of the family, the court shall in particular have regard to the following matters—

(a) the financial needs of the child;

(b) the income, earning capacity (if any), property and other financial resources of the child;

(c) any physical or mental disability of the child;

(d) the manner in which he was being and in which the parties to the marriage expected him to be educated or trained;

(e) the considerations mentioned in relation to the parties to the marriage in paragraphs (a), (b), (c) and (e) of subsection (2) above.

(4) As regards the exercise of the powers of the court under section 23(1)(d), (e) or (f), (2) or (4), 24 or 24A above against a party to a marriage in favour of a child of the family who is not the child of that party, the court shall also have regard—

(a) to whether that party assumed any responsibility for the child's maintenance, and, if so, to the extent to which, and the basis upon which, that party assumed such responsibility and to the length of time for which that party discharged such responsibility;

(b) to whether in assuming and discharging such responsibility that party did so knowing that the child was not his or her own;

(c) to the liability of any other person to maintain the child.

Exercise of court's powers in favour of party to marriage on decree of divorce or nullity of marriage

25A.—(1) Where on or after the grant of a decree of divorce or nullity of marriage the court decides to exercise its powers under section 23(1)(a), (b) or (c), 24, 24A, 24B or 24E above in favour of a party to the marriage, it shall be the duty of the court to consider whether it would be appropriate so to exercise those powers that the financial obligations of each party towards the other will be terminated as soon after the grant of the decree as the court considers just and reasonable.

(2) Where the court decides in such a case to make a periodical payments or secured periodical payments order in favour of a party to the marriage, the court shall in particular consider whether it would be appropriate to require those payments to be made or secured only for such term as would in the opinion of the court be sufficient to enable the party in whose favour the order is made to adjust without undue hardship to the termination of his or her financial dependence on the other party.

(3) Where on or after the grant of a decree of divorce or nullity of marriage an application is made by a party to the marriage for a periodical payments or

secured periodical payments order in his or her favour, then, if the court considers that no continuing obligation should be imposed on either party to make or secure periodical payments in favour of the other, the court may dismiss the application with a direction that the applicant shall not be entitled to make any further application in relation to that marriage for an order under section 23(1)(a) or (b) above.

Pensions

25B.—(1) The matters to which the court is to have regard under section 25(2) above include—
- (a) in the case of paragraph (a), any benefits under a pension arrangement which a party to the marriage has or is likely to have, and
- (b) in the case of paragraph (h), any benefits under a pension arrangement which, by reason of the dissolution or annulment of the marriage, a party to the marriage will lose the chance of acquiring, and, accordingly, in relation to benefits under a pension arrangement, section 25(2)(a) above shall have effect as if "in the foreseeable future" were omitted.

(2) In any proceedings for a financial provision order under section 23 above in a case where a party to the marriage has, or is likely to have, any benefit under a pension scheme, the court shall, in addition to considering any other matter which it is required to consider apart from this subsection, consider—
- (a) whether, having regard to any matter to which it is required to have regard in the proceedings by virtue of subsection (1) above, such an order (whether deferred or not) should be made, and
- (b) where the court determines to make such an order, how the terms of the order should be affected, having regard to any such matter.

(3) The following provisions apply where, having regard to any benefits under a pension arrangement, the court determines to make an order under section 23 above.

(4) To the extent to which the order is made having regard to any benefits under a pension arrangement, the order may require the person responsible for the pension arrangement in question, if at any time any payment in respect of any benefits under the arrangement becomes due to the party with pension rights, to make a payment for the benefit of the other party.

(5) The order must express the amount of any payment required to be made by virtue of subsection (4) above as a percentage of the payment which becomes due to the party with pension rights.

(6) Any such payment by the person responsible for the arrangement—
- (a) shall discharge so much of his liability to the party with pension rights as corresponds to the amount of the payment, and
- (b) shall be treated for all purposes as a payment made by the party with pension rights in or towards the discharge of his liability under the order.

PENSIONS ON DIVORCE

(7) Where the party with pension rights has a right of commutation under the arrangement, the order may require him to exercise it to any extent; and this section applies to the any payment due in consequence of commutation in pursuance of the order as it applies to other payments in respect of benefits under the arrangement.

(7A) The power conferred by subsection (7) above may not be exercised for the purpose of commuting a benefit payable to the party with pension rights to a benefit payable to the other party.

(7B) The power conferred by subsection (4) or (7) above may not be exercised in relation to a pension arrangement which—
   (a) is the subject of a pension sharing order in relation to the marriage, or
   (b) has been the subject of pension sharing between the parties to the marriage.

(7C) In subsection (1) above, references to benefits under a pension arrangement include any benefits by way of pension, whether under a pension arrangement or not.

Pensions: lump sums

25C.—(1) The power of the court under section 23 above to order a party to a marriage to pay a lump sum to the other party includes, where the benefits which the party with pension rights has or is likely to have under a pension arrangement include any lump sum payable in respect of his death, power to make any of the following provision by the order.

(2) The court may—
   (a) if the person responsible for the pension arrangement in question has power to determine the person to whom the sum, or any part of it, is to be paid, require him to pay the whole or part of that sum, when it becomes due, to the other party,
   (b) if the party with pension rights has power to nominate the person to whom the sum, or any part of it, is to be paid, require the party with pension rights to nominate the other party in respect of the whole or part of that sum,
   (c) in any other case, require the person responsible for the pension arrangement in question to pay the whole or part of that sum, when it becomes due, for the benefit of the other party instead of to the person to whom, apart from the order, it would be paid.

(3) Any payment by the person responsible for the arrangement under an order made under section 23 above by virtue of this section shall discharge so much of his liability in respect of the party with pension rights as corresponds to the amount of the payment.

(4) The powers conferred by this section may not be exercised in relation to a pension arrangement which—
   (a) is the subject of a pension sharing order in relation to the marriage, or
   (b) has been the subject of pension sharing between the parties to the marriage.

Pensions: supplementary

25D.—(1) Where—
- (a) an order made under section 23 above by virtue of section 25B or 25C above imposes any requirement on the person responsible for a pension arrangement ("the first arrangement") and the party with pension rights acquires rights under another pension arrangement ("the new arrangement") which are derived (directly or indirectly) from the whole of his rights under the first arrangement, and
- (b) the person responsible for the new arrangement has been given notice in accordance with regulations made by the Lord Chancellor, the order shall have effect as if it had been made instead in respect of the person responsible for the new arrangement.

(2) The Lord Chancellor may by regulations—
- (a) in relation to any provision of sections 25B or 25C above which authorises the court making an order under section 23 above to require the person responsible for a pension arrangement to make a payment for the benefit of the other party, make provision as to the person to whom, and the terms on which, the payment is to be made,
- (ab) make, in relation to payment under a mistaken belief as to the continuation in force of a provision included by virtue of section 25B or 25C above in an order under section 23 above, provision about the rights or liabilities of the payer, the payee or the person to whom the payment was due,
- (b) require notices to be given in respect of changes of circumstances relevant to such orders which include provision made by virtue of sections 25B and 25C above,
- (ba) make provision for the person responsible for a pension arrangement to be discharged in prescribed circumstances from a requirement imposed by virtue of section 25B or 25C above,
- (c) make provision for the trustees or managers of any pension scheme to provide, for the purposes of orders under section 23 above, information as to the value of any benefits under the scheme,
- (d) make provision for the recovery of the administrative expenses of—
  - (i) complying with such orders, so far as they include provision made by virtue of sections 25B and 25C above, and
  - (ii) providing such information, from the party with pension rights or the other party,
- (e) make provision about calculation and verification in relation to the valuation of—
  - (i) benefits under a pension arrangement, or
  - (ii) shareable state scheme rights,

for the purposes of the court's functions in connection with the exercise of any of its powers under this Part of this Act and regulations made by virtue of paragraph (e) above may provide for that value to be calculated and verified in accordance with guidance which is prepared and from time to time revised by a prescribed person and approved by the Secretary of State.

(2A) Regulations under subsection (2)(e) above may include—

(a) provision for calculation or verification in accordance with guidance from time to time prepared by a prescribed person, and
(b) provision by reference to regulations under section 30 or 49(4) of the Welfare Reform and Pensions Act 1999.

(2B) Regulations under subsection (2) above may make different provision for different cases.

(2C) Power to make regulations under this section shall be exercisable by statutory instrument which shall be subject to annulment in pursuance of a resolution of either House of Parliament.

(3) In this section and sections 25B and 25C above—

"occupational pension scheme" has the same meaning as in the Pension Schemes Act 1993;

"the party with pension rights" means the party to the marriage who has or is likely to have benefits under a pension arrangement and "the other party" means the other party to the marriage;

"pension arrangement" means—
- (a) an occupational pension scheme,
- (b) a personal pension scheme,
- (c) a retirement annuity contract,
- (d) an annuity or insurance policy purchased, or transferred, for the purpose of giving effect to rights under an occupational pension scheme or a personal pension scheme, and
- (e) an annuity purchased, or entered into, for the purpose of discharging liability in respect of a pension credit under section 29(1)(b) of the Welfare Reform and Pensions Act 1999 or under corresponding Northern Ireland legislation;

"personal pension scheme" has the same meaning as in the Pension Schemes Act 1993;

"prescribed" means prescribed by regulations;

"retirement annuity contract" means a contract or scheme approved under Chapter III of Part XIV of the Income and Corporation Taxes Act 1988;

"shareable state scheme rights" has the same meaning as in section 21A(1) above; and

"trustees or managers", in relation to an occupational pension scheme or a personal pension scheme, means—
- (a) in the case of a scheme established under a trust, the trustees of the scheme, and
- (b) in any other case, the managers of the scheme.

(4) In this section and sections 25B and 25C above, references to the person responsible for a pension arrangement are—
- (a) in the case of an occupational pension scheme or a personal pension scheme, to the trustees or managers of the scheme,
- (b) in the case of a retirement annuity contract or an annuity falling within paragraph (d) or (e) of the definition of "pension arrangement" above, the provider of the annuity, and
- (c) in the case of an insurance policy falling within paragraph (d) of the definition of that expression, the insurer.

STATUTES AND STATUTORY INSTRUMENTS

The Pension Protection Fund

25E.—(1) The matters to which the court is to have regard under section 25(2) include–
- (a) in the case of paragraph (a), any PPF compensation to which a party to the marriage is or is likely to be entitled, and
- (b) in the case of paragraph (h), any PPF compensation which, by reason of the dissolution or annulment of the marriage, a party to the marriage will lose the chance of acquiring entitlement to,

and, accordingly, in relation to PPF compensation, section 25(2)(a) shall have effect as if "in the foreseeable future" were omitted.

(2) Subsection (3) applies in relation to an order under section 23 so far as it includes provision made by virtue of section 25B(4) which—
- (a) imposed requirements on the trustees or managers of an occupational pension scheme for which the Board has assumed responsibility in accordance with Chapter 3 of Part 2 of the Pensions Act 2004 (pension protection) or any provision in force in Northern Ireland corresponding to that Chapter, and
- (b) was made before the trustees or managers of the scheme received the transfer notice in relation to the scheme.

(3) The order is to have effect from the time when the trustees or managers of the scheme receive the transfer notice—
- (a) as if, except in prescribed descriptions of case—
  - (i) references in the order to the trustees or managers of the scheme were references to the Board, and
  - (ii) references in the order to any pension or lump sum to which the party with pension rights is or may become entitled under the scheme were references to any PPF compensation to which that person is or may become entitled in respect of the pension or lump sum, and
- (b) subject to such other modifications as may be prescribed.

(4) Subsection (5) applies to an order under section 23 if—
- (a) it includes provision made by virtue of section 25B(7) which requires the party with pension rights to exercise his right of commutation under an occupational pension scheme to any extent, and
- (b) before the requirement is complied with the Board has assumed responsibility for the scheme as mentioned in subsection (2)(a).

(5) From the time the trustees or managers of the scheme receive the transfer notice, the order is to have effect with such modifications as may be prescribed.

(6) Regulations may modify section 25C as it applies in relation to an occupational pension scheme at any time when there is an assessment period in relation to the scheme.

(7) Where the court makes a pension sharing order in respect of a person's shareable rights under an occupational pension scheme, or an order which includes provision made by virtue of section 25B(4) or (7) in relation to such a scheme, the Board subsequently assuming responsibility for the scheme as mentioned in subsection (2)(a) does not affect—

(a) the powers of the court under section 31 to vary or discharge the order or to suspend or revive any provision of it, or
(b) on an appeal, the powers of the appeal court to affirm, reinstate, set aside or vary the order.
(8) Regulations may make such consequential modifications of any provision of, or made by virtue of, this Part as appear to the Lord Chancellor necessary or expedient to give effect to the provisions of this section.
(9) In this section—
"assessment period" means an assessment period within the meaning of Part 2 of the Pensions Act 2004 (pension protection) (see sections 132 and 159 of that Act) or an equivalent period under any provision in force in Northern Ireland corresponding to that Part;
"the Board" means the Board of the Pension Protection Fund;
"occupational pension scheme" has the same meaning as in the Pension Schemes Act 1993;
"prescribed" means prescribed by regulations;
"regulations" means regulations made by the Lord Chancellor;
"shareable rights" are rights in relation to which pension sharing is available under Chapter 1 of Part 4 of the Welfare Reform and Pensions Act 1999 or any provision in force in Northern Ireland corresponding to that Chapter;
"transfer notice" has the same meaning as in section 160 of the Pensions Act 2004 or any corresponding provision in force in Northern Ireland.
(10) Any power to make regulations under this section is exercisable by statutory instrument, which shall be subject to annulment in pursuance of a resolution of either House of Parliament.

Attachment of pension compensation

25F.—(1) This section applies where, having regard to any PPF compensation to which a party to the marriage is or is likely to be entitled, the court determines to make an order under section 23.
(2) To the extent to which the order is made having regard to such compensation, the order may require the Board of the Pension Protection Fund, if at any time any payment in respect of PPF compensation becomes due to the party with compensation rights, to make a payment for the benefit of the other party.
(3) The order must express the amount of any payment required to be made by virtue of subsection (2) as a percentage of the payment which becomes due to the party with compensation rights.
(4) Any such payment by the Board of the Pension Protection Fund—
(a) shall discharge so much of its liability to the party with compensation rights as corresponds to the amount of the payment, and
(b) shall be treated for all purposes as a payment made by the party with compensation rights in or towards the discharge of that party's liability under the order.
(5) Where the party with compensation rights has a right to commute any PPF compensation, the order may require that party to exercise it to any extent;

and this section applies to any payment due in consequence of commutation in pursuance of the order as it applies to other payments in respect of PPF compensation.

(6) The power conferred by subsection (5) may not be exercised for the purpose of commuting compensation payable to the party with compensation rights to compensation payable to the other party.

(7) The power conferred by subsection (2) or (5) may not be exercised in relation to rights to PPF compensation that—
   (a) derive from rights under a pension scheme that were at any time the subject of a pension sharing order in relation to the marriage, or a previous marriage between the same parties, or
   (b) are or have ever been the subject of a pension compensation sharing order in relation to the marriage or a previous marriage between the same parties.

Pension compensation: supplementary

25G.—(1) The Lord Chancellor may by regulations—
   (a) make provision, in relation to any provision of section 25F which authorises the court making an order under section 23 to require the Board of the Pension Protection Fund to make a payment for the benefit of the other party, as to the person to whom, and the terms on which, the payment is to be made;
   (b) make provision, in relation to payment under a mistaken belief as to the continuation in force of a provision included by virtue of section 25F in an order under section 23, about the rights or liabilities of the payer, the payee or the person to whom the payment was due;
   (c) require notices to be given in respect of changes of circumstances relevant to orders under section 23 which include provision made by virtue of section 25F;
   (d) make provision for the Board of the Pension Protection Fund to be discharged in prescribed circumstances from a requirement imposed by virtue of section 25F;
   (e) make provision about calculation and verification in relation to the valuation of PPF compensation for the purposes of the court's functions in connection with the exercise of any of its powers under this Part.

(2) Regulations under subsection (1)(e) may include—
   (a) provision for calculation or verification in accordance with guidance from time to time prepared by a prescribed person;
   (b) provision by reference to regulations under section 112 of the Pensions Act 2008.

(3) Regulations under subsection (1) may make different provision for different cases.

(4) The power to make regulations under subsection (1) is exercisable by statutory instrument which shall be subject to annulment in pursuance of a resolution of either House of Parliament.

(5) In this section and section 25F—

"the party with compensation rights" means the party to the marriage who is or is likely to be entitled to PPF compensation, and "the other party" means the other party to the marriage;
"prescribed" means prescribed by regulations.

Duration of continuing financial provision orders in favour of party to marriage, and effect of remarriage or formation of civil partnership

28.—(1) Subject in the case of an order made on or after the grant of a decree of divorce or nullity of marriage to the provisions of sections 25A(2) above and 31(7) below, the term to be specified in a periodical payments or secured periodical payments order in favour of a party to a marriage shall be such term as the court thinks fit, except that the term shall not begin before or extend beyond the following limits, that is to say—
  (a) in the case of a periodical payments order, the term shall begin not earlier than the date of the making of an application for the order, and shall be so defined as not to extend beyond the death of either of the parties to the marriage or, where the order is made on or after the grant of a decree of divorce or nullity of marriage, the remarriage of, or formation of a civil partnership by, the party in whose favour the order is made; and
  (b) in the case of a secured periodical payments order, the term shall begin not earlier than the date of the making of an application for the order, and shall be so defined as not to extend beyond the death or, where the order is made on or after the grant of such a decree, the remarriage of, or formation of a civil partnership by, the party in whose favour the order is made.

(1A) Where a periodical payments or secured periodical payments order in favour of a party to a marriage is made on or after the grant of a decree of divorce or nullity of marriage, the court may direct that that party shall not be entitled to apply under section 31 below for the extension of the term specified in the order

(2) Where a periodical payments or secured periodical payments order in favour of a party to a marriage is made otherwise than on or after the grant of a decree of divorce or nullity of marriage, and the marriage in question is subsequently dissolved or annulled but the order continues in force, the order shall, notwithstanding anything in it, cease to have effect on the remarriage of, or formation of a civil partnership by, that party, except in relation to any arrears due under it on the date of the remarriage or formation of the civil partnership.

(3) If after the grant of a decree dissolving or annulling a marriage either party to that marriage remarries whether at any time before or after the commencement of this Act, or forms a civil partnership that party shall not be entitled to apply, by reference to the grant of that decree, for a financial provision order in his or her favour, or for a property adjustment order, against the other party to that marriage.

STATUTES AND STATUTORY INSTRUMENTS

Variation, discharge, etc., of certain orders for financial relief

31.—(1) Where the court has made an order to which this section applies, then, subject to the provisions of this section and of section 28(1A) above, the court shall have power to vary or discharge the order or to suspend any provision thereof temporarily and to revive the operation of any provision so suspended.

(2) This section applies to the following orders, that is to say—
- (a) any order for maintenance pending suit and any interim order for maintenance;
- (b) any periodical payments order;
- (c) any secured periodical payments order;
- (d) any order made by virtue of section 23(3)(c) or 27(7)(b) above (provision for payment of a lump sum by instalments;
- (dd) any deferred order made by virtue of section 23(1)(c)(lump sums) which includes provision made by virtue of—
  - (i) section 25B(4),
  - (ii) section 25C, or
  - (iii) section 25F(2)

  (provision in respect of pension rights or pension compensation rights)
- (e) any order for a settlement of property under section 24(1)(b) or for a variation of settlement under section 24(1)(c) or (d) above, being an order made on or after the grant of a decree of judicial separation.
- (f) any order made under section 24A(1) above for the sale of property
- (g) a pension sharing order under section 24B above or a pension sharing compensation order under section 24E above which is made at a time before the decree has been made absolute.

(2A) Where the court has made an order referred to in subsection (2)(*a*), (*b*) or (*c*) above, then, subject to the provisions of this section, the court shall have power to remit the payment of any arrears due under the order or of any part thereof.

(2B) Where the court has made an order referred to in subsection (2)(dd)(ii) above, this section shall cease to apply to the order on the death of either of the parties to the marriage

(3) The powers exercisable by the court under this section in relation to an order shall be exercisable also in relation to any instrument executed in pursuance of the order.

(4) The court shall not exercise the powers conferred by this section in relation to an order for a settlement under section 24(1)(b) or for a variation of settlement under section 24(1)(c) or (d) above except on an application made in proceedings—
- (a) for the rescission of the decree of judicial separation by reference to which the order was made, or
- (b) for the dissolution of the marriage in question.

(4A) In relation to an order which falls within paragraph (g) of subsection (2) above ("the subsection (2) order")—
- (a) the powers conferred by this section may be exercised—

(i) only on an application made before the subsection (2) order has or, but for paragraph (b) below, would have taken effect; and

(ii) only if, at the time when the application is made, the decree has not been made absolute; and

(b) an application made in accordance with paragraph (a) above prevents the subsection (2) order from taking effect before the application has been dealt with.

(4B) No variation of a pension sharing order or a pension compensation order shall be made so as to take effect before the decree is made absolute.

(4C) The variation of a pension sharing order or a pension compensation order prevents the order taking effect before the end of such period after the making of the variation as may be prescribed by regulations made by the Lord Chancellor.

(5) Subject to subsections (7A) to (7G) below and without prejudice to any power exercisable by virtue of subsection (2)(d), (dd) , (e) or (g) above or otherwise than by virtue of this section, no property adjustment order or pension sharing order or pension compensation sharing order shall be made on an application for the variation of a periodical payments or secured periodical payments order made (whether in favour of a party to a marriage or in favour of a child of the family) under section 23 above, and no order for the payment of a lump sum shall be made on an application for the variation of a periodical payments or secured periodical payments order in favour of a party to a marriage (whether made under section 23 or under section 27 above).

(6) Where the person liable to make payments under a secured periodical payments order has died, an application under this section relating to that order (and to any order made under section 24A(1) above which requires the proceeds of sale of property to be used for securing those payments) may be made by the person entitled to payments under the periodical payments order. or by the personal representatives of the deceased person, but no such application shall, except with the permission of the court, be made after the end of the period of six months from the date on which representation in regard to the estate of that person is first taken out.

(7) In exercising the powers conferred by this section the court shall have regard to all the circumstances of the case, first consideration being given to the welfare while a minor of any child of the family who has not attained the age of eighteen, and the circumstances of the case shall include any change in any of the matters to which the court was required to have regard when making the order to which the application relates, and—

(a) in the case of a periodical payments or secured periodical payments order made on or after the grant of a decree of divorce or nullity of marriage, the court shall consider whether in all the circumstances and after having regard to any such change it would be appropriate to vary the order so that payments under the order are required to be made or secured only for such further period as will in the opinion of the court be sufficient (in the light of any proposed exercise by the court, where the marriage has been dissolved, of its powers under

subsection (7B) below) to enable the party in whose favour the order was made to adjust without undue hardship to the termination of those payments;
  (b) in a case where the party against whom the order was made has died, the circumstances of the case shall also include the changed circumstances resulting from his or her death.
(7A) Subsection (7B) below applies where, after the dissolution of a marriage, the court—
  (a) discharges a periodical payments order or secured periodical payments order made in favour of a party to the marriage; or
  (b) varies such an order so that payments under the order are required to be made or secured only for such further period as is determined by the court.
(7B) The court has power, in addition to any power it has apart from this subsection, to make supplemental provision consisting of any of—
  (a) an order for the payment of a lump sum in favour of a party to the marriage;
  (b) one or more property adjustment orders in favour of a party to the marriage;
  (ba) one or more pension sharing orders;
  (bb) a pension compensation sharing order;
  (c) a direction that the party in whose favour the original order discharged or varied was made is not entitled to make any further application for—
    (i) a periodical payments or secured periodical payments order, or
    (ii) an extension of the period to which the original order is limited by any variation made by the court.
(7C) An order for the payment of a lump sum made under subsection (7B) above may—
  (a) provide for the payment of that sum by instalments of such amount as may be specified in the order; and
  (b) require the payment of the instalments to be secured to the satisfaction of the court.
(7D) Subsections (7) and (8) of section 22A above apply where the court makes an order for the payment of a lump sum under subsection (7B) above as they apply where it makes such an order under section 22A above.
(7E) If under subsection (7B) above the court makes more than one property adjustment order in favour of the same party to the marriage, each of those orders must fall within a different paragraph of section 21(2) above.
(7F) Sections 24A and 30 above apply where the court makes a property adjustment order under subsection (7B) above as they apply where it makes such an order under section 23A above.
(7G) Subsections (3) to (5) of section 24B above apply in relation to a pension sharing order under subsection (7B) above as they apply in relation to a pension sharing order under that section.
(7H) Subsections (3) to (10) of section 24E above apply in relation to a pension compensation sharing order under section (7B) above as they apply in relation to a pension compensation sharing order under that section.

(8) The personal representatives of a deceased person against whom a secured periodical payments order was made shall not be liable for having distributed any part of the estate of the deceased after the expiration of the period of six months referred to in subsection (6) above on the ground that they ought to have taken into account the possibility that the court might permit an application under this section to be made after that period by the person entitled to payments under the order; but this subsection shall not prejudice any power to recover any part of the estate so distributed arising by virtue of the making of an order in pursuance of this section.

(9) In considering for the purposes of subsection (6) above the question when representation was first taken out, a grant limited to settled land or to trust property shall be left out of account and a grant limited to real estate or to personal estate shall be left out of account unless a grant limited to the remainder of the estate has previously been made or is made at the same time.

(10) Where the court, in exercise of its powers under this section, decides to vary or discharge a periodical payments or secured periodical payments order, then, subject to section 28(1) and (2) above, the court shall have power to direct that the variation or discharge shall not take effect until the expiration of such period as may be specified in the order.

(11) Where—
  (a) a periodical payments or secured periodical payments order in favour of more than one child ("the order") is in force;
  (b) the order requires payments specified in it to be made to or for the benefit of more than one child without apportioning those payments between them;
  (c) a maintenance assessment ("the assessment") is made with respect to one or more, but not all, of the children with respect to whom those payments are to be made; and
  (d) an application is made, before the end of the period of 6 months beginning with the date on which the assessment was made, for the variation or discharge of the order, the court may, in exercise of its powers under this section to vary or discharge the order, direct that the variation or discharge shall take effect from the date on which the assessment took effect or any later date.

(12) Where—
  (a) an order ("the child order") of a kind prescribed for the purposes of section 10(1) of the Child Support Act 1991 is affected by a maintenance assessment;
  (b) on the date on which the child order became so affected there was in force a periodical payments or secured periodical payments order ("the spousal order") in favour of a party to a marriage having the care of the child in whose favour the child order was made; and
  (c) an application is made, before the end of the period of 6 months beginning with the date on which the maintenance assessment was made, for the spousal order to be varied or discharged, the court may, in exercise of its powers under this section to vary or discharge the

spousal order, direct that the variation or discharge shall take effect from the date on which the child order became so affected or any later date.
(13) For the purposes of subsection (12) above, an order is affected if it ceases to have effect or is modified by or under section 10 of the Child Support Act 1991.
(14) Subsections (11) and (12) above are without prejudice to any other power of the court to direct that the variation of discharge of an order under this section shall take effect from a date earlier than that on which the order for variation or discharge was made.
(15) The power to make regulations under subsection (4C) above shall be exercisable by statutory instrument which shall be subject to annulment in pursuance of a resolution of either House of Parliament.

Avoidance of transactions intended to prevent or reduce financial relief

37.—(1) For the purposes of this section "financial relief" means relief under any of the provisions of sections 22, 23, 24, 24B, 27, 31 (except subsection (6)) and 35 above, and any reference in this section to defeating a person's claim for financial relief is a reference to preventing financial relief from being granted to that person, or to that person for the benefit of a child of the family, or reducing the amount of any financial relief which might be so granted, or frustrating or impeding the enforcement of any order which might be or has been made at his instance under any of those provisions.
(2) Where proceedings for financial relief are brought by one person against another, the court may, on the application of the first-mentioned person—
  (a) if it is satisfied that the other party to the proceedings is, with the intention of defeating the claim for financial relief, about to make any disposition or to transfer out of the jurisdiction or otherwise deal with any property, make such order as it thinks fit for restraining the other party from so doing or otherwise for protecting the claim;
  (b) if it is satisfied that the other party has, with that intention, made a reviewable disposition and that if the disposition were set aside financial relief or different financial relief would be granted to the applicant, make an order setting aside the disposition;
  (c) if it is satisfied, in a case where an order has been obtained under any of the provisions mentioned in subsection (1) above by the applicant against the other party, that the other party has, with that intention, made a reviewable disposition, make an order setting aside the disposition; and an application for the purposes of paragraph (b) above shall be made in the proceedings for the financial relief in question.
(3) Where the court makes an order under subsection (2)(b) or (c) above setting aside a disposition it shall give such consequential directions as it thinks fit for giving effect to the order (including directions requiring the making of any payments or the disposal of any property).
(4) Any disposition made by the other party to the proceedings for financial relief in question (whether before or after the commencement of those

proceedings) as is reviewable disposition for the purposes of subsection (2)(b) and (c) above unless it was made for valuable consideration (other than marriage) to a person who, at the time of the disposition, acted in relation to it in good faith and without notice of any intention on the part of the other party to defeat the applicant's claim for financial relief.

(5) Where an application is made under this section with respect to a disposition which took place less than three years before the date of the application or with respect to a disposition or other dealing with property which is about to take place and the court is satisfied—
   (a) in a case falling within subsection (2)(a) or (b) above, that the disposition or other dealing would (apart from this section) have the consequence, or
   (b) in a case falling within subsection (2)(c) above, that the disposition has had the consequence, of defeating the applicant's claim for financial relief, it shall be presumed, unless the contrary is shown, that the person who disposed of or is about to dispose of or deal with the property did so or, as the case may be, is about to do so, with the intention of defeating the applicant's claim for financial relief.

(6) In this section "disposition" does not include any provision contained in a will or codicil but, with that exception, includes any conveyance, assurance or gift of property of any description, whether made by an instrument or otherwise.

(7) This section does not apply to a disposition made before 1st January 1968.

Appeals relating to pension sharing orders which have taken effect

40A.—(1) Subsections (2) and (3) below apply where an appeal against a pension sharing order is begun on or after the day on which the order takes effect.

(2) If the pension sharing order relates to a person's rights under a pension arrangement, the appeal court may not set aside or vary the order if the person responsible for the pension arrangement has acted to his detriment in reliance on the taking effect of the order.

(3) If the pension sharing order relates to a person's shareable state scheme rights, the appeal court may not set aside or vary the order if the Secretary of State has acted to his detriment in reliance on the taking effect of the order.

(4) In determining for the purposes of subsection (2) or (3) above whether a person has acted to his detriment in reliance on the taking effect of the order, the appeal court may disregard any detriment which in its opinion is insignificant.

(5) Where subsection (2) or (3) above applies, the appeal court may make such further orders (including one or more pension sharing orders) as it thinks fit for the purpose of putting the parties in the position it considers appropriate.

(6) Section 24C above only applies to a pension sharing order under this section if the decision of the appeal court can itself be the subject of an appeal.

(7) In subsection (2) above, the reference to the person responsible for the pension arrangement is to be read in accordance with section 25D(4) above.

Appeals relating to pension compensation sharing orders which have taken effect

40B (1) This section applies where an appeal against a pension compensation sharing order is begun on or after the day on which the order takes effect.
(2) If the Board of the Pension Protection Fund has acted to its detriment in reliance on the taking effect of the order the appeal court—
   (a) may not set aside or vary the order;
   (b) may make such further orders (including a pension compensation sharing order) as it thinks fit for the purpose of putting the parties in the position it considers appropriate.
(3) In determining for the purposes of subsection (2) whether the Board has acted to its detriment the appeal court may disregard any detriment which in the court's opinion is insignificant.
(4) Section 24F (duty to stay) only applies to a pension compensation sharing order under this section if the decision of the appeal court can itself be the subject of an appeal.

WELFARE REFORM AND PENSIONS ACT 1999

(Incorporating amendments under Civil Partnership Act 2004, Pensions Act 2004 and The Taxation of Pension Schemes (Consequential Amendments) Order 2006 (SI 2006/745).)

Effect of bankruptcy on pension rights: approved arrangements

11. — (1) Where a bankruptcy order is made against a person on a petition presented after the coming into force of this section, any rights of his under an approved pension arrangement are excluded from his estate.
(2) In this section "approved pension arrangement" means—
   (a) a pension scheme registered under section 153 of the Finance Act 2004;
   [...]
   (c) an occupational pension scheme set up by a government outside the United Kingdom for the benefit, or primarily for the benefit, of its employees;
   [...]
   (g) an annuity purchased for the purpose of giving effect to rights under a scheme falling within paragraph (a), including an annuity in payment before 6th April 2006, giving effect to rights under any scheme approved—
      (i) before that date under Chapters 1, 3 or 4 of Part 14 of the Taxes Act; or
      (ii) any relevant statutory scheme, as defined in section 611 of that Act;

(h) any pension arrangements of any description which may be prescribed by regulations made by the Secretary of State.
[...]

(4) Subsection (5) applies if—
   (a) at the time when a bankruptcy order is made against a person, an appeal against a decision not to register a pension scheme has been made under section 156 of the Finance Act 2004, and
   (b) the decision of the General or Special Commissioners (see section 156(3) of that Act) is to uphold the decision of Her Majesty's Revenue and Customs not to register the scheme.

(5) Any rights of that person under the scheme shall (without any conveyance, assignment or transfer) vest in his trustee in bankruptcy, as part of his estate, immediately on—
   (a) the General or Special Commissioners' decision being made, or
   (b) (if later) the trustee's appointment taking effect or, in the case of the official receiver, his becoming trustee.

(6) Subsection (7) applies if, at any time after a bankruptcy order is made against a person Her Majesty's Revenue and Customs—
   (a) give notice withdrawing registration of the pension scheme under section 157 of the Finance Act 2004, and
   (b) the date specified as being that from which de-registration occurs under sub-section (4) of that section ("the de-registration date") is the date from which the scheme ceases to be a registered pension scheme.

(7) Any rights of that person under the scheme or arising by virtue of the arrangements, and any rights of his under any related annuity, shall (without any conveyance, assignment or transfer) vest in his trustee in bankruptcy, as part of his estate, immediately on—
   (a) the giving of the notice, or
   (b) (if later) the trustee's appointment taking effect or, in the case of the official receiver, his becoming trustee.

(8) In subsection (7) "related annuity" means an annuity purchased on or after the de-registration date for the purpose of giving effect to rights under the scheme or (as the case may be) to rights arising by virtue of the arrangements.

(9) Where under subsection (5) or (7) any rights vest in a person's trustee in bankruptcy, the trustee's title to them has relation back to the commencement of the person's bankruptcy; but where any transaction is entered into by the trustees or managers of the scheme in question—
   (a) in good faith, and
   (b) without notice of the making of the decision mentioned in subsection (4)(b) or (as the case may be) the giving of the notice mentioned in subsection (6),
the trustee in bankruptcy is not in respect of that transaction entitled by virtue of this subsection to any remedy against them or any person whose title to any property derives from them.

(10) Without prejudice to section 83, regulations under subsection (2)(h) may, in the case of any description of arrangements prescribed by the regulations, make provision corresponding to any provision made by subsections (4) to (9).

(11) In this section—
- (a) "occupational pension scheme" has the meaning given in section 150(5) of the Finance Act 2004;
- (b) "pension scheme" has the meaning given in section 150(1) of the Finance Act 2004 and "registered pension scheme" means a pension scheme registered under section 153 of the Finance Act 2004;
- (c) "estate", in relation to a person against whom a bankruptcy order is made, means his estate for the purposes of Parts VIII to XI of the Insolvency Act 1986;
- (d) "the Taxes Act" means the Income and Corporation Taxes Act 1988.

(12) For the purposes of this section a person shall be treated as having a right under an approved pension arrangement where—
- (a) he is entitled to a credit under section 29(1)(b) as against the person responsible for the arrangement (within the meaning of Chapter I of Part IV), and
- (b) the person so responsible has not discharged his liability in respect of the credit.

[…]

Supply of pension information in connection with divorce etc.

23.—(1) The Secretary of State may by regulations—
- (a) make provision imposing on the person responsible for a pension arrangement, or on the Secretary of State, requirements with respect to the supply of information relevant to any power with respect to—
  - (i) financial relief under Part II of the Matrimonial Causes Act 1973 or Part III of the Matrimonial and Family Proceedings Act 1984 (England and Wales powers in relation to domestic and overseas divorce etc.),
  - (ia) financial relief under Schedule 5 or 7 to the Civil Partnership Act 2004 (England and Wales powers in relation to domestic and overseas dissolution of civil partnerships etc.),
  - (ii) financial provision under the Family Law (Scotland) Act 1985 or Part IV of the Matrimonial and Family Proceedings Act 1984 or Schedule 11 to the 2004 Act (corresponding Scottish powers),
  - (iii) financial relief under Part III of the Matrimonial Causes (Northern Ireland) Order 1978 or Part IV of the Matrimonial and Family Proceedings (Northern Ireland) Order 1989 (Northern Ireland powers corresponding to those mentioned in sub-paragraph (i)), or
  - (iv) financial relief under Schedule 15 or 17 to the 2004 Act (Northern Ireland powers corresponding to those mentioned in sub-paragraph (ia));

(b) make provision about calculation and verification in relation to the valuation of—
  (i) benefits under a pension arrangement, or
  (ii) shareable state scheme rights,
  for the purposes of regulations under paragraph (a)(i)(ia), (iii) or (iv);
(c) make provision about calculation and verification in relation to—
  (i) the valuation of shareable rights under a pension arrangement or shareable state scheme rights for the purposes of regulations under paragraph (a)(ii), so far as relating to the making of orders for financial provision (within the meaning of the Family Law (Scotland) Act 1985), or
  (ii) the valuation of benefits under a pension arrangement for the purposes of such regulations, so far as relating to the making of orders under section 12A of that Act;
(d) make provision for the purpose of enabling the person responsible for a pension arrangement to recover prescribed charges in respect of providing information in accordance with regulations under paragraph (a).

(2) Regulations under subsection (1)(b) or (c) may include provision for calculation or verification in accordance with guidance from time to time prepared by a person prescribed by the regulations.

(3) Regulations under subsection (1)(d) may include provision for the application in prescribed circumstances, with or without modification, of any provision made by virtue of section 41(2).

(4) In subsection (1)—
  (a) the reference in paragraph (c)(i) to shareable rights under a pension arrangement is to rights in relation to which pension sharing is available under Chapter I of Part IV, or under corresponding Northern Ireland legislation, and
  (b) the references to shareable state scheme rights are to rights in relation to which pension sharing is available under Chapter II of Part IV, or under corresponding Northern Ireland legislation.

Charges by pension arrangements in relation to earmarking orders

24. The Secretary of State may by regulations make provision for the purpose of enabling the person responsible for a pension arrangement to recover prescribed charges in respect of complying with—
  (a) an order under section 23 of the Matrimonial Causes Act 1973 (financial provision orders in connection with divorce etc.), so far as it includes provision made by virtue of section 25B or 25C of that Act (powers to include provision about pensions),
  (aa) an order under Part 1 of Schedule 5 to the Civil Partnership Act 2004 (financial provision orders in connection with dissolution of civil partnerships etc.) so far as it includes provision made by virtue of Part 6 of that Schedule (powers to include provision about pensions),

STATUTES AND STATUTORY INSTRUMENTS

(b) an order under section 12A(2) or (3) of the Family Law (Scotland) Act 1985 (powers in relation to pensions lump sums when making a capital sum order), or

(c) an order under Article 25 of the Matrimonial Causes (Northern Ireland) Order 1978, so far as it includes provision made by virtue of Article 27B or 27C of that Order (Northern Ireland powers corresponding to those mentioned in paragraph (a)), or

(d) an order under Part 1 of Schedule 15 to the 2004 Act so far as it includes provision made by virtue of Part 5 of that Schedule (Northern Ireland powers corresponding to those mentioned in paragraph (aa)).

[…]

Interpretation of Part III

26.—(1) In this Part—
"occupational pension scheme" has the same meaning as in the Pension Schemes Act 1993;
"pension arrangement" means
    (a) an occupational pension scheme,
    (b) a personal pension scheme,
    (c) a retirement annuity contract,
    (d) an annuity or insurance policy purchased, or transferred, for the purpose of giving effect to rights under an occupational pension scheme or a personal pension scheme, and
    (e) an annuity purchased, or entered into, for the purpose of discharging liability in respect of a pension credit under section 29(1)(b) or under corresponding Northern Ireland legislation;
"personal pension scheme" has the same meaning as in the Pension Schemes Act 1993;
"prescribed" means prescribed by regulations made by the Secretary of State;
"retirement annuity contract" means an annuity contract or trust scheme approved under section 620 or 621 of the Income and Corporation Taxes Act 1988 or a substituted contract within the meaning of section 622(3) of that Act which became a registered pension scheme by virtue of paragraph 1(1)(f) of Schedule 36 to the Finance Act 2004,
"trustees or managers", in relation to an occupational pension scheme or a personal pension scheme, means—
    (a) in the case of a scheme established under a trust, the trustees of the scheme, and
    (b) in any other case, the managers of the scheme.

(2) References to the person responsible for a pension arrangement are—
    (a) in the case of an occupational pension scheme or a personal pension scheme, to the trustees or managers of the scheme,
    (b) in the case of a retirement annuity contract or an annuity falling within paragraph (d) or (e) of the definition of "pension arrangement" above, the provider of the annuity, and

PENSIONS ON DIVORCE

(c) in the case of an insurance policy falling within paragraph (d) of the definition of that expression, the insurer.

Scope of mechanism

27.—(1) Pension sharing is available under this Chapter in relation to a person's shareable rights under any pension arrangement other than an excepted public service pension scheme.
(2) For the purposes of this Chapter, a person's shareable rights under a pension arrangement are any rights of his under the arrangement, other than rights of a description specified by regulations made by the Secretary of State.
(3) For the purposes of subsection (1), a public service pension scheme is excepted if it is specified by order made by such Minister of the Crown or government department as may be designated by the Treasury as having responsibility for the scheme.

Activation of pension sharing

28.—(1) Section 29 applies on the taking effect of any of the following relating to a person's shareable rights under a pension arrangement—
(a) a pension sharing order under the Matrimonial Causes Act 1973,
(aa) a pension sharing order under Schedule 5 to the Civil Partnership Act 2004,
(b) provision which corresponds to the provision which may be made by such an order and which—
  (i) is contained in a qualifying agreement between the parties to a marriage, and
  (ii) takes effect on the dissolution of the marriage under the Family Law Act 1996,
(c) provision which corresponds to the provision which may be made by such an order and which—
  (i) is contained in a qualifying agreement between the parties to a marriage or former marriage, and
  (ii) takes effect after the dissolution of the marriage under the Family Law Act 1996,
(d) an order under Part III of the Matrimonial and Family Proceedings Act 1984 (financial relief in England and Wales in relation to overseas divorce etc.) corresponding to such an order as is mentioned in paragraph (a),
(da) an order under Schedule 7 to the 2004 Act (financial relief in England and Wales after overseas dissolution etc. of a civil partnership) corresponding to such an order as is mentioned in paragraph (aa),
(e) a pension sharing order under the Family Law (Scotland) Act 1985,
(f) provision which corresponds to the provision which may be made by such an order and which—

(i) is contained in a qualifying agreement between the parties to a marriage, or between persons who are civil partners of each other,

(ii) is in such form as the Secretary of State may prescribe by regulations, and

(iii) takes effect on the grant, in relation to the marriage, of decree of divorce under the Divorce (Scotland) Act 1976 or of declarator of nullity, or (as the case may be) on the grant, in relation to the civil partnership, of decree of dissolution or of declarator of nullity,

(g) an order under Part IV of the Matrimonial and Family Proceedings Act 1984 (financial relief in Scotland in relation to overseas divorce etc.) or under Schedule 11 to the 2004 Act (financial provision in Scotland after overseas proceedings) corresponding to such an order as is mentioned in paragraph (e),

(h) a pension sharing order under the Matrimonial Causes (Northern Ireland) Order 1978 (S.I. 1978/1045 (N.I. 15)),

(i) an order under Part IV of the Matrimonial and Family Proceedings (Northern Ireland) Order 1989 (financial relief in Northern Ireland in relation to overseas divorce etc.) corresponding to such an order as is mentioned in paragraph (h).

(j) a pension sharing order under Schedule 15 to the 2004 Act, and

(k) an order under Schedule 17 to the 2004 Act (financial relief in Northern Ireland after overseas dissolution etc. of a civil partnership) corresponding to such an order as is mentioned in paragraph (j).

(2) For the purposes of subsection (1)(b) and (c), a qualifying agreement is one which—

(a) has been entered into in such circumstances as the Lord Chancellor may prescribe by regulations, and

(b) satisfies such requirements as the Lord Chancellor may so prescribe.

(3) For the purposes of subsection (1)(f), a qualifying agreement is one which—

(a) has been entered into in such circumstances as the Secretary of State may prescribe by regulations, and

(b) is registered in the Books of Council and Session.

(4) Subsection (1)(b) does not apply if—

(a) the pension arrangement to which the provision relates is the subject of a pension sharing order under the Matrimonial Causes Act 1973 in relation to the marriage, or

(b) there is in force a requirement imposed by virtue of section 25B or 25C of that Act (powers to include in financial provision orders requirements relating to benefits under pension arrangements) which relates to benefits or future benefits to which the party who is the transferor is entitled under the pension arrangement to which the provision relates.

(5) Subsection (1)(c) does not apply if—

(a) the marriage was dissolved by an order under section 3 of the Family Law Act 1996 (divorce not preceded by separation) and the

satisfaction of the requirements of section 9(2) of that Act (settlement of future financial arrangements) was a precondition to the making of the order,
  (b) the pension arrangement to which the provision relates—
    (i) is the subject of a pension sharing order under the Matrimonial Causes Act 1973 in relation to the marriage, or
    (ii) has already been the subject of pension sharing between the parties, or
  (c) there is in force a requirement imposed by virtue of section 25B or 25C of that Act which relates to benefits or future benefits to which the party who is the transferor is entitled under the pension arrangement to which the provision relates.
(6) Subsection (1)(f) does not apply if there is in force an order under section 12A(2) or (3) of the Family Law (Scotland) Act 1985 which relates to benefits or future benefits to which the party who is the transferor is entitled under the pension arrangement to which the provision relates.
(7) For the purposes of this section, an order or provision falling within subsection (1)(e), (f) or (g) shall be deemed never to have taken effect if the person responsible for the arrangement to which the order or provision relates does not receive before the end of the period of 2 months beginning with the relevant date—
  (a) copies of the relevant documents, and
  (b) such information relating to the transferor and transferee as the Secretary of State may prescribe by regulations under section 34(1)(b)(ii).
(8) The relevant date for the purposes of subsection (7) is—
  (a) in the case of an order or provision falling within subsection (1)(e) or (f), the date of the extract of the decree or declarator responsible for the divorce, dissolution or annulment to which the order or provision relates, and
  (b) in the case of an order falling within subsection (1)(g), the date of disposal of the application under section 28 of the Matrimonial and Family Proceedings Act 1984 or, where the order is under Schedule 11 to the 2004 Act, the date of disposal of the application under paragraph 2 of that Schedule.
(9) The reference in subsection (7)(a) to the relevant documents is—
  (a) in the case of an order falling within subsection (1)(e) or (g), to copies of the order and the order, decree or declarator responsible for the divorce, dissolution or annulment to which it relates, and
  (b) in the case of provision falling within subsection (1)(f), to—
    (i) copies of the provision and the order, decree or declarator responsible for the divorce, dissolution or annulment to which it relates, and
    (ii) documentary evidence that the agreement containing the provision is one to which subsection (3)(a) applies.
(11) In subsections (4)(b), (5)(c) and (6), the reference to the party who is the transferor is to the party to whose rights the provision relates.

STATUTES AND STATUTORY INSTRUMENTS

Creation of pension debits and credits

29.—(1) On the application of this section—
- (a) the transferor's shareable rights under the relevant arrangement become subject to a debit of the appropriate amount, and
- (b) the transferee becomes entitled to a credit of that amount as against the person responsible for that arrangement.

(2) Where the relevant order or provision specifies a percentage value to be transferred, the appropriate amount for the purposes of subsection (1) is the specified percentage of the cash equivalent of the relevant benefits on the valuation day.

(3) Where the relevant order or provision specifies an amount to be transferred, the appropriate amount for the purposes of subsection (1) is the lesser of—
- (a) the specified amount, and
- (b) the cash equivalent of the relevant benefits on the valuation day.

(4) Where the relevant arrangement is an occupational pension scheme and the transferor is in pensionable service under the scheme on the transfer day, the relevant benefits for the purposes of subsections (2) and (3) are the benefits or future benefits to which he would be entitled under the scheme by virtue of his shareable rights under it had his pensionable service terminated immediately before that day.

(5) Otherwise, the relevant benefits for the purposes of subsections (2) and (3) are the benefits or future benefits to which, immediately before the transfer day, the transferor is entitled under the terms of the relevant arrangement by virtue of his shareable rights under it.

(6) The Secretary of State may by regulations provide for any description of benefit to be disregarded for the purposes of subsection (4) or (5).

(7) For the purposes of this section, the valuation day is such day within the implementation period for the credit under subsection (1)(b) as the person responsible for the relevant arrangement may specify by notice in writing to the transferor and transferee.

(8) In this section—
"relevant arrangement" means the arrangement to which the relevant order or provision relates;
"relevant order or provision" means the order or provision by virtue of which this section applies;
"transfer day" means the day on which the relevant order or provision takes effect;
"transferor" means the person to whose rights the relevant order or provision relates;
"transferee" means the person for whose benefit the relevant order or provision is made.
[…]

Reduction of benefit

31.—(1) Subject to subsection (2), where a person's shareable rights under a pension arrangement are subject to a pension debit, each benefit or future benefit—
  (a) to which he is entitled under the arrangement by virtue of those rights, and
  (b) which is a qualifying benefit,
  is reduced by the appropriate percentage.
(2) Where a pension debit relates to the shareable rights under an occupational pension scheme of a person who is in pensionable service under the scheme on the transfer day, each benefit or future benefit—
  (a) to which the person is entitled under the scheme by virtue of those rights, and
  (b) which corresponds to a qualifying benefit,
  is reduced by an amount equal to the appropriate percentage of the corresponding qualifying benefit.
(3) A benefit is a qualifying benefit for the purposes of subsections (1) and (2) if the cash equivalent by reference to which the amount of the pension debit is determined includes an amount in respect of it.
(4) The provisions of this section override any provision of a pension arrangement to which they apply to the extent that the provision conflicts with them.
(5) In this section—
  "appropriate percentage", in relation to a pension debit, means—
    (a) if the relevant order or provision specifies the percentage value to be transferred, that percentage;
    (b) if the relevant order or provision specifies an amount to be transferred, the percentage which the appropriate amount for the purposes of subsection (1) of section 29 represents of the amount mentioned in subsection (3)(b) of that section;
  "relevant order or provision", in relation to a pension debit, means the pension sharing order or provision on which the debit depends;
  "transfer day", in relation to a pension debit, means the day on which the relevant order or provision takes effect.
  [...]

Time for discharge of liability

33.—(1) A person subject to liability in respect of a pension credit shall discharge his liability before the end of the implementation period for the credit.
(2) Where the trustees or managers of an occupational pension scheme have not done what is required to discharge their liability in respect of a pension credit before the end of the implementation period for the credit—
  (a) they shall, except in such cases as the Secretary of State may prescribe by regulations, notify the Regulatory Authority of that fact within such period as the Secretary of State may so prescribe, and

(b) section 10 of the Pensions Act 1995 (power of the Regulatory Authority to impose civil penalties) shall apply to any trustee or manager who has failed to take all such steps as are reasonable to ensure that liability in respect of the credit was discharged before the end of the implementation period for it.

(3) If trustees or managers to whom subsection (2)(a) applies fail to perform the obligation imposed by that provision, section 10 of the Pensions Act 1995 shall apply to any trustee or manager who has failed to take all reasonable steps to ensure that the obligation was performed.

(4) On the application of the trustees or managers of an occupational pension scheme who are subject to liability in respect of a pension credit, the Regulatory Authority may extend the implementation period for the credit for the purposes of this section if it is satisfied that the application is made in such circumstances as the Secretary of State may prescribe by regulations.

(5) In this section "the Regulatory Authority" means the Pensions Regulator.

Implementation period

34.—(1) For the purposes of this Chapter, the implementation period for a pension credit is the period of 4 months beginning with the later of—
   (a) the day on which the relevant order or provision takes effect, and
   (b) the first day on which the person responsible for the pension arrangement to which the relevant order or provision relates is in receipt of—
      (i) the relevant documents, and
      (ii) such information relating to the transferor and transferee as the Secretary of State may prescribe by regulations.

(2) The reference in subsection (1)(b)(i) to the relevant documents is to copies of—
   (a) the relevant order or provision, and
   (b) the order, decree or declarator responsible for the divorce, dissolution or annulment to which it relates,
and, if the pension credit depends on provision falling within subsection (1)(f) of section 28, to documentary evidence that the agreement containing the provision is one to which subsection (3)(a) of that section applies.

(3) Subsection (1) is subject to any provision made by regulations under section 41(2)(a).

(4) The Secretary of State may by regulations—
   (a) make provision requiring a person subject to liability in respect of a pension credit to notify the transferor and transferee of the day on which the implementation period for the credit begins;
   (b) provide for this section to have effect with modifications where the pension arrangement to which the relevant order or provision relates is being wound up;
   (c) provide for this section to have effect with modifications where the pension credit depends on a pension sharing order and the order is the subject of an application for leave to appeal out of time.

(5) In this section—
"relevant order or provision", in relation to a pension credit, means the pension sharing order or provision on which the pension credit depends;
"transferor" means the person to whose rights the relevant order or provision relates;
"transferee" means the person for whose benefit the relevant order or provision is made.

Mode of discharge of liability

35.—(1) Schedule 5 (which makes provision about how liability in respect of a pension credit may be discharged) shall have effect.
(2) Where the person entitled to a pension credit dies before liability in respect of the credit has been discharged—
 (a) Schedule 5 shall cease to have effect in relation to the discharge of liability in respect of the credit, and
 (b) liability in respect of the credit shall be discharged in accordance with regulations made by the Secretary of State.
[…]

Charges in respect of pension sharing costs

41.—(1) The Secretary of State may by regulations make provision for the purpose of enabling the person responsible for a pension arrangement involved in pension sharing to recover from the parties to pension sharing prescribed charges in respect of prescribed descriptions of pension sharing activity.
(2) Regulations under subsection (1) may include—
 (a) provision for the start of the implementation period for a pension credit to be postponed in prescribed circumstances;
 (b) provision, in relation to payments in respect of charges recoverable under the regulations, for reimbursement as between the parties to pension sharing;
 (c) provision, in relation to the recovery of charges by deduction from a pension credit, for the modification of Schedule 5;
 (d) provision for the recovery in prescribed circumstances of such additional amounts as may be determined in accordance with the regulations.
(3) For the purposes of regulations under subsection (1), the question of how much of a charge recoverable under the regulations is attributable to a party to pension sharing is to be determined as follows—
 (a) where the relevant order or provision includes provision about the apportionment of charges under this section, there is attributable to the party so much of the charge as is apportioned to him by that provision;
 (b) where the relevant order or provision does not include such provision, the charge is attributable to the transferor.

(4) For the purposes of subsection (1), a pension arrangement is involved in pension sharing if section 29 applies by virtue of an order or provision which relates to the arrangement.
(5) In that subsection, the reference to pension sharing activity is to activity attributable (directly or indirectly) to the involvement in pension sharing.
(6) In subsection (3)—
- (a) the reference to the relevant order or provision is to the order or provision which gives rise to the pension sharing, and
- (b) the reference to the transferor is to the person to whose rights that order or provision relates.
(7) In this section "prescribed" means prescribed in regulations under subsection (1).
[…]

Interpretation of Chapter I

46.—(1) In this Chapter—
"implementation period", in relation to a pension credit, has the meaning given by section 34;
"occupational pension scheme" has the meaning given by section 1 of the Pension Schemes Act 1993;
"pension arrangement" means—
- (a) an occupational pension scheme,
- (b) a personal pension scheme,
- (c) a retirement annuity contract,
- (d) an annuity or insurance policy purchased, or transferred, for the purpose of giving effect to rights under an occupational pension scheme or a personal pension scheme, and
- (e) an annuity purchased, or entered into, for the purpose of discharging liability in respect of a credit under section 29(1)(b) or under corresponding Northern Ireland legislation;

"pension credit" means a credit under section 29(1)(b);
"pension debit" means a debit under section 29(1)(a);
"pensionable service", in relation to a member of an occupational pension scheme, means service in any description or category of employment to which the scheme relates which qualifies the member (on the assumption that it continues for the appropriate period) for pension or other benefits under the scheme;
"personal pension scheme" has the meaning given by section 1 of the Pension Schemes Act 1993;
"retirement annuity contract" means a contract or scheme approved under Chapter III of Part XIV of the Income and Corporation Taxes Act 1988;
"shareable rights" has the meaning given by section 27(2);
"trustees or managers", in relation to an occupational pension scheme or a personal pension scheme means—
- (a) in the case of a scheme established under a trust, the trustees of the scheme, and
- (b) in any other case, the managers of the scheme.

PENSIONS ON DIVORCE

(2) In this Chapter, references to the person responsible for a pension arrangement are—
  (a) in the case of an occupational pension scheme or a personal pension scheme, to the trustees or managers of the scheme,
  (b) in the case of a retirement annuity contract or an annuity falling within paragraph (d) or (e) of the definition of "pension arrangement" in subsection (1), to the provider of the annuity, and
  (c) in the case of an insurance policy falling within paragraph (d) of the definition of that expression, to the insurer.
(3) In determining what is "pensionable service" for the purposes of this Chapter—
  (a) service notionally attributable for any purpose of the scheme is to be disregarded, and
  (b) no account is to be taken of any rules of the scheme by which a period of service can be treated for any purpose as being longer or shorter than it actually is.

Shareable state scheme rights

47.—(1) Pension sharing is available under this Chapter in relation to a person's shareable state scheme rights.
(2) For the purposes of this Chapter, a person's shareable state scheme rights are—
  (a) his entitlement, or prospective entitlement, to a Category A retirement pension by virtue of section 44(3)(b) of the Contributions and Benefits Act (earnings-related additional pension), and
  (b) his entitlement, or prospective entitlement, to a pension under section 55A of that Act (shared additional pension).
  […]

Transitional provisions

85.—(3) No pension sharing order may be made—
  (a) under section 24B of the Matrimonial Causes Act 1973 if the proceedings in which the decree is granted were begun before the day on which section 19 comes into force, or
  (b) under section 31(7B) of that Act if the marriage was dissolved by a decree granted in proceedings so begun.
  […]

SCHEDULE 5
Section 35

Pension credits: mode of discharge

Funded pension schemes

1.—(1) This paragraph applies to a pension credit which derives from—

STATUTES AND STATUTORY INSTRUMENTS

    (a) a funded occupational pension scheme, or
    (b) a personal pension scheme.

(2) The trustees or managers of the scheme from which a pension credit to which this paragraph applies derives may discharge their liability in respect of the credit by conferring appropriate rights under that scheme on the person entitled to the credit—
    (a) with his consent, or
    (b) in accordance with regulations made by the Secretary of State.

(3) The trustees or managers of the scheme from which a pension credit to which this paragraph applies derives may discharge their liability in respect of the credit by paying the amount of the credit to the person responsible for a qualifying arrangement with a view to acquiring rights under that arrangement for the person entitled to the credit if—
    (a) the qualifying arrangement is not disqualified as a destination for the credit,
    (b) the person responsible for that arrangement is able and willing to accept payment in respect of the credit, and
    (c) payment is made with the consent of the person entitled to the credit, or in accordance with regulations made by the Secretary of State.

(4) For the purposes of sub-paragraph (2), no account is to be taken of consent of the person entitled to the pension credit unless—
    (a) it is given after receipt of notice in writing of an offer to discharge liability in respect of the credit by making a payment under sub-paragraph (3), or
    (b) it is not withdrawn within 7 days of receipt of such notice.

Unfunded public service pension schemes

2.—(1) This paragraph applies to a pension credit which derives from an occupational pension scheme which is—
    (a) not funded, and
    (b) a public service pension scheme.

(2) The trustees or managers of the scheme from which a pension credit to which this paragraph applies derives may discharge their liability in respect of the credit by conferring appropriate rights under that scheme on the person entitled to the credit.

(3) If such a scheme as is mentioned in sub-paragraph (1) is closed to new members, the appropriate authority in relation to that scheme may by regulations specify another public service pension scheme as an alternative to it for the purposes of this paragraph.

(4) Where the trustees or managers of a scheme in relation to which an alternative is specified under sub-paragraph (3) are subject to liability in respect of a pension credit, they may—
    (a) discharge their liability in respect of the credit by securing that appropriate rights are conferred on the person entitled to the credit by the trustees or managers of the alternative scheme, and

(b) for the purpose of so discharging their liability, require the trustees or managers of the alternative scheme to take such steps as may be required.

(5) In sub-paragraph (3), "the appropriate authority", in relation to a public service pension scheme, means such Minister of the Crown or government department as may be designated by the Treasury as having responsibility for the scheme.

Other unfunded occupational pension schemes

3.—(1) This paragraph applies to a pension credit which derives from an occupational pension scheme which is—
  (a) not funded, and
  (b) not a public service pension scheme.

(2) The trustees or managers of the scheme from which a pension credit to which this paragraph applies derives may discharge their liability in respect of the credit by conferring appropriate rights under that scheme on the person entitled to the credit.

(3) The trustees or managers of the scheme from which a pension credit to which this paragraph applies derives may discharge their liability in respect of the credit by paying the amount of the credit to the person responsible for a qualifying arrangement with a view to acquiring rights under that arrangement for the person entitled to the credit if—
  (a) the qualifying arrangement is not disqualified as a destination for the credit,
  (b) the person responsible for that arrangement is able and willing to accept payment in respect of the credit, and
  (c) payment is made with the consent of the person entitled to the credit, or in accordance with regulations made by the Secretary of State.

Other pension arrangements

4.—(1) This paragraph applies to a pension credit which derives from—
  (a) a retirement annuity contract,
  (b) an annuity or insurance policy purchased or transferred for the purpose of giving effect to rights under an occupational pension scheme or a personal pension scheme, or
  (c) an annuity purchased, or entered into, for the purpose of discharging liability in respect of a pension credit.

(2) The person responsible for the pension arrangement from which a pension credit to which this paragraph applies derives may discharge his liability in respect of the credit by paying the amount of the credit to the person responsible for a qualifying arrangement with a view to acquiring rights under that arrangement for the person entitled to the credit if—
  (a) the qualifying arrangement is not disqualified as a destination for the credit,
  (b) the person responsible for that arrangement is able and willing to accept payment in respect of the credit, and

(c) payment is made with the consent of the person entitled to the credit, or in accordance with regulations made by the Secretary of State.
(3) The person responsible for the pension arrangement from which a pension credit to which this paragraph applies derives may discharge his liability in respect of the credit by entering into an annuity contract with the person entitled to the credit if the contract is not disqualified as a destination for the credit.
(4) The person responsible for the pension arrangement from which a pension credit to which this paragraph applies derives may, in such circumstances as the Secretary of State may prescribe by regulations, discharge his liability in respect of the credit by assuming an obligation to provide an annuity for the person entitled to the credit.
(5) In sub-paragraph (1)(c), "pension credit" includes a credit under Northern Ireland legislation corresponding to section 29(1)(b).

Appropriate rights

5. For the purposes of this Schedule, rights conferred on the person entitled to a pension credit are appropriate if—
   (a) they are conferred with effect from, and including, the day on which the order, or provision, under which the credit arises takes effect, and
   (b) their value, when calculated in accordance with regulations made by the Secretary of State, equals the amount of the credit.

Qualifying arrangements

6.—(1) The following are qualifying arrangements for the purposes of this Schedule—
   (a) an occupational pension scheme,
   (b) a personal pension scheme,
   (c) an appropriate annuity contract,
   (d) an appropriate policy of insurance, and
   (e) an overseas arrangement within the meaning of the Contracting-out (Transfer and Transfer Payment) Regulations 1996.
(2) An annuity contract or policy of insurance is appropriate for the purposes of sub-paragraph (1) if, at the time it is entered into or taken out, the insurer with which it is entered into or taken out—
   (a) is carrying on ... long-term insurance business in the United Kingdom or any other EEA State, and
   (b) satisfies such requirements as the Secretary of State may prescribe by regulations.
(3) "Insurer" and "long-term insurance business" have the meaning given in section 180A of the Pension Schemes Act 1993.

Disqualification as destination for pension credit

7.—(1) If a pension credit derives from a pension arrangement which is a registered pension scheme under section 153 of the Finance Act 2004, an arrangement is disqualified as a destination for the credit unless—
    (a)   it is also registered for those purposes, or
    (b)   it satisfies such requirements as the Secretary of State may prescribe by regulations.
(3)   An occupational pension scheme is disqualified as a destination for a pension credit unless the rights to be acquired under the arrangement by the person entitled to the credit are rights whose value, when calculated in accordance with regulations made by the Secretary of State, equals the credit.
(4)   An annuity contract or insurance policy is disqualified as a destination for a pension credit in such circumstances as the Secretary of State may prescribe by regulations.
(5)   The requirements which may be prescribed under sub-paragraph (1)(b) include, in particular, requirements of the Inland Revenue.

Adjustments to amount of pension credit

8.—(1) If—
    (a)   a pension credit derives from an occupational pension scheme,
    (b)   the scheme is one to which Part 3 of the Pensions Act 2004 (scheme funding) applies,
    (c)   the scheme is underfunded on the valuation day, and
    (d)   such circumstances as the Secretary of State may prescribe by regulations apply,
paragraph 1(3) shall have effect in relation to the credit as if the reference to the amount of the credit were to such lesser amount as may be determined in accordance with regulations made by the Secretary of State.
(2)   Whether a scheme is underfunded for the purposes of sub-paragraph (1)(c) shall be determined in accordance with regulations made by the Secretary of State.
(3)   For the purposes of that provision, the valuation day is the day by reference to which the cash equivalent on which the amount of the pension credit depends falls to be calculated.

9.   If—
    (a)   a person's shareable rights under a pension arrangement have become subject to a pension debit, and
    (b)   the person responsible for the arrangement makes a payment which is referable to those rights without knowing of the pension debit,
this Schedule shall have effect as if the amount of the corresponding pension credit were such lesser amount as may be determined in accordance with regulations made by the Secretary of State.

10.   The Secretary of State may by regulations make provision for paragraph 1(3), 3(3) or 4(2) to have effect, where payment is made after the end of the

STATUTES AND STATUTORY INSTRUMENTS

implementation period for the pension credit, as if the reference to the amount of the credit were to such larger amount as may be determined in accordance with the regulations.

General

11. Liability in respect of a pension credit shall be treated as discharged if the effect of paragraph 8(1) or 9 is to reduce it to zero.
12. Liability in respect of a pension credit may not be discharged otherwise than in accordance with this Schedule.
13. Regulations under paragraph 5(b) or 7(3) may provide for calculation of the value of rights in accordance with guidance from time to time prepared by a person specified in the regulations.
13A. The provisions of this Schedule are subject to—
   (a) section 73A(3) and (6) of the Pensions Act 1995 (prohibition on new members during winding up of scheme: exception for discharge of pension credit derived from the scheme), and
   (b) section 133(2) and (8) of the Pensions Act 2004 (prohibition on new members during an assessment period in relation to a scheme: exception for discharge of pension credit derived from the scheme).
14. In this Schedule—
   "funded", in relation to an occupational pension scheme, means that the scheme meets its liabilities out of a fund accumulated for the purpose during the life of the scheme;
   "public service pension scheme" has the same meaning as in the Pension Schemes Act 1993.

SCHEDULE 6
Section 50

Effect of state scheme pension debits and credits

1. The Contributions and Benefits Act is amended as follows.
2. After section 45A there is inserted—

   "*Reduction of additional pension in Category A retirement pension: pension sharing*
   45B.—(1) The weekly rate of the additional pension in a Category A retirement pension shall be reduced as follows in any case where—
      (a) the pensioner has become subject to a state scheme pension debit, and
      (b) the debit is to any extent referable to the additional pension.
   (2) If the pensioner became subject to the debit in or after the final relevant year, the weekly rate of the additional pension shall be reduced by the appropriate weekly amount.
   (3) If the pensioner became subject to the debit before the final relevant year, the weekly rate of the additional pension shall be reduced by the appropriate weekly amount multiplied by the relevant revaluation percentage.

(4) The appropriate weekly amount for the purposes of subsections (2) and (3) above is the weekly rate, expressed in terms of the valuation day, at which the cash equivalent, on that day, of the pension mentioned in subsection (5) below is equal to so much of the debit as is referable to the additional pension.

(5) The pension referred to above is a notional pension for the pensioner by virtue of section 44(3)(b) above which becomes payable on the later of—
  (a) his attaining pensionable age, and
  (b) the valuation day.

(6) For the purposes of subsection (3) above, the relevant revaluation percentage is the percentage specified, in relation to earnings factors for the tax year in which the pensioner became subject to the debit, by the last order under section 148 of the Administration Act to come into force before the end of the final relevant year.

(7) Cash equivalents for the purposes of this section shall be calculated in accordance with regulations.

(8) In this section—
"final relevant year" means the tax year immediately preceding that in which the pensioner attains pensionable age;
"state scheme pension debit" means a debit under section 49(1)(a) of the Welfare Reform and Pensions Act 1999 (debit for the purposes of this Part of this Act);
"valuation day" means the day on which the pensioner became subject to the state scheme pension debit."

3. After section 55 there is inserted—

"*Shared additional pension*

55A.—(1) A person shall be entitled to a shared additional pension if he is—
  (a) over pensionable age, and
  (b) entitled to a state scheme pension credit.

(2) A person's entitlement to a shared additional pension shall continue throughout his life.

(3) The weekly rate of a shared additional pension shall be the appropriate weekly amount, unless the pensioner's entitlement to the state scheme pension credit arose before the final relevant year, in which case it shall be that amount multiplied by the relevant revaluation percentage.

(4) The appropriate weekly amount for the purposes of subsection (3) above is the weekly rate, expressed in terms of the valuation day, at which the cash equivalent, on that day, of the pensioner's entitlement, or prospective entitlement, to the shared additional pension is equal to the state scheme pension credit.

(5) The relevant revaluation percentage for the purposes of that subsection is the percentage specified, in relation to earnings factors for the tax year in which the entitlement to the state scheme pension credit arose, by the last order under section 148 of the Administration Act to come into force before the end of the final relevant year.

(6) Cash equivalents for the purposes of this section shall be calculated in accordance with regulations.

(7) In this section—
"final relevant year" means the tax year immediately preceding that in which the pensioner attains pensionable age;
"state scheme pension credit" means a credit under section 49(1)(b) of the Welfare Reform and Pensions Act 1999 (credit for the purposes of this Part of this Act);

STATUTES AND STATUTORY INSTRUMENTS

"valuation day" means the day on which the pensioner becomes entitled to the state scheme pension credit.

Reduction of shared additional pension: pension sharing

55B.—(1) The weekly rate of a shared additional pension shall be reduced as follows in any case where—
  (a) the pensioner has become subject to a state scheme pension debit, and
  (b) the debit is to any extent referable to the pension.

(2) If the pensioner became subject to the debit in or after the final relevant year, the weekly rate of the pension shall be reduced by the appropriate weekly amount.

(3) If the pensioner became subject to the debit before the final relevant year, the weekly rate of the additional pension shall be reduced by the appropriate weekly amount multiplied by the relevant revaluation percentage.

(4) The appropriate weekly amount for the purposes of subsections (2) and (3) above is the weekly rate, expressed in terms of the valuation day, at which the cash equivalent, on that day, of the pension mentioned in subsection (5) below is equal to so much of the debit as is referable to the shared additional pension.

(5) The pension referred to above is a notional pension for the pensioner by virtue of section 55A above which becomes payable on the later of—
  (a) his attaining pensionable age, and
  (b) the valuation day.

(6) For the purposes of subsection (3) above, the relevant revaluation percentage is the percentage specified, in relation to earnings factors for the tax year in which the pensioner became subject to the debit, by the last order under section 148 of the Administration Act to come into force before the end of the final relevant year.

(7) Cash equivalents for the purposes of this section shall be calculated in accordance with regulations.

(8) In this section—
"final relevant year" means the tax year immediately preceding that in which the pensioner attains pensionable age;
"state scheme pension debit", means a debit under section 49(1)(a) of the Welfare Reform and Pensions Act 1999 (debit for the purposes of this Part of this Act);
"valuation day" means the day on which the pensioner became subject to the state scheme pension debit.

Increase of shared additional pension where entitlement is deferred

55C.—(1) For the purposes of this section, a person's entitlement to a shared additional pension is deferred—
  (a) where he would be entitled to a Category A or Category B retirement pension but for the fact that his entitlement to such a pension is deferred, if and so long as his entitlement to such a pension is deferred, and
  (b) otherwise, if and so long as he does not become entitled to the shared additional pension by reason only of not satisfying the conditions of section 1 of the Administration Act (entitlement to benefit dependent on claim),

and, in relation to a shared additional pension, "period of deferment" shall be construed accordingly.

(2) Where a person's entitlement to a shared additional pension is deferred, the rate of his shared additional pension shall be increased by an amount equal to the aggregate of the increments to which he is entitled under

subsection (3) below, but only if that amount is enough to increase the rate of the pension by at least 1 per cent.

(3) A person is entitled to an increment under this subsection for each complete incremental period in his period of enhancement.

(4) The amount of the increment for an incremental period shall be 1/7th per cent. of the weekly rate of the shared additional pension to which the person would have been entitled for the period if his entitlement had not been deferred.

(5) Amounts under subsection (4) above shall be rounded to the nearest penny, taking any 1/2p as nearest to the next whole penny.

(6) Where an amount under subsection (4) above would, apart from this subsection, be a sum less than 1/2p, the amount shall be taken to be zero, notwithstanding any other provision of this Act, the Pensions Act 1995 or the Administration Act.

(7) Where one or more orders have come into force under section 150 of the Administration Act during the period of enhancement, the rate for any incremental period shall be determined as if the order or orders had come into force before the beginning of the period of enhancement.

(8) The sums which are the increases in the rates of shared additional pensions under this section are subject to alteration by order made by the Secretary of State under section 150 of the Administration Act.

(9) In this section—
"incremental period" means any period of six days which are treated by regulations as days of increment for the purposes of this section in relation to the person and pension in question; and
"period of enhancement", in relation to that person and that pension, means the period which—
(a) begins on the same day as the period of deferment in question, and
(b) ends on the same day as that period or, if earlier, on the day before the 5th anniversary of the beginning of that period."

INSOLVENCY ACT 1986

(Incorporating amendments made by Welfare Reform and Pensions Act 1999)

Recovery of excessive pension contributions

342A.—(1) Where an individual who is adjudged bankrupt—
(a) has rights under an approved pension arrangement, or
(b) has excluded rights under an unapproved pension arrangement,
the trustee of the bankrupt's estate may apply to the court for an order under this section.

(2) If the court is satisfied—
(a) that the rights under the arrangement are to any extent, and whether directly or indirectly, the fruits of relevant contributions, and
(b) that the making of any of the relevant contributions ("the excessive contributions") has unfairly prejudiced the individual's creditors,
the court may make such order as it thinks fit for restoring the position to what it would have been had the excessive contributions not been made.

(3) Subsection (4) applies where the court is satisfied that the value of the rights under the arrangement is, as a result of rights of the individual under the arrangement or any other pension arrangement having at any time

STATUTES AND STATUTORY INSTRUMENTS

become subject to a debit under section 29(1)(a) of the Welfare Reform and Pensions Act 1999 (debits giving effect to pension-sharing), less than it would otherwise have been.

(4) Where this subsection applies—
   (a) any relevant contributions which were represented by the rights which became subject to the debit shall, for the purposes of subsection (2), be taken to be contributions of which the rights under the arrangement are the fruits, and
   (b) where the relevant contributions represented by the rights under the arrangement (including those so represented by virtue of paragraph (a)) are not all excessive contributions, relevant contributions which are represented by the rights under the arrangement otherwise than by virtue of paragraph (a) shall be treated as excessive contributions before any which are so represented by virtue of that paragraph.

(5) In subsections (2) to (4) "relevant contributions" means contributions to the arrangement or any other pension arrangement—
   (a) which the individual has at any time made on his own behalf, or
   (b) which have at any time been made on his behalf.

(6) The court shall, in determining whether it is satisfied under subsection (2)(b), consider in particular—
   (a) whether any of the contributions were made for the purpose of putting assets beyond the reach of the individual's creditors or any of them, and
   (b) whether the total amount of any contributions—
      (i) made by or on behalf of the individual to pension arrangements, and
      (ii) represented (whether directly or indirectly) by rights under approved pension arrangements or excluded rights under unapproved pension arrangements,
      is an amount which is excessive in view of the individual's circumstances when those contributions were made.

(7) For the purposes of this section and sections 342B and 342C ("the recovery provisions"), rights of an individual under an unapproved pension arrangement are excluded rights if they are rights which are excluded from his estate by virtue of regulations under section 12 of the Welfare Reform and Pensions Act 1999.

(8) In the recovery provisions—
   "approved pension arrangement" has the same meaning as in section 11 of the Welfare Reform and Pensions Act 1999;
   "unapproved pension arrangement" has the same meaning as in section 12 of that Act.

Orders under section 342A

342B.—(1) Without prejudice to the generality of section 342A(2), an order under section 342A may include provision—
   (a) requiring the person responsible for the arrangement to pay an amount to the individual's trustee in bankruptcy,

(b) adjusting the liabilities of the arrangement in respect of the individual,

(c) adjusting any liabilities of the arrangement in respect of any other person that derive, directly or indirectly, from rights of the individual under the arrangement,

(d) for the recovery by the person responsible for the arrangement (whether by deduction from any amount which that person is ordered to pay or otherwise) of costs incurred by that person in complying in the bankrupt's case with any requirement under section 342C(1) or in giving effect to the order.

(2) In subsection (1), references to adjusting the liabilities of the arrangement in respect of a person include (in particular) reducing the amount of any benefit or future benefit to which that person is entitled under the arrangement.

(3) In subsection (1)(c), the reference to liabilities of the arrangement does not include liabilities in respect of a person which result from giving effect to an order or provision falling within section 28(1) of the Welfare Reform and Pensions Act 1999 (pension sharing orders and agreements).

(4) The maximum amount which the person responsible for an arrangement may be required to pay by an order under section 342A is the lesser of—
   (a) the amount of the excessive contributions, and
   (b) the value of the individual's rights under the arrangement (if the arrangement is an approved pension arrangement) or of his excluded rights under the arrangement (if the arrangement is an unapproved pension arrangement).

(5) An order under section 342A which requires the person responsible for an arrangement to pay an amount ("the restoration amount") to the individual's trustee in bankruptcy must provide for the liabilities of the arrangement to be correspondingly reduced.

(6) For the purposes of subsection (5), liabilities are correspondingly reduced if the difference between—
   (a) the amount of the liabilities immediately before the reduction, and
   (b) the amount of the liabilities immediately after the reduction,
is equal to the restoration amount.

(7) An order under section 342A in respect of an arrangement—
   (a) shall be binding on the person responsible for the arrangement, and
   (b) overrides provisions of the arrangement to the extent that they conflict with the provisions of the order.

Orders under section 342A: supplementary

342C.—(1) The person responsible for—
   (a) an approved pension arrangement under which a bankrupt has rights,
   (b) an unapproved pension arrangement under which a bankrupt has excluded rights, or
   (c) a pension arrangement under which a bankrupt has at any time had rights,

shall, on the bankrupt's trustee in bankruptcy making a written request, provide the trustee with such information about the arrangement and rights as the trustee may reasonably require for, or in connection with, the making of applications under section 342A.

(2) Nothing in—
  (a) any provision of section 159 of the Pension Schemes Act 1993 or section 91 of the Pensions Act 1995 (which prevent assignment and the making of orders that restrain a person from receiving anything which he is prevented from assigning),
  (b) any provision of any enactment (whether passed or made before or after the passing of the Welfare Reform and Pensions Act 1999) corresponding to any of the provisions mentioned in paragraph (a), or
  (c) any provision of the arrangement in question corresponding to any of those provisions,
  applies to a court exercising its powers under section 342A.
(3) Where any sum is required by an order under section 342A to be paid to the trustee in bankruptcy, that sum shall be comprised in the bankrupt's estate.
(4) Regulations may, for the purposes of the recovery provisions, make provision about the calculation and verification of—
  (a) any such value as is mentioned in section 342B(4)(b);
  (b) any such amounts as are mentioned in section 342B(6)(a) and (b).
(5) The power conferred by subsection (4) includes power to provide for calculation or verification—
  (a) in such manner as may, in the particular case, be approved by a prescribed person; or
  (b) in accordance with guidance—
    (i) from time to time prepared by a prescribed person, and
    (ii) approved by the Secretary of State.
(6) References in the recovery provisions to the person responsible for a pension arrangement are to—
  (a) the trustees, managers or provider of the arrangement, or
  (b) the person having functions in relation to the arrangement corresponding to those of a trustee, manager or provider.
(7) In this section and sections 342A and 342B—
  "prescribed" means prescribed by regulations;
  "the recovery provisions" means this section and sections 342A and 342B;
  "regulations" means regulations made by the Secretary of State.
(8) Regulations under the recovery provisions may—
  (a) make different provision for different cases;
  (b) contain such incidental, supplemental and transitional provisions as appear to the Secretary of State necessary or expedient.
(9) Regulations under the recovery provisions shall be made by statutory instrument subject to annulment in pursuance of a resolution of either House of Parliament.

MATRIMONIAL AND FAMILY PROCEEDINGS ACT 1984

(Incorporating amendments under Pensions Act 1995, Welfare Reform and Pensions Act 1999, Pensions Act 2004 and Pensions Act 2008)

Orders for financial provision and property adjustment

17.—(1) Subject to section 20 below, on an application by a party to a marriage for an order for financial relief under this section, the court may—
    (a) make any one or more of the orders which it could make under Part II of the 1973 Act if a decree of divorce, a decree of nullity of marriage or a decree of judicial separation in respect of the marriage had been granted in England and Wales, that is to say—
        (i) any order mentioned in section 23(1) of the 1973 Act (financial provision orders); and
        (ii) any order mentioned in section 24(1) of that Act (property adjustment orders); and
    (b) if the marriage has been dissolved or annulled, make one or more orders each of which would, within the meaning of that Part of that Act, be a pension sharing order in relation to the marriage.
    (c) if the marriage has been dissolved or annulled, make an order which would, within the meaning of that Part of that Act, be a pension compensation sharing order in relation to the marriage.

(2) Subject to section 20 below, where the court makes a secured periodical payments order, an order for the payment of a lump sum or a property adjustment order under subsection (1) above, then, on making that order or at any time thereafter, the court may make any order mentioned in section 24A(1) of the 1973 Act (orders for sale of property) which the court would have power to make if the order under subsection (1) above had been made under Part II of the 1973 Act.

Matters to which the court is to have regard in exercising its powers under s.17

18.—(1) In deciding whether to exercise its powers under section 17 above and, if so, in what manner the court shall act in accordance with this section.

(2) The court shall have regard to all the circumstances of the case, first consideration being given to the welfare while a minor of any child of the family who has not attained the age of eighteen.

(3) As regards the exercise of those powers in relation to a party to the marriage, the court shall in particular have regard to the matters mentioned in section 25(2)(a) to (h) of the 1973 Act and shall be under duties corresponding with those imposed by section 25A(1) and (2) of the 1973 Act where it decides to exercise under section 17 above powers corresponding with the powers referred to in those subsections.

(3A) The matters to which the court is to have regard under subsection (3) above—

(a) so far as relating to paragraph (a) of section 25(2) of the 1973 Act, include any benefits under a pension arrangement which a party to the marriage has or is likely to have and any PPF compensation to which a party to the marriage is or is likely to be entitled,(whether or not in the foreseeable future), and

(b) so far as relating to paragraph (h) of that provision, include–
  (i) any benefits under a pension arrangement which, by reason of the dissolution or annulment of the marriage, a party to the marriage will lose the chance of acquiring, and
  (ii) any PPF compensation which, by reason of the dissolution or annulment of the marriage, a party to the marriage will lose the chance of acquiring entitlement to.

(4) As regards the exercise of those powers in relation to a child of the family, the court shall in particular have regard to the matters mentioned in section 25(3)(a) to (e) of the 1973 Act.

(5) As regards the exercise of those powers against a party to the marriage in favour of a child of the family who is not the child of that party, the court shall also have regard to the matters mentioned in section 25(4)(a) to (c) of the 1973 Act.

(6) Where an order has been made by a court outside England and Wales for the making of payments or the transfer of property by a party to the marriage, the court in considering in accordance with this section the financial resources of the other party to the marriage or a child of the family shall have regard to the extent to which that order has been complied with or is likely to be complied with.

(7) In this section—
  (a) "pension arrangement" has the meaning given by section 25D(3) of the 1973 Act,
  (b) references to benefits under a pension arrangement include any benefits by way of pension, whether under a pension arrangement or not [, and]
  (c) "PPF compensation" means compensation payable under—
    (i) Chapter 3 of Part 2 of the Pensions Act 2004 (pension protection) or any regulations or order made under it,
    (ii) Chapter 1 of Part 3 of the Pensions Act 2008 (pension compensation sharing) or any regulations or order made under it, or
    (iii) any provision corresponding to the provisions mentioned in sub-paragraph (i) or (ii) in force in Northern Ireland.

Consent orders for financial provision or property adjustment

19.—(1) Notwithstanding anything in section 18 above, on an application for a consent order for financial relief the court may, unless it has reason to think that there are other circumstances into which it ought to inquire, make an order in the terms agreed on the basis only of the prescribed information furnished with the application.

(2) Subsection (1) above applies to an application for a consent order varying or discharging an order for financial relief as it applies to an application for an order for financial relief.

(3) In this section—

"consent order", in relation to an application for an order, means an order in the terms applied for to which the respondent agrees;

"order for financial relief" means an order under section 17 above; and

"prescribed" means prescribed by rules of court.

Restriction of powers of court where jurisdiction depends on matrimonial home in England or Wales

20.—(1) Where the court has jurisdiction to entertain an application for an order for financial relief by reason only of the situation in England or Wales of a dwelling-house which was a matrimonial home of the parties, the court may make under section 17 above any one or more of the following orders (but no other)—

(a) an order that either party to the marriage shall pay to the other such lump sum as may be specified in the order;

(b) an order that a party to the marriage shall pay to such person as may be so specified for the benefit of a child of the family, or to such a child, such lump sum as may be so specified;

(c) an order that a party to the marriage shall transfer to the other party, to any child of the family or to such person as may be so specified for the benefit of such a child, the interest of the first-mentioned party in the dwelling-house, or such part of that interest as may be so specified;

(d) an order that a settlement of the interest of a party to the marriage in the dwelling-house, or such part of that interest as may be so specified, be made to the satisfaction of the court for the benefit of the other party to the marriage and of the children of the family or either or any of them;

(e) an order varying for the benefit of the parties to the marriage and of the children of the family or either or any of them any ante-nuptial or post-nuptial settlement (including such a settlement made by will or codicil) made on the parties to the marriage so far as that settlement relates to an interest in the dwelling-house;

(f) an order extinguishing or reducing the interest of either of the parties to the marriage under any such settlement so far as that interest is an interest in the dwelling-house;

(g) an order for the sale of the interest of a party to the marriage in the dwelling-house.

(2) Where, in the circumstances mentioned in subsection (1) above, the court makes an order for the payment of a lump sum by a party to the marriage, the amount of the lump sum shall not exceed, or where more than one such order is made the total amount of the lump sums shall not exceed in aggregate, the following amount, that is to say—

(a) if the interest of that party in the dwelling-house is sold in pursuance of an order made under subsection (1)(g) above, the amount of the proceeds of the sale of that interest after deducting therefrom any costs incurred in the sale thereof;

(b) if the interest of that party is not so sold, the amount which in the opinion of the court represents the value of that interest.

(3) Where the interest of a party to the marriage in the dwelling-house is held jointly or in common with any other person or persons—

(a) the reference in subsection (1)(g) above to the interest of a party to the marriage shall be construed as including a reference to the interest of that other person, or the interest of those other persons, in the dwelling-house, and

(b) the reference in subsection (2)(a) above to the amount of the proceeds of a sale ordered under subsection (1)(g) above shall be construed as a reference to that part of those proceeds which is attributable to the interest of that party to the marriage in the dwelling-house.

Application to orders under ss.14 and 17 of certain provisions of Part II of Matrimonial Causes Act 1973

21.—(1) The following provisions of Part II of the 1973 Act (financial relief for parties to marriage and children of family) shall apply in relation to an order under section 14 or 17 above as they apply in relation to a like order under that Part of that Act, that is to say—

(a) section 23(3) (provisions as to lump sums);

(b) section 24A(2), (4), (5) and (6) (provisions as to orders for sale);

(ba) section 24B(3) to (5) (provisions about pension sharing orders in relation to divorce and nullity);

(bb) section 24C (duty to stay pension sharing orders);

(bc) section 24D (apportionment of pension sharing charges);

(bca) section 24E(3) to (10) (provisions about pension compensation orders in relation to divorce and nullity);

(bcb) section 24F (duty to stay pension compensation sharing orders);

(bcc) section 24G (apportionment of pension compensation sharing charges);

(bd) section 25B(3) to (7B) (power, by financial provision order, to attach payments under a pension arrangement, or to require the exercise of a right of commutation under such an arrangement);

(be) section 25C (extension of lump sum powers in relation to death benefits under a pension arrangement);

(bf) section 25E(2) to (10) (the Pension Protection Fund);

(bg) section 25F (power, by financial provision order, to attach pension compensation payments, or to require the exercise of a right of commutation of pension compensation);

(c) section 28(1) and (2) (duration of continuing financial provision orders in favour of party to marriage);

(d) section 29 (duration of continuing financial provision orders in favour of children, and age limit on making certain orders in their favour);
(e) section 30 (direction for settlement of instrument for securing payments or effecting property adjustment), except paragraph (b);
(f) section 31 (variation, discharge etc. of certain orders for financial relief), except subsection (2)(e) and subsection (4);
(g) section 32 (payment of certain arrears unenforceable without the leave of the court);
(h) section 33 (orders for repayment of sums paid under certain orders);
(i) section 38 (orders for repayment of sums paid after cessation of order by reason of remarriage);
(j) section 39 (settlements etc. made in compliance with a property adjustment order may be avoided on bankruptcy of settlor); [. . .]5
(k) section 40 (payments etc. under order made in favour of person suffering from mental disorder);
(l) section 40A (appeals relating to pension sharing orders which have taken effect); and
(m) section 40B (appeals relating to pension compensation sharing orders which have taken effect);

(2) Subsection (1)(bd), (be) and (bg) above shall not apply where the court has jurisdiction to entertain an application for an order for financial relief by reason only of the situation in England or Wales of a dwelling-house which was a matrimonial home of the parties.

(3) Section 25D(1) of the 1973 Act (effect of transfers on orders relating to rights under a pension arrangement) shall apply in relation to an order made under section 17 above by virtue of subsection (1)(bd) or (be) above as it applies in relation to an order made under section 23 of that Act by virtue of section 25B or 25C of the 1973 Act.

(4) The Lord Chancellor may by regulations make for the purposes of this Part of this Act provision corresponding to any provision which may be made by him under subsections (2) to (2B) of section 25D of the 1973 Act or under subsections (1) to (3) of section 25G of that Act.

(5) Power to make regulations under this section shall be exercisable by statutory instrument which shall be subject to annulment in pursuance of a resolution of either House of Parliament.

PENSION SCHEMES ACT 1993

(Incorporating amendments under Pensions Act 2004)

Categories of pension schemes

1.—(1) In this Act, unless the context otherwise requires—
   "occupational pension scheme" means a pension scheme—
      (a) that—
         (i) for the purpose of providing benefits to, or in respect of, people with service in employments of a description, or

(ii) for that purpose and also for the purpose of providing benefits to, or in respect of, other people,

is established by, or by persons who include, a person to whom subsection (2) applies when the scheme is established or (as the case may be) to whom that subsection would have applied when the scheme was established had that subsection then been in force, and

(b) that has its main administration in the United Kingdom or outside the EEA States, or a pension scheme that is prescribed or is of a prescribed description;

"personal pension scheme" means a pension scheme that—
(a) is not an occupational pension scheme, and
(b) is established by a person within section 154(1) of the Finance Act 2004.

"public service pension scheme" means an occupational pension scheme established by or under an enactment or the Royal prerogative or a Royal charter, being a scheme—

(a) all the particulars of which are set out in, or in a legislative instrument made under, an enactment, Royal warrant or charter, or
(b) which cannot come into force, or be amended, without the scheme or amendment being approved by a Minister of the Crown or government department,

and includes any occupational pension scheme established, with the concurrence of the Treasury, by or with the approval of any Minister of the Crown and any occupational pension scheme prescribed by regulations made by the Secretary of State and the Treasury jointly as being a scheme which ought in their opinion to be treated as a public service pension scheme for the purposes of this Act.

(2) This subsection applies—
(a) where people in employments of the description concerned are employed by someone, to a person who employs such people,
(b) to a person in an employment of that description, and
(c) to a person representing interests of a description framed so as to include—
(i) interests of persons who employ people in employments of the description mentioned in paragraph (a), or
(ii) interests of people in employments of that description.

(3) For the purposes of subsection (2), if a person is in an employment of the description concerned by reason of holding an office (including an elective office) and is entitled to remuneration for holding it, the person responsible for paying the remuneration shall be taken to employ the office-holder.

(4) In the definition in subsection (1) of "occupational pension scheme", the reference to a description includes a description framed by reference to an employment being of any of two or more kinds.

(5) In subsection (1) "pension scheme"(except in the phrases "occupational pension scheme", "personal pension scheme" and "public service pension scheme") means a scheme or other arrangements, comprised in one or more

instruments or agreements, having or capable of having effect so as to provide benefits to or in respect of people—
(a) on retirement,
(b) on having reached a particular age, or
(c) on termination of service in an employment.

(6) The power of the Treasury under section 154(4) of the Finance Act 2004 (power to amend sections 154 and 155) includes power consequentially to amend—
(a) paragraph (a) of the definition in subsection (1) of "personal pension scheme", and
(b) any provision in force in Northern Ireland corresponding to that paragraph.

PENSIONS ACT 2008

107.—(1) Pension compensation sharing is available under this Chapter in relation to a person's shareable rights to PPF compensation.
(2) For the purposes of this Chapter, a right of a person to PPF compensation is "shareable" unless it is of a description specified by regulations made by the Secretary of State.

Interpretation

108. In this Chapter—
"the Board" means the Board of the Pension Protection Fund;
"PPF compensation" means compensation payable under the pension compensation provisions;
"the pension compensation provisions" means—
(a) Chapter 3 of Part 2 of the Pensions Act 2004 (pension protection) and any regulations or order made under it,
(b) this Chapter and any regulations or order made under it, and
(c) any provision corresponding to the provisions mentioned in paragraph (a) or (b) in force in Northern Ireland;
"prescribed" means prescribed by regulations made by the Secretary of State;
"the relevant order or provision" means the pension compensation sharing order, or provision contained in a qualifying agreement, which gives rise to the pension compensation sharing;
"the transfer day" means the day on which the relevant order or provision takes effect;
"the transferee" means the person for whose benefit the relevant order or provision is made;
"the transferor" means the person to whose rights the relevant order or provision relates.

STATUTES AND STATUTORY INSTRUMENTS

Activation of pension compensation sharing

109. Section 111 applies on the taking effect of any of the following relating to a person's shareable rights to PPF compensation—
    (a) a pension compensation sharing order under the Matrimonial Causes Act 1973 (c. 18);
    (b) a pension compensation sharing order under Schedule 5 to the Civil Partnership Act 2004 (c. 33);
    (c) an order under Part 3 of the Matrimonial and Family Proceedings Act 1984 (c. 42) (financial relief in England and Wales in relation to overseas divorce etc) corresponding to such an order as is mentioned in paragraph (a);
    (d) an order under Schedule 7 to the Civil Partnership Act 2004 (c. 33) (financial relief in England and Wales after overseas dissolution etc of a civil partnership) corresponding to such an order as is mentioned in paragraph (b);
    (e) an order under any provision corresponding to a provision mentioned in any of paragraphs (a) to (d) in force in Northern Ireland.
    (f) a pension compensation sharing order under section 8 of the Family Law (Scotland) Act 1985 (c. 37) (orders for financial provision);
    (g) any provision corresponding to provision which may be made by such an order, and which—
        (i) is contained in a qualifying agreement between the parties to a marriage or the partners in a civil partnership,
        (ii) is in such form as the Secretary of State may prescribe by regulations, and
        (iii) takes effect on the grant, in relation to the marriage, of decree of divorce or of declarator of nullity or (as the case may be) on the grant, in relation to the civil partnership, of decree of dissolution or of declarator of nullity,
    except where the provision relates to the same rights to PPF compensation as are the subject of an order made under section 12B(2) of the Family Law (Scotland) Act 1985 (order for payment of capital sum: pension compensation)[...]

Creation of pension compensation debits and credits

111.—(1) On the application of this section—
    (a) the transferor's shareable rights to PPF compensation that derive from rights under the specified scheme become subject to a debit of the appropriate amount, and
    (b) the transferee becomes entitled to a credit of that amount as against the Board.
(2) For the purposes of subsection (1) "the appropriate amount" means—
    (a) where the relevant order or provision specifies a percentage to be transferred, that percentage of the cash equivalent of the relevant compensation on the valuation day;

(b) where the relevant order or provision specifies an amount to be transferred, the lesser of—
  (i) that specified amount, and
  (ii) the cash equivalent of the relevant compensation on the valuation day.

(3) For the purposes of subsection (2) "the relevant compensation" means the payments or future payments to which, immediately before the transfer day, the transferor is entitled under the pension compensation provisions by virtue of the transferor's shareable rights to PPF compensation that derive from rights under the specified scheme.

(4) The Secretary of State may by regulations provide for any description of payment to be disregarded for the purposes of subsection (3).

(5) For the purposes of this section—
"the specified scheme" means the pension scheme specified in the relevant order or provision;
"the valuation day" means such day within the implementation period for the credit under subsection (1)(b) as the Board may specify by notice in writing to the transferor and transferee.

(6) The credit to which the transferee becomes entitled under subsection (1)(b) is referred to in this Chapter as a "pension compensation credit".

Cash equivalents

112.—(1) The Secretary of State may by regulations make provision about the calculation and verification of cash equivalents for the purposes of section 111.

(2) Regulations under this section may include provision for calculation and verification in a manner approved by the Board[...]

Discharge of liability

116.—(1) This section applies where the Board is subject to a liability in respect of a pension compensation credit.

(2) The Board must discharge the liability by sending a notice to the transferee.

(3) On the sending of the notice the transferee becomes entitled, with effect from (and including) the transfer day, to compensation calculated in accordance with Schedule 5.

(4) For the purposes of that calculation, the initial annual rate of compensation is an amount determined by the Board.

(5) The Board must determine that amount in such a way as to secure that the cash equivalent value of the compensation to which the transferee becomes entitled under subsection (3) equals the amount of the credit.

(6) The Secretary of State may by regulations make provision about the calculation of cash equivalents for the purposes of subsection (5).

(7) The notice sent under this section must—
 (a) state that the transferee is entitled to periodic pension compensation calculated under Schedule 5, and
 (b) specify the amount determined under subsection (4).

(8) Where the transferee dies before liability in respect of the credit has been discharged—
   (a) subsections (2) to (7) do not have effect in relation to the discharge of liability in respect of the credit, and
   (b) liability in respect of the credit must be discharged in accordance with regulations made by the Secretary of State.

Charges in respect of pension compensation sharing costs

117.—(1) The Secretary of State may by regulations make provision for the purpose of enabling the Board to recover from the parties to pension compensation sharing prescribed charges in respect of prescribed descriptions of pension compensation sharing activity.

(2) Regulations under subsection (1) may include—
   (a) provision for the start of the implementation period for a pension compensation credit to be postponed in prescribed circumstances;
   (b) provision enabling the Board to set off against any PPF compensation payable to a party to pension compensation sharing any charges owed to it by that party under the regulations;
   (c) provision, in relation to payments in respect of charges recoverable under the regulations, for reimbursement as between the parties to pension compensation sharing.

(3) For the purposes of regulations under subsection (1), the question of how much of a charge recoverable under the regulations is attributable to a party to pension compensation sharing is to be determined as follows—
   (a) where the relevant order or provision includes provision ("provision for apportionment") about the apportionment of charges under this section, there is attributable to the party so much of the charge as is apportioned to that party by that provision for apportionment;
   (b) where the relevant order or provision does not include provision for apportionment, the charge is attributable to the transferor.

(4) In subsection (1), the reference to pension compensation sharing activity is to activity attributable directly or indirectly to the application of section 111 by virtue of the relevant order or provision.

Supply of information about pension compensation in relation to divorce etc.

118.—(1) The Secretary of State may by regulations—
   (a) make provision imposing on the Board requirements with respect to the supply of information relevant to any power with respect to—
      (i) financial relief under Part 2 of the Matrimonial Causes Act 1973 (c. 18) or Part 3 of the Matrimonial and Family Proceedings Act 1984 (c. 42) (England and Wales powers in relation to domestic and overseas divorce etc),
      (ii) financial relief under Schedule 5 or 7 to the Civil Partnership Act 2004 (c. 33) (England and Wales powers in relation to domestic and overseas dissolution of civil partnerships etc),

(iii) financial relief under any provision corresponding to a provision mentioned in sub-paragraph (i) or (ii) in force in Northern Ireland,
(iv) orders for financial provision under section 8 of the Family Law (Scotland) Act 1985 (c. 37) (orders for financial provision), or
(v) provision as to pension sharing, or pension compensation sharing, that is contained in an agreement that is a qualifying agreement for the purposes of section 28(1)(b) and (c) of the Welfare Reform and Pensions Act 1999 (c. 30) (activation of pension sharing) or this Chapter;
(b) make provision about calculation and verification in relation to the valuation of PPF compensation for the purposes of regulations under paragraph (a);
(c) make provision for the purpose of enabling the Board to recover prescribed charges in respect of providing information in accordance with regulations under paragraph (a).
(2) Regulations under subsection (1)(b) may include provision for calculation and verification in a manner approved by the Board.
(3) Regulations under subsection (1)(c) may include provision for the application in prescribed circumstances, with or without modification, of any provision made by virtue of section 117(2).

Pension compensation sharing and attachment on divorce etc.

120. Schedule 6 (which amends matrimonial and civil partnership legislation for the purpose of enabling the court to make pension compensation sharing orders, and orders for the attachment of pension compensation, in connection with proceedings in England and Wales) and Schedule 7 (which amends in relation to pension compensation sharing orders similar legislation applying in Scotland) have effect.

Statutory Instruments

FAMILY PROCEDURE RULES 2010 (SI 2010/2955) (as amended)

Interpretation
  Rule 9.3

(1) In this Part—
"the Board" means the Board of the Pension Protection Fund;
"pension arrangement" means—
(a) an occupational pension scheme;
(b) a personal pension scheme;
(c) shareable state scheme rights;
(d) a retirement annuity contract;

(e) an annuity or insurance policy purchased, or transferred, for the purpose of giving effect to rights under an occupational pension scheme or a personal pension scheme; and

(f) an annuity purchased, or entered into, for the purpose of discharging liability in respect of a pension credit under section 29(1)(b) of the Welfare Reform and Pensions Act 1999 or under corresponding Northern Ireland legislation;

"pension attachment order" means—

(a) in proceedings under the 1973 Act, an order making provision under section 25B or 25C of that Act;

(b) in proceedings under the 1984 Act, an order under section 17(1)(a)(i) of that Act making provision equivalent to an order referred to in paragraph (a);

(c) in proceedings under Schedule 5 to the 2004 Act, an order making provision under paragraph 25 or paragraph 26; or

(d) in proceedings under Schedule 7 to the 2004 Act, an order under paragraph 9(2) or (3) making provision equivalent to an order referred to in paragraph (c);

"pension compensation attachment order" means—

(a) in proceedings under the 1973 Act, an order making provision under section 25F of that Act;

(b) in proceedings under the 1984 Act, an order under section 17(1)(a)(i) of that Act making provision equivalent to an order referred in to paragraph (a);

(c) in proceedings under Schedule 5 to the 2004 Act, an order under paragraph 34A; and

(d) in proceedings under Schedule 7 to the 2004 Act, an order under paragraph 9(2) or (3) making provision equivalent to an order referred to in paragraph (c);

"pension compensation sharing order" means—

(a) in proceedings under the 1973 Act, an order under section 24E of that Act;

(b) in proceedings under the 1984 Act, an order under section 17(1)(c) of that Act;

(c) in proceedings under Schedule 5 to the 2004 Act, an order under paragraph 19A; and

(d) in proceedings under Schedule 7 to the 2004 Act, an order under paragraph 9(2) or (3) making provision equivalent to an order referred to in paragraph (c);

"pension sharing order" means—

(a) in proceedings under the 1973 Act, an order making provision under section 24B of that Act;

(b) in proceedings under the 1984 Act, an order under section 17(1)(b) of that Act;

(c) in proceedings under Schedule 5 to the 2004 Act, an order under paragraph 15; or

(d) in proceedings under Schedule 7 to the 2004 Act, an order under paragraph 9(2) or (3) making provision equivalent to an order referred to in paragraph (c);

"pension scheme" means, unless the context otherwise requires, a scheme for which the Board has assumed responsibility in accordance with Chapter 3 of Part 2 of the Pensions Act 2004 (pension protection) or any provision in force in Northern Ireland corresponding to that Chapter;

"PPF compensation" has the meaning given to it—

(a) in proceedings under the 1973 Act, by section 21C of the 1973 Act;

(b) in proceedings under the 1984 Act, by section 18(7) of the 1984 Act; and

(c) in proceedings under the 2004 Act, by paragraph 19F of Schedule 5 to the 2004 Act;

"relevant valuation" means a valuation of pension rights or benefits as at a date not more than 12 months earlier than the date fixed for the first appointment which has been furnished or requested for the purposes of any of the following provisions—

(a) the Pensions on Divorce etc (Provision of Information) Regulations 2000;

(b) regulation 5 of and Schedule 2 to the Occupational Pension Schemes (Disclosure of Information) Regulations 1996 and regulation 11 of and Schedule 1 to the Occupational Pension Schemes (Transfer Value) Regulations 1996;

(c) section 93A or 94(1)(a) or (aa) of the Pension Schemes Act 1993;

(d) section 94(1)(b) of the Pension Schemes Act 1993 or paragraph 2(a) (or, where applicable, 2(b)) of Schedule 2 to the Personal Pension Schemes (Disclosure of Information) Regulations 1987;

(e) the Dissolution etc. (Pensions) Regulations 2005.

When an Application for a financial order may be made
Rule 9.4

An application for a financial order may be made—
(a) in an application for a matrimonial or civil partnership order; or
(b) at any time after an application for a matrimonial or civil partnership order has been made.

Procedure before the first appointment
Rule 9.14

(1) Not less than 35 days before the first appointment both parties must simultaneously exchange with each other and file with the court a financial statement in the form referred to in Practice Direction 5A[…]

Duties of the court at the first appointment
Rule 9.15

(1) The first appointment must be conducted with the objective of defining the issues and saving costs[. . .]

(3) The court must give directions where appropriate about—
   (a) the valuation of assets (including the joint instruction of joint experts);
   (b) obtaining and exchanging expert evidence, if required;
   (c) the evidence to be adduced by each party; and
   (d) further chronologies or schedules to be filed by each party[. . .]

(7) The court may[. . .]
   (c) in a case where a pension sharing order or a pension attachment order is requested, direct any party with pension rights to file and serve a Pension Inquiry Form, completed in full or in part as the court may direct; and
   (d) in a case where a pension compensation sharing order or a pension compensation attachment order is requested, direct any party with PPF compensation rights to file and serve a Pension Protection Fund Inquiry Form, completed in full or in part as the court may direct.

Application and interpretation of this Chapter
Rule 9.29

(1) This Chapter applies—
   (a) where an application for a financial remedy has been made; and
   (b) the applicant or respondent is the party with pension rights.

(2) In this Chapter—
   (a) in proceedings under the 1973 Act and the 1984 Act, all words and phrases defined in sections 25D(3) and (4) of the 1973 Act have the meaning assigned by those subsections;
   (b) in proceedings under the 2004 Act—
      (i) all words and phrases defined in paragraphs 16(4) to (5) and 29 of Schedule 5 to that Act have the meanings assigned by those paragraphs; and
      (ii) "the party with pension rights" has the meaning given to "civil partner with pension rights" by paragraph 29 of Schedule 5 to the 2004 Act;
   (c) all words and phrases defined in section 46 of the Welfare Reform and Pensions Act 1999 have the meanings assigned by that section.

What the party with pension rights must do when the court fixes a first appointment
Rule 9.30

(1) Where the court fixes a first appointment as required by rule 9.12(1)(a) the party with pension rights must request the person responsible for each pension arrangement under which the party has or is likely to have benefits

to provide the information referred to in regulation 2(2) of the Pensions on Divorce etc (Provision of Information) Regulations 2000.

(The information referred to in regulation 2 of the Pensions on Divorce etc (Provision of Information) Regulations 2000 relates to the valuation of pension rights or benefits.)

(2) The party with pension rights must comply with paragraph (1) within 7 days beginning with the date on which that party receives notification of the date of the first appointment.

(3) Within 7 days beginning with the date on which the party with pension rights receives the information under paragraph (1) that party must send a copy of it to the other party, together with the name and address of the person responsible for each pension arrangement.

(4) A request under paragraph (1) need not be made where the party with pension rights is in possession of, or has requested, a relevant valuation of the pension rights or benefits accrued under the pension arrangement in question.

Applications for pension sharing orders
Rule 9.31

Where an application for a financial remedy includes an application for a pension sharing order, or where a request for such an order is added to an existing application for a financial remedy, the applicant must serve a copy of the application on the person responsible for the pension arrangement concerned.

Applications for consent orders for pension sharing
Rule 9.32

(1) This rule applies where—
  (a) the parties have agreed on the terms of an order and the agreement includes a pension sharing order;
  (b) service has not been effected under rule 9.31; and
  (c) the information referred to in paragraph (2) has not otherwise been provided.

(2) The party with pension rights must—
  (a) request the person responsible for the pension arrangement concerned to provide the information set out in Section C of the Pension Inquiry Form; and
  (b) on receipt, send a copy of the information referred to in sub-paragraph (a) to the other party.

Applications for pension attachment orders
Rule 9.33

(1) Where an application for a financial remedy includes an application for a pension attachment order, or where a request for such an order is added to an existing application for a financial remedy, the applicant must serve a

STATUTES AND STATUTORY INSTRUMENTS

copy of the application on the person responsible for the pension arrangement concerned and must at the same time send—
- (a) an address to which any notice which the person responsible is required to serve on the applicant is to be sent;
- (b) an address to which any payment which the person responsible is required to make to the applicant is to be sent; and
- (c) where the address in sub-paragraph (b) is that of a bank, a building society or the Department of National Savings, sufficient details to enable the payment to be made into the account of the applicant.

(2) A person responsible for a pension arrangement who receives a copy of the application under paragraph (1) may, within 21 days beginning with the date of service of the application, request the party with the pension rights to provide that person with the information disclosed in the financial statement relating to the party's pension rights or benefits under that arrangement.

(3) If the person responsible for a pension arrangement makes a request under paragraph (2), the party with the pension rights must provide that person with a copy of the section of that party's financial statement that relates to that party's pension rights or benefits under that arrangement.

(4) The party with the pension rights must comply with paragraph (3)—
- (a) within the time limited for filing the financial statement by rule 9.14(1); or
- (b) within 21 days beginning with the date on which the person responsible for the pension arrangement makes the request,

whichever is the later.

(5) A person responsible for a pension arrangement who receives a copy of the section of a financial statement as required pursuant to paragraph (4) may, within 21 days beginning with the date on which that person receives it, send to the court, the applicant and the respondent a statement in answer.

(6) A person responsible for a pension arrangement who files a statement in answer pursuant to paragraph (5) will be entitled to be represented at the first appointment, or such other hearing as the court may direct, and the court must within 4 days, beginning with the date on which that person files the statement in answer, give the person notice of the date of the first appointment or other hearing as the case may be.

Applications for consent orders for pension attachment
Rule 9.34

(1) This rule applies where service has not been effected under rule 9.33(1).

(2) Where the parties have agreed on the terms of an order and the agreement includes a pension attachment order, then they must serve on the person responsible for the pension arrangement concerned—
- (a) a copy of the application for a consent order;
- (b) a draft of the proposed order, complying with rule 9.35; and
- (c) the particulars set out in rule 9.33(1).

(3) No consent order that includes a pension attachment order must be made unless either—

(a) the person responsible for the pension arrangement has not made any objection within 21 days beginning with the date on which the application for a consent order was served on that person; or
(b) the court has considered any such objection, and for the purpose of considering any objection the court may make such direction as it sees fit for the person responsible to attend before it or to furnish written details of the objection.

Pension sharing orders or pension attachment orders
Rule 9.35

An order for a financial remedy, whether by consent or not, which includes a pension sharing order or a pension attachment order, must—
(a) in the body of the order, state that there is to be provision by way of pension sharing or pension attachment in accordance with the annex or annexes to the order; and
(b) be accompanied by a pension sharing annex or a pension attachment annex as the case may require, and if provision is made in relation to more than one pension arrangement there must be one annex for each pension arrangement.

Duty of the court upon making a pension sharing order or a pension attachment order
Rule 9.36

(1) A court which varies or discharges a pension sharing order or a pension attachment order, must send, or direct one of the parties to send—
   (a) to the person responsible for the pension arrangement concerned; or
   (b) where the Board has assumed responsibility for the pension scheme or part of it, the Board;
   the documents referred to in paragraph (4).
(2) A court which makes a pension sharing order or pension attachment order, must send, or direct one of the parties to send to the person responsible for the pension arrangement concerned, the documents referred to in paragraph (4).
(3) Where the Board has assumed responsibility for the pension scheme or part of it after the making of a pension sharing order or attachment order but before the documents have been sent to the person responsible for the pension arrangement in accordance with paragraph (2), the court which makes the pension sharing order or the pension attachment order, must send, or direct one of the parties to send to the Board the documents referred to in paragraph (4).
(4) The documents to be sent in accordance with paragraph (1) to (3) are—
   (a) in the case of—
      (i) proceedings under the 1973 Act, a copy of the decree of judicial separation;
      (ii) proceedings under Schedule 5 to the 2004 Act, a copy of the separation order;

STATUTES AND STATUTORY INSTRUMENTS

        (iii) proceedings under Part 3 of the 1984 Act, a copy of the document of divorce, annulment or legal separation;
        (iv) proceedings under Schedule 7 to the 2004 Act, a copy of the document of dissolution, annulment or legal separation;
  (b) in the case of divorce or nullity of marriage, a copy of the decree absolute under rule 7.31or 7.32; or
  (c) in the case of dissolution or nullity of civil partnership, a copy of the order making the conditional order final under rule 7.31 or 7.32; and
  (d) a copy of the pension sharing order or the pension attachment order, or as the case may be of the order varying or discharging that order, including any annex to that order relating to that pension arrangement but no other annex to that order.

(5) The documents referred to in paragraph (4) must be sent—
  (a) in proceedings under the 1973 Act and the 1984 Act, within 7 days beginning with the date on which—
        (i) the relevant pension sharing or pension attachment order or any order varying or discharging such an order is made; or
        (ii) the decree absolute of divorce or nullity or decree of judicial separation is made,
    whichever is the later; and
  (b) in proceedings under the 2004 Act, within 7 days beginning with the date on which—
        (i) the relevant pension sharing or pension attachment order or any order varying or discharging such an order is made; or
        (ii) the final order of dissolution or nullity or separation order is made,
    whichever is the later.

Procedure where Pension Protection Fund becomes involved with the pension scheme
Rule 9.37

(1) This rule applies where—
  (a) rules 9.30 to 9.34 or 9.36 apply; and
  (b) the party with the pension rights ("the member") receives or has received notification in compliance with the Pension Protection Fund (Provision of Information) Regulations 2005 ("the 2005 Regulations")—
        (i) from the trustees or managers of a pension scheme, that there is an assessment period in relation to that scheme; or
        (ii) from the Board that it has assumed responsibility for the pension scheme or part of it.
(2) If the trustees or managers of the pension scheme notify or have notified the member that there is an assessment period in relation to that scheme, the member must send to the other party, all the information which the Board is required from time to time to provide to the member under the 2005 Regulations including—
  (a) a copy of the notification; and

(b) a copy of the valuation summary,
in accordance with paragraph (3).
(3) The member must send the information or any part of it referred to in paragraph (2)—
   (a) if available, when the member sends the information received under rule 9.30(1); or
   (b) otherwise, within 7 days of receipt.
(4) If the Board notifies the member that it has assumed responsibility for the pension scheme, or part of it, the member must—
   (a) send a copy of the notification to the other party within 7 days of receipt; and
   (b) comply with paragraph (5).
(5) Where paragraph (4) applies, the member must—
   (a) within 7 days of receipt of the notification, request the Board in writing to provide a forecast of the member's compensation entitlement as described in the 2005 Regulations; and
   (b) send a copy of the forecast of the member's compensation entitlement to the other party within 7 days of receipt.
(6) In this rule—
   (a) "assessment period" means an assessment period within the meaning of Part 2 of the Pensions Act 2004; and
   (b) "valuation summary" has the meaning assigned to it by the 2005 Regulations.

Application and interpretation of this Chapter
Rule 9.38

(1) This Chapter applies—
   (a) where an application for a financial remedy has been made; and
   (b) the applicant or respondent is, the party with compensation rights.
(2) In this Chapter "party with compensation rights"—
   (a) in proceedings under the 1973 Act and the 1984 Act, has the meaning given to it by section 25G(5) of the 1973 Act;
   (b) in proceedings under the 2004 Act, has the meaning given to "civil partner with compensation rights" by paragraph 37(1) of Schedule 5 to the 2004 Act

What the party with compensation rights must do when the court fixes a first appointment
Rule 9.39

(1) Where the court fixes a first appointment as required by rule 9.12(1)(a) the party with compensation rights must request the Board to provide the information about the valuation of entitlement to PPF compensation referred to in regulations made by the Secretary of State under section 118 of the Pensions Act 2008.

STATUTES AND STATUTORY INSTRUMENTS

(2) The party with compensation rights must comply with paragraph (1) within 7 days beginning with the date on which that party receives notification of the date of the first appointment.

(3) Within 7 days beginning with the date on which the party with compensation rights receives the information under paragraph (1) that party must send a copy of it to the other party, together with the name and address of the trustees or managers responsible for each pension scheme.

(4) Where the rights to PPF Compensation are derived from rights under more than one pension scheme, the party with compensation rights must comply with this rule in relation to each entitlement.

Applications for pension compensation sharing orders
Rule 9.40

Where an application for a financial remedy includes an application for a pension compensation sharing order or where a request for such an order is added to an existing application for a financial remedy, the applicant must serve a copy of the application on the Board.

Applications for consent orders for pension compensation sharing
Rule 9.41

(1) This rule applies where—
  (a) the parties have agreed on the terms of an order and the agreement includes a pension compensation sharing order;
  (b) service has not been effected under rule 9.40; and
  (c) the information referred to in paragraph (2) has not otherwise been provided.

(2) The party with compensation rights must—
  (a) request the Board to provide the information set out in Section C of the Pension Protection Fund Inquiry Form; and
  (b) on receipt, send a copy of the information referred to in sub-paragraph (a) to the other party.

Applications for pension compensation attachment orders
Rule 9.42

Where an application for a financial remedy includes an application for a pension compensation attachment order or where a request for such an order is added to an existing application for a financial remedy, the applicant must serve a copy of the application on the Board and must at the same time send—
  (a) an address to which any notice which the Board is required to serve on the applicant is to be sent;
  (b) an address to which any payment which the Board is required to make to the applicant is to be sent; and
  (c) where the address in sub-paragraph (b) is that of a bank, a building society or the Department of National Savings, sufficient details to enable the payment to be made into the account of the applicant.

PENSIONS ON DIVORCE

Applications for consent orders for pension compensation attachment orders
Rule 9.43

(1) This rule applies where service has not been effected under rule 9.42.
(2) Where the parties have agreed on the terms of an order and the agreement includes a pension compensation attachment order, then they must serve on the Board—
    (a) a copy of the application for a consent order;
    (b) a draft of the proposed order, complying with rule 9.44; and
    (c) the particulars set out in rule 9.42.

Pension compensation sharing orders or pension compensation attachment orders
Rule 9.44

An order for a financial remedy, whether by consent or not, which includes a pension compensation sharing order or a pension compensation attachment order, must—
    (a) in the body of the order, state that there is to be provision by way of pension compensation sharing or pension compensation attachment in accordance with the annex or annexes to the order; and
    (b) be accompanied by a pension compensation sharing annex or a pension compensation attachment annex as the case may require, and if provision is made in relation to entitlement to PPF compensation that derives from rights under more than one pension scheme there must be one annex for each such entitlement.

Duty of the court upon making a pension compensation sharing order or a pension compensation attachment order
Rule 9.45

(1) A court which makes, varies or discharges a pension compensation sharing order or a pension compensation attachment order, must send, or direct one of the parties to send, to the Board—
    (a) in the case of—
        (i) proceedings under Part 3 of the 1984 Act, a copy of the document of divorce, annulment or legal separation;
        (ii) proceedings under Schedule 7 to the 2004 Act, a copy of the document of dissolution, annulment or legal separation;
    (b) in the case of—
        (i) divorce or nullity of marriage, a copy of the decree absolute under rule 7.32 or 7.33;
        (ii) dissolution or nullity of civil partnership, a copy of the order making the conditional order final under rule 7.32 or 7.33;
    (c) in the case of separation—
        (i) in the matrimonial proceedings, a copy of the decree of judicial separation;

(ii) in civil partnership proceedings, a copy of the separation order; and

(d) a copy of the pension compensation sharing order or the pension compensation attachment order, or as the case may be of the order varying or discharging that order, including any annex to that order relating to that PPF compensation but no other annex to that order.

(2) The documents referred to in paragraph (1) must be sent—
   (a) in proceedings under the 1973 Act and the 1984 Act, within 7 days beginning with the date on which—
      (i) the relevant pension compensation sharing or pension compensation attachment order is made; or
      (ii) the decree absolute of divorce or nullity or the decree of judicial separation is made,
      whichever is the later; and
   (b) in proceedings under the 2004 Act, within 7 days beginning with the date on which—
      (i) the relevant pension compensation sharing or pension compensation attachment order is made; or
      (ii) the final order of dissolution or nullity or separation order is made,
      whichever is the later.

Practice Direction 9A, Family Procedure Rules 2010
Pensions

10.1 The phrase "party with pension rights" is used in FPR Part 9, Chapter 8. For matrimonial proceedings, this phrase has the meaning given to it by section 25D(3) of the Matrimonial Causes Act 1973 and means "the party to the marriage who has or is likely to have benefits under a pension arrangement". There is a definition of "civil partner with pension rights" in paragraph 29 of Schedule 5 to the Civil Partnership Act 2004 which mirrors the definition of "party with pension rights" in section 25D(3) of the 1973 Act. The phrase "is likely to have benefits" in these definitions refers to accrued rights to pension benefits which are not yet in payment.

PPF Compensation

11.1 The phrase "party with compensation rights" is used in FPR Part 9, Chapter 9. For matrimonial proceedings, the phrase has the meaning given to it by section 25G(5) of the Matrimonial Causes Act 1973 and means the party to the marriage who is or is likely to be entitled to PPF compensation. There is a definition of "civil partner with compensation rights" in paragraph 37(1) of Schedule 5 to the Civil Partnership Act 2004 which mirrors the definition of "party with compensation rights" in section 25G(5). The phrase "is likely to be entitled to PPF Compensation" in those definitions refers to statutory entitlement to PPF Compensation which is not yet in payment.

PENSIONS ON DIVORCE

Practice Direction 25D, Family Procedure Rules 2010
Scope of this Practice Direction

1.1 This Practice Direction applies to financial remedy proceedings and other family proceedings except children proceedings and contains guidance on—
    (a) the use of single joint experts;
    (b) how to prepare for the hearing at which the court will consider whether to give permission for putting expert evidence (in any form) before the court including—
        (i) preliminary enquiries of experts;
        (ii) information to be given to the court before the hearing;
    (c) the letter of instruction to the expert.

Single joint experts

2.1 FPR 25.4 applies to a single joint expert ("SJE") in addition to an expert instructed by one party. This means that the court's permission is required to put expert evidence from an SJE (in any form) before the court. However, in family proceedings (except children proceedings) there is no requirement for the court's permission to be obtained before instructing an expert. Wherever possible, expert evidence should be obtained from a single joint expert instructed by both or all the parties ("SJE").To that end, a party wishing to instruct an expert should first give the other party or parties a list of the names of one or more experts in the relevant speciality whom they consider suitable to be instructed.

2.2 **Within 10 business days after receipt of the list of proposed experts**, the other party or parties should indicate any objection to one or more of the named experts and, if so, supply the name(s) of one or more experts whom they consider suitable.

2.3 Each party should disclose whether they have already consulted any of the proposed experts about the issue(s) in question.

2.4 Where the parties cannot agree on the identity of the expert, each party should think carefully before instructing their own expert and seeking the permission of the court to put that expert evidence before it because of the costs implications. Disagreements about the use and identity of an expert may be better managed by the court in the context of an application or the court's permission to put the expert evidence before the court and for directions for the use of an SJE (see paragraph 2.6 below).

Agreement to instruct separate experts

2.5 If the parties agree to instruct separate experts and to seek the permission of the court to put the separate expert evidence before it—
    (a) they should agree in advance that the reports will be disclosed; and
    (b) the instructions to each expert should comply, so far as appropriate, with paragraphs 4.1 and 6.1 below

STATUTES AND STATUTORY INSTRUMENTS

Agreement to instruct an SJE

2.6 If there is agreement to instruct an SJE, **before applying to the court for permission to put the expert evidence before it and directions for the use of an SJE**, the parties should—
   (a) so far as appropriate, comply with the guidance in paragraphs 3.3 (Preliminary enquiries of the expert) and paragraphs 3.11 and 3.12 below;
   (b) receive the expert's confirmation in response to preliminary enquiries referred to in paragraph 8.1 of Practice Direction 25B;
   (c) have agreed in what proportion the SJE's fee is to be shared between them (at least in the first instance) and when it is to be paid; and
   (d) if applicable, have obtained agreement for public funding.
2.7 The instructions to the SJE should comply, so far as appropriate, with paragraphs 4.1 and 6.1 below

The test for permission and preparation for the permission hearing

3.1 The test in FPR 25.1 which the court is to apply to determine whether permission should be given for expert evidence to be put before the court has been altered from one which refers to expert evidence being restricted by the court to that which is reasonably required to resolve the proceedings to one which refers to the expert evidence being in the opinion of the court necessary to assist the court to resolve the proceedings. The overriding objective of the FPR, which is to enable the court to deal with cases justly, having regard to any welfare issues involved, continues to apply when the court is making the decision whether to give permission. In addition, the rules (FPR 25.5(2)) now tell the court what factors it is to have particular regard to when deciding whether to give permission. In financial remedy proceedings the expectation is that the new test and factors are a reflection of current practice and so are unlikely in practice to alter the use of expert evidence in these proceedings.
3.2 Paragraphs 3.3 to 3.12 below give guidance on how to prepare for the hearing at which the court will apply the test in FPR 25.1 and the factors in FPR 25.5(2) and decide whether to give permission for expert evidence to be put before the court. The purpose of the preparation is to ensure that the court has the information required to enable it to exercise its powers under FPR 25.4 and 25.5 in line with FPR 25.1.

Preliminary enquiries of the expert

3.3 **In good time for the information requested to be available for the hearing** at which the court will consider whether to give permission for expert evidence to be put before the court, the party or parties intending to instruct the expert shall approach the expert with the following information—
   (a) the nature of the proceedings and the issues likely to require determination by the court;

(b) the issues in the proceedings to which the expert evidence is to relate;
(c) the questions about which the expert is to be asked to give an opinion and which relate to the issues in the case;
(d) whether permission is to be asked of the court for the use of another expert in the same or any related field (that is, to give an opinion on the same or related questions);
(e) the volume of reading which the expert will need to undertake;
(f) whether or not it will be necessary for the expert to conduct interviews and, if so, with whom;
(g) the likely timetable of legal steps;
(h) when the expert's report is likely to be required;
(i) whether and, if so, what date has been fixed by the court for any hearing at which the expert may be required to give evidence (in particular the Final Hearing); and whether it may be possible for the expert to give evidence by telephone conference or video link: see paragraphs 10.1 and 10.2 **(Arrangements for experts to give evidence)** of Practice Direction 25B;
(j) the possibility of making, through their instructing solicitors, representations to the court about being named or otherwise identified in any public judgment given by the court;
(k) whether the instructing party has public funding and the legal aid rates of payment which are applicable.

Expert's response to preliminary enquiries

3.4 In good time for the hearing at which the court will consider whether to give permission for expert evidence to be put before the court, the solicitors or party intending to instruct the expert must obtain the confirmations from the expert referred to in paragraph 8.1 of Practice Direction 25B. These confirmations include that the work is within the expert's expertise, the expert is available to do the work within the relevant timescale and the expert's costs.

3.5 Where parties **cannot agree who should be the single joint expert** before the hearing at which the court will consider whether to give permission for expert evidence to be put before the court, they should obtain the above confirmations in respect of all experts whom they intend to put to the court for the purposes of rule 25.11(2)(a) as candidates for the appointment.

The application for the court's permission to put expert evidence before the court

Timing and oral applications for the court's permission

3.6 An application for the court's permission to put expert evidence before the court should be made as soon as it becomes apparent that it is necessary to make it. FPR 25.6 makes provision about the time by which applications for the court's permission should be made.

3.7 Applications should, wherever possible, be made so that they are considered at any directions hearing or other hearing for which a date has been fixed or for which a date is about to be fixed. It should be noted that one application notice can be used by a party to make more than one application for an order or direction at a hearing held during the course of proceedings. An application for the court's permission to put expert evidence before the court may therefore be included in an application notice requesting other orders to be made at such a hearing.

3.8 Where a date for a hearing has been fixed, a party who wishes to make an application at that hearing but does not have sufficient time to file an application notice should as soon as possible inform the court (if possible in writing) and, if possible, the other parties of the nature of the application and the reason for it. The party should provide the court and the other party with as much as possible of the information referred to in FPR 25.7and paragraph 3.11 below. That party should then make the application orally at the hearing. An oral application of this kind should be the exception and reserved for genuine cases where circumstances are such that it has only become apparent shortly before the hearing that an expert opinion is necessary.

3.9 In financial remedy proceedings, unless the court directs otherwise, parties must apply for permission to put expert evidence before the court as soon as possible and no later than the first appointment. The expectation is that the court will give directions extending the time by which permission should be obtained where there is good reason for parties to delay the decision whether to use expert evidence and make an application for the court's permission.

3.10 Examples of situations where the time for requesting permission to put expert evidence before the court is likely to be extended are where—
 (a) a decision about the need for expert evidence cannot be made until replies to questionnaires in relation to Forms E have been fully considered; or
 (b) valuations of property are agreed for the purposes of the Financial Dispute Resolution appointment but no agreement is reached to resolve the proceedings at that appointment and the court cannot make a consent order as mentioned in FPR 9.17(8). In these circumstances, it may become clear to a party that he or she will want to use expert valuations of property and an application for the court's permission for such valuation to be put before it may be made orally at the end of the appointment to avoid the need for a separate hearing about this issue. As with other oral applications, the party should provide the court and the other party with as much as possible of the information referred to in FPR 25.7 and paragraph 3.11 below. FPR 9.17(9) requires the court to give directions for the future course of the proceedings where it has not made a consent order including, where appropriate, the filing of evidence.

The application

3.11 In addition to the matters specified in FPR 25.7(2)(a), an application for the court's permission to put expert evidence before the court must state—

(a) the discipline, qualifications and expertise of the expert (by way of C.V. where possible);
(b) the expert's availability to undertake the work;
(c) the timetable for the report;
(d) the responsibility for instruction;
(e) whether the expert evidence can properly be obtained by only one party;
(f) why the expert evidence proposed cannot properly be given by an expert already instructed in the proceedings;
(g) the likely cost of the report on an hourly or other charging basis:
(h) the proposed apportionment (at least in the first instance) of any jointly instructed expert's fee; when it is to be paid; and, if applicable, whether public funding has been approved.

The draft order to be attached to the application for the court's permission

3.12 FPR 25.7(2)(b) provides that a draft of the order giving the court's permission to put expert evidence before the court is to be attached to the application for the court's permission. That draft order must set out the following matters—
(a) the issues in the proceedings to which the expert evidence is to relate;
(b) the party who is to be responsible for drafting the letter of instruction and providing the documents to the expert;
(c) the timetable within which the report is to be prepared, filed and served;
(d) the disclosure of the report to the parties and to any other expert;
(e) the organisation of, preparation or and conduct of any experts' discussion (see Practice Direction25E—Discussions between Experts in Family Proceedings);
(f) the preparation of a statement of agreement and disagreement by the experts following an experts' discussion;
(g) making available to the court at an early opportunity the expert reports in electronic form;
(h) the attendance of the expert at court to give oral evidence (alternatively, the expert giving his or her evidence in writing or remotely by video link), whether at or for the Final Hearing or another hearing; unless agreement about the opinions given by the expert is reached by a date specified by the court prior to the hearing at which the expert is to give oral evidence.

Letter of instruction

4.1 The party responsible for instructing the expert shall, **within 5 business days after the permission hearing**, prepare (in agreement with the other parties where appropriate), file and serve a letter of instruction to the expert which shall—

(a) set out the context in which the expert's opinion is sought (including any ethnic, cultural, religious or linguistic contexts);
(b) set out the questions which the expert is required to answer and ensuring that they –
   (i) are within the ambit of the expert's area of expertise;
   (ii) do not contain unnecessary or irrelevant detail;
   (iii) are kept to a manageable number and are clear, focused and direct; and
   (iv) reflect what the expert has been requested to do by the court;
(c) list the documentation provided, or provide for the expert an indexed and paginated bundle which shall include—
   (i) an agreed list of essential reading; and
   (ii) a copy of this Practice Direction and Practice Directions 25B, 25E and where appropriate Practice Direction 15B;
(d) identify any materials provided to the expert which have not been produced either as original medical (or other professional) records or in response to an instruction from a party, and state the source of that material (such materials may contain an assumption as to the standard of proof, the admissibility or otherwise of hearsay evidence, and other important procedural and substantive questions relating to the different purposes of other enquiries);
(e) identify all requests to third parties for disclosure and their responses in order to avoid partial disclosure, which tends only to prove a case rather than give full and frank information;
(f) identify the relevant people concerned with the proceedings and inform the expert of his or her right to talk to them provided that an accurate record is made of the discussions;
(g) identify any other expert instructed in the proceedings and advise the expert of their right to talk to the other experts provided that an accurate record is made of the discussions;
(h) subject to any public funding requirement for prior authority, define the contractual basis upon which the expert is retained and in particular the funding mechanism including how much the expert will be paid (an hourly rate and overall estimate should already have been obtained), when the expert will be paid, and what limitation there might be on the amount the expert can charge for the work which they will have to do. In cases where the parties are publicly funded, there may also be a brief explanation of the costs and expenses excluded from public funding by Funding Code criterion 1.3 and the detailed assessment process.

Asking the court to settle the letter of instruction to a single joint expert

6.1 Where possible, the written request for the court to consider the letter of instruction referred to in rule 25.12(2) should be set out in an e-mail to the court and copied by e-mail to the other instructing parties. The request should be sent to the relevant court or (by prior arrangement only) directly to the judge dealing with the proceedings. In the magistrates' court, the request should be sent to the relevant court or (by prior arrangement only) to any district judge (magistrates' courts) hearing the proceedings (and copied to the legal adviser) or to the legal adviser. The court will settle the letter of instruction, usually without a hearing to avoid delay; and will send (where practicable, by e-mail) the settled letter to the party responsible for instructing the expert for transmission forthwith to the expert, and copy it to the other instructing parties for information.

PENSIONS ON DIVORCE ETC. (PROVISION OF INFORMATION) REGULATIONS 2000 (SI 2000/1048)

(Incorporating amendments under The Pension Sharing (Consequential and Miscellaneous Amendments) Regulations 2000 (SI 2000/2691))

Basic information about pensions and divorce

2.—(1) The requirements imposed on a person responsible for a pension arrangement for the purposes of section 23(1)(a) of the 1999 Act (supply of pension information in connection with divorce etc.) are that he shall furnish—
   (a) on request from a member, the information referred to in paragraphs (2) and (3)(b) to (f);
   (b) on request from the spouse of a member, the information referred to in paragraph (3); or
   (c) pursuant to an order of the court, the information referred to in paragraph (2), (3) or (4),
   to the member, the spouse of the member, or, as the case may be, to the court.
(2) The information in this paragraph is a valuation of pension rights or benefits accrued under that member's pension arrangement.
(3) The information in this paragraph is—
   (a) a statement that on request from the member, or pursuant to an order of the court, a valuation of pension rights or benefits accrued under that member's pension arrangement, will be provided to the member, or, as the case may be, to the court;
   (b) a statement summarising the way in which the valuation referred to in paragraph (2) and sub-paragraph (a) is calculated;
   (c) the pension benefits which are included in a valuation referred to in paragraph (2) and sub-paragraph (a);
   (d) whether the person responsible for the pension arrangement offers membership to a person entitled to a pension credit, and if so, the types of benefits available to pension credit members under that arrangement;
   (e) whether the person responsible for the pension arrangements intends to discharge his liability for a pension credit other than by offering membership to a person entitled to a pension credit; and

(f) the schedule of charges which the person responsible for the pension arrangement will levy in accordance with regulation 2(2) of the Charging Regulations (general requirements as to charges).

(4) The information in this paragraph is any other information relevant to any power with respect to the matters specified in section 23(1)(a) of the 1999 Act and which is not specified in Schedule 1 or 2 to the Occupational Pension Schemes (Disclosure of Information) Regulations 1996 (basic information about the scheme and information to be made available to individuals), or in Schedule 1 or 2 to the Personal Pension Schemes (Disclosure of Information) Regulations 1987 (basic information about the scheme and information to be made available to individuals), in a case where either of those Regulations applies.

(5) Where the member's request for, or the court order for the provision of, information includes a request for, or an order for the provision of, a valuation under paragraph (2), the person responsible for the pension arrangement shall furnish all the information requested, or ordered, to the member—
  (a) within 3 months beginning with the date the person responsible for the pension arrangement receives that request or order for the provision of the information;
  (b) within 6 weeks beginning with the date the person responsible for the pension arrangement receives the request, or order, for the provision of the information, if the member has notified that person on the date of the request or order that the information is needed in connection with proceedings commenced under any of the provisions referred to in section 23(1)(a) of the 1999 Act; or
  (c) within such shorter period specified by the court in an order requiring the person responsible for the pension arrangement to provide a valuation in accordance with paragraph (2).

(6) Where—
  (a) the member's request for, or the court order for the provision of, information does not include a request or an order for a valuation under paragraph (2); or
  (b) the member's spouse requests the information specified in paragraph (3),
  the person responsible for the pension arrangement shall furnish that information to the member, his spouse, or the court, as the case may be, within one month beginning with the date that person responsible for the pension arrangement receives the request for, or the court order for the provision of, the information.

(7) At the same time as furnishing the information referred to in paragraph (1), the person responsible for a pension arrangement may furnish the information specified in regulation 4(2) (provision of information in response to a notification that a pension sharing order or provision may be made).

PENSIONS ON DIVORCE

Information about pensions and divorce: valuation of pension benefits

3.—(1) Where an application for financial relief under any of the provisions referred to in section 23(1)(a)(i) or (iii) of the 1999 Act (supply of pension information in connection with domestic and overseas divorce etc. in England and Wales and corresponding Northern Ireland powers) has been made or is in contemplation, the valuation of benefits under a pension arrangement shall be calculated and verified for the purposes of regulation 2 of these Regulations in accordance with—
  (a) paragraph (3), if the person with pension rights is a deferred member of an occupational pension scheme;
  (b) paragraph (4), if the person with pension rights is an active member of an occupational pension scheme;
  (c) paragraphs (5) and (6), if—
    (i) the person with pension rights is a member of a personal pension scheme; or
    (ii) those pension rights are contained in a retirement annuity contract; or
  (d) paragraphs (7) to (9), if—
    (i) the pension of the person with pension rights is in payment;
    (ii) the rights of the person with pension rights are contained in an annuity contract other than a retirement annuity contract; or
    (iii) the rights of the person with pension rights are contained in a deferred annuity contract other than a retirement annuity contract.

(2) Where an application for financial provision under any of the provisions referred to in section 23(1)(a)(ii) of the 1999 Act (corresponding Scottish powers) has been made, or is in contemplation, the valuation of benefits under a pension arrangement shall be calculated and verified for the purposes of regulation 2 of these Regulations in accordance with regulation 3 of the Divorce etc. (Pensions) (Scotland) Regulations 2000 (valuation).

(3) Where the person with pension rights is a deferred member of an occupational pension scheme, the value of the benefits which he has under that scheme shall be taken to be—
  (a) in the case of an occupational pension scheme other than a salary related scheme, the cash equivalent to which he acquired a right under section 94(1)(a) of the 1993 Act (right to cash equivalent) on the termination of his pensionable service, calculated on the assumption that he has made an application under section 95 of that Act (ways of taking right to cash equivalent) on the date on which the request for the valuation was received; or
  (b) in the case of a salary related occupational pension scheme, the guaranteed cash equivalent to which he would have acquired a right under section 94(1)(aa) of the 1993 Act if he had made an application under section 95(1) of that Act, calculated on the assumption that he has made such an application on the date on which the request for the valuation was received.

(4) Where the person with pension rights is an active member of an occupational pension scheme, the valuation of the benefits which he has accrued under that scheme shall be calculated and verified—
  (a) on the assumption that the member had made a request for an estimate of the cash equivalent that would be available to him were his pensionable service to terminate on the date on which the request for the valuation was received; and
  (b) in accordance with regulation 11 of and Schedule 1 to the Occupational Pension Schemes (Transfer Values) Regulations 1996 (disclosure).
(5) Where the person with pension rights is a member of a personal pension scheme, or those rights are contained in a retirement annuity contract, the value of the benefits which he has under that scheme or contract shall be taken to be the cash equivalent to which he would have acquired a right under section 94(1)(b) of the 1993 Act, if he had made an application under section 95(1) of that Act on the date on which the request for the valuation was received.
(6) In relation to a personal pension scheme which is comprised in a retirement annuity contract made before 4th January 1988, paragraph (5) shall apply as if such a scheme were not excluded from the scope of Chapter IV of Part IV of the 1993 Act by section 93(1)(b) of that Act (scope of Chapter IV).
(7) Except in a case to which, or to the extent to which, paragraph (9) applies, the cash equivalent of benefits in respect of a person referred to in paragraph (1)(d) shall be calculated and verified in such manner as may be approved in a particular case by—
  (a) a Fellow of the Institute of Actuaries;
  (b) a Fellow of the Faculty of Actuaries; or
  (c) a person with other actuarial qualifications who is approved by the Secretary of State, at the request of the person responsible for the pension arrangement in question, as being a proper person to act for the purposes of this regulation in connection with that arrangement.
(8) Except in a case to which paragraph (9) applies, cash equivalents are to be calculated and verified by adopting methods and making assumptions which—
  (a) if not determined by the person responsible for the pension arrangement in question, are notified to him by an actuary referred to in paragraph (7); and
  (b) are certified by the actuary to the person responsible for the pension arrangement in question as being consistent with "Retirement Benefit Schemes—Transfer Values (GN11)" published by the Institute of Actuaries and the Faculty of Actuaries and current at the date on which the request for the valuation is received.
(9) Where the cash equivalent, or any portion of it represents rights to money purchase benefits under the pension arrangement in question of the person with pension rights, and those rights do not fall, either wholly or in part, to be valued in a manner which involves making estimates of the value of benefits, then that cash equivalent, or that portion of it, shall be calculated and verified in such manner as may be approved in a particular case by the

person responsible for the pension arrangement in question, and by adopting methods consistent with the requirements of Chapter IV of Part IV of the 1993 Act (protection for early leavers—transfer values).

(10) Where paragraph (3), (4) or (9) has effect by reference to provisions of Chapter IV of Part IV of the 1993 Act, section 93(1)(a)(i) of that Act (scope of Chapter IV) shall apply to those provisions as if the words "at least one year" had been omitted from section 93(1)(a)(i).

Provision of information in response to a notification that a pension sharing order or provision may be made

4.—(1) A person responsible for a pension arrangement shall furnish the information specified in paragraph (2) to the member or to the court, as the case may be—
  (a) within 21 days beginning with the date that the person responsible for the pension arrangement received the notification that a pension sharing order or provision may be made; or
  (b) if the court has specified a date which is outside the 21 days referred to in sub-paragraph (a), by that date.
(2) The information referred to in paragraph (1) is—
  (a) the full name of the pension arrangement and address to which any order or provision referred to in section 28(1) of the 1999 Act (activation of pension sharing) should be sent;
  (b) in the case of an occupational pension scheme, whether the scheme is winding up, and, if so,—
    (i) the date on which the winding up commenced; and
    (ii) the name and address of the trustees who are dealing with the winding up;
  (c) in the case of an occupational pension scheme, whether a cash equivalent of the member's pension rights, if calculated on the date the notification referred to in paragraph (1)(a) was received by the trustees or managers of that scheme, would be reduced in accordance with the provisions of regulation 8(4), (6) or (12) of the Occupational Pension Schemes (Transfer Values) Regulations 1996 (further provisions as to reductions of cash equivalents);
  (d) whether the person responsible for the pension arrangement is aware that the member's rights under the pension arrangement are subject to any, and if so, to specify which, of the following—
    (i) any order or provision specified in section 28(1) of the 1999 Act;
    (ii) an order under section 23 of the Matrimonial Causes Act 1973 (financial provision orders in connection with divorce etc.), so far as it includes provision made by virtue of section 25B or 25C of that Act (powers to include provisions about pensions);
    (iii) an order under section 12A(2) or (3) of the Family Law (Scotland) Act 1985 (powers in relation to pensions lump sums

STATUTES AND STATUTORY INSTRUMENTS

when making a capital sum order) which relates to benefits or future benefits to which the member is entitled under the pension arrangement;

 (iv) an order under Article 25 of the Matrimonial Causes (Northern Ireland) Order 1978, so far as it includes provision made by virtue of Article 27B or 27C of that Order (Northern Ireland powers corresponding to those mentioned in paragraph (2)(d)(ii));

 (v) a forfeiture order;

 (vi) a bankruptcy order;

 (vii) an award of sequestration on a member's estate or the making of the appointment on his estate of a judicial factor under section 41 of the Solicitors (Scotland) Act 1980 (appointment of judicial factor);

(e) whether the member's rights under the pension arrangement include rights specified in regulation 2 of the Valuation Regulations (rights under a pension arrangement which are not shareable);

(f) if the person responsible for the pension arrangement has not at an earlier stage provided the following information, whether that person requires the charges specified in regulation 3 (charges recoverable in respect of the provision of basic information), 5 (charges in respect of pension sharing activity), or 6 (additional amounts recoverable in respect of pension sharing activity) of the Charging Regulations to be paid before the commencement of the implementation period, and if so,—

 (i) whether that person requires those charges to be paid in full; or

 (ii) the proportion of those charges which he requires to be paid;

(g) whether the person responsible for the pension arrangement may levy additional charges specified in regulation 6 of the Charging Regulations, and if so, the scale of the additional charges which are likely to be made;

(h) whether the member is a trustee of the pension arrangement;

(i) whether the person responsible for the pension arrangement may request information about the member's state of health from the member if a pension sharing order or provision were to be made;

(k) whether the person responsible for the pension arrangement requires information additional to that specified in regulation 5 (information required by the person responsible for the pension arrangement before the implementation period may begin) in order to implement the pension sharing order or provision.

Information required by the person responsible for the pension arrangement before the implementation period may begin

5. The information prescribed for the purposes of section 34(1)(b) of the 1999 Act (information relating to the transferor and the transferee which the person responsible for the pension arrangement must receive) is—

 (a) in relation to the transferor—

(i) all names by which the transferor has been known;
(ii) date of birth;
(iii) address;
(iv) National Insurance number;
(v) the name of the pension arrangement to which the pension sharing order or provision relates; and
(vi) the transferor's membership or policy number in that pension arrangement;
(b) in relation to the transferee—
(i) all names by which the transferee has been known;
(ii) date of birth;
(iii) address;
(iv) National Insurance number; and
(v) if the transferee is a member of the pension arrangement from which the pension credit is derived, his membership or policy number in that pension arrangement;
(c) where the transferee has given his consent in accordance with paragraph 1(3)(c), 3(3)(c) or 4(2)(c) of Schedule 5 to the 1999 Act (mode of discharge of liability for a pension credit) to the payment of the pension credit to the person responsible for a qualifying arrangement—
(i) the full name of that qualifying arrangement;
(ii) its address;
(iii) if known, the transferee's membership number or policy number in that arrangement; and
(iv) the name or title, business address, business telephone number, and, where available, the business facsimile number and electronic mail address of a person who may be contacted in respect of the discharge of liability for the pension credit;
(d) where the rights from which the pension credit is derived are held in an occupational pension scheme which is being wound up, whether the transferee has given an indication whether he wishes to transfer his pension credit rights which may have been reduced in accordance with the provisions of regulation 16(1) of the Implementation and Discharge of Liability Regulations (adjustments to the amount of the pension credit—occupational pension schemes which are underfunded on the valuation day) to a qualifying arrangement; and
(e) any information requested by the person responsible for the pension arrangement in accordance with regulation 4(2)(i) or (k).
[…]

Provision of information after receiving a pension sharing order or provision

7.— (1) A person responsible for a pension arrangement who is in receipt of a pension sharing order or provision relating to that arrangement shall provide in writing to the transferor and transferee, or, where regulation 6(1) applies, to the person other than the person entitled to the pension credit

STATUTES AND STATUTORY INSTRUMENTS

referred to in regulation 6 of the Implementation and Discharge of Liability Regulations (discharge of liability in respect of a pension credit following the death of the person entitled to the pension credit), as the case may be,—
- (a) a notice in accordance with the provisions of regulation 7(1) of the Charging Regulations (charges in respect of pension sharing activity—postponement of implementation period);
- (b) a list of information relating to the transferor or the transferee, or, where regulation 6(1) applies, the person other than the person entitled to the pension credit referred to in regulation 6 of the Implementation and Discharge of Liability Regulations, as the case may be, which—
    - (i) has been requested in accordance with regulation 4(2)(i) and (k), or, where appropriate, 6(2)(c), or should have been provided in accordance with regulation 5;
    - (ii) the person responsible for the pension arrangement considers he needs in order to begin to implement the pension sharing order or provision; and
    - (iii) remains outstanding;
- (c) a notice of implementation; or
- (d) a statement by the person responsible for the pension arrangement explaining why he is unable to implement the pension sharing order or agreement.

(2) The information specified in paragraph (1) shall be furnished in accordance with that paragraph within 21 days beginning with—
- (a) in the case of sub-paragraph (a), (b) or (d) of that paragraph, the day on which the person responsible for the pension arrangement receives the pension sharing order or provision; or
- (b) in the case of sub-paragraph (c) of that paragraph, the later of the days specified in section 34(1)(a) and (b) of the 1999 Act (implementation period).

Provision of information after the implementation of a pension sharing order or provision

8.—(1) The person responsible for the pension arrangement shall issue a notice of discharge of liability to the transferor and the transferee, or, as the case may be, the person entitled to the pension credit by virtue of regulation 6 of the Implementation and Discharge of Liability Regulations no later than the end of the period of 21 days beginning with the day on which the discharge of liability in respect of the pension credit is completed.

(2) In the case of a transferor whose pension is not in payment, the notice of discharge of liability shall include the following details—
- (a) the value of the transferor's accrued rights as determined by reference to the cash equivalent value of those rights calculated and verified in accordance with regulation 3 of the Valuation Regulations (calculation and verification of cash equivalents for the purposes of the creation of pension debits and credits);
- (b) the value of the pension debit;

(c) any amount deducted from the value of the pension rights in accordance with regulation 9(2)(c) of the Charging Regulations (charges in respect of pension sharing activity—method of recovery);
(d) the value of the transferor's rights after the amounts referred to in sub-paragraphs (b) and (c) have been deducted; and
(e) the transfer day.

(3) In the case of a transferor whose pension is in payment, the notice of discharge of liability shall include the following details—
    (a) the value of the transferor's benefits under the pension arrangement as determined by reference to the cash equivalent value of those rights calculated and verified in accordance with regulation 3 of the Valuation Regulations;
    (b) the value of the pension debit;
    (c) the amount of the pension which was in payment before liability in respect of the pension credit was discharged;
    (d) the amount of pension which is payable following the deduction of the pension debit from the transferor's pension benefits;
    (e) the transfer day;
    (f) if the person responsible for the pension arrangement intends to recover charges, the amount of any unpaid charges—
        (i) not prohibited by regulation 2 of the Charging Regulations (general requirements as to charges); and
        (ii) specified in regulations 3 and 6 of those Regulations;
    (g) how the person responsible for the pension arrangement will recover the charges referred to in sub-paragraph (f), including—
        (i) whether the method of recovery specified in regulation 9(2)(d) of the Charging Regulations will be used;
        (ii) the date when payment of those charges in whole or in part is required; and
        (iii) the sum which will be payable by the transferor, or which will be deducted from his pension benefits, on that date.

(4) In the case of a transferee—
    (a) whose pension is not in payment; and
    (b) who will become a member of the pension arrangement from which the pension credit rights were derived,
the notice of discharge of liability to the transferee shall include the following details—
    (i) the value of the pension credit;
    (ii) any amount deducted from the value of the pension credit in accordance with regulation 9(2)(b) of the Charging Regulations;
    (iii) the value of the pension credit after the amount referred to in sub-paragraph (b)(ii) has been deducted;
    (iv) the transfer day;
    (v) any periodical charges the person responsible for the pension arrangement intends to make, including how and when those charges will be recovered from the transferee; and

STATUTES AND STATUTORY INSTRUMENTS

      (vi)   information concerning membership of the pension arrangement which is relevant to the transferee as a pension credit member.

(5) In the case of a transferee who is transferring his pension credit rights out of the pension arrangement from which those rights were derived, the notice of discharge of liability to the transferee shall include the following details—
  (a) the value of the pension credit;
  (b) any amount deducted from the value of the pension credit in accordance with regulation 9(2)(b) of the Charging Regulations;
  (c) the value of the pension credit after the amount referred to in sub-paragraph (b) has been deducted;
  (d) the transfer day; and
  (e) details of the pension arrangement, including its name, address, reference number, telephone number, and, where available, the business facsimile number and electronic mail address, to which the pension credit has been transferred.

(6) In the case of a transferee, who has reached normal benefit age on the transfer day, and in respect of whose pension credit liability has been discharged in accordance with paragraph 1(2), 2(2), 3(2) or 4(4) of Schedule 5 to the 1999 Act (pension credits: mode of discharge—funded pension schemes, unfunded public service pension schemes, other unfunded pension schemes, or other pension arrangements), the notice of discharge of liability to the transferee shall include the following details—
  (a) the amount of pension credit benefit which is to be paid to the transferee;
  (b) the date when the pension credit benefit is to be paid to the transferee;
  (c) the transfer day;
  (d) if the person responsible for the pension arrangement intends to recover charges, the amount of any unpaid charges—
    (i) not prohibited by regulation 2 of the Charging Regulations; and
    (ii) specified in regulations 3 and 6 of those Regulations; and
  (e) how the person responsible for the pension arrangement will recover the charges referred to in sub-paragraph (d), including—
    (i) whether the method of recovery specified in regulation 9(2)(e) of the Charging Regulations will be used;
    (ii) the date when payment of those charges in whole or in part is required; and
    (iii) the sum which will be payable by the transferee, or which will be deducted from his pension credit benefits, on that date.

(7) In the case of a person entitled to the pension credit by virtue of regulation 6 of the Implementation and Discharge of Liability Regulations, the notice of discharge of liability shall include the following details—
  (a) the value of the pension credit rights as determined in accordance with regulation 10 of the Implementation and Discharge of Liability Regulations (calculation of the value of appropriate rights);
  (b) any amount deducted from the value of the pension credit in accordance with regulation 9(2)(b) of the Charging Regulations;

(c) the value of the pension credit;
(d) the transfer day; and
(e) any periodical charges the person responsible for the pension arrangement intends to make, including how and when those charges will be recovered from the payments made to the person entitled to the pension credit by virtue of regulation 6 of the Implementation and Discharge of Liability Regulations.

PENSIONS ON DIVORCE (CHARGING) REGULATIONS 2000 (SI 2000/1049)

Charges in respect of pension sharing activity—method of recovery

9.—(1) Subject to paragraphs (7) and (8), a person responsible for a pension arrangement may recover the charges specified in regulations 3, 5 and 6 by using any of the methods described in paragraph (2).

(2) The methods of recovery described in this paragraph are—
  (a) subject to regulation 7 requiring the charges referred to in paragraph (1) to be paid before the implementation period for the pension sharing order or provision is commenced;
  (b) deduction from a pension credit;
  (c) deduction from the accrued rights of the member;
  (d) where a pension sharing order or provision is made in respect of a pension which is in payment, deduction from the member's pension benefits;
  (e) where liability in respect of a pension credit is discharged by the person responsible for the pension arrangement in accordance with paragraph 1(2), 2(2), or 3(2) of Schedule 5 to the 1999 Act (mode of discharge of liability for pension credits), deduction from payments of pension credit benefit; or
  (f) deduction from the amount of a transfer value which is calculated in accordance with—
    (i) regulation 7 of the Occupational Pension Schemes (Transfer Values) Regulations 1996 (manner of calculation and verification of cash equivalents); or
    (ii) regulation 3 of the Personal Pension Schemes (Transfer Values) Regulations 1987 (manner of calculation and verification of cash equivalents).

(3) A person responsible for a pension arrangement shall not recover charges referred to in paragraph (1) by using any of the methods described in paragraph (2)(b), (c), (d), (e) or (f) unless—
  (a) a pension sharing order or provision corresponding to any order or provision specified in subsection (1) of section 28 of the 1999 Act has been made;
  (b) the implementation period has commenced;
  (c) where a pension sharing order has been made, the person responsible for a pension arrangement is not aware of an appeal against the order having begun on or after the day on which the order takes effect;

STATUTES AND STATUTORY INSTRUMENTS

- (d) there are charges which are unpaid and for which the party, to whom paragraph (2)(b), (c), (d), (e) or (f) applies, is liable;
- (e) the person responsible for the pension arrangement has issued a notice of implementation in accordance with regulation 7 of the Provision of Information Regulations;
- (f) the person responsible for a pension arrangement specifies in the notice of implementation that recovery of the charges may be made by using any of those methods; and
- (g) 21 days have elapsed since the notice of implementation was issued to the parties to pension sharing in accordance with the requirements of regulation 7 of the Provision of Information Regulations.

(4) If a pension sharing order or provision includes provision about the apportionment between the parties to pension sharing of any charge under section 41 of the 1999 Act or under corresponding Northern Ireland legislation, by virtue of section 24D of the Matrimonial Causes Act 1973 (pension sharing orders: apportionment of charges) or section 8A of the Family Law (Scotland) Act 1985 (pension sharing orders: apportionment of charges), the recovery of charges using any of the methods described in paragraph (2) by the person responsible for the pension arrangement shall comply with the terms of the order or provision.

(5) A person responsible for a pension arrangement shall not recover charges referred to in paragraph (1) by using any of the methods described in paragraph (2), from a party to pension sharing, if that party has paid in full the proportion of the charges for which he is liable.

(6) A person responsible for a pension arrangement may recover charges by using any of the methods described in paragraph (2)(b), (c) or (d)—
- (a) at any time within the implementation period prescribed by section 34 of the 1999 Act ("implementation period");
- (b) following an application by the trustees or managers of an occupational pension scheme, such longer period as the Regulatory Authority may allow in accordance with section 33(4) of the 1999 Act (extension of time for discharge of liability); or
- (c) within 21 days after the end of the period referred to in sub-paragraph (a) or (b).

(7) Where the commencement of the implementation period is postponed, or its operation ceases in accordance with regulation 4 of the Pension Sharing (Implementation and Discharge of Liability) Regulations 2000 (postponement or cessation of implementation period where an application is made for leave to appeal out of time) a person responsible for a pension arrangement may require any outstanding charges referred to in paragraph (1) to be paid immediately, in respect of—
- (a) all costs which have been incurred prior to the date of postponement or cessation; or
- (b) any reasonable costs related to—
  - (i) the application for leave to appeal out of time; or
  - (ii) the appeal out of time itself.

(8) Paragraph (7) applies even if, prior to receiving the notification of the application for leave to appeal out of time, a person responsible for a

pension arrangement has indicated to the parties to pension sharing that he will not be using the method of recovery specified in paragraph (2)(a).

PENSION SHARING (VALUATION) REGULATIONS 2000 (SI 2000/1052)

(Incorporating amendments under The Pension Sharing (Consequential and Miscellaneous Amendments) Regulations 2000 (SI 2000/2691))

Citation, commencement and interpretation

1.—(1) These Regulations may be cited as the Pension Sharing (Valuation) Regulations 2000 and shall come into force on 1st December 2000.
(2) In these Regulations—
"the 1993 Act" means the Pension Schemes Act 1993;
"the 1995 Act" means the Pensions Act 1995;
"the 1999 Act" means the Welfare Reform and Pensions Act 1999;
"employer" has the meaning given by section 181(1) of the 1993 Act;
"occupational pension scheme" has the meaning given by section 1 of the 1993 Act;
"pension arrangement" has the meaning given by section 46(1) of the 1999 Act;
"relevant arrangement" has the meaning given by section 29(8) of the 1999 Act;
"relevant benefits" has the meaning given by section 612 of the Income and Corporation Taxes Act 1988;
"scheme" means an occupational pension scheme;
"scheme actuary", in relation to a scheme to which section 47(1)(b) of the 1995 Act applies, means the actuary mentioned in section 47(1)(b) of that Act;
"transfer credits" has the meaning given by section 181(1) of the 1993 Act;
"transfer day" has the meaning given by section 29(8) of the 1999 Act;
"transferor" has the meaning given by section 29(8) of the 1999 Act;
"trustees or managers" has the meaning given by section 46(1) of the 1999 Act;
"valuation day" has the meaning given by section 29(7) of the 1999 Act.

Rights under a pension arrangement which are not shareable

2.—(1) Rights under a pension arrangement which are not shareable are—
  (a) subject to paragraph (2), any rights accrued between 1961 and 1975 which relate to contracted-out equivalent pension benefit within the meaning of section 57 of the National Insurance Act 1965 (equivalent pension benefits, etc.);
  (b) any rights in respect of which a person is in receipt of—
    (i) a pension;
    (ii) an annuity;

(iii) payments under an interim arrangement within the meaning of section 28(1A) of the 1993 Act (ways of giving effect to protected rights); or
(iv) income withdrawal within the meaning of section 630(1) of the Income and Corporation Taxes Act 1988 (interpretation), by virtue of being the widow, widower or other dependant of a deceased person with pension rights under a pension arrangement; and
(c) any rights which do not result in the payment of relevant benefits.
(2) Paragraph (1)(a) applies only when those rights are the only rights held by a person under a pension arrangement.

PENSION SHARING (IMPLEMENTATION AND DISCHARGE OF LIABILITY) REGULATIONS 2000 (SI 2000/1053)

(Incorporating amendments under The Pension Sharing (Consequential and Miscellaneous Amendments) Regulations 2000 (SI 2000/2691))

Circumstances in which an application for an extension of the implementation period may be made

3. The circumstances in which an application may be made for the purposes of section 33(4) of the 1999 Act (application for extension of period within which pension credit liability is to be discharged) are that the application is made to the Regulatory Authority before the end of the implementation period; and—
   (a) the Regulatory Authority is satisfied that—
      (i) the scheme is being wound up or is about to be wound up;
      (ii) the scheme is ceasing to be a contracted-out scheme;
      (iii) the financial interests of the members of the scheme generally will be prejudiced if the trustees or managers do what is needed to discharge their liability for the pension credit within that period;
      (iv) the transferor or the transferee has not taken such steps as the trustees or managers can reasonably expect in order to satisfy them of any matter which falls to be established before they can properly discharge their liability for the pension credit;
      (v) the trustees or managers have not been provided with such information as they reasonably require properly to discharge their liability for the pension credit within the implementation period;
      (vi) the transferor or the transferee has disputed the amount of the cash equivalent calculated and verified for the purposes of section 29 of the 1999 Act (creation of pension debits and credits);
   (b) the provisions of section 53 of the 1993 Act (supervision: former contracted-out schemes) apply; or

(c) the application has been made on one or more of the grounds specified in paragraph (a) or (b), and the Regulatory Authority's consideration of the application cannot be completed before the end of the implementation period.
[...]

Civil penalties

5. For the purpose of section 33(2)(b) or (3) of the 1999 Act, the maximum amount of the penalty which may be imposed by the Regulatory Authority under section 10(2)(b) of the 1995 Act is—
   (a) £1,000 in the case of an individual, and
   (b) £10,000 in any other case.

Discharge of liability in respect of a pension credit following the death of the person entitled to the pension credit

6.—(1) The person responsible for the pension arrangement shall following the death of the person entitled to the pension credit discharge his liability in respect of a pension credit in accordance with this regulation.

(2) Where the rules or provisions of a pension arrangement so provide and provided that any requirements of the Inland Revenue under Part XIV of the Income and Corporation Taxes Act 1988 are satisfied, the person responsible for the pension arrangement shall discharge his liability in respect of a pension credit by undertaking to—
   (a) make—
      (i) a payment of a lump sum; or
      (ii) payments of a pension; or
      (iii) payments of both a lump sum and a pension, to one or more persons; or
   (b) enter into an annuity contract or take out a policy of insurance with an insurance company for the benefit of one or more persons; or
   (c) make a payment or, as the case may be, payments under sub-paragraph (a) and enter into an annuity contract or take out an insurance policy under sub-paragraph (b).

(3) Where paragraph (2)(b) or (c) applies, the annuity contract entered into or insurance policy taken out must satisfy the requirements of paragraph 6(2) of Schedule 5 to the 1999 Act (qualifying arrangements) and regulation 11 of these Regulations.

(4) Where the provisions of paragraph (2) do not apply, liability in respect of a pension credit shall be discharged by retaining the value of the pension credit in the pension arrangement from which that pension credit was derived.

(5) Where—
   (a) liability in respect of a pension credit has been discharged in accordance with paragraph (2); and

(b) the value of the payment or payments made, the annuity contract entered into or the insurance policy taken out, as the case may be, is less than the value of the pension credit,

the value of an amount equal to the difference between the value of the pension credit and the value of that payment or those payments, that contract or policy, as the case may be, shall be retained in the pension arrangement from which that pension credit was derived.

DIVORCE ETC. (PENSIONS) REGULATIONS 2000 (SI 2000/1123)

Valuation

3.—(1) For the purposes of the court's functions in connection with the exercise of any of its powers under Part II of the Matrimonial Causes Act 1973, benefits under a pension arrangement shall be calculated and verified in the manner set out in regulation 3 of the Pensions on Divorce etc. (Provision of Information) Regulations 2000, and—
  (a) the benefits shall be valued as at a date to be specified by the court (being not earlier than one year before the date of the petition and not later than the date on which the court is exercising its power);
  (b) in determining that value the court may have regard to information furnished by the person responsible for the pension arrangement pursuant to any of the provisions set out in paragraph (2); and
  (c) in specifying a date under sub-paragraph (a) above the court may have regard to the date specified in any information furnished as mentioned in sub-paragraph (b) above.
(2) The relevant provisions for the purposes of paragraph (1)(b) above are:
  (a) the Pensions on Divorce etc. (Provision of Information) Regulations 2000;
  (b) regulation 5 of and Schedule 2 to the Occupational Pension Schemes (Disclosure of Information) Regulations 1996 and regulation 11 of and Schedule 1 to the Occupational Pension Schemes (Transfer Value) Regulations 1996;
  (c) section 93A or 94(1)(a) or (aa) of the Pension Schemes Act 1993;
  (d) section 94(1)(b) of the Pension Schemes Act 1993 or paragraph 2(a) (or, where applicable, 2(b)) of Schedule 2 to the Personal Pension Schemes (Disclosure of Information) Regulations 1987.
  […]

Pension sharing order not to take effect pending appeal

9.—(1) No pension sharing order under section 24B or variation of a pension sharing order under section 31 shall take effect earlier than 7 days after the end of the period for filing notice of appeal against the order.
(2) The filing of a notice of appeal within the time allowed for doing so prevents the order taking effect before the appeal has been dealt with.

SHARING OF STATE SCHEME RIGHTS (PROVISION OF INFORMATION AND VALUATION) REGULATIONS 2000 (SI 2000/2693)

Citation, commencement and interpretation

1.—(1) These Regulations may be cited as the Sharing of State Scheme Rights (Provision of Information and Valuation) Regulations 2000 and shall come into force on 1st December 2000.
(2) In these Regulations—
"the 1992 Act" means the Social Security Contributions and Benefits Act 1992;
"the 1999 Act" means the Welfare Reform and Pensions Act 1999;
"shareable state scheme rights" has the meaning given by section 47(2) of the 1999 Act.

Basic information about the sharing of state scheme rights and divorce

2.—(1) The requirements imposed on the Secretary of State for the purposes of section 23(1)(a) of the 1999 Act (supply of pension information in connection with divorce etc.) are that he shall furnish—
  (a) the information specified in paragraphs (2) and (3)—
    (i) to a person who has shareable state scheme rights on request from that person; or
    (ii) to the court, pursuant to an order of the court; or
  (b) the information specified in paragraph (3) to the spouse of a person who has shareable state scheme rights, on request from that spouse.
(2) The information specified in this paragraph is a valuation of the person's shareable state scheme rights.
(3) The information in this paragraph is an explanation of—
  (a) the state scheme rights which are shareable;
  (b) how a pension sharing order or provision will affect a person's shareable state scheme rights; and
  (c) how a pension sharing order or provision in respect of a person's shareable state scheme rights will result in the spouse of the person who has shareable state scheme rights becoming entitled to a shared additional pension.
(4) The Secretary of State shall furnish the information specified in paragraphs (2) and (3) to the court or, as the case may be, to the person who has shareable state scheme rights within—
  (a) 3 months beginning with the date the Secretary of State receives the request or, as the case may be, the order for the provision of that information;
  (b) 6 weeks beginning with the date the Secretary of State receives the request or, as the case may be, the order for the provision of the information, if the person who has shareable state scheme rights has notified the Secretary of State on the date of the request or order that

the information is needed in connection with proceedings commenced under any of the provisions referred to in section 23(1)(a) of the 1999 Act; or
  (c) such shorter period specified by the court in an order requiring the Secretary of State to provide a valuation in accordance with paragraph (2).
(5) Where—
  (a) the request made by the person with shareable state scheme rights for, or the court order requiring, the provision of information does not include a request or, as the case may be, an order for a valuation under paragraph (2); or
  (b) the spouse of the person with shareable state scheme rights requests the information specified in paragraph (3),
  the Secretary of State shall furnish that information to the person who has shareable state scheme rights, his spouse, or the court, as the case may be, within one month beginning with the date the Secretary of State receives the request or the court order for the provision of that information.

Information about the sharing of state scheme rights and divorce: valuation of shareable state scheme rights

3. Where an application for financial relief or financial provision under any of the provisions referred to in section 23(1)(a) of the 1999 Act has been made or is in contemplation, the valuation of shareable state scheme rights shall be calculated and verified for the purposes of regulation 2(2) of these Regulations in such manner as may be approved by or on behalf of the Government Actuary.

Calculation and verification of cash equivalents for the purposes of the creation of state scheme pension debits and credits

4. For the purposes of—
  (a) section 49 of the 1999 Act (creation of state scheme pension debits and credits);
  (b) section 45B of the 1992 Act (reduction of additional pension in Category A retirement pension: pension sharing);
  (c) section 55A of the 1992 Act (shared additional pension); and
  (d) section 55B of the 1992 Act (reduction of shared additional pension: pension sharing),
  cash equivalents shall be calculated and verified in such manner as may be approved by or on behalf of the Government Actuary.

OCCUPATIONAL PENSION SCHEMES (TRANSFER VALUES) REGULATIONS 1996 (SI 1996/1847)

(As amended by the Occupational Pension Schemes (Transfer Values)(Amendment) Regulations 2008 (SI 2008/1050))

PENSIONS ON DIVORCE

Manner of calculation and verification of cash equivalents—general provisions

7.—(1) Subject to paragraphs (4) and (7), cash equivalents are to be calculated and verified—
  (a) by calculating the initial cash equivalent—
    (i) for salary related benefits, in accordance with regulations 7A and 7B; or
    (ii) for money purchase benefits, in accordance with regulation 7C, and then making any reductions in accordance with regulation 7D; or
  (b) in accordance with regulation 7E.
(2) The trustees must decide whether to calculate and verify the cash equivalent in accordance with paragraph (1)(a) or (b), but they can only choose paragraph (1)(b) if they have had regard to any requirement for consent to paying a cash equivalent which is higher than the amount calculated and verified in accordance with paragraph (1)(a).
(3) The trustees are responsible for the calculation and verification of cash equivalents and initial cash equivalents.
(4) Where a member, in relation to whom a cash equivalent is to be calculated and verified, is a member of a scheme modified by—
  (a) the British Coal Staff Superannuation Scheme (Modification) Regulations 1994; or
  (b) the Mineworkers' Pension Scheme (Modification) Regulations 1994, the cash equivalent of his bonus is to be calculated and verified by the trustees, having obtained the advice of the actuary, to reflect the fact that a reduced bonus, or no bonus, may become payable in accordance with the provisions governing the scheme in question.
(5) For the purposes of paragraph (4) "bonus" means any—
  (a) augmentation of his benefits; or
  (b) new, additional or alternative benefits,
which the trustees of the scheme in question have applied to the member's benefits, or granted to him in accordance with the provisions governing that scheme, on the basis of findings as to that scheme's funding position.
(6) Paragraph (7) applies where the cash equivalent is calculated and verified in accordance with paragraph (1)(a).
(7) Where a portion of the cash equivalent relates to a salary related benefit and a portion relates to a money purchase benefit, the initial cash equivalent is to be calculated—
  (a) for the salary related benefit portion, in accordance with regulations 7A and 7B; and
  (b) for the money purchase benefit portion, in accordance with regulation 7C.

Manner of calculation of initial cash equivalents for salary related benefits

7A.—(1) For salary related benefits, the initial cash equivalent is to be calculated—

STATUTES AND STATUTORY INSTRUMENTS

    (a)   on an actuarial basis; and

    (b)   in accordance with paragraph (2) and regulation 7B.

(2) The initial cash equivalent is the amount at the guarantee date which is required to make provision within the scheme for a member's accrued benefits, options and discretionary benefits.

(3) For the purposes of paragraph (2), the trustees must determine the extent—

    (a)   of any options the member has which would increase the value of his benefits under the scheme;

    (b)   of any adjustments they decide to make to reflect the proportion of members likely to exercise those options; and

    (c)   to which any discretionary benefits should be taken into account, having regard to any established custom for awarding them and any requirement for consent before they are awarded.

Initial cash equivalents for salary related benefits: assumptions and guidance

7B.—(1) The trustees must calculate the initial cash equivalent for salary related benefits—

    (a)   by using the assumptions determined under this regulation; and

    (b)   where the scheme falls within paragraph (6), in accordance with the guidance referred to in that paragraph.

(2) Having taken the advice of the actuary, the trustees must determine the economic, financial and demographic assumptions.

(3) In determining the demographic assumptions, the trustees must have regard to—

    (a)   the main characteristics of the members of the scheme; or

    (b)   where the members of the scheme do not form a large enough group to allow demographic assumptions to be made, the characteristics of a wider population sharing similar characteristics to the members.

(4) Except where the scheme falls within paragraph (6), the trustees must have regard to the scheme's investment strategy when deciding what assumptions will be included in calculating the discount rates in respect of the member.

(5) The trustees must determine the assumptions under this regulation with the aim that, taken as a whole, they should lead to the best estimate of the initial cash equivalent.

(6) A scheme falls within this paragraph if it is a public service pension scheme in respect of which guidance has been prepared, and from time to time revised, by the Treasury for calculating the discount rates.

Manner of calculation of initial cash equivalents for money purchase benefits

7C.—(1) For money purchase benefits, the initial cash equivalent is to be calculated in accordance with this regulation.

(2) The initial cash equivalent is the realisable value at the date of calculation of any benefits to which the member is entitled.

(3) The trustees must calculate that realisable value—
   (a) in accordance with the scheme rules; and
   (b) in a manner which is—
       (i) approved by the trustees; and
       (ii) consistent with Chapter IV of Part IV of the 1993 Act.
(4) The realisable value must include any increases to the benefits resulting from a payment of interest made in accordance with the scheme rules.

Reductions to initial cash equivalents

7D.—(1) An initial cash equivalent may, or as the case may be must, be reduced in accordance with Schedule 1A (reductions in initial cash equivalents).
(2) The trustees may request an insufficiency report from the actuary in accordance with Schedule 1B.
(3) The trustees may treat the actuary's last relevant GN11 report as an insufficiency report.

Alternative manner of calculating and verifying cash equivalents

7E.—(1) This regulation applies where the trustees have decided to calculate and verify the cash equivalent in accordance with regulation 7(1)(b).
(2) The cash equivalent is to be calculated and verified in such manner as may be approved by the trustees.
(3) The cash equivalent must be higher than it would be if it was calculated and verified in accordance with regulation 7(1)(a).
(4) For the purposes of calculating and verifying the cash equivalent, the trustees may request an insufficiency report from the actuary in accordance with Schedule 1B.
(5) The trustees may treat the actuary's last relevant GN11 report as an insufficiency report.

PERSONAL PENSION SCHEMES (TRANSFER VALUES) REGULATIONS 1987 (SI 1987/1112)

(As amended by the Occupational Pension Schemes (Transfer Values)(Amendment) Regulations 2008 (SI 2008/1050) and the Occupational Pension Schemes (Transfer Values)(Amendment) Regulations 2008 (SI 2008/2450))

Manner of calculation and verification of cash equivalents

3.—(1) Cash equivalents are to be calculated and verified by calculating the initial cash equivalent in accordance with this regulation and then making any increases or reductions in accordance with regulation 4.
(2) The initial cash equivalent is the realisable value at the date of calculation of any benefits to which the member is entitled.
(3) The trustees must calculate that realisable value—
   (a) in accordance with the scheme rules; and
   (b) in a manner which is—

STATUTES AND STATUTORY INSTRUMENTS

      (i)   approved by the trustees; and

      (ii)   consistent with Chapter IV of Part IV of the Act.

(4)   The realisable value must include any increases to the benefits resulting from a payment of interest made in accordance with the scheme rules.

PART D

MISCELLANEOUS MATERIALS

FORM E—PARAGRAPH 2.13

2 Financial Details   Part 4 Capital: Pensions and Pension Protection Fund (PPF) Compensation

2.13 Give details of all your pension rights and all PPF compensation entitlements, including prospective entitlements. Complete a separate page for each pension or PPF compensation entitlement.

EXCLUDE:
- Basic State Pension

INCLUDE (complete a separate page for each one):
- Additional State Pension (SERPS and State Second Pension (S2P))
- Free Standing Additional Voluntary Contribution Schemes (FSAVC) separate from the scheme of your employer
- Membership of ALL pension plans or schemes
- PPF compensation entitlement for each scheme you were a member of which has transferred to PPF

Documentation required for attachment to this section:
a) A recent statement showing the cash equivalent (CE) provided by the trustees or managers of each pension arrangement; for the additional state pension, a valuation of these rights or for PPF a valuation of PPF compensation entitlement
b) If any valuation is not available, give the estimated date when it will be available and attach a copy of your letter to the pension company, administrators, or PPF Board from whom the information was sought and/or state the date on which an application for a valuation of an Additional State Pension was submitted to the Department of Work and Pensions

Name and address of pension arrangement or PPF Board			
Your National Insurance Number			
Number of pension arrangement or reference number or PPF compensation reference number			
Type of scheme e.g. occupational or personal, final salary, money purchase, additional state pension, PPF or other (if other, please give details)			
Date the CE, PPF compensation or additional state pension was calculated	Date	Month	Year
Is the pension in payment or drawdown? (please answer Yes or No)	☐ Yes ☐ No		
State the CE quotation, the additional state pension valuation or PPF valuation of those rights			
If the arrangement is an occupational pension arrangement that is paying reduced CEs, please quote what the CE would have been if not reduced. If this is not possible, please indicate if the CE quoted is a reduced CE			
Is the PPF compensation capped? (please answer Yes or No)	☐ Yes ☐ No		

TOTAL value of ALL your pension assets: TOTAL F   £

FORM P—PENSION ENQUIRY FORM

Pension Inquiry Form

Information needed when a Pension Sharing Order or Pension Attachment Order may be made

Insert details of pension scheme here	
To:	
of:	
Reference No:	

A. To be completed by Pension Scheme member or policy holder:

1. Pension scheme member or policy holder's details:

   Name

   Address (including postcode)

   Postcode

   Reference

2. Solicitors details:

   Name

   Address (including postcode)

   Postcode

   Reference

   Telephone

3. Address to which the form should be sent once completed if different from 2 above:

   Address (including postcode)

   Postcode

   Signature

   of Pension Scheme member or policy holder

   (The scheme member's signature is necessary to authorise the release of the requested information, unless a court or requiring the information is attached to this form.)

Form P Pension Inquiry Form (04.11) © Crown Copyright 2011

MISCELLANEOUS MATERIALS

B. To be completed by the pension arrangement

This section deals with information required to be provided under the Pensions on Divorce etc (Provision of Information) Regulations 2000 S.I.1048/2000, Regulations 2 and 3 and Chapter 8 of Part 9 to the Family Procedure Rules 2010. If a request for a Cash Equivalent Value has been made, the pension arrangement has 3 months to provide the information or 6 weeks if notified that the information is needed in connection with matrimonial or civil partnership proceedings, or such shorter time as notified by the court. Otherwise, the information should be provided within one month or such shorter time as notified by the court. The valuation referred to in paragraph 1(a) below must have been made not more than 12 months before the date fixed for the first appointment.

If this information has already been prepared in a standard form please send this instead.

1. (a) Please confirm that you have already provided a valuation of the member's pension rights to the scheme member or to the Court. ☐ Yes ☐ No

   (b) If the answer to (a) is No, details of the CEV quotation should be attached and the date on which it was calculated.

2. Provide a statement summarising the way in which the valuation referred to above has been or will be calculated.

3. State the pension benefits included in the valuation referred to in B1 above.

4. (a) Does the person responsible for the pension arrangement offer scheme membership to the person entitled to a pension credit? ☐ Yes ☐ No

   (b) If Yes, does this depend on Employer and/or trustee approval? ☐ Yes ☐ No

5. If the answer to 4(a) is Yes, what benefits are available to the person with the pension credit?

6. **Charging Policy**
   - Does the arrangement charge for providing information or implementing a pension sharing order? ☐ Yes ☐ No

   If Yes, please:
   - provide a list of charges
   - indicate when these must be paid, and
   - whether they can be paid directly from benefits held in the scheme or policy, or the pension credit.

PENSIONS ON DIVORCE

C. To be completed by the pension arrangement

This information is required to be provided by the pension arrangement under the Pension on Divorce (Provision of Information) Regulations 2000 S.I. 1048, Regulation 4 within 21 days of being notified that a pension sharing order may be made. If such notification has not already been given, please treat this document as notification that such an order may be made. Alternatively the Court may specify a date by which this information should be provided.

If this information has already been prepared in a standard form please send this instead.

1. The full name of the pension arrangement and address to which a pension sharing order should be sent.

   Postcode

2. In the case of an occupational pension scheme only, is the scheme winding up?

   ☐ Yes   ☐ No

   If Yes:
   - when did the winding up commence, and
   - give the name and address of the trustees who are dealing with the winding up.

3. In the case of an occupational pension scheme only, assuming that a calculation of the member's CEV was carried out on the day the pension scheme received notification that a pension sharing order may be made, would that CEV be reduced?

   ☐ Yes   ☐ No

4. As far as you are aware, are the member's rights under the pension scheme subject to any of the following:
   - a pension sharing order   ☐ Yes   ☐ No
   - a pension attachment order made under section 23 of the Matrimonial Causes Act 1973 (England and Wales), section 12A(2) or (3) of the Family Law (Scotland) Act 1985 or under Article 25 of the Matrimonial Causes (Northern Ireland) Order 1978   ☐ Yes   ☐ No
   - a pension attachment order made under Part 1 of Schedule 5 to the Civil Partnership Act 2004 (England and Wales), section 12A(2) or (3) of the Family Law (Scotland) Act 1985 or under Part 1 of Schedule 15 to the Civil Partnership Act 2004 (Northern Ireland)   ☐ Yes   ☐ No
   - a forfeiture order   ☐ Yes   ☐ No
   - a bankruptcy order   ☐ Yes   ☐ No
   - an award of sequestration on a member's estate or the making of the appointment on his estate of a judicial factor under section 41 of the Solicitors (Scotland) Act 1980.   ☐ Yes   ☐ No

5. Do the member's rights include rights which are not shareable by virtue of regulation 2 of the Pension Sharing (Valuation) Regulations 2000?

   ☐ Yes   ☐ No

   If Yes, please provide details.

MISCELLANEOUS MATERIALS

6. Does the pension arrangement propose to levy additional charges specified in Regulation 6 of the Pensions on Divorce (Charging) Regulations 2000? ☐ Yes ☐ No

   If Yes, please provide the scale of the additional charges likely to made.

7. Is the scheme member a trustee of the pension scheme? ☐ Yes ☐ No

8. If a pension sharing order is made, will the person responsible for the pension arrangement require information regarding the scheme member's state of health before implementing the pension sharing order? ☐ Yes ☐ No

9. Does the person responsible for the pension sharing arrangement require any further information other than that contained in regulation 5 of the Pensions on Divorce etc. (Provision of Information Regulations) 2000, before implementing any Pension Sharing Order? ☐ Yes ☐ No

   If Yes, specify what.

D. To be completed by the pension arrangement

The following information should be provided if the scheme member requests it or the Court orders it pursuant to its powers under the Pensions on Divorce etc (Provision of Information) Regulations 2000, S.I. 1048/2000. Please note that pension arrangements may make an additional charge for providing this information.

1. Disregarding any future service or premiums that might be paid and future inflation, what is the largest lump sum payment that the member would be entitled to take if s/he were to retire at a normal retirement age?

2. What is the earliest date on which the member has the right to take benefits, excluding retirement on grounds of ill health? DD/MM/YYYY

3. Are spouse's or civil partner's benefits payable? ☐ Yes ☐ No

4. What lump sum would be payable on death at the date of completion of this form?

5. What proportion of the member's pension would be payable as of right to the spouse or civil partner of the member if the member were to die:

   (a) before retirement, and

   (b) after retirement, disregarding any future service or premiums that might be paid and future inflation?

6. Is the pension in payment, drawdown or deferment? ☐ Yes ☐ No

   If Yes, which?

7. Please provide a copy of the scheme booklet.

Dated ☐☐/☐☐/☐☐☐☐

FORM P1—PENSION SHARING ANNEX

Pension Sharing Annex under [section 24B of the Matrimonial Causes Act 1973] [paragraph 15 of Schedule 5 to the Civil Partnership Act 2004]

In the	
	*[County Court] *[Principal Registry of the Family Division]
Case No. (Always quote this)	
Transferor's Solicitor's reference	
Transferee's Solicitor's reference	

Between _____ **(Petitioner)**

and _____ **(Respondent)**

Take Notice that:

On _____ the court   *(delete as appropriate)

- made a pension sharing order under Part IV of the Welfare Reform and Pensions Act 1999.

- [varied] [discharged] an order which included provision for pension sharing under Part IV of the Welfare Reform and Pensions Act 1999 dated D D / M M / Y Y Y Y .

This annex to the order provides the person responsible for the pension arrangement with the information required by virtue of rules of court:

A. Transferor's details

(i) The full name by which the Transferor is known:

(ii) All names by which the Transferor has been known:

(iii) The Transferor's date of birth: D D / M M / Y Y Y Y

(iv) The Transferor's address:

(v) The Transferor's National Insurance Number:

B. Transferee's Details

(i) The full name by which the Transferee is known:

(ii) All names by which the Transferee has been known:

MISCELLANEOUS MATERIALS

(iii) The Transferee's date of birth: D D / M M / Y Y Y Y

(iv) The Transferee's address:

(v) The Transferee's National Insurance Number:

(vi) If the Transferee is also a member of the pension scheme from which the credit is derived, or a beneficiary of the same scheme because of survivor's benefits, the membership number:

C. Details of the Transferor's Pension Arrangement

(i) Name of the arrangement:

(ii) Name and address of the person responsible for the pension arrangement:

(iii) Reference Number:

(iv) If appropriate, such other details to enable the pension arrangement to be identified:

(v) The specified percentage of the member's CEV to be transferred: _ . _ %

D. Pension Sharing Charges

It is directed that: (*delete as appropriate)

*The pension sharing charges be apportioned between the parties as follows:

or

*The pension sharing charges be paid in full by the Transferor.

E. Have you filed Form D81 (Statement of Information for a Consent Order for a financial remedy)?   ☐ Yes   ☐ No

If 'Yes' delete the text opposite.

The parties certify that:

(i) they have received the information required by Regulation 4 of the Pensions on Divorce etc (Provisions of Information) Regulations 2000; and

(ii) it appears from that information that there is power to make an order including provision under [section 24B of the Matrimonial Causes Act 1973] [paragraph 15 of Schedule 5 to the Civil Partnership Act 2004].

PENSIONS ON DIVORCE

F. In cases where the Transferee has a choice of an internal or external transfer, if the Transferee has indicated a preference, indicate what this is.

☐ Internal transfer   ☐ External transfer

G. In the case of external transfer only (recommended but optional information)

(i) The name of the qualifying arrangement which has agreed to accept the pension credit:

(ii) The address of the qualifying arrangement:

(iii) If known, the Transferee's membership or policy number in the qualifying arrangement and reference number of the new provider:

(iv) The name, or title, business address, phone and fax numbers and email address of the person who may be contacted in respect of the discharge of liability for the pension credit on behalf of the Transferee:
(This may be an Independent Financial Advisor, for example, if one is advising the Transferee or the new pension scheme itself.)

(v) Please attach a copy of the letter from the qualifying arrangement indicating its willingness to accept the pension credit   ☐

Please complete boxes H to J where applicable

H. Where the credit is derived from an occupational scheme which is being wound up, has the Transferee indicated whether he wishes to transfer his pension credit rights to a qualifying arrangement?   ☐ Yes   ☐ No

I. Where the pension arrangement has requested details of the Transferor's health, has that information been provided?   ☐ Yes   ☐ No

J. Where the pension arrangement has requested further information, has that information been provided?   ☐ Yes   ☐ No

---

Note: Until the information requested in A, B, (and as far as applicable G, H, I and J) is provided the pension sharing order cannot be implemented although it may be made. Even if all the information requested has been provided, further information may be required before implementation can begin. If so, reasons why implementation cannot begin should be sent by the pension arrangement to the Transferor and Transferee within 21 days of receipt of the pension sharing order and this annex.

MISCELLANEOUS MATERIALS

THIS ORDER TAKES EFFECT FROM the later of

a. the date on which the Decree Absolute of Divorce or Nullity of marriage is granted, or the Final Order of Dissolution or Nullity of civil partnership is made;

b. 28 days from the date of this order or, where the court has specified a period for filing an appeal notice, 7 days after the end of that period;

c. where an appeal has been lodged, the effective date of the order determining that appeal.

To the person responsible for the pension arrangement:

*(delete as appropriate)

*1. Take notice that you must discharge your liability within the period of 4 months beginning with the later of:
   - the day on which this order takes effect; or
   - the first day on which you are in receipt of –
   a. the pension sharing order including this annex (and where appropriate any attachments);
   b. in a matrimonial case, a copy of the decree absolute of divorce or nullity of marriage;
   c. in a civil partnership case, a copy of the final order of dissolution or order of nullity of civil partnership;
   d. the information specified in paragraphs A, B and C of this annex and, where applicable, paragraphs G to J of this annex; and
   e. payment of all outstanding charges requested by the pension scheme.

*2. The court directs that the implementation period for discharging your liability should be determined by regulations made under section 34(4) or 41(2)(a) of the Welfare Reform and Pensions Act 1999, in that:

FORM P2—PENSION ATTACHMENT ANNEX

Pension Attachment Annex under [section 25B or 25C of the Matrimonial Causes Act 1973] [paragraph 25 or 26 of Schedule 5 to the Civil Partnership Act 2004]

In the	
	*[County Court] *[Principal Registry of the Family Division]
Case No. (Always quote this)	
Applicant's Solicitor's reference	
Respondent's Solicitor's reference	

Between [   ] **(Petitioner)**

and [   ] **(Respondent)**

Take Notice that:

On [   ] the court   *(delete as appropriate)

- made an order including provision under [section [25B][25C]* of the Matrimonial Causes Act 1973]* [paragraph [25][26]* or Schedule 5 to the Civil Partnership Act 2004]*.

- [varied] [discharged] an order which included provision under [section [25B][25C]* of the Matrimonial Causes Act 1973] [paragraph [25][26] of Schedule 5 to the Civil Partnership Act 2004]* and dated D D / M M / Y Y Y Y

This annex to the order provides the person responsible for the pension arrangement with the information required by virtue of rules of court:

1. Name of the party with the pension rights:

2. Name of the other party:

3. The National Insurance Number of the party with pension rights:

4. Details of the Pension Arrangement:
   (i) Name and address of the person responsible for the pension arrangement:

   (ii) Policy Reference Number:

   (iii) *if appropriate, such other details to enable the pension arrangement to be identified:*

Form P2 Pension Attachment Annex under [section 25B or 25C of the Matrimonial Causes Act 1973] [paragraph 25 or 26 of Schedule 5 to the Civil Partnership Act 2004] (04.11)

© Crown Copyright 2011

5A. **(i) To be completed where a Periodical Payments Order is made under s.25B of the Matrimonial Causes Act 1973.**

The specified percentage of any payment due to the party with the pension rights that is to be paid for the benefit of the other party: _ . _ %

(ii) To be completed where the court orders that the party with pension rights commutes a percentage of his pension to a tax free lump sum on retirement under s.25B of the Matrimonial Causes Act 1973.

(a) the specified percentage of the maximum lump sum available that is to be commuted: _ . _ %

(b) the specified percentage of the commuted sum which is to be paid to the spouse or the former spouse of the party with pension rights: _ . _ %

(iii) To be completed where the court orders, under s.25C of the Matrimonial Causes Act 1973, that all or part of a lump sum payable to the party with pension rights in respect of his death be paid to the other party.

(a) the percentage of the lump sum to be paid by the person responsible for the pension arrangement to the other party: _ . _ %

(b) the percentage of the lump sum payable (in accordance with a nomination by the party with pension rights) to the other party: _ . _ %

(c) the percentage of the lump sum to be paid by the person responsible for the pension arrangement for the benefit of the other party: _ . _ %

5B. **(i) To be completed where a Periodical Payments Order is made under paragraph 25 of Schedule 5 to the Civil Partnership Act 2004.**

The specified percentage of any payment due to the civil partner with the pension rights that is to be paid for the benefit of the other civil partner: _ . _ %

(ii) To be completed where the court orders that the civil partner with pension rights commutes a percentage of his pension to a tax free lump sum on retirement under paragraph 25 of Schedule 5 to the Civil Partnership Act 2004.

(a) the specified percentage of the maximum lump sum available that is to be commuted: _ . _ %

(b) the specified percentage of the commuted sum which is to be paid to the civil partner or the former civil partner of the civil partner with pension rights: _ . _ %

PENSIONS ON DIVORCE

(iii) To be completed where the court orders, under paragraph 26 of Schedule 5 to the Civil Partnership Act 2004, that all or part of a lump sum payable to the civil partner with pension rights in respect of his death be paid to the other civil partner.

(a) the percentage of the lump sum to be paid by the person responsible for the pension arrangement to the other civil partner: __.__ %

(b) the percentage of the lump sum payable (in accordance with a nomination by the civil partner with pension rights) to the other civil partner: __.__ %

(c) the percentage of the lump sum to be paid by the person responsible for the pension arrangement for the benefit of the other civil partner: __.__ %

To the person responsible for the pension arrangement:
*(delete if this information has already been provided to the person responsible for the pension arrangement)

1. *You are required to serve any notice under the Divorce etc. (Pensions) Regulations 2000 or the Dissolution etc. (Pensions) Regulations 2005 on the other party at the following address:

2. *You are required to make any payments due under the pension arrangement to the other party at the following address:

3. *If the address at 2. above is that of a bank, building society or the Department of National Savings the following details will enable you to make payment into the account of the other party (e.g. Account Name, Number, Bank/Building Society/etc. Sort code):

Note: Where the order to which this annex applies was made by consent the following section should also be completed.

The court also confirms: *(delete as appropriate)

- *That notice has been served on the person responsible for the pension arrangement and that no objection has been received.
- *That notice has been served on the person responsible for the pension arrangement and that the court has considered any objection received.

FORM PPF—PENSION PROTECTION FUND INQUIRY FORM

Pension Protection Fund (PPF) Inquiry Form

Information needed when a Pension Compensation Sharing Order or Pension Compensation Attachment Order may be made

Insert details of pension scheme here	
To:	
of:	
Reference No:	

A. To be completed by PPF member:

1. The PPF member's details:

   - Name
   - Address (including postcode)
   - Postcode
   - Reference

2. Solicitors details:

   - Name
   - Address (including postcode)
   - Postcode
   - Reference
   - Telephone

3. Address to which the form should be sent once completed if different from 2 above:

   - Address (including postcode)
   - Postcode

Signature

of PPF member

(The PPF member's signature is necessary to authorise the release of the requested information, unless a court order requiring the information is attached to this form.)

Form PPF Pension Protection Fund (PPF) Inquiry Form (04.11) © Crown Copyright 2011

PENSIONS ON DIVORCE

B. To be completed by the PPF

This section deals with information required to be provided under the Pension Protection Fund (Pension Compensation Sharing and Attachment on Divorce etc) Regulations 2011 S.I.731/2011, Regulations 3 and 4 and Rule 9.39(1) of the Family Procedure Rules 2010. If a request for a Cash Equivalent Valuation (CEV) has been made, the PPF has 3 months to provide the information or 6 weeks if notified that the information is needed in connection with matrimonial or civil partnership proceedings, or such shorter time as notified by the court. Otherwise, the information should be provided within one month or such shorter time as notified by the court.

If this information has already been prepared in a standard form please send this instead.

1. (a) Please confirm that you have already provided a valuation of the member's entitlement to the relevant member and/or to the Court. ☐ Yes ☐ No

   (b) If the answer to (a) is No, details of the CEV quotation should be attached and the date on which it was calculated.

2. Provide a statement summarising the way in which the valuation referred to above has been or will be calculated.

3. State the pension compensation entitlement included in the valuation referred to in B1 above.

4. **Charging Policy**

   Please
   - provide a list of charges for information provision and implementing sharing and attachment orders
   - indicate when these must be paid .

MISCELLANEOUS MATERIALS

C. To be completed by the PPF

This information is required to be provided by the PPF under the Pension Protection Fund (Pension Compensation Sharing and Attachment on Divorce etc) Regulations 2011 S.I.731/2011, Regulation 5 within 21 days of being notified that a pension sharing order may be made. If such notification has not already been given, please treat this document as notification that such an order may be made. Alternatively the Court may specify a date by which this information should be provided.

If this information has already been prepared in a standard form please send this instead.

---

1. The address to which a pension compensation sharing order should be sent is:

    Pension Protection Fund
    Operations Team
    P O Box 128
    Mowden Hall
    Darlington DL1 9DA

2. Is the member's compensation subject to capping? ☐ Yes ☐ No

3. As far as you are aware, is the member's pension compensation, or are the pension rights from which the compensation derives subject to any of the following:
   - a pension compensation sharing order ☐ Yes ☐ No
   - a pension compensation attachment order ☐ Yes ☐ No
   - a pension sharing order ☐ Yes ☐ No
   - a pension attachment order ☐ Yes ☐ No
   - a forfeiture order ☐ Yes ☐ No
   - a bankruptcy order ☐ Yes ☐ No
   - any other order or provision referred to in regulation 5(2)(b) of the Pension Protection Fund (Pension Compensation Sharing and Attachment on Divorce etc) Regulations 2011, SI 2011/731. ☐ Yes ☐ No

    If Yes, give details.

4. Does the member's pension compensation entitlement include rights which are not shareable by virtue of regulation 2 of Pension Protection Fund (Pension Compensation Sharing and Attachment on Divorce etc) Regulations 2011 S.I.731/2011? ☐ Yes ☐ No

    If Yes, please provide details.

PENSIONS ON DIVORCE

5. Does the Board require any further information other than that contained in regulation 9 of the Pension Protection Fund (Pension Compensation Sharing and Attachment on Divorce etc) Regulations 2011 S.I.731/2011, before implementing any pension compensation sharing order? ☐ Yes ☐ No

   If Yes, specify what.

D. To be completed by the PPF

The following information should be provided if the PPF member requests it or the Court orders it pursuant to its powers under the Pension Protection Fund (Pension Compensation Sharing and Attachment on Divorce etc) Regulations 2011 S.I.731/2011.

1. What is the largest lump sum payment that the member would be entitled to take if s/he were to retire at a normal retirement age?

2. What is the earliest date on which the member has the right to take compensation? DD/MM/YYYY

3. Are spouse's/civil partner's or children's benefits payable? ☐ Yes ☐ No

   If Yes, please give details.

4. Is the compensation in payment or deferment? ☐ Yes ☐ No

   If Yes, which?

5. Please provide a copy of the PPF Guidance.

Dated ☐☐/☐☐/☐☐☐☐

FORM PPF1—PENSION PROTECTION FUND PENSION COMPENSATION SHARING ANNEX

Pension Protection Fund (PPF) Sharing Annex to a Pension Compensation Sharing Order [section 24E of the Matrimonial Causes Act 1973] [paragraph 19A of Schedule 5 to the Civil Partnership Act 2004]

In the	*[County Court] *[Principal Registry of the Family Division]
Case No. (Always quote this)	
Transferor's Solicitor's reference	
Transferee's Solicitor's reference	

Between _____ (Petitioner)

and _____ (Respondent)

Take Notice that:

On _____ the court   *(delete as appropriate)

- made a pension compensation sharing order under s24E of the Matrimonial Causes Act 1973, or paragraph 19A of Schedule 5 of the Civil Partnership Act 2004.*

- [varied] [discharged]* an order dated [D D]/[M M]/[Y Y Y Y] which included provision for pension compensation sharing under s24E of the Matrimonial Causes Act 1973, or paragraph 19A of Schedule 5 of the Civil Partnership Act 2004.*

This annex to the order provides the PPF Board with the information required by virtue of rules of court:

A. Transferor's details

(i) The full name by which the Transferor is known:

(ii) All names by which the Transferor has been known:

(iii) The Transferor's date of birth: [D D]/[M M]/[Y Y Y Y]

(iv) The Transferor's address:

(v) The Transferor's National Insurance Number:

(vi) The name of the pension scheme for which the Board assumed responsibility and to which the pension compensation relates:

Form **PPF1** Pension Protection Fund (PPF) Sharing Annex to a Pension Compensation Sharing order (04.11)   © Crown Copyright 2011

PENSIONS ON DIVORCE

B. Transferee's Details

(i) The full name by which the Transferee is known:

(ii) If the Transferee is entitled to PPF compensation other than by reason of the pension compensation, all names by which the Transferee has been known:

(iii) The Transferee's date of birth: D D / M M / Y Y Y Y

(iv) The Transferee's address:

(v) The Transferee's National Insurance Number:

C. Details of the Transferor's Pension Compensation

(i) If pension compensation is in payment, please provide the Reference number:

(ii) If appropriate, such other details to enable the pension compensation to be identified:

(iii) The specified percentage of the member's CEV to be transferred: _ _ . _ _ %

D. Pension Compensation Sharing Charges

It is directed that: (*delete as appropriate)

*The pension compensation sharing charges be apportioned between the parties as follows:

or

*The pension compensation sharing charges be paid in full by the Transferor.

E. Have you filed Form D81 (Statement of Information for a Consent Order for a financial remedy)? ☐ Yes   ☐ No

If 'Yes' delete the text opposite.

The parties certify that:

(i) they have received the information required by Regulation 5 of the Pension Protection Fund (Pension Compensation Sharing and Attachment on Divorce etc) Regulations 2011;

(ii) that information is attached on Form PPF (Pension Protection Fund Inquiry Form); and

(iii) it appears from that information that there is power to make an order section 24E of the Matrimonial Causes Act 1973 or paragraph 19A of Schedule 5 to the Civil Partnership Act 2004.

MISCELLANEOUS MATERIALS

F. Where the PPF has requested further information, has that information been provided? ☐ Yes ☐ No

Note: If the information requested in A, B, (and as far as applicable F) is **not** provided the pension compensation sharing order may still be implemented. Even if all the information requested has been provided, further information may be required before implementation can begin. If so, reasons why implementation cannot begin should be sent by the PPF to the Transferor and Transferee within 21 days of receipt of the pension compensation sharing order and this annex.

THIS ORDER TAKES EFFECT FROM the later of

a. the date on which the Decree Absolute of Divorce or Nullity of marriage is granted, or the Final Order of Dissolution or Nullity of civil partnership is made;

b. 28 days from the date of this order or, where the court has specified a period for filing an appeal notice, 7 days after the end of that period;

c. where an appeal has been lodged, the effective date of the order determining that appeal.

To the PPF Board:

*(delete as appropriate)

*1. Take notice that you must discharge your liability within the period of 4 months beginning with the later of:
- the day on which this order takes effect; or
- the first day on which you are in receipt of –
  a. the pension compensation sharing order including this annex (and where appropriate any attachments);
  b. in a matrimonial cause, a copy of the Decree Absolute of Divorce or Nullity of marriage;
  c. in a civil partnership cause, a copy of the Final Order of Dissolution or Nullity of civil partnership;
  d. the information specified in paragraphs A, B and C of this annex and, where applicable, paragraph F of this annex; and
  e. payment of all outstanding charges requested by the PPF.

*2. The court directs that the implementation period for discharging your liability should be determined by Regulation 5(4) of the Divorce and Dissolution etc (Pension Protection Fund) Regulations 2011 in that:

FORM PPF2—PENSION PROTECTION FUND PENSION COMPENSATION ATTACHMENT ANNEX

Pension Protection Fund (PPF) Attachment Annex to a Pension Compensation Attachment Order [section 25F of the Matrimonial Causes Act 1973] [paragraph 34A of Schedule 5 to the Civil Partnership Act 2004]

In the	*[County Court] *[Principal Registry of the Family Division]
Case No. (Always quote this)	
Applicant's Solicitor's reference	
Respondent's Solicitor's reference	

Between _____ (Petitioner)

and _____ (Respondent)

Take Notice that:

On _____ the court   *(delete as appropriate)

- made an order including provision under section 25F of the Matrimonial Causes Act 1973 or paragraph 34A of Schedule 5 to the Civil Partnership Act 2004*
- [varied] [discharged]* an order dated D D / M M / Y Y Y Y which included provision under section 25F of the Matrimonial Causes Act 1973 or paragraph 34A of Schedule 5 to the Civil Partnership Act 2004*

This annex to the order provides the PPF Board with the information required by virtue of rules of court:

1. Name of the party who has the PPF compensation entitlement:

2. Name of the other party:

3. The National Insurance Number of the party with PPF compensation entitlement:

4. The name of the pension scheme for which the PPF Board assumed responsibility and to which the pension compensation relates:

   (i) if appropriate, such other details to enable the PPF compensation to be identified:

continued over the page ⇨

Form PPF2 Pension Protection Fund (PPF) Attachment Annex to a Pension Compensation Attachment Order (04.11)   © Crown Copyright 2011

MISCELLANEOUS MATERIALS

5A. **(i) To be completed where a periodical payments order is made under s.23 of the Matrimonial Causes Act 1973 making provision under s25F of the 1973 Act.**

The specified percentage of any payment due to the party with the PPF compensation entitlement that is to be paid for the benefit of the other party: _ _ . _ _ %

(ii) To be completed where the court orders that the party with PPF compensation entitlement commutes a percentage of his PPF compensation to a tax free lump sum on retirement under s.25F(5) of the Matrimonial Causes Act 1973.

(a) the specified percentage of the maximum lump sum available that is to be commuted: _ _ . _ _ %

(b) the specified percentage of the commuted sum which is to be paid to the spouse or the former spouse of the party with PPF compensation entitlement: _ _ . _ _ %

5B. **(i) To be completed where a periodical payments order is made under Part 1 of Schedule 5 of the Civil Partnership Act 2004 making provision under paragraph 34A of Schedule 5 of the 2004 Act.**

The specified percentage of any payment due to the civil partner with the PPF compensation entitlement that is to be paid for the benefit of the other civil partner: _ _ . _ _ %

(ii) To be completed where the court orders that the civil partner with PPF compensation entitlement commutes a percentage of the PPF compensation to a tax free lump sum on retirement under paragraph 34A(5) of Schedule 5 to the Civil Partnership Act 2004.

(a) the specified percentage of the maximum lump sum available that is to be commuted: _ _ . _ _ %

(b) the specified percentage of the commuted sum which is to be paid to the civil partner or the former civil partner of the civil partner with PPF compensation entitlement: _ _ . _ _ %

continued over the page ⇨

PENSIONS ON DIVORCE

To the PPF Board:
(*delete if this information has already been provided to the PPF Board)

1.* You are required to make any payments due under the PPF compensation to the other party at the following address:

2.* If the address at 1. above is that of a bank, building society or the Department of National Savings the following details will enable you to make payment into the account of the other party (e.g. Account Name, Number, Bank/Building Society/etc. Sort code):

Note: Where the order to which this annex applies was made by consent the following section should also be completed.

The court also confirms:
(*delete as appropriate)

- That notice has been served on the PPF Board and the Board is not aware of the member's PPF compensation, or the pension rights from which it was derived, being subject to any order or provision referred to in regulation 5(2)(b) of the Pension Protection Fund (Pension Compensation Sharing and Attachment on Divorce etc) Regulations 2011, SI 2011/731.*

- That notice has been served on the PPF Board and that any order or provision referred to in regulation 5(2)(b) of the Pension Protection Fund (Pension Compensation Sharing and Attachment on Divorce etc) Regulations 2011, SI 2011/731 has been considered and that there is the power to make this order.*

FORM D81—STATEMENT OF INFORMATION FOR CONSENT ORDER

Statement of information for a consent order in relation to a financial remedy

To be completed by the parties	
Name of court	Case No.
Name of Petitioner/Applicant	
Name of Respondent	

If completing this form by hand, please use **black ink and BLOCK CAPITAL LETTERS** and tick the boxes that apply.

You may complete separate forms if you wish. However both parties must confirm they have read the contents of each statement of information.

Details of the marriage/civil partnership

1. Please give the date of the ☐ marriage ☐ civil partnership   D D / M M / Y Y Y Y

2. On what date did you separate?   D D / M M / Y Y Y Y

3. On what date was your decree nisi/conditional order of divorce/ dissolution/nullity or (judicial) separation decree/order pronounced?   D D / M M / Y Y Y Y

   (Please note that a consent order cannot be made until the court has pronounced a decree nisi/conditional order unless it is a consent order for maintenance pending suit.)

4. On what date was your decree absolute/final order of divorce/ dissolution/nullity granted?   D D / M M / Y Y Y Y

   If this has not yet been pronounced please write 'not applicable'

Dates of birth of the parties

5. Please give the date of birth of the parties along with the date of birth of any child(ren) of the family aged under 18, or any other child(ren) dependant upon the family.

   Date of birth

   Petitioner/Applicant   D D / M M / Y Y Y Y

   Respondent   D D / M M / Y Y Y Y

   Child(ren) (if applicable)   D D / M M / Y Y Y Y   D D / M M / Y Y Y Y   D D / M M / Y Y Y Y

   D D / M M / Y Y Y Y   D D / M M / Y Y Y Y   D D / M M / Y Y Y Y

Financial agreements

6. Please state how the attached proposed consent order was reached e.g. discussions between parties, negotiations through solicitors, Mediation, Collaborative Process or other out of court dispute resolution process.

D81 Statement of information for a consent order in relation to a financial r   dy (04.12)   © Crown Copyright 2012

PENSIONS ON DIVORCE

Summary of means

The information in this section should so far as possible be correct as at the time this statement is signed.

The information should therefore be stated before implementation of the proposed consent order.

If the application is made only for an order for interim periodical payments or for variation of an order for periodical payments, you need only give details of 'net income'.

Capital

7. Please give the following information for each party and the child(ren) (if applicable). Use additional sheets if necessary. Jointly owned capital should be divided as appropriate and listed below. If no agreement has been reached regarding shares, it should be divided equally.

Type of capital	Petitioner/Applicant	Respondent	Child(ren) if applicable
a. Property (net of any mortgage(s))	£	£	£
b. Other capital e.g. savings, investments, ISAs etc	£	£	£
c. Gross capital (a. plus b.)	£	£	£
d. Liabilities (excluding mortgages deducted at a.) e.g. loans and overdrafts	£	£	£
e. Net capital excluding pensions and Pension Protection Fund (PPF) compensation (c. less d.)	£	£	£
f. Pensions valuation including the Additional State Pension (cash equivalent)	£	£	£
g. PPF compensation valuation	£	£	£
h. Total capital (e. plus f. plus g.)	£	£	£

Income

8. Please state for each party, their total **net** (after deductions for tax and NI contributions only) monthly income from all sources e.g. wages, state benefits, child support and maintenance payments, pension or PPF compensation payments, interest from bank accounts, tips etc.

Petitioner/Applicant	£
Respondent	£
Child(ren) (if applicable)	£

MISCELLANEOUS MATERIALS

9. Are there any other matters relating to the proposed consent order that the court should consider e.g. medical conditions, change of employment, any significant change in circumstances, any prior agreement reached between the parties etc?

Where the parties and the children will live

10. Please give details of where the named parties will live and the basis on which you will occupy the property e.g. owner, tenant etc.

	Address	Basis of occupation in property
Petitioner/Applicant		
Respondent		
Child(ren) (if applicable)		

New relationships

11. Please tick the appropriate box below

Petitioner/Applicant

☐ I have no intention at present to remarry/enter into a new civil partnership or cohabit.

☐ I have remarried/formed a civil partnership.
The date of the marriage/civil partnership was DD/MM/YYYY

☐ I intend to remarry/form a civil partnership.
The date of the intended marriage/civil partnership is DD/MM/YYYY

☐ I am in a cohabiting relationship with another person.

☐ I intend to cohabit.

Respondent

☐ I have no intention at present to remarry/enter into a new civil partnership or cohabit.

☐ I have remarried/formed a civil partnership.
The date of the marriage/civil partnership was DD/MM/YYYY

☐ I intend to remarry/form a civil partnership.
The date of the intended marriage/civil partnership is DD/MM/YYYY

☐ I am in a cohabiting relationship with another person.

☐ I intend to cohabit.

continued over the page ⇨

PENSIONS ON DIVORCE

Notice to mortgagee

These questions are to be answered by the Petitioner/Applicant where the terms of the order provide for a transfer of property.

12. Has every mortgagee (if any) of the property been served with notice of the application?

    ☐ Yes   ☐ No

13. Has any objection to a transfer of property been made by any mortgagee, within 14 days from the date when the notice of the application was served?

    ☐ Yes   ☐ No

Notice to pension arrangement/PPF Board

Question 14 is to be answered by the Petitioner/Applicant where the terms of an order include provision for a pension attachment order and/or a PPF pension compensation attachment order. Question 15 is to be answered by the Petitioner/Applicant only where the terms of the order include provision for a pension attachment order.

(Please note that if you wish to include provision relating to a pension or to PPF compensation in your consent order you should first seek legal advice as this area of law is complex. Court staff are unable to assist, as they are not trained to give legal advice.)

14. Has notice been served on every person responsible for any pension arrangement under Rules 9.33(1) or 9.34, and/or the PPF Board under 9.42 or 9.43 of the Family Procedure Rules 2010?

    ☐ Yes   ☐ No

15. Has any objection to an attachment order been made by the person responsible for the pension arrangements within 21 days from the date when the notice of the application was served?

    ☐ Yes   ☐ No

Pension or PPF compensation sharing on divorce, dissolution or nullity

These questions are to be answered by the Petitioner/Applicant where the terms of an order include provision for a pension or a PPF compensation sharing order.

(Please note that if you wish to include provision relating to a pension or a PPF compensation in your consent order you should first seek legal advice. Court staff are unable to assist, as they are not trained to give legal advice.)

16. (For pension sharing only) Has the Pension Arrangement furnished the information required by Regulation 4 of the Pensions on Divorce etc. (Provision of Information) Regulations 2000?

    ☐ Yes   ☐ No

    (For PPF compensation sharing only) Has the PPF Board provided the information required by Regulation 5 of The Pension Protection Fund (Pension Compensation Sharing and Attachment on Divorce etc) Regulations 2011?

    ☐ Yes   ☐ No

MISCELLANEOUS MATERIALS

17. (For pension sharing only) Does it appear from that information that there is power to make an order including provision under section 24B of the Matrimonial Causes Act 1973 or under paragraph 15 of Schedule 5 to the Civil Partnership Act 2004 (Pension Sharing)?

☐ Yes   ☐ No

(For PPF compensation sharing only) Does it appear from that information that there is power to make an order for compensation sharing?

☐ Yes   ☐ No

Proposed consent order

Please ensure that you attach the proposed consent order with this completed form when lodging at court, and if appropriate, any pension sharing/attachment annex or compensation sharing/annex.

I _____
[(Petitioner/Applicant's full name)]

confirm that I have read a fully completed Statement of information for a consent order from the [Respondent].

Signed _____   Dated D D / M M / Y Y Y Y

I _____
[(Respondent's full name)]

confirm that I have read a fully completed Statement of information for a consent order from the [Applicant/Petitioner].

Signed _____   Dated D D / M M / Y Y Y Y

continued over the page ⇨

PENSIONS ON DIVORCE

Petitioner/Applicant's Statement of Truth

*delete as appropriate

*I [_____] [(Petitioner/Applicant's full name)]

believe that the facts stated in this Statement of information for a consent order are true and I have made full disclosure of all relevant facts.

*I am duly authorised by the Petitioner/Applicant to sign this statement

Print full name [_____]

Name of Petitioner/ Applicant's solicitor's firm [_____]

Signed [_____] Dated [D D]/[M M]/[Y Y Y Y]

*Petitioner/Applicant('s solicitor)('s litigation friend)

Position or office held (if signing on behalf of firm or company) [_____]

Proceedings for contempt of court may be brought against a person who makes or causes to be made, a false statement in a document verified by a statement of truth.

Respondent's Statement of Truth

*delete as appropriate

*I [_____] [(Respondent's full name)]

believe that the facts stated in this Statement of information for a consent order are true and I have made full disclosure of all relevant facts.

*I am duly authorised by the Respondent to sign this statement

Print full name [_____]

Name of Respondent's solicitor's firm [_____]

Signed [_____] Dated [D D]/[M M]/[Y Y Y Y]

*(Respondent('s solicitor)('s litigation friend)

Position or office held (if signing on behalf of firm or company) [_____]

Proceedings for contempt of court may be brought against a person who makes or causes to be made, a false statement in a document verified by a statement of truth.

FORM BR19—STATE PENSION FORECAST

Help using this PDF claim form

In this PDF form we have introduced a special feature that lets you save it in Adobe Reader 8.1.2 and later. This means that you no longer have to complete the form in one session.

This form will only work if you:
- save it to your computer, then
- open it in Acrobat Reader version 8.1.2 or later.

The form will not work in:
- older versions of Acrobat Reader
- other pdf readers, for example *Preview* on a Mac or *Foxit* on a PC
- your web browser window.

If you are having technical difficulties:
- downloading the form
- Navigating around the form, or
- printing the form

Please contact the **eService helpdesk**.
Phone: **0845 601 80 40**
Minicom (textphone): **0845 601 80 39**
Email: **eservicehelpdesk@dwp.gsi.gov.uk**

Opening hours
Monday to Friday: 08.00am - 09.00pm
Weekend: 08.00am - 04.00pm
Closed on all Public and Bank Holidays.

For help and advice on the information you need to put on the form or about the benefit you want to claim, contact the office that deals with the benefit.

We would like your feedback about this PDF claim form

We would like your feedback about this form. We will use any comments to improve future versions. Please email your comments to:
forms.feedback@dwp.gsi.gov.uk

State Pension Forecast

The Pension Service
Department for Work and Pensions

Who can get a State Pension forecast

You can get a State Pension forecast if you are more than 30 days away from State Pension age when we process your application. It will take an average of 10 working days to prepare your forecast from the date we receive your application form.

Completing the form

If you need any help, please phone us on **0845 3000 168** (if you live in the UK) or **+44 191 218 3600** (if you live outside the UK), or write to us at:

**Future Pension Centre
The Pension Service
Tyneview Park
Whitley Road
Newcastle upon Tyne
NE98 1BA
United Kingdom**

Other ways to get a State Pension forecast

If you live in the UK you can get a forecast:
- online by visiting the website **www.direct.gov.uk/pensionforecast** and following the State Pension Forecasting links.
- by calling the Future Pension Centre and we will take your application over the phone. Our phone number is **0845 3000 168**. Our opening hours are Monday to Friday 8am to 8pm. For security and quality purposes your call may be monitored and recorded.

  If you have speech or hearing difficulties you can call us using a textphone on **0845 3000 169**. Or you can use Text Relay by dialling **18001 0845 3000 168**.

If you live outside the UK
You can call us at the Future Pension Centre by dialling **+44 191 2183600** and we will take your application over the phone. Lines are open 8am to 5pm Monday to Friday. For security and quality purposes your call may be monitored and recorded. If you have speech or hearing difficulties you can call us using a textphone on **+44 191 2182051**.

BR19 10/11

What your State Pension forecast will tell you

Your forecast will give you, using today's values, estimates of the basic and additional State Pension (and Graduated Retirement Benefit if appropriate) that you may get at State Pension age, based on:
- your National Insurance (NI) contributions so far, and
- what we expect your future NI contributions to be.

Your forecast will also tell you if there is anything you can do to improve your basic State Pension. If you have little or no basic State Pension and you have a spouse or civil partner, you may be able to get a basic State Pension based on their NI contributions.

Your forecast will be based on your own NI contributions record unless:
- at the time the forecast is prepared you were widowed, or your civil partner had died, and you had given us details of your late husband, late wife, or late civil partner, or
- at the time the forecast is prepared you were divorced or had your civil partnership dissolved, and you had given us details of your ex-husband, ex-wife, or former civil partner.

If you are divorced or your civil partnership has been dissolved, your forecast may also tell you the amount of any additional State Pension gained or lost as a result of any pension sharing order made by the Court during your divorce or dissolution proceedings.

If you have a spouse or civil partner, your forecast does not include details of any State Pension they may receive.

MISCELLANEOUS MATERIALS

Sending your forecast to someone else

Our records are strictly confidential and we cannot send your forecast to someone else unless they are authorised to act on your behalf (for example, they have Power of Attorney) or we have your permission in writing. If your representative is authorised to act on your behalf we need to see proof of that authority before we can send your forecast to them. If you would like us to send your forecast to someone else, please tick the box in **Part 9** and fill in **Part 10**.

Tracing a lost occupational or personal pension

The Pension Tracing Service

It's easy to lose contact with a previous employer and their pension scheme if, for example, you have changed jobs several times. If you think you have one or more old company or personal pensions, but you don't know the full details, contact the Pension Tracing Service. If you can give details of the company who you worked for, or the provider you had your pension(s) with, the Pension Tracing Service may be able to give you the scheme's contact details. You do not have to pay for this service.

Once you have the contact details, you can ask the pension provider to check whether you have a pension with them.

You can contact the Pension Tracing Service by:

- phoning **0845 600 2537** (lines are open from 8am to 6pm Monday to Friday). If you are calling from outside the UK, the phone number is **+44 191 2154491**
- textphone on **0845 3000 169**. Or you can use Text Relay by dialling **18001 0845 600 2537**. These numbers are not available for customers who are calling from outside the UK.
- going to the website at **www.direct.gov.uk/pensions**
- writing to:
  The Pension Tracing Service
  Tyneview Park
  Whitley Road
  Newcastle upon Tyne
  NE98 1BA
  United Kingdom

Claiming State Pension

You cannot use this form to claim your State Pension.

To find out how to claim your State Pension go to **www.direct.gov.uk/pensions**

However, further information will be sent to you with your forecast.

How we collect and use information

The information we collect about you and how we use it depends mainly on the reason for your business with us. But we may use it for any of the Department's purposes, which include:

- social security benefits and allowances
- child support
- employment and training
- private pensions policy, and
- retirement planning.

We may get information from others to check the information you give to us and to improve our services. We may give information to other organisations as the law allows, for example to protect against crime.

To find out more about how we use information, visit our website **www.dwp.gov.uk/privacy-policy** or contact any of our offices.

329

PENSIONS ON DIVORCE

State Pension Forecast

- **Application for a State Pension forecast**
- **Part 1   About you**

Please tell us about yourself. Use BLOCK CAPITALS.

National Insurance (NI) number	Letters Numbers Letter
Current surname or family name	Title
First name and any middle names	
Any other surnames or family names you have previously been known by	
Full address including postcode or zip code	
Correspondence address if different. Give us the full address, including the postcode or zip code.	
If you are living outside the UK now, please give us full details of your last two UK addresses, including postcodes	
Address 1	
Postcode	
Address 2	
Postcode	
Date of birth	DD/MM/YYYY

BR19   10/11

MISCELLANEOUS MATERIALS

• Application for a State Pension forecast continued

○ Part 2   Marital status

Please tick the description that applies to you and give exact dates. If you do not know exact dates, we can still give you a forecast but it will be based only on your own NI contributions. If you are no longer married or in a civil partnership we will ask you for more information later in the form.

Single	☐		
Married	☐	Date of marriage	DD/MM/YYYY
Civil partner	☐	Date of formation of civil partnership	DD/MM/YYYY
Divorced	☐	Date of divorce	DD/MM/YYYY
Civil partnership dissolved	☐	Date of dissolution	DD/MM/YYYY
Widowed	☐	Date you were widowed	DD/MM/YYYY
Surviving civil partner	☐	Date your civil partner died	DD/MM/YYYY
Marriage annulled	☐	Date of annulment	DD/MM/YYYY
		Please send your certificate of annulment	
Civil partnership annulled	☐	Date of annulment	DD/MM/YYYY
		Please send your certificate of annulment	

○ Part 3   Contact details

If we need to contact you before we send you your forecast, how would you prefer us to get in touch with you?	By letter to the address given in Part 1 ☐	By phone. Please give number below ☐	
Home phone number	Code [ ]	Number [ ]	
Daytime phone number, if different	Code [ ]	Number [ ]	Ext [ ]
What is this number?	Work ☐ Mobile ☐ Textphone ☐		
If you live in Wales, we can send your forecast in English or Welsh. Which language do you prefer?	English ☐ Welsh ☐		
We can send you information in braille or large print. Please tick the box if you prefer one of these choices.	Braille ☐ Large print ☐		

- **Application for a State Pension forecast** continued

○ **Part 4 What you are doing now**

Please tick **all** the boxes that describe what you are doing now.

a Working for an employer ☐

b Working for an employer and getting Working Tax Credit ☐

c Self-employed ☐

d Self-employed and getting Working Tax Credit ☐

e Not working ☐

f Getting Statutory Sick Pay ☐

g Registered for Jobseeker's Allowance ☐

h Getting Incapacity Benefit ☐

i Getting Employment and Support Allowance ☐

j Getting Carer's Allowance
previously known as Invalid Care Allowance ☐

k Getting Severe Disablement Allowance ☐

About NI contributions

If you have ticked any of the boxes **a** to **d** shown above, we need to know about the NI contributions you are paying.

If you can improve your basic State Pension by paying Class 3 voluntary NI contributions, we will tell you about this in your forecast.

Please tick **all** the boxes that apply to you.

Paying full-rate United Kingdom (UK) NI contributions ☐

Paying married woman's or widow's reduced-rate NI contributions ☐

Paying Class 2 self-employed NI contributions ☐

Paying Class 3 voluntary NI contributions ☐

Not paying NI contributions ☐

If you are working for a UK employer, please tell us your current earnings **before** tax and National Insurance.

£ _____

Each week ☐
Each month ☐
Each year ☐

MISCELLANEOUS MATERIALS

• Application for a State Pension forecast continued

○ Part 5 Living outside the United Kingdom (UK)

We use *United Kingdom (UK)* to mean England, Scotland, Wales and Northern Ireland.
If you have not lived outside the UK please go to **Part 6**.
If you have lived outside the UK at any time since the age of 16, please tell us where you have been. Do not include holidays or periods served in HM forces.

Please tick the boxes that apply to you.

Australia – please give dates. ☐ from [DD/MM/YYYY] to [DD/MM/YYYY]
Australia is the only country we need exact dates for.

Canada ☐

New Zealand ☐

Any other country ☐   Which countries?

[   ]

If you are currently living outside the UK, please provide details of the country you are living in and when you went to live there:

Country [   ]

From [DD/MM/YYYY]

What date did you leave the UK? [DD/MM/YYYY]

○ Part 6 Widowed or a surviving civil partner?

If this does not apply to you, please go to **Part 7**.
If you are currently widowed or a surviving civil partner, please tick the boxes that apply to you.

Are you getting or did you get

Widow's Benefit or bereavement benefits ☐

War Widow's Pension ☐

War Widower's Pension ☐

Industrial Death Benefit ☐   How much Industrial Death Benefit do you get each week?
£ [   ]

Please also tell us if

You were getting bereavement benefits which have now stopped ☐

You have voluntarily given up your entitlement to Widow's Benefit ☐

You are currently disqualified from getting Widow's Benefit ☐

333

PENSIONS ON DIVORCE

• Application for a State Pension forecast continued

○ Part 7   Extra information

We can also tell you what may happen to your State Pension in different situations. If you want extra information in your forecast, please tick the things you want to know about. If not, go to **Part 8**.

If you put off claiming your State Pension	☐ Please tell us the date when you may want to start claiming your State Pension	DD/MM/YYYY
If you stop work before you reach State Pension age	☐ Please tell us the date you may stop working	DD/MM/YYYY
If you currently live in the UK but may go to live outside the UK	☐ Please tell us the country you may go to	
If your annual earnings change Do not include pension income	☐ Please tell us what they might change to	£
If you are married or a civil partner but are about to get divorced or dissolve your civil partnership	☐ Please tell us your expected date of divorce or dissolution	DD/MM/YYYY

○ Part 8   Former marital or civil partner status

Only fill in this part if
- you are widowed or a surviving civil partner
- you are divorced or your civil partnership has been dissolved
- you are about to be divorced or have your civil partnership dissolved, or
- your marriage or civil partnership has been annulled.

If this does not apply to you, or it does but you would like us to provide you with a forecast based on your own NI contributions only, please go to **Part 9**.

Do not fill in this part if you have since remarried or formed a new civil partnership.

Please give as much information as you can to help us trace your last spouse or civil partner's NI contribution record.

We will not contact your former spouse or civil partner. Any information you give us about them will only be used to trace their NI contribution record.

	Letters Numbers Letter
Your ex or late spouse's or former or late civil partner's NI number	☐☐ ☐☐☐☐☐☐ ☐
Their full name	
Their date of birth	DD/MM/YYYY
Please tell us their last two addresses in the UK if you know them	
Postcode	
Date you married or formed a civil partnership	DD/MM/YYYY

MISCELLANEOUS MATERIALS

• Application for a State Pension forecast continued

○ **Part 9 What to do now**

Where do you want your forecast sent?

Please tick the box that applies to you.

To me at the address I have given in **Part 1**	☐ Please go to **Part 11**.
To my representative. I want my representative to handle any follow-up enquiries that relate to my State Pension forecast	☐ Please go to **Part 10**.

Where to send the form

Please send the form to the address below.

State Pension Forecasting Team
The Pension Service
Tyneview Park
Whitley Road
Newcastle upon Tyne
NE98 1BA

Please note that
- this authorisation relates only to enquiries made to the Future Pension Centre, and
- we can only provide information to your representative for the period that your forecast is held on our computer records.

If you request another forecast in the future, you would need to provide further authorisation for us to provide/discuss that forecast with your representative.

I am a Personal Acting Body. Send the forecast to me	☐	Please go to **Part 10**. Please provide proof of your authority, for example, power of attorney.

○ **Part 10 Your representative**

Please give details of your representative.
If you are a Personal Acting Body, please give your name and address.

Surname or family name   Title [   ] [   ]

Other names   [   ]

Organisation's name
if this applies   [   ]

**Full address including
postcode or zip code**   [   ]

Daytime phone number   Code [   ]   Number [   ]   Ext [   ]

Fax number   Code [   ]   Number [   ]

Reference number
if you know it   [   ]

Please go to **Part 11**.

○ **Part 11 Signature**

Please sign and date this form.

Signature   [Please remember to sign the form in pen after printing.]

Date   [DD/MM/YYYY]

335

FORM BR20—ADDITIONAL STATE PENSION VALUATION

Pensions and divorce or dissolution

The Pension Service
Department for Work and Pensions

○ **Pension sharing**

If you get divorced or dissolve your civil partnership, the court is allowed to consider your additional State Pension as a financial asset, which can be shared in a financial settlement through the making of a pension sharing order. This means that part of the value of any additional State Pension you have earned could be shared with a former husband, wife or civil partner.

The court will need the details of any additional State Pension you may be entitled to. Both parties will have to complete a separate BR20 to enable all financial assets to be considered.

What is additional State Pension?
Additional State Pension is an amount you may be entitled to in addition to your basic State Pension. It is based on your National Insurance (NI) contributions and earnings since April 1978.

A lump sum valuation will give this information and will help the court make a decision.

How do I get a lump sum valuation?
Fill in form BR20 and send it to the address below. You must complete the form in full, in BLOCK CAPITALS, giving as much information as possible.

If your valuation is more than 12 months old at the date of the court hearing, you must apply for a new valuation, as this can change.

What happens to my additional State Pension?
If a pension sharing order is made, your additional State Pension may either increase or decrease, depending on the decision of the court.

Please return your form to:
Future Pension Centre
The Pension Service
Tyneview Park
Whitley Road
Newcastle upon Tyne
NE98 1BA

The telephone number is **0845 3000 168**.

If you have speech or hearing difficulties you can contact us using a textphone on **0845 3000 169**. Or you can use text relay by dialling **18001 0845 3000 168**.

MISCELLANEOUS MATERIALS

14-May-13

- **Pensions and divorce or dissolution** continued

  ○ **Part 1   About you**

  Please tell us about yourself. Use BLOCK CAPITALS.

National Insurance (NI) number	Letters Numbers Letter
Title	Mr/Mrs/Miss/Ms
Surname or family name	
Your first names	
All other surnames or family names you have used	
Date of birth	/ /
Address	Postcode
Home phone number	Code Number

  ○ **Part 2   About your pending divorce or dissolution of your civil partnership**

  Are you divorcing or dissolving your civil partnership under Scottish Matrimonial Law?

  No ○

  Yes ○ Please give the relevant date.

  / /

  The 'relevant date' is either
  - the date you and your spouse or civil partner stopped living together, or
  - the date the summons for divorce or dissolution of a civil partnership was served,

  whichever is earliest.

- **Pensions and divorce or dissolution** continued

○ **Part 3 About your spouse or civil partner**

Title	Mr/Mrs/Miss/Ms
Surname or family name	
Their first names	
Date of birth	/ /

Letters Numbers   Letter

National Insurance (NI) number

Address

Postcode

Date of marriage or civil partnership   /   /

○ **Part 4 About your representative or legal adviser**

If you want your valuation sent to someone else, please tell us about them.

Surname	Mr/Mrs/Miss/Ms
Organisation's name if this applies	
Address	

Postcode

Telephone number   Code   Number

Reference number

○ **Part 5 Declaration**

I declare that the information I have given on this form is correct and complete as far as I know and believe.

Signature

Date   /   /

○ **Part 6 What to do now**

When you have filled in this form, please send it to the address on the front page.

○ **What happens next**

We will send you your valuation as soon as we can.

Sample Letters of Instruction to a Pensions Actuary for an Expert's Report

A. Confirmation of accuracy of Cash Equivalent

Pension share required to provide equal income at retirement at various ages

Dear Sirs,
   [*Instructing solicitors*]
   We are instructed on behalf of [ ] and [ ] are instructed on behalf of [ ]. [ ] is the Applicant in divorce proceedings/Civil partnership dissolution proceedings numbered [ ] proceeding in [ ] court. [ ] is the Respondent in those proceedings.
   [*Agreed instruction or Court directed instruction*]
   [You are instructed jointly by the parties to provide a report as to their pension rights and pension sharing].
   [You are instructed in accordance with the terms of Paragraph [ ] of the order of [ ]. The order is attached.
   [*Information to be provided to the actuary*]
   The Applicant [Wife] is aged having been born on [ ]
   The Respondent [Husband] is aged having been born on [ ]
   The Applicant has the following pensions:

(i) [provider] [address of provider] [number of policy]: etc.

   The Respondent has the following pensions:

(ii) [provider] [address of provider] [number of policy]

   The parties have the following Additional State Pension provision.
   [*Letters of authority*]
   We provide herewith letters of authority to enable you to correspond with the pension providers if necessary.
   Timing
   You are instructed to provide a report by [ ] in advance of [FDA] [FDR] [Round table meeting]. If you cannot comply with this timescale please notify both parties immediately. If you require any information that has not been provided please notify the parties immediately and further information will be provided.

PENSIONS ON DIVORCE

[*Questions*]

1. Please consider the CE values provided by [pension providers A/B/C] and please advise as to whether they are an accurate reflection of the benefits provided by the schemes.
2. If any of the CE values provided are not an accurate reflection of the benefits in the scheme please advise the parties as to the level of CE that would in your opinion reflect the value of the benefits. Please explain the reasoning behind the figure proposed.
3. Please set out the income that each pension scheme will provide to the Applicant and/or the Respondent at age:
   (a) [60] and
   (b) [65] and
   (c) [68],
   if no pension share were to be implemented.
4. Please advise as to the appropriate pension share to provide each party with equal income at age:
   (a) [60],
   (b) [65] and
   (c) [68].
[5. [If applicable] Given that the Normal Retirement Age for Pension A is 60 and that the Applicant will therefore in scenario 4 (b) or (c) above receive pension income earlier than the Respondent please identify the benefits to the Applicant in the period before the Respondent can receive pension income]
6. Please set out the parties' respective incomes at 60, 65 and 68 if a pension share were to be implemented of 35%, 40%, 45%, 50%, 55% or 60% of [pension A].
7. Please set out the costs to the parties of any pension share that may be contemplated and please indicate whether the costs can be deducted from the fund or must be paid before implementation.

Practice Direction [to be used whether instructed in court proceedings or pre-issue]

You are instructed in accordance with Family Procedure Rules 2010 the relevant extract of which we enclose.

Your report should be addressed to the Court at [ ] /both parties

The report should contain details of the individual expert's qualifications and must set out any literature, documents or other material relied on in compiling the report. In particular, may we draw your attention to Practice Direction 25 of the Family Procedure Rules 2010, specifically paragraph 3.3(h) which states that the report must contain a statement that the expert:—

"
Has no conflict of any kind, other than any conflict disclosed in his or her report;

Does not consider that any interest disclosed affects his or her suitability as an expert witness on any issue in which he or she has given evidence;

SAMPLE LETTERS OF INSTRUCTION TO A PENSIONS ACTUARY

Will advise the instructing party if, between the date of the experts report and the final hearing, if there is any change in the circumstances which affects the experts answers to the above;

Understands their duty to the Court and has complied with that duty; and

Is aware of the requirements of Part 25 and this Practice Direction."

The rules also require the report to contain a signed Statement of Truth in the following terms:—

"*I confirm that I have made clear which facts and matters referred to in this report are within my knowledge and which are not. Those that are within my knowledge I confirm to be true. The opinions I have expressed represent my true and complete professional opinion on the matters to which they refer.*"

This wording is mandatory and must not be modified. If you knowingly sign a Statement of Truth that is untrue, then you may be held in contempt of Court and liable of imprisonment. It is important that your report is entirely independent and not influenced by either party.

B. Non marital contributions

Dear Sirs,
   [*Instructing solicitors*]
   We are instructed on behalf of [ ] and [ ] are instructed on behalf of [ ]. [ ] is the Applicant in divorce proceedings/Civil partnership dissolution proceedings numbered [ ] proceeding in [ ] court. [ ] is the Respondent in those proceedings.
   [*Agreed instruction or Court directed instruction*]
   [You are instructed jointly by the parties to provide a report as to their pension rights and pension sharing].
   [You are instructed in accordance with the terms of Paragraph [ ] of the order of [ ]. The order is attached.
   [*Information to be provided to the actuary*]
   The Applicant [Wife] is aged having been born on [ ]
   The Respondent [Husband] is aged having been born on [ ]
   The Applicant has the following pensions:

(i) [provider] [address of provider] [number of policy]: etc.

   The Respondent has the following pensions:

(ii) [provider] [address of provider] [number of policy]

   The parties have the following Additional State Pension provision.
   [*Letters of authority*]
   We provide herewith letters of authority to enable you to correspond with the pension providers if necessary.
   Timing

PENSIONS ON DIVORCE

You are instructed to provide a report by [ ] in advance of [FDA] [FDR] [Round table meeting]. If you cannot comply with this timescale please notify both parties immediately. If you require any information that has not been provided please notify the parties immediately and further information will be provided.

[*Relevant factual information*]

In relation to pension [A] [B] you should note the following chronology:

00/00/00 The Applicant began work for [A]
00/00/00 The parties married.
00/00/00 The Applicant left his employment with [A]
00/00/00 The Applicant began work with [B]
00/00/00 The parties separated.

It is the Applicant's case that his pre-marital and post separation contributions should be excluded from consideration when division of pension is considered. The Respondent's case is that the entire pension should be included. The court will determine which approach is correct but you are asked to provide an opinion on the alternative bases in accordance with the questions set out below.

[*Questions*]

1. Please consider the CE values provided by [pension providers A/B/C] and please advise as to whether they are an accurate reflection of the benefits provided by the schemes.
2. If any of the CE values provided are not an accurate reflection of the benefits provided please advise the parties as to the level of CE that would in your opinion reflect the value of the benefits. Please explain the reasoning behind the figure proposed.
3. Please advise as to the relevant CE for that part of pension A that was accrued during the marriage and that part of pension B that was accrued before separation. Please explain the basis of your calculations. If the calculation is based upon a straight line discount please explain why that is considered the appropriate basis for the calculation. If the calculation is based upon another actuarial approach please explain the basis of the calculation and why that is considered an appropriate basis for the calculation.
4. Please set out the income that each pension scheme will provide to the Applicant and/or the Respondent at age:
   (a) [60]
   (b) [65] and
   (c) [68]
   If no pension share were implemented.
5. Please carry out the calculation referred to in paragraph 4 on the basis that pre-marital and post separation pension is excluded.
6. Please carry out the calculation referred to in paragraph 4 on the basis that pre-marital pension is excluded but post separation pension included.
7. Please carry out the calculation referred to in paragraph 4 on the basis that pre-marital pension is included and post separation excluded.
8. Please advise as to the appropriate pension share to provide each party with equal income at age:

SAMPLE LETTERS OF INSTRUCTION TO A PENSIONS ACTUARY

(a) [60],
(b) [65] and
(c) [68].

9. Please carry out the calculation referred to in paragraph 8 on the basis that pre-marital pension and post separation pension is excluded.
10. Please carry out the calculation referred to in paragraph 8 on the basis that pre-marital pension is excluded but post separation pension included.
11. Please carry out the calculation referred to in paragraph 4 on the basis that pre-marital pension is included and post separation excluded.
[12. [If applicable] Given that the Normal Retirement Age for Pension A is 60 and that the Applicant will therefore in scenario 8 (b) or (c) above receive pension income earlier than the Respondent please identify the benefits to the Applicant in the period before the Respondent can receive pension income]
13. Please set out the parties' respective incomes at 60, 65 and 68 if a pension share were to be implemented of 35%, 40%, 45%, 50%, 55% or 60% of pension [A].
14. Please set out the costs to the parties of any pension share that may be contemplated and please indicate whether the costs can be deducted from the fund or must be paid before implementation.

Practice Direction [to be used whether instructed in court proceedings or pre-issue]

You are instructed in accordance Family Procedure Rules 2010, the relevant extract, of which we enclose.

Your report should be addressed to the Court at [ ] /both parties

The report should contain details of the individual expert's qualifications and must set out any literature, documents or other material relied on in compiling the report. In particular, may we draw your attention to Practice Direction 25 of the Family Procedure Rules 2010, specifically paragraph 3.3(h) which states that the report must contain a statement that the expert:—

"

Has no conflict of any kind, other than any conflict disclosed in his or her report;

Does not consider that any interest disclosed affects his or her suitability as an expert witness on any issue in which he or she has given evidence;

Will advise the instructing party if, between the date of the experts report and the final hearing, if there is any change in the circumstances which affects the experts answers to the above;

Understands their duty to the Court and has complied with that duty; and

Is aware of the requirements of Part 25 and this Practice Direction."

The rules also require the report to contain a signed Statement of Truth in the following terms:—

"I confirm that I have made clear which facts and matters referred to in this report are within my knowledge and which are not. Those that are within my knowledge I

confirm to be true. The opinions I have expressed represent my true and complete professional opinion on the matters to which they refer."

This wording is mandatory and must not be modified. If you knowingly sign a Statement of Truth that is untrue, then you may be held in contempt of Court and liable of imprisonment. It is important that your report is entirely independent and not influenced by either party.

C. Post implementation accrual

Dear Sirs,
[*Instructing solicitors*]
We are instructed on behalf of [ ] and [ ] are instructed on behalf of [ ]. [ ] is the Applicant in divorce proceedings/Civil partnership dissolution proceedings numbered [ ] proceedings in [ ] court. [ ] is the Respondent in those proceedings.
[*Agreed instruction or Court directed instruction*]
[You are instructed jointly by the parties to provide a report as to their pension rights and pension sharing].
[You are instructed in accordance with the terms of Paragraph [ ] of the order of [ ]. The order is attached.
[*Information to be provided to the actuary*]
The Applicant [Wife] is aged having been born on [ ]
The Respondent [Husband] is aged having been born on [ ]
The Applicant has the following pensions:

(i) [provider] [address of provider] [number of policy]: etc.

The Respondent has the following pensions:

(ii) [provider] [address of provider] [number of policy]

The parties have the following Additional State Pension provision.
[*Letters of authority*]
We provide herewith letters of authority to enable you to correspond with the pension providers if necessary.
Timing
You are instructed to provide a report by [ ] in advance of [FDA] [FDR] [Round table meeting]. If you cannot comply with this timescale please notify both parties immediately. If you require any information that has not been provided please notify the parties immediately and further information will be provided.
[*Relevant factual information*]
The parties are agreed that the Applicant will retire in 12 months' time on his [65th] birthday. The Applicant's case is that the Respondent will continue to work until age [65] and that she will continue to make pension contributions to pension [C] as she is at present. The Respondent does not accept that she will work until 65 but agrees that she may work until age 60. Her case is that the court should place no reliance on her continuing pension contributions. The correct approach

SAMPLE LETTERS OF INSTRUCTION TO A PENSIONS ACTUARY

will be a matter for the court. You are asked to provide an opinion on the alternative bases set out in the questions below.

[Questions]

1. Please consider the CE values provided by [pension providers A/B/C] and please advise as to whether they are an accurate reflection of the benefits provided by the schemes.
2. If any of the CE values provided are not an accurate reflection of the benefits provided please advise the parties as to the level of CE that would in your opinion reflect the value of the benefits. Please explain the reasoning behind the figure proposed.
4. Please set out the income that each pension scheme will provide to the Applicant and/or the Respondent at age:
    (a) [60],
    (b) [65] and
    (c) [68]
    On the basis that no pension sharing orders are made.
    Please carry out the calculation on the basis that the Respondent ceases work now, works to until 60 or works until 65.
5. Please advise as to the appropriate pension share to provide each party with equal income at age:
    (a) [60],
    (b) [65] and
    (c) [68].
    Please carry out the calculation on the basis that the Respondent ceases work now, works until 60 or works until 65.
6. Please set out the parties' respective incomes at 60, 65 and 68 if a pension share were to be implemented of 35%, 40%, 45%, 50%, 55% or 60% of pension [A]. Please carry out the calculation on the basis that the Respondent eases work now, works until 60 or works until 65.
7. Please set out the costs to the parties of any pension share that may be contemplated and please indicate whether the costs can be deducted from the fund or must be paid before implementation.

Practice Direction [to be used whether instructed in court proceedings or pre-issue]

You are instructed in accordance Family Procedure Rules 2010, the relevant extract, of which we enclose.

Your report should be addressed to the Court at [ ] /both parties

The report should contain details of the individual expert's qualifications and must set out any literature, documents or other material relied on in compiling the report. In particular, may we draw your attention to Practice Direction 25 of the Family Procedure Rules 2010, specifically paragraph 3.3(h) which states that the report must contain a statement that the expert: -

"

> *Has no conflict of any kind, other than any conflict disclosed in his or her report;*
>
> *Does not consider that any interest disclosed affects his or her suitability as an expert witness on any issue in which he or she has given evidence;*

Will advise the instructing party if, between the date of the experts report and the final hearing, if there is any change in the circumstances which affects the experts answers to the above;

Understands their duty to the Court and has complied with that duty; and

Is aware of the requirements of Part 25 and this Practice Direction."

The rules also require the report to contain a signed Statement of Truth in the following terms:—

"I confirm that I have made clear which facts and matters referred to in this report are within my knowledge and which are not. Those that are within my knowledge I confirm to be true. The opinions I have expressed represent my true and complete professional opinion on the matters to which they refer."

This wording is mandatory and must not be modified. If you knowingly sign a Statement of Truth that is untrue, then you may be held in contempt of Court and liable of imprisonment. It is important that your report is entirely independent and not influenced by either party.

D. CPI/RPI

Dear Sirs,
   [Instructing solicitors]
   We are instructed on behalf of [ ] and [ ] are instructed on behalf of [ ]. [ ] is the Applicant in divorce proceedings/Civil partnership dissolution proceedings numbered [ ] proceedings in [ ] court. [ ] is the Respondent in those proceedings.
   [Agreed instruction or Court directed instruction]
   [You are instructed jointly by the parties to provide a report as to their pension rights and pension sharing].
   [You are instructed in accordance with the terms of Paragraph [ ] of the order of [ ]. The order is attached.
   [Information to be provided to the actuary]
   The Applicant [Wife] is aged having been born on [ ]
   The Respondent [Husband} is aged having been born on [ ]
   The Applicant has the following pensions:

(i) [provider] [address of provider] [number of policy]: etc.

The Respondent has the following pensions:

(ii) [provider] [address of provider] [number of policy]

The parties have the following Additional State Pension provision.
   [Letters of authority]
   We provide herewith letters of authority to enable you to correspond with the pension providers if necessary.
   Timing

SAMPLE LETTERS OF INSTRUCTION TO A PENSIONS ACTUARY

You are instructed to provide a report by [ ] in advance of [FDA] [FDR] [Round table meeting]. If you cannot comply with this timescale please notify both parties immediately. If you require any information that has not been provided please notify the parties immediately and further information will be provided.

[*Relevant factual information*]

The CE of Pension [A] has been calculated by the provider in accordance with the CPI. The parties' understanding is that the CE in relation to pension [B] is at present based on the RPI. There appears to be a risk that this may change at some point in the future and the benefits payable in relation to pension [B] will be recalculated in accordance with CPI. The court will need to make a decision as to how to reflect this consideration in its orders but you are asked in accordance with the questions below to provide calculations based on both possible outcomes.

[*Questions*]

1. Please consider the CE values provided by [pension providers A/B/C] and please advise as to whether they are an accurate reflection of the benefits provided by the schemes.
2. If any of the CE values provided are not an accurate reflection of the benefits provided please advise the parties as to the level of CE that would in your opinion reflect the value of the benefits. Please explain the reasoning behind the figure proposed.
4. Please set out the income that each pension scheme will provide to the Applicant and/or the Respondent at age:
   (a) [60],
   (b) [65] and
   (c) [68]
   On the basis that no pension sharing orders are made.
   Please carry out the calculation referred to on the basis that pension [B] is RPI based at the date of retirement and on the basis that it is CPI based at that date.
5. Please advise as to the appropriate pension share to provide each party with equal income at age:
   (a) [60],
   (b) [65] and
   (c) [68].
   Please carry out the calculation on the basis that pension [B] is RPI based at the date or retirement and on the basis that it is CPI based.
6. Please set out the parties' respective incomes at 60, 65 and 68 if a pension share were to be implemented of 35%, 40%, 45%, 50%, 55% or 60% of pension [A]. Please carry out the calculation on the basis that pension [B] is RPI based at retirement or CPI based at retirement.
7. Please set out the costs to the parties of any pension share that may be contemplated and please indicate whether the costs can be deducted from the fund or must be paid before implementation.

Practice Direction [to be used whether instructed in court proceedings or pre-issue]

You are instructed in accordance Family Procedure Rules 2010, the relevant extract, of which we enclose.

Your report should be addressed to the Court at [ ] /both parties

The report should contain details of the individual expert's qualifications and must set out any literature, documents or other material relied on in compiling the report. In particular, may we draw your attention to Practice Direction 25 of the Family Procedure Rules 2010, specifically paragraph 3.3(h) which states that the report must contain a statement that the expert:—

> *Has no conflict of any kind, other than any conflict disclosed in his or her report;*
>
> *Does not consider that any interest disclosed affects his or her suitability as an expert witness on any issue in which he or she has given evidence;*
>
> *Will advise the instructing party if, between the date of the experts report and the final hearing, if there is any change in the circumstances which affects the experts answers to the above;*
>
> *Understands their duty to the Court and has complied with that duty; and*
>
> *Is aware of the requirements of Part 25 and this Practice Direction."*

The rules also require the report to contain a signed Statement of Truth in the following terms:—

> *"I confirm that I have made clear which facts and matters referred to in this report are within my knowledge and which are not. Those that are within my knowledge I confirm to be true. The opinions I have expressed represent my true and complete professional opinion on the matters to which they refer."*

This wording is mandatory and must not be modified. If you knowingly sign a Statement of Truth that is untrue, then you may be held in contempt of Court and liable of imprisonment. It is important that your report is entirely independent and not influenced by either party.

Income Equality and Pension Age Tables

Income Equality Tables

We have produced calculations of the percentage required by a non member spouse of the total pension funds to create equality of income.

These are not going to be accurate at all times as annuity rates vary and they assume there are no Market Value Adjustments or Guaranteed Annuity Rates available on the policies and allow for investment returns in future where applicable.

If any of the above features are available on the policies then this is not appropriate but it does give an indication where there are one or a number of Stakeholder or Unit-Linked contracts.

This cannot be relied on for complete accuracy.

Assume Retirement Age 67
Assume inflation linked annuities

Member spouse Age	Non member spouse Age										
	35	36	37	38	39	40	41	42	43	44
35	50.00%	50.48%	50.97%	51.45%	51.93%	52.41%	52.90%	53.38%	53.86%	54.34%
36	49.52%	50.00%	50.48%	50.97%	51.45%	51.93%	52.41%	52.90%	53.38%	53.86%
37	49.03%	49.52%	50.00%	50.48%	50.97%	51.45%	51.93%	52.41%	52.90%	53.38%
38	48.55%	49.03%	49.52%	50.00%	50.48%	50.97%	51.45%	51.93%	52.41%	52.90%
39	48.07%	48.55%	49.03%	49.52%	50.00%	50.48%	50.97%	51.45%	51.93%	52.41%
40	47.59%	48.07%	48.55%	49.03%	49.52%	50.00%	50.48%	50.97%	51.45%	51.93%
41	47.10%	47.59%	48.07%	48.55%	49.03%	49.52%	50.00%	50.48%	50.97%	51.45%
42	46.62%	47.10%	47.59%	48.07%	48.55%	49.03%	49.52%	50.00%	50.48%	50.97%
43	46.14%	46.62%	47.10%	47.59%	48.07%	48.55%	49.03%	49.52%	50.00%	50.48%
44	45.66%	46.14%	46.62%	47.10%	47.59%	48.07%	48.55%	49.03%	49.52%	50.00%
45	45.18%	45.66%	46.14%	46.62%	47.10%	47.59%	48.07%	48.55%	49.03%	49.52%
46	44.71%	45.18%	45.66%	46.14%	46.62%	47.10%	47.59%	48.07%	48.55%	49.03%
47	44.23%	44.71%	45.18%	45.66%	46.14%	46.62%	47.10%	47.59%	48.07%	48.55%
48	43.75%	44.23%	44.71%	45.18%	45.66%	46.14%	46.62%	47.10%	47.59%	48.07%
49	43.28%	43.75%	44.23%	44.71%	45.18%	45.66%	46.14%	46.62%	47.10%	47.59%
50	42.80%	43.28%	43.75%	44.23%	44.71%	45.18%	45.66%	46.14%	46.62%	47.10%
51	42.33%	42.80%	43.28%	43.75%	44.23%	44.71%	45.18%	45.66%	46.14%	46.62%
52	41.86%	42.33%	42.80%	43.28%	43.75%	44.23%	44.71%	45.18%	45.66%	46.14%
53	41.39%	41.86%	42.33%	42.80%	43.28%	43.75%	44.23%	44.71%	45.18%	45.66%

INCOME EQUALITY AND PENSION AGE TABLES

Age	45	46	47	48	49	50	51	52	53	54
54	40.92%	41.39%	41.86%	42.33%	42.80%	43.28%	43.75%	44.23%	44.71%	45.18%
55	40.46%	40.92%	41.39%	41.86%	42.33%	42.80%	43.28%	43.75%	44.23%	44.71%
56	39.99%	40.46%	40.92%	41.39%	41.86%	42.33%	42.80%	43.28%	43.75%	44.23%
57	39.53%	39.99%	40.46%	40.92%	41.39%	41.86%	42.33%	42.80%	43.28%	43.75%
58	39.07%	39.53%	39.99%	40.46%	40.92%	41.39%	41.86%	42.33%	42.80%	43.28%
59	38.61%	39.07%	39.53%	39.99%	40.46%	40.92%	41.39%	41.86%	42.33%	42.80%
60	38.15%	38.61%	39.07%	39.53%	39.99%	40.46%	40.92%	41.39%	41.86%	42.33%
61	37.70%	38.15%	38.61%	39.07%	39.53%	39.99%	40.46%	40.92%	41.39%	41.86%
62	37.24%	37.70%	38.15%	38.61%	39.07%	39.53%	39.99%	40.46%	40.92%	41.39%
63	36.79%	37.24%	37.70%	38.15%	38.61%	39.07%	39.53%	39.99%	40.46%	40.92%
64	36.35%	36.79%	37.24%	37.70%	38.15%	38.61%	39.07%	39.53%	39.99%	40.46%
65	35.90%	36.35%	36.79%	37.24%	37.70%	38.15%	38.61%	39.07%	39.53%	39.99%
66	35.46%	35.90%	36.35%	36.79%	37.24%	37.70%	38.15%	38.61%	39.07%	39.53%

Age

Age	45	46	47	48	49	50	51	52	53	54
35	54.82%	55.29%	55.77%	56.25%	56.72%	57.20%	57.67%	58.14%	58.61%	59.08%
36	54.34%	54.82%	55.29%	55.77%	56.25%	56.72%	57.20%	57.67%	58.14%	58.61%
37	53.86%	54.34%	54.82%	55.29%	55.77%	56.25%	56.72%	57.20%	57.67%	58.14%
38	53.38%	53.86%	54.34%	54.82%	55.29%	55.77%	56.25%	56.72%	57.20%	57.67%
39	52.90%	53.38%	53.86%	54.34%	54.82%	55.29%	55.77%	56.25%	56.72%	57.20%
40	52.41%	52.90%	53.38%	53.86%	54.34%	54.82%	55.29%	55.77%	56.25%	56.72%
41	51.93%	52.41%	52.90%	53.38%	53.86%	54.34%	54.82%	55.29%	55.77%	56.25%
42	51.45%	51.93%	52.41%	52.90%	53.38%	53.86%	54.34%	54.82%	55.29%	55.77%
43	50.97%	51.45%	51.93%	52.41%	52.90%	53.38%	53.86%	54.34%	54.82%	55.29%

PENSIONS ON DIVORCE

Age										
44	50.48%	50.97%	51.45%	51.93%	52.41%	52.90%	53.38%	53.86%	54.34%	54.82%
45	50.00%	50.48%	50.97%	51.45%	51.93%	52.41%	52.90%	53.38%	53.86%	54.34%
46	49.52%	50.00%	50.48%	50.97%	51.45%	51.93%	52.41%	52.90%	53.38%	53.86%
47	49.03%	49.52%	50.00%	50.48%	50.97%	51.45%	51.93%	52.41%	52.90%	53.38%
48	48.55%	49.03%	49.52%	50.00%	50.48%	50.97%	51.45%	51.93%	52.41%	52.90%
49	48.07%	48.55%	49.03%	49.52%	50.00%	50.48%	50.97%	51.45%	51.93%	52.41%
50	47.59%	48.07%	48.55%	49.03%	49.52%	50.00%	50.48%	50.97%	51.45%	51.93%
51	47.10%	47.59%	48.07%	48.55%	49.03%	49.52%	50.00%	50.48%	50.97%	51.45%
52	46.62%	47.10%	47.59%	48.07%	48.55%	49.03%	49.52%	50.00%	50.48%	50.97%
53	46.14%	46.62%	47.10%	47.59%	48.07%	48.55%	49.03%	49.52%	50.00%	50.48%
54	45.66%	46.14%	46.62%	47.10%	47.59%	48.07%	48.55%	49.03%	49.52%	50.00%
55	45.18%	45.66%	46.14%	46.62%	47.10%	47.59%	48.07%	48.55%	49.03%	49.52%
56	44.71%	45.18%	45.66%	46.14%	46.62%	47.10%	47.59%	48.07%	48.55%	49.03%
57	44.23%	44.71%	45.18%	45.66%	46.14%	46.62%	47.10%	47.59%	48.07%	48.55%
58	43.75%	44.23%	44.71%	45.18%	45.66%	46.14%	46.62%	47.10%	47.59%	48.07%
59	43.28%	43.75%	44.23%	44.71%	45.18%	45.66%	46.14%	46.62%	47.10%	47.59%
60	42.80%	43.28%	43.75%	44.23%	44.71%	45.18%	45.66%	46.14%	46.62%	47.10%
61	42.33%	42.80%	43.28%	43.75%	44.23%	44.71%	45.18%	45.66%	46.14%	46.62%
62	41.86%	42.33%	42.80%	43.28%	43.75%	44.23%	44.71%	45.18%	45.66%	46.14%
63	41.39%	41.86%	42.33%	42.80%	43.28%	43.75%	44.23%	44.71%	45.18%	45.66%
64	40.92%	41.39%	41.86%	42.33%	42.80%	43.28%	43.75%	44.23%	44.71%	45.18%
65	40.46%	40.92%	41.39%	41.86%	42.33%	42.80%	43.28%	43.75%	44.23%	44.71%
66	39.99%	40.46%	40.92%	41.39%	41.86%	42.33%	42.80%	43.28%	43.75%	44.23%

INCOME EQUALITY AND PENSION AGE TABLES

Age	55	56	57	58	59	60	61	62	63	64
35	59.54%	60.01%	60.47%	60.93%	61.39%	61.85%	62.30%	62.76%	63.21%	63.65%
36	59.08%	59.54%	60.01%	60.47%	60.93%	61.39%	61.85%	62.30%	62.76%	63.21%
37	58.61%	59.08%	59.54%	60.01%	60.47%	60.93%	61.39%	61.85%	62.30%	62.76%
38	58.14%	58.61%	59.08%	59.54%	60.01%	60.47%	60.93%	61.39%	61.85%	62.30%
39	57.67%	58.14%	58.61%	59.08%	59.54%	60.01%	60.47%	60.93%	61.39%	61.85%
40	57.20%	57.67%	58.14%	58.61%	59.08%	59.54%	60.01%	60.47%	60.93%	61.39%
41	56.72%	57.20%	57.67%	58.14%	58.61%	59.08%	59.54%	60.01%	60.47%	60.93%
42	56.25%	56.72%	57.20%	57.67%	58.14%	58.61%	59.08%	59.54%	60.01%	60.47%
43	55.77%	56.25%	56.72%	57.20%	57.67%	58.14%	58.61%	59.08%	59.54%	60.01%
44	55.29%	55.77%	56.25%	56.72%	57.20%	57.67%	58.14%	58.61%	59.08%	59.54%
45	54.82%	55.29%	55.77%	56.25%	56.72%	57.20%	57.67%	58.14%	58.61%	59.08%
46	54.34%	54.82%	55.29%	55.77%	56.25%	56.72%	57.20%	57.67%	58.14%	58.61%
47	53.86%	54.34%	54.82%	55.29%	55.77%	56.25%	56.72%	57.20%	57.67%	58.14%
48	53.38%	53.86%	54.34%	54.82%	55.29%	55.77%	56.25%	56.72%	57.20%	57.67%
49	52.90%	53.38%	53.86%	54.34%	54.82%	55.29%	55.77%	56.25%	56.72%	57.20%
50	52.41%	52.90%	53.38%	53.86%	54.34%	54.82%	55.29%	55.77%	56.25%	56.72%
51	51.93%	52.41%	52.90%	53.38%	53.86%	54.34%	54.82%	55.29%	55.77%	56.25%
52	51.45%	51.93%	52.41%	52.90%	53.38%	53.86%	54.34%	54.82%	55.29%	55.77%
53	50.97%	51.45%	51.93%	52.41%	52.90%	53.38%	53.86%	54.34%	54.82%	55.29%
54	50.48%	50.97%	51.45%	51.93%	52.41%	52.90%	53.38%	53.86%	54.34%	54.82%
55	50.00%	50.48%	50.97%	51.45%	51.93%	52.41%	52.90%	53.38%	53.86%	54.34%
56	49.52%	50.00%	50.48%	50.97%	51.45%	51.93%	52.41%	52.90%	53.38%	53.86%
57	49.03%	49.52%	50.00%	50.48%	50.97%	51.45%	51.93%	52.41%	52.90%	53.38%

58	48.55%	49.03%	49.52%	50.00%	50.48%	50.97%	51.45%	51.93%	52.41%	52.90%
59	48.07%	48.55%	49.03%	49.52%	50.00%	50.48%	50.97%	51.45%	51.93%	52.41%
60	47.59%	48.07%	48.55%	49.03%	49.52%	50.00%	50.48%	50.97%	51.45%	51.93%
61	47.10%	47.59%	48.07%	48.55%	49.03%	49.52%	50.00%	50.48%	50.97%	51.45%
62	46.62%	47.10%	47.59%	48.07%	48.55%	49.03%	49.52%	50.00%	50.48%	50.97%
63	46.14%	46.62%	47.10%	47.59%	48.07%	48.55%	49.03%	49.52%	50.00%	50.48%
64	45.66%	46.14%	46.62%	47.10%	47.59%	48.07%	48.55%	49.03%	49.52%	50.00%
65	45.18%	45.66%	46.14%	46.62%	47.10%	47.59%	48.07%	48.55%	49.03%	49.52%
66	44.71%	45.18%	45.66%	46.14%	46.62%	47.10%	47.59%	48.07%	48.55%	49.03%

INCOME EQUALITY AND PENSION AGE TABLES

Assume Retirement Age 67, continued		
Assume inflation linked annuities, continued		
	Non-member spouse age	
Member spouse age	65	66
35	64.10%	64.54%
36	63.65%	64.10%
37	63.21%	63.65%
38	62.76%	63.21%
39	62.30%	62.76%
40	61.85%	62.30%
41	61.39%	61.85%
42	60.93%	61.39%
43	60.47%	60.93%
44	60.01%	60.47%
45	59.54%	60.01%
46	59.08%	59.54%
47	58.61%	59.08%
48	58.14%	58.61%
49	57.67%	58.14%
50	57.20%	57.67%
51	56.72%	57.20%
52	56.25%	56.72%
53	55.77%	56.25%
54	55.29%	55.77%
55	54.82%	55.29%
56	54.34%	54.82%
57	53.86%	54.34%
58	53.38%	53.86%
59	52.90%	53.38%
60	52.41%	52.90%
61	51.93%	52.41%
62	51.45%	51.93%
63	50.97%	51.45%
64	50.48%	50.97%
65	50.00%	50.48%
66	49.52%	50.00%

PENSIONS ON DIVORCE

Assume Immediate Retirement
Assume inflation linked annuities

Age	55	56	57	58	59	60	61	62	63	64
55	50.00%	49.28%	48.57%	47.89%	47.01%	46.16%	45.24%	44.31%	43.33%	42.30%
56	50.72%	50.00%	49.30%	48.61%	47.73%	46.88%	45.96%	45.03%	44.04%	43.00%
57	51.43%	50.70%	50.00%	49.32%	48.43%	47.58%	46.66%	45.72%	44.73%	43.69%
58	52.11%	51.39%	50.68%	50.00%	49.12%	48.26%	47.34%	46.40%	45.41%	44.37%
59	52.99%	52.27%	51.57%	50.88%	50.00%	49.15%	48.22%	47.28%	46.29%	45.24%
60	53.84%	53.12%	52.42%	51.74%	50.85%	50.00%	49.07%	48.13%	47.13%	46.09%
61	54.76%	54.04%	53.34%	52.66%	51.78%	50.93%	50.00%	49.06%	48.06%	47.01%
62	55.69%	54.97%	54.28%	53.60%	52.72%	51.87%	50.94%	50.00%	49.00%	47.95%
63	56.67%	55.96%	55.27%	54.59%	53.71%	52.87%	51.94%	51.00%	50.00%	48.95%
64	57.70%	57.00%	56.31%	55.63%	54.76%	53.91%	52.99%	52.05%	51.05%	50.00%
65	58.77%	58.07%	57.38%	56.71%	55.84%	55.00%	54.08%	53.14%	52.15%	51.10%
66	59.66%	58.97%	58.29%	57.62%	56.75%	55.91%	55.00%	54.07%	53.07%	52.02%
67	60.60%	59.90%	59.23%	58.57%	57.71%	56.87%	55.96%	55.03%	54.04%	52.99%
68	61.52%	60.84%	60.17%	59.51%	58.65%	57.82%	56.92%	55.99%	55.00%	53.96%
69	62.48%	61.80%	61.13%	60.48%	59.63%	58.81%	57.91%	56.99%	56.00%	54.96%
70	63.45%	62.78%	62.12%	61.47%	60.63%	59.81%	58.92%	58.01%	57.03%	55.99%
71	64.50%	63.83%	63.18%	62.54%	61.71%	60.90%	60.02%	59.11%	58.14%	57.11%
72	65.57%	64.92%	64.27%	63.64%	62.82%	62.02%	61.15%	60.25%	59.28%	58.26%
73	66.64%	65.99%	65.36%	64.74%	63.93%	63.14%	62.27%	61.38%	60.43%	59.42%
74	67.80%	67.16%	66.54%	65.93%	65.13%	64.35%	63.50%	62.62%	61.68%	60.68%

INCOME EQUALITY AND PENSION AGE TABLES

Age	65	66	67	68	69	70	71	72	73	74
55	41.23%	40.34%	39.40%	38.48%	37.52%	36.55%	35.50%	34.43%	33.36%	32.20%
56	41.93%	41.03%	40.10%	39.16%	38.20%	37.22%	36.17%	35.08%	34.01%	32.84%
57	42.62%	41.71%	40.77%	39.83%	38.87%	37.88%	36.82%	35.73%	34.64%	33.46%
58	43.29%	42.38%	41.43%	40.49%	39.52%	38.53%	37.46%	36.36%	35.26%	34.07%
59	44.16%	43.25%	42.29%	41.35%	40.37%	39.37%	38.29%	37.18%	36.07%	34.87%
60	45.00%	44.09%	43.13%	42.18%	41.19%	40.19%	39.10%	37.98%	36.86%	35.65%
61	45.92%	45.00%	44.04%	43.08%	42.09%	41.08%	39.98%	38.85%	37.73%	36.50%
62	46.86%	45.93%	44.97%	44.01%	43.01%	41.99%	40.89%	39.75%	38.62%	37.38%
63	47.85%	46.93%	45.96%	45.00%	44.00%	42.97%	41.86%	40.72%	39.57%	38.32%
64	48.90%	47.98%	47.01%	46.04%	45.04%	44.01%	42.89%	41.74%	40.58%	39.32%
65	50.00%	49.07%	48.10%	47.13%	46.12%	45.09%	43.97%	42.80%	41.64%	40.37%
66	50.93%	50.00%	49.03%	48.05%	47.05%	46.01%	44.88%	43.71%	42.55%	41.27%
67	51.90%	50.97%	50.00%	49.03%	48.02%	46.98%	45.85%	44.67%	43.50%	42.21%
68	52.87%	51.95%	50.97%	50.00%	48.99%	47.95%	46.81%	45.64%	44.46%	43.17%
69	53.88%	52.95%	51.98%	51.01%	50.00%	48.96%	47.82%	46.64%	45.46%	44.16%
70	54.91%	53.99%	53.02%	52.05%	51.04%	50.00%	48.86%	47.68%	46.50%	45.19%
71	56.03%	55.12%	54.15%	53.19%	52.18%	51.14%	50.00%	48.82%	47.63%	46.32%
72	57.20%	56.29%	55.33%	54.36%	53.36%	52.32%	51.18%	50.00%	48.81%	47.50%
73	58.36%	57.45%	56.50%	55.54%	54.54%	53.50%	52.37%	51.19%	50.00%	48.69%
74	59.63%	58.73%	57.79%	56.83%	55.84%	54.81%	53.68%	52.50%	51.31%	50.00%

PENSIONS ON DIVORCE

Assume Immediate Retirement
Assume non increasing annuities

Age	55	56	57	58	59	60	61	62	63	64
55	50.00%	49.61%	49.19%	48.75%	48.29%	47.78%	47.31%	46.80%	46.25%	45.68%
56	50.39%	50.00%	49.58%	49.14%	48.68%	48.18%	47.71%	47.19%	46.64%	46.07%
57	50.81%	50.42%	50.00%	49.56%	49.10%	48.59%	48.12%	47.61%	47.05%	46.48%
58	51.25%	50.86%	50.44%	50.00%	49.54%	49.03%	48.56%	48.05%	47.49%	46.92%
59	51.71%	51.32%	50.90%	50.46%	50.00%	49.49%	49.02%	48.51%	47.95%	47.38%
60	52.22%	51.82%	51.41%	50.97%	50.51%	50.00%	49.53%	49.01%	48.46%	47.89%
61	52.69%	52.29%	51.88%	51.44%	50.98%	50.47%	50.00%	49.48%	48.93%	48.36%
62	53.20%	52.81%	52.39%	51.95%	51.49%	50.99%	50.52%	50.00%	49.44%	48.87%
63	53.75%	53.36%	52.95%	52.51%	52.05%	51.54%	51.07%	50.56%	50.00%	49.43%
64	54.32%	53.93%	53.52%	53.08%	52.62%	52.11%	51.64%	51.13%	50.57%	50.00%
65	54.93%	54.54%	54.12%	53.68%	53.23%	52.72%	52.25%	51.74%	51.18%	50.61%
66	55.44%	55.05%	54.64%	54.20%	53.74%	53.24%	52.77%	52.26%	51.70%	51.13%
67	55.97%	55.58%	55.17%	54.73%	54.28%	53.77%	53.30%	52.79%	52.23%	51.66%
68	56.55%	56.16%	55.75%	55.32%	54.86%	54.36%	53.89%	53.38%	52.82%	52.25%
69	57.17%	56.78%	56.37%	55.94%	55.48%	54.98%	54.51%	54.00%	53.45%	52.88%
70	57.81%	57.42%	57.01%	56.58%	56.13%	55.63%	55.16%	54.65%	54.10%	53.53%
71	58.51%	58.13%	57.72%	57.29%	56.84%	56.34%	55.88%	55.37%	54.82%	54.25%
72	59.25%	58.87%	58.47%	58.04%	57.59%	57.09%	56.63%	56.13%	55.58%	55.01%
73	60.05%	59.67%	59.27%	58.84%	58.40%	57.90%	57.44%	56.94%	56.39%	55.83%
74	60.85%	60.48%	60.08%	59.65%	59.21%	58.72%	58.26%	57.76%	57.21%	56.65%

INCOME EQUALITY AND PENSION AGE TABLES

Age	65	66	67	68	69	70	71	72	73	74
55	45.07%	44.56%	44.03%	43.45%	42.83%	42.19%	41.49%	40.75%	39.95%	39.15%
56	45.46%	44.95%	44.42%	43.84%	43.22%	42.58%	41.87%	41.13%	40.33%	39.52%
57	45.88%	45.36%	44.83%	44.25%	43.63%	42.99%	42.28%	41.53%	40.73%	39.92%
58	46.32%	45.80%	45.27%	44.68%	44.06%	43.42%	42.71%	41.96%	41.16%	40.35%
59	46.77%	46.26%	45.72%	45.14%	44.52%	43.87%	43.16%	42.41%	41.60%	40.79%
60	47.28%	46.76%	46.23%	45.64%	45.02%	44.37%	43.66%	42.91%	42.10%	41.28%
61	47.75%	47.23%	46.70%	46.11%	45.49%	44.84%	44.12%	43.37%	42.56%	41.74%
62	48.26%	47.74%	47.21%	46.62%	46.00%	45.35%	44.63%	43.87%	43.06%	42.24%
63	48.82%	48.30%	47.77%	47.18%	46.55%	45.90%	45.18%	44.42%	43.61%	42.79%
64	49.39%	48.87%	48.34%	47.75%	47.12%	46.47%	45.75%	44.99%	44.17%	43.35%
65	50.00%	49.48%	48.95%	48.35%	47.73%	47.08%	46.35%	45.59%	44.77%	43.95%
66	50.52%	50.00%	49.47%	48.87%	48.25%	47.59%	46.87%	46.11%	45.29%	44.46%
67	51.05%	50.53%	50.00%	49.41%	48.78%	48.13%	47.40%	46.64%	45.82%	44.99%
68	51.65%	51.13%	50.59%	50.00%	49.37%	48.72%	48.00%	47.23%	46.41%	45.58%
69	52.27%	51.75%	51.22%	50.63%	50.00%	49.35%	48.62%	47.85%	47.03%	46.20%
70	52.92%	52.41%	51.87%	51.28%	50.65%	50.00%	49.28%	48.51%	47.68%	46.85%
71	53.65%	53.13%	52.60%	52.00%	51.38%	50.72%	50.00%	49.23%	48.41%	47.57%
72	54.41%	53.89%	53.36%	52.77%	52.15%	51.49%	50.77%	50.00%	49.17%	48.34%
73	55.23%	54.71%	54.18%	53.59%	52.97%	52.32%	51.59%	50.83%	50.00%	49.16%
74	56.05%	55.54%	55.01%	54.42%	53.80%	53.15%	52.43%	51.66%	50.84%	50.00%

State Pension Age calculation table

(Assuming implementation of proposals in draft Pensions Bill 2013: following the implementation of Pensions Act 2011 state pension ages will now be as follows)

For WOMEN born:	Retirement Date	Age at retirement
On or before 5th April 1950	Age 60	60
6th April 1950 to 5th May 1950	6th May 2010	
6th May 1950 to 5th June 1950	6th July 2010	
6th June 1950 to 5th July 1950	6th September 2010	
6th July 1950 to 5th August 1950	6th November 2010	
6th August 1950 to 5th September 1950	6th January 2011	
6th September 1950 to 5th October 1950	6th March 2011	
6th October 1950 to 5th November 1950	6th May 2011	
6th November 1950 to 5th December 1950	6th July 2011	
6th December 1950 to 5th January 1951	6th September 2011	
6th January 1951 to 5th February 1951	6th November 2011	
6th February 1951 to 5th March 1951	6th January 2012	
6th March 1951 to 5th April 1951	6th March 2012	61
6th April 1951 to 5th May 1951	6th May 2012	
6th May 1951 to 5th June 1951	6th July 2012	
6th June 1951 to 5th July 1951	6th September 2012	
6th July 1951 to 5th August 1951	6th November 2012	
6th August 1951 to 5th September 1951	6th January 2013	
6th September 1951 to 5th October 1951	6th March 2013	
6th October 1951 to 5th November 1951	6th May 2013	
6th November 1951 to 5th December 1951	6th July 2013	
6th December 1951 to 5th January 1952	6th September 2013	
6th January 1952 to 5th February 1952	6th November 2013	
6th February 1952 to 5th March 1952	6th January 2014	
6th March 1952 to 5th April 1952	6th March 2014	62

INCOME EQUALITY AND PENSION AGE TABLES

6th April 1952 to 5th May 1952	6th May 2014	
6th May 1952 to 5th June 1952	6th July 2014	
6th June 1952 to 5th July 1952	6th September 2014	
6th July 1952 to 5th August 1952	6th November 2014	
6th August 1952 to 5th September 1952	6th January 2015	
6th September 1952 to 5th October 1952	6th March 2015	
6th October 1952 to 5th November 1952	6th May 2015	
6th November 1952 to 5th December 1952	6th July 2015	
6th December 1952 to 5th January 1953	6th September 2015	
6th January 1953 to 5th February 1953	6th November 2015	
6th February 1953 to 5th March 1953	6th January 2016	
6th March 1953 to 5th April 1953	6th March 2016	63
6th April 1953 to 5th May 1953	6th July 2016	
6th May 1953 to 5th June 1953	6th November 2016	
6th June 1953 to 5th July 1953	6th March 2017	
6th July 1953 to 5th August 1953	6th July 2017	64
6th August 1953 to 5th September 1953	6th November 2017	
6th September 1953 to 5th October 1953	6th March 2018	
6th October 1953 to 5th November 1953	6th July 2018	
6th November 1953 to 5th December 1953	6th November 2018	65
For MEN born:	**Retirement Date**	**Age at retirement**
On or before 5th December 1953	Age 65	65
For MEN and WOMEN born	**Retirement Date**	**Age at retirement**
6th December 1953 to 5th January 1954	6th March 2019	
6th January 1954 to 5th February 1954	6th May 2019	
6th February 1954 to 5th March 1954	6th July 2019	
6th March 1954 to 5th April 1954	6th September 2019	
6th April 1954 to 5th May 1954	6th November 2019	
6th May 1954 to 5th June 1954	6th January 2020	
6th June 1954 to 5th July 1954	6th March 2020	
6th July 1954 to 5th August 1954	6th May 2020	

6th August 1954 to 5th September 1954	6th July 2020	
6th September 1954 to 5th April 1960	Age 66	**66**
6th April 1960 to 5th May 1960	Age 66 and 1 month	
6th May 1960 to 5th June 1960	Age 66 and 2 months	
6th June 1960 to 5th July 1960	Age 66 and 3 months	
6th July 1960 to 5th August 1960	Age 66 and 4 months	
6th August 1960 to 5th September 1960	Age 66 and 5 months	
6th September 1960 to 5th October 1960	Age 66 and 6 months	
6th October to 5th November 1960	Age 66 and 7 months	
6th November 1960 to 5th December 1960	Age 66 and 8 months	
6th December 1960 to 5th January 1961	Age 66 and 9 months	
6th January 1961 to 5th February 1961	Age 66 and 10 months	
6th February 1961 to 5th March 1961	Age 66 and 11 months	
6th March 1961 to 5th April 1977	Age 67	**67**
6th April 1977 and 5th May 1977	6th May 2044	
6th May 1977 and 5th June 1977	6th July 2044	
6th June 1977 and 5th July 1977	6th September 2044	
6th July 1977 and 5th August 1977	6th November 2044	
6th August 1977 and 5th September 1977	6th January 2045	
6th September 1977 and 5th October 1977	6th March 2045	
6th October 1977 and 5th November 1977	6th May 2045	
6th November 1977 and 5th December 1977	6th July 2045	
6th December 1977 and 5th January 1978	6th September 2045	
6th January 1978 and 5th February 1978	6th November 2045	
6th February 1978 and 5th March 1978	6th January 2046	
6th March 1978 and 5th April 1978	6th March 2046	
On or after 6th April 1978	Age 68	**68**

INDEX

This index has been prepared using Sweet and Maxwell's Legal Taxonomy. Main index entries conform to keywords provided by the Legal Taxonomy except where references to specific documents or non-standard terms (denoted by quotation marks) have been included. These keywords provide a means of identifying similar concepts in other Sweet and Maxwell publications and online services to which keywords from the Legal Taxonomy have been applied. Readers may find some minor differences between terms used in the text and those which appear in the index. Suggestions to *sweetandmaxwell.taxonomy@thomson.com*.

All references are to paragraph number

Actuarial valuations
  apportionment of pension rights,
    14–033—14–035
  cash equivalent
    external option, 14–009—14–014
    market value adjustment factors,
      14–018—14–019
    nature as method of calculation, 14–002
  external option, 14–009—14–014
  guaranteed annuity rates, 14–015—14–017
  health issues, 14–040
  income gap, 14–020—14–034
  introduction, 14–001
  market value adjustment factors,
    14–018—14–019
  nature of CE as valuation method,
    14–002—14–004
  offsetting, and
    comparison of approaches, 13–018
    conclusion, 13–019
    Duxbury value, 13–017
    full replacement value, 13–012
    fund account value, 13–014
    introduction, 13–011
    net actuarial value, 13–015
    net replacement value, 13–013
    replacement of pension sharing value, 13–016
  pension rights at different dates,
    14–036—14–039
  security of benefits in final salary scheme,
    14–005—14–008

Actuaries
  reports
    pension sharing orders, 4–008
    section 25 MCA 1973 factors, 12–005

Additional voluntary contributions
  pension sharing orders, 4–002

Age
  parties, of
    section 25 MCA 1973 factors,
      12–027—12–029

Alternatively secured pensions
  generally, 1–028—1–029

Annuities
  alternatively secured, 1–028—1–029
  generally, 1–027
  unsecured, 1–028—1–029

Appeals
  setting aside
    pension attachment orders, 5–011
    pension sharing orders, 4–014

Armed forces
  Pension Scheme 1975 – Non-Officers Section
    case studies, 15–008—15–011
    cash equivalent, 15–005
    contact details, 15–001
    eligibility, 15–002
    equal income calculations, 15–007
    features, 15–003—15–004
    miscellaneous, 15–012
    pension sharing, 15–006—15–007
  Pension Scheme 1975 – Officers Section
    case studies, 15–020—15–023
    cash equivalent, 15–017
    contact details, 15–013
    eligibility, 15–014
    equal income calculations, 15–019
    features, 15–015—15–016
    miscellaneous, 15–024
    pension sharing, 15–018—15–019
  Pension Scheme 2005
    case studies, 15–032—15–034
    cash equivalent, 15–029
    contact details, 15–025
    eligibility, 15–026

equal income calculations, 15–031
features, 15–027—15–028
miscellaneous, 15–035
pension sharing, 15–030—15–031
Bankruptcy
civil partnerships, and, 7–024
excessive contributions
  recovery by trustee, 7–006
  setting aside pension sharing orders, 7–007
fraud compensation, 7–026
income payment orders, 7–004
introduction, 7–001
lump sum orders, 7–002—7–003
market value reductions
  generally, 7–011
  introduction, 7–001
pension attachment orders, 7–005
Pension Protection Fund
  aims, 7–013
  assessment period, 7–015
  charges, 7–023
  compensation, 7–016
  eligibility, 7–015
  funding, 7–014
  notification of insolvency event, 7–012
  pension attachment orders against compensation rights, 7–022
  pension compensation sharing orders, 7–020
  pension sharing in assessment period, 7–019
  pre-existing pension attachment orders, 7–021
  pre-existing pension sharing orders, 7–018
  section 25E MCA 1973, 7–017
  transfer notice, 7–016
pension sharing orders, 7–005
property adjustment orders, 7–002—7–003
underfunded occupational pension schemes, 7–008—7–010
winding up of schemes, 7–025
"Barder appeals"
unexpected death, 10–003
Cash equivalent
actuarial calculations
  external option, 14–009—14–014
  market value adjustment factors, 14–018—14–019
  nature as method of calculation, 14–002
definition, 2–001
issues affecting, 2–002—2–003
offsetting
  courts' approach, 13–002
  valuation, 13–008
  without expert evidence, 13–009
pension sharing orders, 4–003
private sector pension schemes
  BP – Final Salary Section, 17–028
  British Airways – APS, 17–006
  British Airways – New APS, 17–019
  British Telecom – Defined Benefit Section, 17–040

generally, 2–001
Shell Contributory Pension Scheme, 17–047
Shell Overseas Contributory Pension Scheme, 17–054
Universities Superannuation Scheme – Final Salary Section, 17–060
public sector pension schemes
  armed forces (1975 – non-officers), 15–005
  armed forces (1975 – officers), 15–017
  armed forces (2005), 15–029
  civil service (classic section), 16–043
  civil service (classic section plus), 16–036
  civil service (nuvos section), 16–052
  civil service (premium section), 16–058
  firefighters (1992), 15–062
  firefighters (2006), 15–073
  introduction, 15–001
  local government, 16–005
  NHS (1995), 16–019
  NHS (2008), 16–029
  police (1987), 15–040
  police (2008), 15–051
  teachers, 16–012
Cash equivalent of the benefits *see* **Cash equivalent**
Civil partnerships
entitlement to pension provision
  death, 11–002
  dissolution, 11–003
insolvency, 7–024
new civil partnership, and, 11–004
pension attachment orders, 11–003
pension compensation attachment orders
  generally, 11–007
  pre-existing orders, 11–008
pension compensation sharing orders
  generally, 11–005
  pre-existing orders, 11–006
Pension Protection Fund, and
  introduction, 11–005
  pension compensation attachment orders, 11–007—11–008
  pension compensation sharing orders, 11–005—11–006
pension sharing orders
  generally, 11–003
  Pension Protection Fund, 11–005
  remarriage, after, 11–004
remarriage, and, 11–004
statutory framework, 11–001
Civil service
Pension Scheme (Classic Section)
  case studies, 16–046
  cash equivalent, 16–043
  contact details, 16–039
  eligibility, 16–040
  equal income calculations, 16–045
  features, 16–041—16–042

INDEX

miscellaneous, 16–047
pension sharing, 16–044—16–045
Pension Scheme (Classic Section Plus)
  cash equivalent, 16–036
  contact details, 16–032
  eligibility, 16–033
  features, 16–034—16–035
  miscellaneous, 16–038
  pension sharing, 16–037
Pension Scheme (Nuvos Section)
  cash equivalent, 16–052
  contact details, 16–048
  eligibility, 16–049
  features, 16–050—16–051
  miscellaneous, 16–047
  pension sharing, 16–053
Pension Scheme (Premium Section)
  cash equivalent, 16–058
  contact details, 16–054
  eligibility, 16–055
  features, 16–056—16–057
  miscellaneous, 16–060
  pension sharing, 16–059

Clawback
implementation, 10–011

Commencement of proceedings
pension sharing orders, 4–006

Cross-border disputes
pension sharing orders
  applications under MFPA 1984, 6–006
  between the UK and other countries, 6–002—6–007
  exporting pension rights, 6–004
  importing pension rights, 6–004
  undertaking to obtaining of equivalent overseas provision, 6–004
  within the UK, 6–001

Death
pension attachment orders, 10–008
pension sharing orders
  after decree absolute but before order takes effect, 10–004
  after implementation of order, 10–007
  after order taken effect but before implementation, 10–005—10–006
  Barder appeals, 10–003
  basis of PSO, 10–001
  before decree absolute, 10–002

Defined benefit schemes
generally, 1–003—1–005

Defined contribution schemes
generally, 1–002

Delay
section 25 MCA 1973 factors, 12–025

"Destination arrangement"
pension sharing orders, 4–012

Divorce
insolvency, and
  excessive contributions, 7–006—7–007

fraud compensation, 7–026
income payment orders, 7–004
introduction, 7–001
lump sum orders, 7–002—7–003
market value reductions, 7–011
Pension Protection Fund, 7–012—7–023
pensions, 7–005
property adjustment orders, 7–002—7–003
underfunded occupational pension schemes, 7–008—7–010
winding up of schemes, 7–025
offsetting
  actuarially calculation, 13–011—13–019
  appropriate circumstances, 13–001
  capitalisation of periodical payments, 13–020
  courts' approach, 13–002—13–007
  valuation, 13–008
  without expert evidence, 13–009—13–010
pension sharing
see also **Pension sharing**
  actuarial issues, 14–001—14–042
  alternative remedies, 8–001—8–015
  cross-border issues, 6–001—6–007
  implementation issues, 10–001—10–013
  insolvency, and, 7–001—7–026
  'longer career' public sector schemes, 16–001—16–060
  pension attachment orders, 5–001—5–016
  pension sharing orders, 4–001—4–021
  Pensions Ombudsman's role, 9–001—9–002
  prior to 1996, 3–001—3–009
  private sector schemes, 17–001—17–061
  s 25 factors, 12–001—12–029

"Double orders"
pension attachment orders
  earlier pension sharing order, 5–013
pension sharing orders
  earlier pension attachment order, 4–016
  earlier pension sharing order, 4–017
  more than one pension sharing order, 4–018
  'shorter career' public sector schemes, 15–001—15–078

Drawdown
flexible, 1–030
generally, 1–028—1–029

Earmarking *see* **Pension sharing**

Excessive pension contributions
insolvency
  recovery by trustee, 7–006
  setting aside pension sharing orders, 7–007

Family Procedure Rules
pension sharing orders, 4–005

Final salary schemes *see* **Defined benefit schemes**

Firefighters
Pension Scheme 1992
  case studies, 15–065—15–067
  cash equivalent, 15–062

contact details, 15–057
eligibility, 15–058
equal income calculations, 15–064
features, 15–059—15–061
miscellaneous, 15–068
pension sharing, 15–063—15–064
Pension Scheme 2006
  case studies, 15–076—15–077
  cash equivalent, 15–073
  contact details, 15–069
  eligibility, 15–070
  equal income calculations, 15–075
  features, 15–071—15–072
  miscellaneous, 15–078
  pension sharing, 15–074—15–075
Fraud compensation levy
insolvency, 7–026
Funded unapproved schemes
generally, 1–020
pension sharing orders, 8–004
FURBS see **Funded unapproved schemes**
Further information
pension sharing orders, 4–008
Graduated retirement benefit
generally, 1–010
"Guaranteed annuities"
actuarial calculations, 14–015—14–017
generally, 1–024
pension sharing orders, 8–006
Health
actuarial calculations, 14–040
section 25 MCA 1973 factors, 12–010
Hutton Report
generally, 1–031
Implementation
clawback, 10–011
death (PAO), 10–008
death (PSO)
  after decree absolute but before order takes effect, 10–004
  after implementation of order, 10–007
  after order taken effect but before implementation, 10–005—10–006
  Barder appeals, 10–003
  basis of PSO, 10–001
  before decree absolute, 10–002
income gap, 10–012
'moving target' syndrome, 10–009—10–010
pension sharing orders
  generally, 4–004
  procedure, 4–011
  unexpected death, 10–001—10–008
"Income gap"
actuarial calculations, 14–020—14–034
generally, 8–007
implementation issues, 10–012
pension sharing orders, 8–007
Income payment orders
insolvency, 7–004

Insolvency
civil partnerships, and, 7–024
excessive contributions
  recovery by trustee, 7–006
  setting aside pension sharing orders, 7–007
fraud compensation, 7–026
income payment orders, 7–004
introduction, 7–001
lump sum orders, 7–002—7–003
market value reductions
  generally, 7–011
  introduction, 7–001
pension attachment orders, 7–005
Pension Protection Fund
  aims, 7–013
  assessment period, 7–015
  charges, 7–023
  compensation, 7–016
  eligibility, 7–015
  funding, 7–014
  notification of insolvency event, 7–012
  pension attachment orders against compensation rights, 7–022
  pension compensation sharing orders, 7–020
  pension sharing in assessment period, 7–019
  pre-existing pension attachment orders, 7–021
  pre-existing pension sharing orders, 7–018
  section 25E MCA 1973, 7–017
  transfer notice, 7–016
pension sharing orders, 7–005
property adjustment orders, 7–002—7–003
underfunded occupational pension schemes, 7–008—7–010
winding up of schemes, 7–025
Local government
Pension Scheme
  cash equivalent, 16–005
  contact details, 16–001
  eligibility, 16–002
  features, 16–003—16–004
  miscellaneous, 16–007
  pension sharing, 16–006
Lump sum orders
insolvency, 7–002—7–003
Maintenance orders
joint lives
  pension sharing orders, 8–014
"Market value adjustment factors"
actuarial calculations, 14–018—14–019
"Market value reductions"
insolvency
  generally, 7–011
  introduction, 7–001
Money purchase schemes see **Defined contribution schemes**
"Moving target syndrome"
generally, 10–009—10–010

INDEX

NHS
  Pension Scheme (1995 Section)
    case studies, 16–022—16–023
    cash equivalent, 16–019
    contact details, 16–015
    eligibility, 16–016
    equal income calculations, 16–021
    features, 16–017—16–018
    miscellaneous, 16–024
    pension sharing, 16–020—16–021
  Pension Scheme (2008 Section)
    cash equivalent, 16–029
    contact details, 16–025
    eligibility, 16–026
    features, 16–027—16–028
    miscellaneous, 16–031
    pension sharing, 16–030

Occupational pensions
  BP – Final Salary Section
    cash equivalent, 17–028
    contact details, 17–022
    eligibility, 17–023
    features, 17–024—17–027
    miscellaneous, 17–030
    pension sharing, 17–029
  British Airways – APS
    cash equivalent, 17–006
    contact details, 17–001
    eligibility, 17–002
    features, 17–003—17–005
    miscellaneous, 17–008
    pension sharing, 17–007
  British Airways – New APS
    cash equivalent, 17–019
    contact details, 17–009
    eligibility, 17–010
    features, 17–011—17–018
    increasing build up rate, 17–012—17–017
    miscellaneous, 17–021
    Option 55, 17–018
    pension sharing, 17–020
    Plan 65, 17–012—17–017
  British Telecom – Defined Benefit Section
    cash equivalent, 17–040
    contact details, 17–031
    contributions, 17–035—17–039
    eligibility, 17–032
    features, 17–033—17–034
    miscellaneous, 17–042
    pension sharing, 17–041
  cash equivalent
    BP – Final Salary Section, 17–028
    British Airways – APS, 17–006
    British Airways – New APS, 17–019
    British Telecom – Defined Benefit Section, 17–040
    generally, 2–001
    Shell Contributory Pension Scheme, 17–047
    Shell Overseas Contributory Pension Scheme, 17–054
    Universities Superannuation Scheme – Final Salary Section, 17–060
  defined benefit schemes, 1–003—1–005
  defined contribution schemes, 1–002
  examples
    BP Final Salary Section, 17–029
    British Airways APS, 17–007
    British Airways New APS, 17–020
    British Telecom Defined Benefit Section, 17–041
    introduction, 17–001
    Shell Contributory Pension Scheme, 17–048
    Shell Overseas Contributory Pension Scheme, 17–055
    Universities Superannuation Scheme Final Salary Section, 17–061
  funded schemes, 1–017—1–020
  funded unapproved schemes, 1–020
  pension sharing
    BP Final Salary Section, 17–029
    British Airways APS, 17–007
    British Airways New APS, 17–020
    British Telecom Defined Benefit Section, 17–041
    Shell Contributory Pension Scheme, 17–048
    Shell Overseas Contributory Pension Scheme, 17–055
    Universities Superannuation Scheme Final Salary Section, 17–061
  Shell Contributory Pension Scheme
    cash equivalent, 17–047
    contact details, 17–043
    eligibility, 17–044
    features, 17–045—17–046
    miscellaneous, 17–049
    pension sharing, 17–048
  Shell Overseas Contributory Pension Scheme
    cash equivalent, 17–054
    contact details, 17–050
    eligibility, 17–051
    features, 17–052—17–053
    pension sharing, 17–055
  small self-administered schemes, 1–019
  unfunded from public sector employers, 1–016
  unfunded unapproved schemes, 1–020
  Universities Superannuation Scheme – Final Salary Section
    cash equivalent, 17–060
    contact details, 17–056
    eligibility, 17–057
    features, 17–058—17–059
    pension sharing, 17–061

Offsetting
  actuarially calculated
    comparison of approaches, 13–018
    conclusion, 13–019
    Duxbury value, 13–017

full replacement value, 13–012
fund account value, 13–014
introduction, 13–011
net actuarial value, 13–015
net replacement value, 13–013
replacement of pension sharing value, 13–016
appropriate circumstances, 13–001
capitalisation of periodical payments, 13–020
cash equivalent
    courts' approach, 13–002
    valuation, 13–008
    without expert evidence, 13–009
courts' approach, 13–002—13–007
pension sharing orders
    capitalisation of periodical payments, 13–020
    generally, 8–011
valuation, 13–008
without expert evidence, 13–009—13–010

"Pension arrangement"
pension sharing orders, 4–002

Pension attachment orders
appeals, 5–011
civil partnerships, 11–003
cross-border issues
    applications under MFPA 1984, 6–006
    between the UK and other countries, 6–002—6–007
    exporting pension rights, 6–004
    importing pension rights, 6–004
    undertaking to obtaining of equivalent overseas provision, 6–004
    within the UK, 6–001
death, 10–008
definition, 5–002
double orders
    earlier pension sharing order, 5–013
insolvency, 7–005
law, 5–001—5–004
nature, 5–003
pre-legislation decrees, 5–014
procedure
    commencement of proceedings, 5–006—5–007
    implementation, 5–010
    making an order, 5–009
    statutory framework, 5–005
    valuation information, 5–008
s 37 MCA 1973 orders, 5–016
setting aside, 5–011
statutory charge, 5–015
statutory framework
    general, 5–001
    procedure, 5–005
subsidiary powers, 5–004
unexpected death, 10–008
variation, 5–012

Pension compensation attachment orders
civil partnerships
    generally, 11–007
    introduction, 11–003
    pre-existing orders, 11–008
cross-border issues, 6–006
introduction, 3–008
Pension Protection Fund
    charges, 7–023
    generally, 7–022

Pension compensation sharing orders
civil partnerships
    generally, 11–005
    introduction, 11–003
    pre-existing orders, 11–006
cross-border issues, 6–006
introduction, 3–008
Pension Protection Fund
    charges, 7–023
    generally, 7–020
s 37 MCA 1973, 4–021

"Pension credits"
pension sharing orders, 4–012

"Pension inquiry forms"
pension sharing orders, 4–008

Pension Protection Fund
aims, 7–013
assessment period, 7–015
charges, 7–023
civil partnerships
    introduction, 11–005
    pension compensation attachment orders, 11–007—11–008
    pension compensation sharing orders, 11–005—11–006
compensation, 7–016
eligibility, 7–015
funding, 7–014
notification of insolvency event, 7–012
pension attachment orders against compensation rights, 7–022
pension compensation sharing orders, 7–020
pension sharing in assessment period, 7–019
pension sharing orders, 8–008
pre-existing pension attachment orders, 7–021
pre-existing pension sharing orders, 7–018
section 25E MCA 1973, 7–017
transfer notice, 7–016

Pension sharing
actuarial issues
    apportionment of pension rights, 14–033—14–035
    external option, 14–009—14–014
    guaranteed annuity rates, 14–015—14–017
    health issues, 14–040
    income gap, 14–020—14–034
    introduction, 14–001
    market value adjustment factors, 14–018—14–019
    nature of CE as valuation method, 14–002—14–004

INDEX

pension rights at different dates, 14–036—14–039
security of benefits in final salary scheme, 14–005—14–008
alternative remedies
  actuarial solution, 8–015
  deferring sharing, 8–010
  diminution of assets, resulting in, 8–005—8–006
  funded unapproved schemes, 8–004
  income gap, 8–007
  introduction, 8–001
  joint lives maintenance orders, 8–014
  lump sums in instalments, 8–012
  offsetting, 8–011
  other cases, 8–009
  pension attachment, 8–013
  Pension Protection Fund, 8–008
  self-invested personal pensions, 8–003
  series of lump sums, 8–012
  small self-administered schemes, 8–002
  unfunded unapproved schemes, 8–004
background
  earmarking, 3–005
  pension sharing, 3–006—3–009
  post 1996, 3–005—3–009
  prior to 1996, 3–001—3–004
civil partnerships, and
  entitlement to pension provision on death, 11–002
  pension attachment orders, 11–003
  Pension Protection Fund, and, 11–005—11–008
  pension sharing orders, 11–003
  remarriage, after, 11–004
  statutory framework, 11–001
clawback, 10–011
cross-border issues
  applications under MFPA 1984, 6–006
  between the UK and other countries, 6–002—6–007
  exporting pension rights, 6–004
  importing pension rights, 6–004
  undertaking to obtaining of equivalent overseas provision, 6–004
  within the UK, 6–001
death (PAO), 10–008
death (PSO)
  after decree absolute but before order takes effect, 10–004
  after implementation of order, 10–007
  after order taken effect but before implementation, 10–005—10–006
  Barder appeals, 10–003
  basis of PSO, 10–001
  before decree absolute, 10–002
earmarking, 3–005
implementation issues
  clawback, 10–011

income gap, 10–012
'moving target' syndrome, 10–009—10–010
unexpected death, 10–001—10–008
income gap
  actuarial issues, 14–020—14–034
  generally, 8–007
  implementation issues, 10–012
insolvency, and
  excessive contributions, 7–006—7–007
  fraud compensation, 7–026
  income payment orders, 7–004
  introduction, 7–001
  lump sum orders, 7–002—7–003
  market value reductions, 7–011
  Pension Protection Fund, 7–012—7–023
  pensions, 7–005
  property adjustment orders, 7–002—7–003
  underfunded occupational pension schemes, 7–008—7–010
  winding up of schemes, 7–025
legislative development
  earmarking, 3–005
  pension sharing, 3–006—3–009
  post 1996, 3–005—3–009
  prior to 1996, 3–001—3–004
'longer career' public sector schemes
  civil service (classic section), 16–044
  civil service (classic section plus), 16–037
  civil service (nuvos section), 16–053
  civil service (premium section), 16–059
  local government, 16–006
  NHS (1995), 16–020
  NHS (2008), 16–030
  teachers, 16–013
'moving target' syndrome, 10–009—10–010
pension attachment orders
  appeals, 5–011
  cross-border issues, 6–001—6–007
  double orders, 5–013
  law, 5–001—5–004
  pre-legislation decrees, 5–014
  procedure, 5–005—5–010
  s 37 MCA 1973 orders, 5–016
  setting aside, 5–011
  statutory charge, 5–015
  variation, 5–012
pension sharing orders
  appeals, 4–014
  cases in which PSOs are not appropriate, 8–001—8–015
  cross-border issues, 6–001—6–007
  double orders, 4–016—4–018
  law, 4–001—4–004
  pre-legislation decrees, 4–019
  procedure, 4–005—4–013
  s 37 MCA 1973 orders, 4–021
  statutory charge, 4–020
  variation, 4–015

Pensions Ombudsman's role
    relevance to divorce practitioner, 9–002
    status, 9–001
position prior to 1996
    reforms, 3–004
    traditional remedies, 3–001—3–003
private sector schemes
    BP Final Salary Section, 17–029
    British Airways APS, 17–007
    British Airways New APS, 17–020
    British Telecom Defined Benefit Section, 17–041
    introduction, 17–001
    Shell Contributory Pension Scheme, 17–048
    Shell Overseas Contributory Pension Scheme, 17–055
    Universities Superannuation Scheme Final Salary Section, 17–061
public sector schemes
    armed forces (1975 – non-officers), 15–006
    armed forces (1975 – officers), 15–018
    armed forces (2005), 15–030
    civil service (classic section), 16–044
    civil service (classic section plus), 16–037
    civil service (nuvos section), 16–053
    civil service (premium section), 16–059
    firefighters (1992), 15–063
    firefighters (2006), 15–074
    introduction, 15–001
    local government, 16–006
    NHS (1995), 16–020
    NHS (2008), 16–030
    police (1987), 15–041
    police (2008), 15–052
    teachers, 16–013
s 25 factors
    contributions, 12–011—12–025
    duration of marriage, 12–027—12–029
    financial needs and obligations, 12–007—12–009
    'foreseeable future', 12–002
    future accrual, 12–026
    health, 12–010
    introduction, 12–001
    matrimonial acquest, 12–011
    post-separation contributions, 12–018—12–025
    pre-marital contributions, 12–012—12–017
    quantification of asset, 12–004—12–006
    relevant factors, 12–003
'shorter career' public sector schemes
    armed forces (1975 – non-officers), 15–006
    armed forces (1975 – officers), 15–018
    armed forces (2005), 15–030
    firefighters (1992), 15–063
    firefighters (2006), 15–074
    introduction, 15–001
    police (1987), 15–041
    police (2008), 15–052

unexpected death (PAO), 10–008
unexpected death (PSO)
    after decree absolute but before order takes effect, 10–004
    after implementation of order, 10–007
    after order taken effect but before implementation, 10–005—10–006
    Barder appeals, 10–003
    basis of PSO, 10–001
    before decree absolute, 10–002
Pension sharing orders
    actuary's report, 4–008
    additional voluntary contributions, 4–002
    appeals, 4–014
    availability, 4–003
    background
        earmarking, 3–005
        pension sharing, 3–006—3–009
        post 1996, 3–005—3–009
        prior to 1996, 3–001—3–004
    cases in which not appropriate
        actuarial solution, 8–015
        deferring pension sharing, 8–010
        diminution of assets, resulting in, 8–005—8–006
        funded unapproved schemes, 8–004
        guaranteed annuities, 8–006
        income gap, 8–007
        introduction, 8–001
        joint lives maintenance orders, 8–014
        lump sums in instalments, 8–012
        offsetting, 8–011
        other cases, 8–009
        pension attachment, 8–013
        Pension Protection Fund, 8–008
        self-invested personal pensions, 8–003
        series of lump sums, 8–012
        small self-administered schemes, 8–002
        solutions, 8–010—8–015
        transfer out of defined benefit schemes, 8–005
        unfunded unapproved schemes, 8–004
    cash equivalent, 4–003
    civil partnerships
        generally, 11–003
        Pension Protection Fund, 11–005
        remarriage, after, 11–004
    clawback, 10–011
    commencement of proceedings, 4–006
    completion of process, 4–013
    cross-border issues
        applications under MFPA 1984, 6–006
        between the UK and other countries, 6–002—6–007
        exporting pension rights, 6–004
        importing pension rights, 6–004
        undertaking to obtaining of equivalent overseas provision, 6–004
        within the UK, 6–001

INDEX

death
- after decree absolute but before order takes effect, 10–004
- after implementation of order, 10–007
- after order taken effect but before implementation, 10–005—10–006
- Barder appeals, 10–003
- basis of PSO, 10–001
- before decree absolute, 10–002

deferring pension sharing, and, 8–010
definition, 4–002
diminution of assets, and, 8–005—8–006
double orders
- earlier pension attachment order, 4–016
- earlier pension sharing order, 4–017
- more than one pension sharing order, 4–018

Family Procedure Rules, 4–005
Form P, 4–008
funded unapproved schemes, and, 8–004
further information, 4–008
guaranteed annuities, and, 8–006
implementation
- generally, 4–004
- procedure, 4–011

income gap, and
- generally, 8–007
- implementation issue, 10–012

insolvency, 7–005
joint lives maintenance orders, and, 8–014
law, 4–001—4–004
lump sums in instalments, and, 8–012
making, 4–009—4–010
'moving target' syndrome, 10–009—10–010
offsetting
- capitalisation of periodical payments, 13–020
- generally, 8–011

'pension arrangement', 4–002
pension credits, 4–012
pension inquiry forms, 4–008
Pension Protection Fund, and, 8–008
pre-legislation decrees, 4–019
procedure
- actuary's report, 4–008
- commencement, 4–006
- completion of process, 4–013
- Family Procedure Rules, 4–005
- Form P, 4–008
- further information, 4–008
- implementation, 4–011
- making an order, 4–009—4–010
- pension credits, 4–012
- pension inquiry forms, 4–008
- statutory framework, 4–005
- valuations, 4–007

'relevant valuation', 4–003
s 37 MCA 1973 orders, 4–021
self-invested personal pensions, and, 8–003
series of lump sums, and, 8–012
setting aside, 4–014

'shareable rights', 4–002
'shareable state scheme right', 4–002
small self-administered schemes, and, 8–002
'specified', 4–002
statutory charge, 4–020
statutory framework
- general, 4–001
- procedure, 4–005

transfer out of defined benefit schemes, and, 8–005
unexpected death
- after decree absolute but before order takes effect, 10–004
- after implementation of order, 10–007
- after order taken effect but before implementation, 10–005—10–006
- Barder appeals, 10–003
- basis of PSO, 10–001
- before decree absolute, 10–002

unfunded unapproved schemes, and, 8–004
valuations, 4–007
'value', 4–003
variation, 4–015

Pensions
alternatively secured pensions, 1–028—1–029
annuities
- alternatively secured, 1–028—1–029
- generally, 1–027
- unsecured, 1–028—1–029

defined benefit schemes, 1–003—1–005
defined contribution schemes, 1–002
drawdown
- flexible, 1–030
- generally, 1–028—1–029

final salary schemes, 1–003—1–005
funded unapproved schemes, 1–020
FURBS, 1–020
graduated retirement benefit, 1–010
guaranteed annuity options, 1–024
Hutton Report, 1–031
in payment
- alternatively secured annuities, 1–028—1–029
- annuities, 1–027
- drawdown, 1–028—1–029
- flexible drawdown, 1–030
- unsecured annuities, 1–028—1–029

money purchase schemes, 1–002
occupational pensions
- defined benefit schemes, 1–003—1–005
- defined contribution schemes, 1–002
- funded schemes, 1–017—1–020
- funded unapproved schemes, 1–020
- small self-administered schemes, 1–019
- unfunded from public sector employers, 1–016
- unfunded unapproved schemes, 1–020

offsetting
- actuarially calculation, 13–011—13–019

371

appropriate circumstances, 13–001
capitalisation of periodical payments, 13–020
courts' approach, 13–002—13–007
valuation, 13–008
without expert evidence, 13–009—13–010
personal pensions
  guaranteed annuity options, 1–024
  introduction, 1–021—1–022
  retirement annuity contracts, 1–025
  self-invested personal pensions, 1–026
  stakeholder pensions, 1–023
retirement annuity contracts, 1–025
self-invested personal pensions, 1–026
SERPS, 1–009
sharing
see also **Pension sharing**
  actuarial issues, 14–001—14–042
  alternative remedies, 8–001—8–015
  cross-border issues, 6–001—6–007
  implementation issues, 10–001—10–013
  insolvency, and, 7–001—7–026
  'longer career' public sector schemes, 16–001—16–060
  pension attachment orders, 5–001—5–016
  pension sharing orders, 4–001—4–021
  Pensions Ombudsman's role, 9–001—9–002
  prior to 1996, 3–001—3–009
  private sector schemes, 17–001—17–061
  s 25 factors, 12–001—12–029
  'shorter career' public sector schemes, 15–001—15–078
small self-administered schemes, 1–019
stakeholder pensions, 1–023
state retirements pension
  additional state pensions, 1–009
  basic state pension, 1–008
  contracting out, 1–011
  graduated retirement benefit, 1–010
  introduction, 1–006
  reform proposals, 1–014—1–0115
  S2P, 1–009
  SERPS, 1–009
  sharing, 1–013
  state pension age, 1–007
  valuation, 1–012
state second pension, 1–009
types, 1–001
unfunded unapproved schemes, 1–020
UURBS, 1–020

Pensions Ombudsman
relevance to divorce practitioner, 9–002
status, 9–001

Personal pensions
guaranteed annuity options, 1–024
introduction, 1–021—1–022
retirement annuity contracts, 1–025
self-invested personal pensions, 1–026
stakeholder pensions, 1–023

Police
Pension Scheme 1987
  case studies, 15–054—15–055
  cash equivalent, 15–040
  contact details, 15–036
  eligibility, 15–037
  equal income calculations, 15–053
  features, 15–038—15–039
  miscellaneous, 15–056
  pension sharing, 15–052—15–053
Pension Scheme 2008
  case studies, 15–043—15–045
  cash equivalent, 15–051
  contact details, 15–047
  eligibility, 15–048
  equal income calculations, 15–042
  features, 15–049—15–050
  miscellaneous, 15–046
  pension sharing, 15–041—15–042

Private sector schemes *see* **occupational pension schemes**

Property adjustment orders
insolvency, 7–002—7–003

Public sector (pension schemes)
armed forces (1975 – non-officers)
  case studies, 15–008—15–011
  cash equivalent, 15–005
  contact details, 15–001
  eligibility, 15–002
  equal income calculations, 15–007
  features, 15–003—15–004
  miscellaneous, 15–012
  pension sharing, 15–006—15–007
armed forces (1975 – officers)
  case studies, 15–020—15–023
  cash equivalent, 15–017
  contact details, 15–013
  eligibility, 15–014
  equal income calculations, 15–019
  features, 15–015—15–016
  miscellaneous, 15–024
  pension sharing, 15–018—15–019
armed forces (2005)
  case studies, 15–032—15–034
  cash equivalent, 15–029
  contact details, 15–025
  eligibility, 15–026
  equal income calculations, 15–031
  features, 15–027—15–028
  miscellaneous, 15–035
  pension sharing, 15–030—15–031
cash equivalent
  armed forces (1975 – non-officers), 15–005
  armed forces (1975 – officers), 15–017
  armed forces (2005), 15–029
  civil service (classic section), 16–043
  civil service (classic section plus), 16–036
  civil service (nuvos section), 16–052

INDEX

civil service (premium section), 16–058
  firefighters (1992), 15–062
  firefighters (2006), 15–073
  introduction, 15–001
  local government, 16–005
  NHS (1995), 16–019
  NHS (2008), 16–029
  police (1987), 15–040
  police (2008), 15–051
  teachers, 16–012
civil service (classic section)
  case studies, 16–046
  cash equivalent, 16–043
  contact details, 16–039
  eligibility, 16–040
  equal income calculations, 16–045
  features, 16–041—16–042
  miscellaneous, 16–047
  pension sharing, 16–044—16–045
civil service (classic section plus)
  cash equivalent, 16–036
  contact details, 16–032
  eligibility, 16–033
  features, 16–034—16–035
  miscellaneous, 16–038
  pension sharing, 16–037
civil service (nuvos section)
  cash equivalent, 16–052
  contact details, 16–048
  eligibility, 16–049
  features, 16–050—16–051
  miscellaneous, 16–047
  pension sharing, 16–053
civil service (premium section)
  cash equivalent, 16–058
  contact details, 16–054
  eligibility, 16–055
  features, 16–056—16–057
  miscellaneous, 16–060
  pension sharing, 16–059
firefighters (1992)
  case studies, 15–065—15–067
  cash equivalent, 15–062
  contact details, 15–057
  eligibility, 15–058
  equal income calculations, 15–064
  features, 15–059—15–061
  miscellaneous, 15–068
  pension sharing, 15–063—15–064
firefighters (2006)
  case studies, 15–076—15–077
  cash equivalent, 15–073
  contact details, 15–069
  eligibility, 15–070
  equal income calculations, 15–075
  features, 15–071—15–072
  miscellaneous, 15–078
  pension sharing, 15–074—15–075

local government
  cash equivalent, 16–005
  contact details, 16–001
  eligibility, 16–002
  features, 16–003—16–004
  miscellaneous, 16–007
  pension sharing, 16–006
'longer career' schemes
  civil service (classic section),
    16–039—16–047
  civil service (classic section plus),
    16–032—16–038
  civil service (nuvos section),
    16–048—16–053
  civil service (premium section),
    16–054—16–060
  local government, 16–001—16–007
  NHS (1995), 16–015—16–024
  NHS (2008), 16–025—16–031
  teachers, 16–008—16–014
NHS (1995)
  case studies, 16–022—16–023
  cash equivalent, 16–019
  contact details, 16–015
  eligibility, 16–016
  equal income calculations, 16–021
  features, 16–017—16–018
  miscellaneous, 16–024
  pension sharing, 16–020—16–021
NHS (2008)
  cash equivalent, 16–029
  contact details, 16–025
  eligibility, 16–026
  features, 16–027—16–028
  miscellaneous, 16–031
  pension sharing, 16–030
pension sharing
  armed forces (1975 – non-officers), 15–006
  armed forces (1975 – officers), 15–018
  armed forces (2005), 15–030
  civil service (classic section), 16–044
  civil service (classic section plus), 16–037
  civil service (nuvos section), 16–053
  civil service (premium section), 16–059
  firefighters (1992), 15–063
  firefighters (2006), 15–074
  introduction, 15–001
  local government, 16–006
  NHS (1995), 16–020
  NHS (2008), 16–030
  police (1987), 15–041
  police (2008), 15–052
  teachers, 16–013
police (1987)
  case studies, 15–054—15–055
  cash equivalent, 15–040
  contact details, 15–036
  eligibility, 15–037
  equal income calculations, 15–053

features, 15–038—15–039
miscellaneous, 15–056
pension sharing, 15–052—15–053
police (2008)
  case studies, 15–043—15–045
  cash equivalent, 15–051
  contact details, 15–047
  eligibility, 15–048
  equal income calculations, 15–042
  features, 15–049—15–050
  miscellaneous, 15–046
  pension sharing, 15–041—15–042
'shorter career' schemes
  armed forces (1975 – non-officers), 15–001—15–012
  armed forces (1975 – officers), 15–013—15–024
  armed forces (2005), 15–025—15–035
  firefighters (1992), 15–057—15–068
  firefighters (2006), 15–069—15–078
  introduction, 15–001
  police (1987), 15–036—15–046
  police (2008), 15–047—15–056
teachers (pre 2007)
  cash equivalent, 16–012
  contact details, 16–008
  eligibility, 16–009
  features, 16–010—16–011
  miscellaneous, 16–014
  pension sharing, 16–013

Remarriage
civil partnerships, 11–004

Retirement annuity contracts
generally, 1–025

"Section 25 MCA 1973 factors"
actuary's report, 12–005
age of parties, 12–027—12–029
continuing periodical payments, 12–028
contributions
  future accrual, 12–026
  introduction, 12–011
  post-separation contributions, 12–018—12–025
  pre-marital contributions, 12–012—12–017
delay, 12–025
duration of marriage, 12–027—12–029
financial needs and obligations
  equalisation of cash equivalent or income, 12–007—12–008
  maintaining value of pension, 12–009
'foreseeable future', 12–002
future accrual, 12–026
health of parties, 12–010
introduction, 12–001
matrimonial acquest, 12–011
post-separation contributions, 12–018—12–025
pre-marital contributions, 12–012—12–017
quantification of asset
  generally, 12–004—12–005

widow's/widower's pensions, 12–006
re-building lifetime allowance, 12–029
relevant factors
  age of parties, 12–027—12–029
  contributions, 12–011—12–025
  duration of marriage, 12–027—12–029
  financial needs and obligations, 12–007—12–009
  future accrual, 12–026
  health of parties, 12–010
  introduction, 12–003
  quantification of asset, 12–004—12–006
  widow's/widower's pensions, 12–006

"Section 37 MCA 1973 orders"
pension attachment orders, 5–016
pension sharing orders, 4–021

Self-invested personal pensions
generally, 1–026
pension sharing orders, 8–003

SERPS
generally, 1–009

Setting aside
appeals
  pension attachment orders, 5–011
  pension sharing orders, 4–014

"Shareable rights"
pension sharing orders, 4–002

Small self-administered schemes
generally, 1–019
pension sharing orders, 8–002

Stakeholder pensions
generally, 1–023

State pension
generally, 1–009

State retirement pension
additional state pensions, 1–009
basic state pension, 1–008
contracting out, 1–011
graduated retirement benefit, 1–010
introduction, 1–006
reform proposals, 1–014—1–0115
S2P, 1–009
SERPS, 1–009
sharing, 1–013
state pension age, 1–007
valuation, 1–012

Statutory charge
pension attachment orders, 5–015
pension sharing orders, 4–020

Teachers
Pension Scheme (pre 2007)
  cash equivalent, 16–012
  contact details, 16–008
  eligibility, 16–009
  features, 16–010—16–011
  miscellaneous, 16–014
  pension sharing, 16–013

"Underfunded pension schemes"
occupational pension schemes, 7–008—7–010

INDEX

Unexpected death *see* **Death**
Unfunded unapproved schemes
  generally, 1–020
  pension sharing orders, 8–004
UURBS *see* **Unfunded unapproved schemes**
Valuation
  offsetting, 13–008
  pension sharing orders, 4–007
Value
  offsetting
    comparison of approaches, 13–018
    conclusion, 13–019
    Duxbury value, 13–017
    full replacement value, 13–012
    fund account value, 13–014
    introduction, 13–011
    net actuarial value, 13–015
    net replacement value, 13–013
    replacement of pension sharing value, 13–016
  pension sharing orders, 4–003
Variation
  pension attachment orders, 5–012
  pension sharing orders, 4–015
Widower's pension *see* **Widow's pension**
Widow's pension
  section 25 MCA 1973 factors, 12–006
Winding up
  pension schemes, 7–025